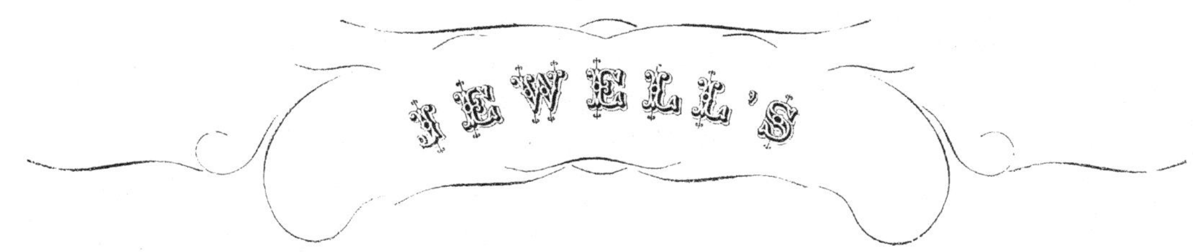

CRESCENT CITY ILLUSTRATED.

EDITED AND COMPILED BY

EDWIN L. JEWELL.

The Commercial, Social, Political and General History

—OF—

INCLUDING

Biographical Sketches of its Distinguished Citizens,

TOGETHER WITH

NEW ORLEANS:
1873.

JEWELL'S

Crescent City Illustrated.

INTRODUCTION.

NO City in the United States, of equal population, commercial importance and material wealth, is so little known by the outside world as New Orleans. And yet its history, full of romantic incident and legendary lore is in itself sufficient to fill a volume, whilst its peculiar characteristics, local institutions, and singular manners and customs of its people would furnish material for a work of larger scope than is designed by the author of this publication.

It is, however, his object and desire to present to the reader, in an attractive and succinct form, a brief historical outline of the most prominent features that contribute to make the Crescent City the great metropolis of the South and South=West, and prove the intelligence, enterprise and progressive spirit of its citizens. It is also his design to produce such a work as will disseminate a more general knowledge of the local history of New Orleans and will, in a great degree, demonstrate its immense resources, advantages and attractions, and at the same time furnish such information as will engage the attention of the casual reader and command the serious consideration of capitalists, immigrants and the commercial world.

In the preparation of this volume, comprising as it does, a vast amount of information and a great variety of subjects, the author has been materially assisted by the contributions of a number of literary friends whose valuable services he desires to publicly acknowledge. The Hon. Charles Gayarre, Prof. D. K. Whittaker, Prof. Alex. Dimitry, Hon. Wm. M. Burrell, Albert Fabre, Esq., E. W. Halsey, Esq., Judge Alexander Walker and Mr. E. C. Hancock, of the New Orleans "Times," and Mr. J. A. Quintero, of the "Picayune," have all lent the aid of their graceful pens to the pages of the **Crescent City Illustrated.** To say that all of these gentlemen are recognized as writers of the highest order of literary talent would only be to accord them their well=merited reputation. Extracts also have been made from "Norman's History of New Orleans," and other volumes have contributed interesting statistics which have been carefully compiled and arranged.

If this volume, prepared with much care and labor, will in any way contribute towards giving additional information or throwing more light upon the general history of New Orleans and tend to remove the unreasonable and unjust prejudices that exist through ignorance of its true character, the highest object in view will have been fully attained and the richest reward obtained by

THE AUTHOR.

To

E. J. HART, Esq.,

The successful and highly esteemed Merchant;

The enterprising, liberal, and public=spirited Citizen;

The honorable, high=toned, and exemplary Man;

The generous Friend and devoted Father and Husband,

THIS WORK IS

Respectfully Dedicated,

AS AN

Evidence of Appreciation of True Moral Worth, and as a Token of Remembrance
of years gone by so fondly cherished

BY THE AUTHOR.

New Orleans, January, 1873.

THE CRESCENT CITY.

Slow sweeping from a bleak northwestern clime,
Where snow=storms beat and forests rise sublime,
Till, gathering strength, as southward rolls his course,
To Mexicana's Gulf descends his force;
Monarch of streams! great Mississippi flows,
While on his breast the fervid sunbeam flows.

And, rising near his disemboguing tide,
The Crescent City sits in queenly pride;
The spires ascend, a coronet on high,
Her gardens bloom with every floral dye;
Her thronging marts a varied crowd display,
The merchant prince, the dame in rich array,
The wan=eyed beggar, and the tradesman keen,
The brisk attorney with his eager mien,
And sapient age, with tottering step and slow,
Walks side by side with youth in freshest glow;
From different lands collected strangers meet,
Are borne in cars or move along the street.

But white and solemn, midst the ceaseless tread,
Rise, here and there, the dwellings of the dead!
Whose peopled mansions never sound repeat,
Save song=birds' wail, at evening, clear and sweet.

The floating palace on the grand old stream,
The thundering iron horse impelled by steam,
Pour in her lap rich treasures from all lands,
As, Queen of Trade, the Crescent Empress stands!

New Orleans, January, 1873.

BIRD'S EYE VIEW OF NEW ORLEANS.

THE CITY OF NEW ORLEANS.

New Orleans, the Metropolis of the South, stands on the right side of the Mississippi, in ascending, ninety-two miles from its mouth. The river here makes a considerable bend to the northeast, and the city occupies the northwestern side, although its situation is east of the general course of the stream. It is in latitude 29° 57 north, longitude 90° 8′ west; by the river 301 miles below Natchez; 1220 miles below St. Louis; 1040 below Cairo, at the mouth of the Ohio; 2004 below Pittsburg; and 1244 southwest from Washington city.

In 1718, Bienville, then Governor of the province, explored the banks of the Mississippi, in order to choose a spot for the chief settlement, which had hitherto been at Biloxi. He selected the present site, and left fifty men to clear the ground, and erect the necessary buildings. Much opposition was made, both by the military and the directors of the Western Company, to removing the seat of government to this place. Another obstacle, for a while, threatened almost insurmountable difficulties to his design. In 1719, the Mississippi rose to an extraordinary height; and, as the company did not possess sufficient force to protect the spot from inundation, by dykes and levees, it was for a time abandoned. In the November of 1722, however, in pursuance of orders, Delorme removed the principal establishment to New Orleans. In the following year, agreeably to Charlevoix, it consisted only of one hundred cabins, placed with little order, a large wooden warehouse, two or three dwelling-houses, and a miserable store-house, which had been used as a chapel, a mere shed being then the only accommodation afforded for a house of prayer. The population did not exceed two hundred. Thus commenced what is now called the "Crescent City;' which, in a commercial point of view, and in proportion to the number of its inhabitants, has not an equal on the face of the globe.

During the same year, a party of German emigrants, who had been disappointed by the financier, Law, of settling on lands granted to him in Arkansas, descended the river to New Orleans, in the hope of obtaining passage to France; but the government being either unwilling or unable to grant it, small allotments of land were apportioned them, on what is now called the German Coast. These people supplied the city with garden stuffs; and most of their descendants, with large accessions from the old country, still cultivate the same land, upon a much improved scale.

In September of this year, the capital was visited by a terrible hurricane, which levelled to the ground the church, if such it might be called, the hospital, and thirty houses; and three vessels that lay in the river were driven ashore. So destructive was it to the crops and gardens, that a scarcity of provisions was the consequence; and such was the distress, that several of the inhabitants seriously thought of abandoning the colony.

In the summer of 1727, the Jesuits and Ursuline nuns arrived. The fathers were placed on a tract of land now forming the lowest part of the fauxbourg St. Mary. The nuns were temporarily lodged in a house in the corner of Chartres and Bienville streets—but, soon after, the company laid the foundation of the edifice in Condé and Ursuline streets, to which they were removed in 1730; this place was occupied by them until the great value of the land induced them to divide the larger portion of it into lots. Their new convent was erected about two miles below the city, and there they removed in 1824. At this period, the council house and jail were built, on the upper side of the Cathedral.

In 1763, Clement XIII expelled the Jesuits from the dominions of the kings of France, Spain and Naples. They were, consequently, obliged to leave Louisiana. Their property in New Orleans was seized, and sold for about one hundred and eighty thousand dollars. At the time of the expulsion of this order, they owned the grounds which are now occupied by the first District. The valuable buildings in which they dwelt, were situated in Gravier and Magazine streets. Some of them were pulled down to make room for the late banking-house of the Canal bank, on the corner of those streets. It is computed, that more than one half of the real estate in this city, is derived from the confiscation of the property of the Jesuits, under legal proceedings had by order of the French government. The archives of the city contain many interesting and curious documents in relation to these proceedings, that are well worth examination.

The first visitation of the yellow fever was in 1769. Since that time it has continued to be almost an annual visitor. It was introduced into this contitent, in the above named year, *by a British vessel*, from the coast of Africa, *with a cargo of slaves.* In addition to this affliction, (the yellow fever above alluded to,) the colony was, during the year 1769, transferred to Spain, and the capital was taken possession of by O'Reilly, with a show of military power, and an individual disposition to oppress, that brought equal disgrace upon himself, and upon the government that commissioned him. The commerce of this city suffered very much from the restrictive colonial system of Spain. This, however, was removed in 1778, (a year memorable for a fire that burnt nine hundred houses at one time) and, in 1782, the mercantile interest of the place was benefited by still further extended privileges of trade.

The census of 1785 gives to the city a population of 4,780, exclusive of the settlements in the immediate vicinity.

In consequence of the commercial advantages above alluded to, a number of merchants from France established themselves here, and British trading vessels navigated the Mississippi. They were a species of marine pedlers, stopping to trade at any house, by making fast to a tree, and receiving in payment for merchandize, whatever the planter had to spare, or giving him long credits. The Americans, at that time, commenced the establishment of that trade from the west to New Orleans, which has been steadily increasing ever since. The idea of this traffic was first conceived by General Wilkinson. A lucrative business was also conducted by the Philadelphians, which the colonial authorities winked at for a while; but the Spanish minister, finding that he did not participate in the profits of it, as the Americans refused to comply with his hints to consign to his friends, put a stop to it. He procured a list of the names of the vessels, severely reprimanded the intendant, Navarro, and so worked upon his fears that he began to prosecute all infringements of the revenue laws, seizing the vessels, confiscating the goods and imprisoning the owners, captains and crews. The venal minister, perceiving that he had rendered himself extremely unpopular by his intermeddling with the commerce between Philadelphia and New Orleans, finally released all the individuals he had imprisoned, restoring the confiscated property, and discontinuing any further interference. The trade immediately received a new impulse and was greatly increased. General Wilkinson at the same time obtained permission to send one or more launches loaded with tobacco, from Kentucky.

Soon after, many Americans availed themselves of a privilege which was granted, of settling in the country.

The first company of French comedians arrived here in 1791. They came from Cape Francois, whence they made their escape from the revolted slaves. Others from the same quarter opened academies—the education of youth having hitherto been confined to the priests and nuns.

The baron Carondelet, in 1792, divided the city into four wards. He recommended lighting it, and employing watchmen. The revenue did not amount to seven thousand dollars, and to meet the charges for the purchases of lamps and oil, and to pay watchmen, a tax of one dollar and an eighth was levied upon chimneys.

He also commenced new fortifications around the capital. A fort was erected where the mint now stands, and another at the foot of Canal street. A strong redoubt was built in Rampart street, and at each of the angles of the now city proper. The Baron also paid some attention to training the militia. In the city, there were four companies of volunteers, one of artillery, and two of riflemen, consisting of one hundred men each, making an aggregate force of 700 men.

A great extension was given to business in February of this year. The inhabitants were now permitted to trade freely in Europe and America, wherever Spain had formed treaties for the regulation of commerce. The merchandise thus imported, was subject to a duty of fifteen per cent.; and exports to six per cent. With the Peninsula it was free.

In 1795 permission was granted by the king to citizens of the United States, during a period of ten years, to deposit merchandise at New Orleans. The succeeding year, the city was visited by another conflagration, which destroyed many houses. This reduced the tax upon chimneys so much, that recourse was had to assessing wheat bread and meat, to defray the expense of the city light and watch.

At the time of the transfer to the United States, the public property consisted of two large brick stores, running from the levee on each side of Main street, (which were burnt in 1822,)—a government house, at the corner of Levee and Toulouse streets, (which also suffered a similar fate in 1826,)—a military hospital, and a powder magazine, on the opposite side of the river, which was abandoned some years since—an old frame custom house—extensive barracks below those now remaining—five miserable redoubts, a town house, market house, assembly room and prison, a cathedral and presbytery, and a charity hospital. At this memorable era, the grounds which now constitute that thriving portion of the city, then known as the second municipality, were mostly used as a plantation. It was the property of a wealthy citizen named Gravier, after whom one of the principal streets that runs through the property has been called. How has the scene changed? At this moment it contains a population of nearly fifty thousand, and has become the centre of the business, and enterprise, and beauty of the city.

In 1804, New Orleans was made a port of entry and delivery, and Bayou St. John a port of delivery. The first act of incorporation was granted to the city, by the legislative council of the territory, in 1805, under the style of "the Mayor, Aldermen and inhabitants of the city of New Orleans." The officers were a mayor, a recorder, fourteen aldermen and a treasurer. This year a branch of the United States Bank was established in this capital.

The population of the city and suburbs in 1810, amounted to 24,552; having been trebled in seven years, under the administration of its new government. The prosperity of its trade increased in an equal ratio.

At that time the city extended no further down than Esplanade street, with the exception of here and there a villa scattered along the leeve; nor above, further than Canal street, unless occasionally a house occupying a square of ground. A few dwellings had been erected on Canal and Magazine streets, but it was considered to be getting quite into the country, to go beyond the *Polar Star Lodge*, which was at the corner of Camp and Gravier streets.

There was not then a paved street in the city. The late Benjamin Morgan, who, some time after, made the first attempt, was looked upon as a visionary. The circumstance which gave an impulse to improvements in the second municipality, was the erection of the American theatre, on Camp street, by James H. Caldwell, Esq., the only access to which, for a long time, was over flatboat gunwales. This was in 1823—4. He was ridiculed for his folly, and derided as a madman—but time proved his foresight. He was soon followed by a crowd that gave life and energy to that section; and, in a few years, through the enterprise of others of a similar spirit, the then suburb of St. Mary reached its present advanced state of elegance and prosperity.

LANE'S COTTON MILLS.

JEWELL'S CRESCENT CITY ILLUSTRATED.

The block where the Auctioneer's Exchange has since been built, was then occupied by a row of frail wooden shanties; and the corner of Royal and Custom house streets, where the bank now stands, was tenanted by Scott, who furnished food for his hundreds a day directly opposite, and who laid the foundation of his fortune in the tenement that was removed to make room for the present beautiful edifice.

ARCHITECTURE.

The houses are chiefly constructed with bricks; except a few ancient and dilapidated dwellings in the heart of the city, and some new ones in the outskirts. Wooden buildings are not permitted to be built, under present regulations, within what are denominated the fire limits. The modern structures, particularly in the First District, are generally three and four stories high, and are embellished with handsome and substantial granite, marble or iron fronts. The public buildings are numerous; and many of them will vie with any of the kind in our sister cities.

The view of New Orleans from the river, in ascending or descend.ng, is beautiful and imposing—seen from the spire of St. Patrick's Church, it presents a panorama at once magnificent and surprising. In taking a lounge through the lower part of the city, the stranger finds a difficulty in believing himself to be in an American city. The older buildings are of ancient and foreign construction, and the manners, customs and language are various—the population being composed, in nearly equal proportions, of American, French, Creoles, and Spaniards, together with a large portion of Germans and Irish and a good sprinkling from almost every other nation upon the globe.

In the summer of 1844, a fire destroyed about seven blocks of buildings b.tween Common and Canal streets, near the charity Hospital. The ground has since been occupied with much better buildings, and presents a very improved appearance.

POPULATION,

The population of New Orleans, after it was ceded to the United States, increased very rapidly. At the time of the transfer, there were not eight thousand inhabitants.

	Blacks.	Whites.	Total.
In 1810	8,001	16,551	24,552
1815	——	——	32,947
1820	19,737	21,614	41,350
1825	——	——	45,336
1830	21,280	28,530	49,826
1840	——	59,519	102,191
1850	——	91,431	119,460
1860	——	149,063	174,491
1870	——	140,923	191,413

and at the present period there are, probably two hundred and twenty thousand. During 1844 there were more buildings erected than any previous year—notwithstanding which, tenements are in great demand, and rents continue high.

BOARD OF HEALTH.

The first ordinance for the establishment of a board of health in this city, (so far as known,) was passed by the general council in June, of 1 1. The board consisted of nine members—three aldermen, three physicians, and three private citizens. It was invested with ample powers to adopt and enforce such sanitary regulations as were thought conducive to the health of the city. This board performed all its functions well during the first year of its existence. The second year there was a falling off; but a dissolution did not take place till 1843. In 1844, the board of health having ceased to officiate, the general council invited the medico-chirurgical society to take charge of this duty. This proposition was accepted, and a committee of nine members appointed, with full power to act as a board of health.

SOCIETY.

Society, as at present constituted in New Orleans, has very little resemblance to that of any other city in the Union. It is made up of a heterogeneous mixture of almost all nations. First, and foremost, is the Creole population. All who are born here, come under this designation, without reference to the birth place of their parents. They form the foundation, on which the superstructure of what is termed "society," is erected. They are remarkably exclusive in their intercourse with others, and, with strangers, enter into business arrangements with extreme caution. They were once, and very properly, considered as the patricians of the land. But they are not more distinguished for their exclusiveness, and pride of family, than for their habits of punctuality, temperance and good faith.

CHARACTER OF THE POPULATION.

Till about the commencement of the present century, the period of the transfer of Louisiana to the United States, the Creoles were almost entirely of French and Spanish parentage. Now, the industrious Germans, the shrewd and persevering Irishmen, are beginning to be quite numerous, and many of them have advanced to a condition of wealth and respectability.

Next come the emigrants from the sister States, from the mighty west, from the older sections of the south, and (last not least) from the colder regions of the north, the enterprising, calculating, hardy Yankee.

Then come the nondescript watermen. Our river steam navigation, averaging, during half the year, some three hundred arrivals per month, furnishes a class of fifteen thousand men, who have few if any parallels in the world. The numberless flatboats that throng the levees for an immense distance, are peopled and managed by an amphibious race of human beings, whose mode of living is much like that of the alligator, with whom they ironically claim relationship, but who carry under their rough exterior and uncouth manners, a heart as generous and noble as beats in any human breast. They are the children of the Mississippi, as the Arabs are of the great desert, and, like them, accustomed to encounter danger in every shape. Combining all the most striking peculiarities of the common sailor, the whaleman, the backwoodsman, and the Yankee, without imitating, or particularly resembling any one of them, they are a class entirely by themselves, unique, eccentric, original, a distinct and unmistakeable feature in the floating mass that swarms on the levees, and treads the streets, of the Cresent City.

Among them may be found the representatives of nearly all the states. Some are descendants of the Pilgrims, and have carried with them the industrious habits, and the strict moral principles, of their Puritan forefathers, into the wilds of the West. They are all active, enterprising, fearless, shrewd, independent, and self-sufficient, and often aspiring and ambitious, as our halls of legislation, and our business circles can testify. They are just the stuff to lay the broad foundations of freedom in a new country—able to clear the forest, and till the soil, in time of peace, to defend it in war, and to govern it at all times.

SOCIAL CHARACTERISTICS.

Of the two hundred and fifty thousand souls, who now occupy this capital, about twenty thousand may be estimated as migratory. These are principally males, engaged in the various departments of business. Some of them have families at the North, where they pass the summer. Many are bachelors, who have no home for one half the year, and, if the poets are to be believed, less than half a home for the remainder. As these two classes of migratory citizens, who live at the hotels and boarding-houses, embrace nearly, if not quite, one third the business men of the city, it may serve to some extent, to accout for the seemingly severe restrictions by which the avenues to good native society are protected. Unexceptionable character, certified beyound mistake, is the only passport to the domestic circle of the Creole. With such credentials their hospitality knows no limits. The resident Americans are less suspicious in admitting you to their hospitality, though not more liberal than their Creole neighbors, when once their confidence is secured.

The restrictions thus thrown around society, and the great difficulty which the new comer experiences in securing a share in those social enjoyments to which he has been accustomed in other places, have had an unfavorable effect upon the morals of the place. Having no other resource for pastime, when the hours of business are over, he flies to such public entertainments as the city affords. And if these are not always what they should be, it behooves us to provide better. Public libraries, reading rooms, galleries for the exhibition of the fine arts, lyceums for lectures, and other kindred rational amusements, would do much to establish a new and better order, and to break down those artificial barriers, which separate so many refined and pure minded men from the pleasures and advantages of general society, condemning them to live alone and secluded, in the midst of all that is lovely and attractive in the social relations of life.

HEALTH OF THE CITY.

The character of New Orleans. in respect to health, has been much and unjustly abused. At the north, in ratio to their population, the consumption annually destroys more than the yellow fever of the south. Patients with pulmonary complaints, resort to these latitudes for relief, where such diseases are otherwise rarely known. In truth, this capital shows a more favorable bill of mortality, than any seaport town in the United States.

MORALS.

There is little to be said in favor of the morals of New Orleans, during the first few years after its cession. Report made them much worse than they were. As the community was composed of some of the worst classes of society, gathered from every region under the sun, nothing very good was to be expected. But circumstances have changed. A system of wholesome police regulations has been introduced and enforced, which has either brought the desperate and the lawless under subjection, or expelled them from the community. By reference to the statistics of crime, in other commercial cities in proportion to the number of inhabitants, the stranger will be convinced that this City has reason to be proud of her standing. Personal security in the public streets, at all hours, is never endangered—and females may venture out after dark, without a protector, and be free from insult and molestation.

THE PROFESSIONS.

The learned professions here, generally, stand preeminently high. The science of medicine may boast of a talent and a skill, that would confer honor upon any city in the Union—and the few empirics that disgrace the practice, are so well known, that the evil is circumscribed within very narrow limits. The clergy are proverbial for their learning and eloquence—and the same remarks will apply with equal force to members of the bar.

PUBLIC LIBRARY.

This city, at the present time, possesses no public library. Considering the population, and their ability, this must be regarded as a blot upon the intelligence of its citizens. This is completely a commercial community, however, and money is the universal ambition. Thence springs that acknowledged deficiency in literature and the fine arts, observable to the stranger. But shall it still remain? Is there no Girard—no Astor—among our millionaires, who will leave behind them a monument which shall make their names dearer and more honored in all coming time, than those of heroes and conquerors?

SOCIETIES.

The Masonic fraternity in New Orleans appears to enjoy all their ancient privileges. There are some sixty-five lodges, besides a grand lodge and an encampement. Here is a large number of the order of Odd Fellows, and one of Equal Fellows—a Typographical Union, and Mechanics, Hibernian, St. Andrews, German, and Swiss societies. These are all, more or less, of a benevolent nature; and within their own circles, have all been extremely serviceable.

THE MISSISSIPPI.

The navigation of the Mississipi, even by steamboats, in 1818, was extremely tedious. The Etna is recorded as arriving at Shipping port, a few miles below Louisville, in

THE STEAMBOAT LANDING.

thirty-two days. The Governor Shelby in *twenty-two* days, was considered as a remarkably short passage. An hermaphrodite brig was *seventy one* days from New Orleans—and a keel boat *one hundred and one*; the latter to Louisville. Now the time occupied is *four to five* days.

During the business season, which continues from the first of November to July, the levee, to the extent of five miles, is crowded with vessels of all sizes, but more especially ships, from every part of the world—with hundreds of immense floating castles and palaces, called steamboats; and barges and flatboats innumerable. No place can present a more busy, bustling scene. The loading and unloading of vessels and steamboats—the transportation, by some three thousand drays, of cotton, sugar, tobacco and the various and extensive produce of the great West, strikes the stranger with wonder and admiration. The levee and piers that range along the whole length of the city, extending back on an average of some two hundred feet, are continually covered with moving merchandize. This was once a pleasant promenade, where the citizen enjoyed his delightful morning and evening walk; but now there is scarcely room amid hogsheads, boxes and bales, for the business men to crowd along, without a sharp lookout for his personal safety.

COMMERCIAL EMPORIUM.

The position of New Orleans, as a vast commercial emporium, is unrivalled—as will be seen by a single glance at the map of the United States. As the depot of the West, and the half-way house of foreign trade, it is almost impossible to anticipate its future magnitude.

Take a view, for instance, of the immense regions known under the name of the Mississippi valley. Its boundaries on the West are the Rocky Mountains, and Mexico; on the South, the Gulf of Mexico; on the East the Alleghany mountains; and, on the North, the Lakes and British possessions. It contains nearly as many square miles, and more tillable ground, than all continental Europe, and, if peopled as densely as England, would sustain a population of five hundred millions—more than half of the present inhabitants of the earth. Its surface is generally cultivable, and its soil rich, with a climate varying to suit all products, for home consumption or a foreign market. The Mississippi is navigable twenty-one hundred miles—passing a small portage three thousand may be achieved. It embraces the productions of many climates, and a mining country abounding in coal, lead, iron and copper ore, all in veins of wonderful richness. The Missouri stretches thirty-nine hundred miles to the Great Falls, among the Flat Foot Indians, and five thousand miles from New Orleans. The Yellow Stone, navigable for eleven hundred miles, the Platte for sixteen hundred, and the Kansas for twelve hundred, are only tributaries to the latter river. The Ohio is two thousand miles to Pittsburgh, receiving into her bosom from numerous streams, the products of New York, Pennylvania, Ohio, Kentucky, Western Virginia, Tennesee, Indiana, and Illinois. The Arkansas, Big Black, Yazoo, Red River, and many others, all pouring their wealth into the main artery, the Mississippi, upon whose mighty current it floats down to its grand reservoir, New Orleans.

ALGIERS.

DRY DOCKS.

For the repair of shipping and river craft, our port is supplied with several extensive dry docks along the Algiers Levee.

THE OCEAN DOCK.

This is located near the landing of the First and Second District ferryboats at Bartholomew street. It is 203 feet long in the clear and 60 feet beam, with capacity for a ship of a thousand tons, 225 feet keel and drawing fifteen feet. For the service of the dock there is a steam saw mill, and a smith's shop is also attached. The number of mechanics and laborers employed during a busy season is from fifty to one hundred. The officers of the Ocean Dock company for 1872 were Messrs. Spencer Field, President and Treasurer, J. B. Williams, Secretary and F. G. Mackie and J. F. Follett, Managers.

THE MARINE DOCK.

This adjoins the Ocean Dock below, and has a front of 500 feet by 250 feet deep. It has capacity for a ship of 1600 tons. The two Peruvian Monitors were recently repaired in this dock. The officers of the company are Messrs. S. Hopkins, Jr., President; C. E. Morrison, Secretary and J. Geddes, Treasurer.

THE VALLETTE DOCK.

This is located at the foot of Vallette street, a block below the landing of the Third District ferry. It has a frontage of about 100 feet on Patterson street, with a depth of 200 feet to the river. The dock is 315 feet long by 84 feet beam, with capacity for the largest ships that come into this port. It employs a blacksmith shop and a saw mill, with several gangs of saws. From 75 to 150 men are employed in ship building and repairing. The dock is owned by a joint stock company, under the special management of Messrs. François Vallette and Octave F. Vallette, Paul Fouchy, President; and Roger T. Boyle, Secretary.

THE GOOD INTENT DRY DOCK.

This is located just above the Algiers landing of the Canal street ferry. The grounds of the company have a river frontage of one and a half squares and a depth of 150 feet. The dock measures 200 feet in length by 50 feet in breadth inboard. The works employ from 60 to 100 men. The affairs of the company are managed by four directors, the present being Messrs. S. Hopkins, Jr., G. Busing, Hermann Schroeder, Secretary, and John H. Reiners.

The manufacture of ice, in New Orleans, is now successfully and profitably carried on. A view of the works is to be found on another page, and will give some idea of the extensive scale on which the business is conducted.

HON. CHARLES GAYARRÉ.

THIS distinguished Louisianian, whose historical and literary labors have made his name familiar to the *literati* of this country and of Europe, was born in New Orleans in 1801. He is of mixed Spanish and French descent, his paternal ancestor, Don Esteban Gayarré, having come here in 1766 with Governor Ulloa as *Contad* or Comptroller of the province of Louisiana, which had just then been ceded by France to Spain. His grand-mother in the female line was the daughter of Destrehan, who, for a long time, had been the treasurer of the colony under the French, and his maternal grand-father was Etienne Boré, who was the first to make sugar in Louisiana in 1795, and was Mayor of New Orleans under the French Republic in 1803. Among his ancestors were also the Grandprés who were the companions of Bienville and Iberville, and whose descendants occupied important military positions under the French and Spanish dominions. Charles Gayarré was educated at the "College d'Orléans" then conducted by Lakanal, the celebrated member of the French Convention, who was then an exile in Louisiana. In this college some of the most distinguished men of this state received their diplomas. In 1826, Mr. Gayarré went to Philadelphia and studied law in the office of William Rawle, then at the head of the bar of that city and well known as the author of an excellent work on the constitution of the United States. In 1829 the subject of this sketch was admitted to the bar, and in 1830 he returned to Louisiana, where he published, in French, an "Historical Essay on Louisiana." In the same year, he was almost unanimously elected to the State Legislature, and was chosen by that body to write the complimentary address sent by them to the French people on the occasion of the Revolution of 1830. He was appointed assistant Attorney General in 1831, and two years later, he was called to the office of presiding judge of the City Court

of New Orleans. In 1835, although he was a Democrat, and the Whigs had a majority of the legislature, Mr. Gayarré was elected to the Senate of the U. S. for six years, three of his political opponents having voted for him. Unfortunately the wretched condition of Mr. Gayarré's health prevented him from taking his seat, and in obedience to the advice of his physicians, he had to go to Europe, where he remained until the end of 1843. Shortly after his return he was elected to the legislature from the city of N. O., and carried several important measures, among others a bill to provide for the liabilities of the State, whereby a reduction of two millions and a half of the State debt was effected during Gov. Mouton's administration. Having been re-elected in 1846, he accepted the office of Secretary of State tendered to him by Gov. Isaac Johnson, an office of very great importance and responsibility at the time, as in addition to his other duties, the Secretary of State was *ex officio* Superintendent of Public Education, and constituted jointly with the State Treasurer, the "Board of Currency." In this laborious position, the multifarious duties of which he discharged with great benefit to the State, Mr. Gayarré remained till 1853, having been re-appointed by Governor Walker in 1850. During that period, Mr. Gayarré published in two volumes a "History of Louisiana," in the French language, and in which all the most interesting and curious documents he had collected from the archives of France were textually reproduced. He also published through Harper & Co., of New York, a series of lectures in English under the title of the "Romance of the History of Louisiana."

The State library of Baton Rouge, with its valuable historical works and documents collected by Mr. Gayarré during his seven years term of office, was almost totally destroyed during the war. A few years before that event, Mr. Gayarré had succeeded in obtaining from the Spanish government important documents from the archives of the Kingdom, the substance of which he embodied in his "History of Louisiana," in three volumes, octavo, embracing the French, Spanish and American régimes, from the earliest settlement of the colony to the year 1861—a work which may justly be considered as the most valuable contribution ever made to the history of our State. This work has already passed through several editions. After a brief connection with the American or Know-nothing party, which he left at once when his efforts to strike out the anti-catholic plank of their platform proved unavailing, and an unsuccessful run for Congress as an independent candidate, Mr. Gayarré supported the candidacy of President Pierce, and his name was prominently mentioned in connection with the Mission to Spain on the accession of the new administration. That appointment, however, having been first tendered to Senator Soulé, Mr. Marcy, then Secretary of State, offered to Mr. Gayarré the position of Assistant Secretary, just then created, and in which his extensive knowledge of European affairs and fine linguistic attainments would have proved eminently useful to the Administration. His offer, however, was declined by Mr. Gayarré. In 1861, Mr. Gayarré, having been called upon for his views on the right of Secession, addressed an immense meeting of citizens at Odd Fellows' Hall, taking a strong

Louisiana National Bank,

—OF—

NEW ORLEANS.

United States Depository & Financial Agent,

OFFICERS:

JOSEPH H. OGLESBY, President,

A. LURIA, Cashier.

DIRECTORS:

J. F. D. LANIER,	W. A. JOHNSON.
J. N. LEA,	T. L. AIREY,
JULIUS VAIRIN,	W. J. FRIERSON,
JOSEPH H. OGLESBY.	

Incorporated, December 30th, 1865.

Commenced Business, January 18th, 1866.

CAPITAL STOCK, $1,000,000.

SURPLUS FUND, *$150,000.*

Total Net Earnings, Commencement of Business, [exclusive of taxes] to
July 1, 1872. $712,272.37.

Total Dividends, Commencement of Business, [exclusive of taxes] to
July 1, 1872, $530,000.

State rights view of the subject. During the war, Mr. Gayarré advocated the arming of the slaves and the conclusion of a treaty with England and France recognizing the independence of the Southern Confederacy on the basis of a gradual emancipation of the African race. In 1866, when Louisiana was presumed to be reconstructed, Mr. Gayarré's name was put forward by his friends in the Legislature, and came within a few votes of obtaining the honor of an election to the United States Senate—Messrs. Randal Hunt and G. Williamson, his successful competitors, having been denied admittance to that body. Since the war, Mr. Gayarré, besides the last volume of his great historical work on Louisiana, has published a "*History of Philip II*," of Spain—a work of great research and sound historical philosophy and a novel based on the early history of Louisiana, "*Fernando de Limos*," which has elicited great praise from all the literary journals of the country. He is now preparing for publication, another historical novel, "Aubert Dubayet," in which the hero goes through the American Revolution of 1776 and the French revolution of 1789. It will doubtless prove highly interesting, and give ample scope to the writer's wide field of information and fertility of conception.

HON. MILES TAYLOR.

THIS gentleman, who is one of the best civil lawyers in this State, was born in New York about sixty years ago. He is small of stature, gray haired, fair complexioned and bright eyed.

When quite young he came to this State and devoted his attention to the study of the law. He passed an excellent examination before the Supreme Court, and obtained his license to practice. As Mr. Taylor had previously studied pharmacy, old Judge Ilsley with naïveté said at the time of his admission to the bar, that Mr. Taylor would be unrivaled in bringing an apothecary (hypothecary) action.

Mr. Taylor has proved to be one of our most eminent lawyers. He is certainly a gentleman of vast talents, profoundly read in law, and trained to grapple closely with every question. He is distinguished for grace and ease of manner, and for happy and polished address.

He exerts great influence on the mind and affection of those who know him.

He is a good speaker, clear and correct in diction. Endowed by nature with a quick and vigorous understanding, his arguments are vivid, and he shows in all the cases intrusted to him, honesty of purpose, earnestness and faithfulness. Even at his advanced age he is most diligent and attentive to business.

Mr. Taylor has represented Louisiana in the Congress of the United States when that body contained the most brilliant array of ability ever seen in any deliberate assembly. He there distinguished himself as a polished debater, achieved a high position, and stood on the same plane as the most prominent stateman who adorned the halls of the National Legislature.

THE ST. MARY'S MARKET fronts on Tchoupitoulas street and runs to New Levee. It was completed in 1836 in the rusticated Doric order at a cost of about $48,000.

MAYOR JOHN L. LEWIS.

OF all the members of the old population of New Orleans, there is no one who is better known, and more universally esteemed by all classes, than the subject of this sketch. John Lawson Lewis is the son of Judge Lewis, who was appointed to the Sppreme Bench of the then Territory of Orleans by Thomas Jefferson, immediately after the purchase of Louisiana from France. Mr. Lewis was then only three years old, and was brought up at the school of Mr. D'Hébécourt, on the old Bayou Road, where he had for his schoolmates many of the creoles who afterward took a leading part in the politics of the State, and afterward completed his studies at the Academy of the Rev. James F. Hull, on Canal street. In 1819, young Lewis left school and read law under his father, entering shortly after the office of Martin Gordon, Sr., then Chief Clerk of the First District Court, to which position he succeeded upon the resignation of Mr. Gordon, in 1826. In 1842, John L. Lewis was unanimously elected Commanding General of the First Division of the Louisiana Militia, an office for which he was peculiarly fitted by his previous military training and his great personal influence, and to which he was invariable re-elected without the shadow of an opposition. In 1845, he ran as an independent candidate for the Shrievalty of the Parish of Orleans, and though opposed by several of our most popular citizens, was returned at the head of the poll. So ably did he administer the office, that on three successive occasions he was re-elected by handsome majorities, sometimes in the face of a formidable party opposition, and when, some years later, an effort was made to defeat the hitherto invincible A. D. Crossman, Gen. Lewis accepted the nomination of the Democratic Party for the Mayoralty, and although the ticket upon which he ran was beaten, so great was his personal popularity that he was returned over his competitor by a small majority. When the war broke out Gen. Lewis, although not liable to military service, promptly offered his sword to the Confederate Government, and served throughout the war with great gallantry and distinction in the Trans-Mississippi Department. As a public officer, Gen. Lewis has always maintained the reputation of an able, courteous and incorruptible public servant. A high-toned, affable gentleman, ever generous and open-handed whenever his means allowed him to indulge the warm impulses of his nature, few men of his generation can claim a larger circle of attached friends, or after occupying so many responsible positions, are able to exhibit more unexceptionable record than John L. Lewis.

The following letter, written by Gov. H. W. Allen to Gen. Lewis, soon after the battle of Mansfield, shows the high estimation in which Gen. Lewis's services were held by that distinguished official :—

SHREVEPORT, LA., April 27, 1864.

GEN. LEWIS :

MY DEAR SIR.—I have just heard from you through Mr. Wagner. I am rejoiced to hear that you are doing well. I sent my Surgeon-General down to take care of you. He reported that you were doing well.

Receive my thanks, my dear sir, and the thanks of Louisiana for your gallant conduct on the battle-field of one of the best fought battles of this war. If you visit Shreveport do not fail to call on me. I shall be glad to receive you at the Executive Mansion and extend all the courtesy due a brave patriot and gallant soldier.

Very truly your obedient servant,

(Signed.) HENRY W. ALLEN, Gov. Louisiana.

To Gen. John L. Lewis, Mansfield, La.

ROBERT MOTT ESQ.

Is a native of Baltimore, Md., of fair complexion, classical features, of commanding appearance and about fifty-seven years of age. He is open and above everything like dissimulation, warmly affectionate and steadfast in friendship.

As a lawyer, the clearness of his statement presents at once a picture to the mind. In his arguments he appeals forcibly to strict reason, and his tone, though deferential and courtly, is manly. He indulges very sparingly in declamation.

He is one of the best civil, commercial and chancery lawyers in this State, with an uncommon capacity for effective and untiring industry. His legal studies have been comprehensive. He writes with great facility and cleverness, exhibiting philosophical research and maturity of judgment.

Several years ago, he served as a member in the State Legislature of Louisiana with much ability. After our late war, he went to Europe and visited the principal cities of the Old World.

Mr. Mott is now in the full vigor of all his faculties, active in his movements and in turning off business with as much ease as when he entered public life thirty years ago. He is kindly in his disposition, so as to devote some of his time and resources to making others happy—domestic and affectionate in his habits, and religious without intolerance.

He is a cautious and safe counselor, a diligent man of business, punctual to his appointments, regular in the distribution of his time, never suffering pleasure or distraction of any kind to interfere with his duties.

JOSEPH H. OGLESBY

IS DESCENDED from Scottish ancestry. His father, the Rev. Joseph Oglesby, D.D., was born in West Moreland, Virginia, the native county of Washington and Lee. His mother, Elizabeth Hite, was born in the Valley of the Shenandoah. His grandfather removed to Kentucky, and the father and mother of Mr. Oglesby subsequently removed from Kentucky to Madison, in Indiana, at which place the subject of this sketch was born September 14, 1822. In 1839, Mr. Oglesby came to New Orleans, and was employed as a clerk in the house of Hyde & Comstock, Poydras street. In the year 1842, Mr. Comstock retired, and at the early age of twenty, Mr. Oglesby became a partner in the Western produce commission house of Hyde & Oglesby. The house did a large and profitable business, and upon the withdrawal of Mr. Hyde, was continued under the style of Oglesby & McCaulay, which was a leading house in the Western trade, at the declaration of civil hostilities in 1861.

Upon the termination of the war, Mr. Oglesby resumed business under his own name, in the same street in which he has been engaged in the same trade for a period of about thirty years. Perhaps few cities have undergone the same mutations of commerce within the same period. An inspection of the Directory of 1856, shows that of about 300 firms engaged in the commission business at that date, only eleven exist at present under the same style, while very few of the members who composed these firms are in business at all. To have pursued the same business, in the same community, amid such vicissitudes of commerce, and for so long a period, displays a sound texture of character and systematic business habits. After a period of mercantile probation so long and so successful, it was natural that Mr. Oglesby should have been promoted to the charge of the associated interests of his fellow merchants. The highest and most disinterested evidence of commercial ap-

TOURO BUILDINGS.

ST. CHARLES HOTEL.

RIVERS & LONSDALE, Proprietors.

prsdiation was, of course, his election as President of the Chamber of Commerce, in which office he is now serving his second term.

In 1869, he was elected President of the Louisiana National Bank, one of our largest financial institutions. As we believe much of the capital stock has been subscribed abroad, the appointment shows that the reputation of Mr. Oglesby is appreciated by other commercial communities besides his own. In the same year he was chosen President of the Commercial Insurance Company, of New Orleans. He was also tendered, at the same period, the office of Mayor of the City of New Orleans, and was solicited by citizens, without distinction of party, to accept it. This important position he was, after much deliberation and in consequence of official and domestic obligations, compelled to decline. The discharge of the trusts accepted by Mr. Oglesby with the superintendence and consultations of his own commercial house demands very unusual faculties. It requires moreover that extended experience which, by knowing and being known to the men and commerce of a community, assures accuracy and dispatch of administration. Nothing except the combination of these qualities could enable Mr. Oglesby to wield the vast and complicated duties so conferred upon him. This, however, he seems to do with comparative ease. He has even, by dint of systematic organization and judicious choice of subordinates, been enabled to spare extended portions of the years 1869–70–71 to be devoted to a tour in Europe. In addition to the education of his children and the care of the health of Mrs. Oglesby, he has thus had an opportunity to observe the commercial and social systems of other countries. It may be mentioned at this point that Mr. Oglesby married Miss Margaret Hendricks. This estimable lady died August 24, 1871, at Paris, France, leaving to her afflicted husband the comparative consolation of a family of interesting and well-reared children.

Mr. Oglesby has been enabled by his experience at home and his observations abroad to render to New Orleans invaluable services toward the restoration of her commerce. The extraordinary result to which we have adverted elsesewhere, by which an artificial system of transportation has wrested from New Orleans so much of her natural and immediate territory, has compelled her to adopt a countervailing economy and dispatch in conducting the trade of this debateable region ; no one has been more sagacious than Mr. Oglesby in perceiving this inevitable conflict, or more prompt in adopting a counteracting commercial strategy. The ancient mode of receiving, storing, and forwarding by produce sail vessels, no longer met the demands of the interior. Even a port of the cotton crop immediately adjacent to our market began to feel the influence of these competing facilities. The Western surplus of provisions once exclusively exported, foreign and coastwise, through our port, was taken *across* direct to Eastern Atlantic ports for exportation, while the European imports, *consumed* in the interior, took the same route. This formidable *invasion* rendered necessary the construction of new and the extension of incomplete railroads into Louisiana, Texas, and Mexico. It also required improved facilities

of importation and transmission of goods in bond. It was also necessary to establish close connection between the rail and river, with all other facilities for protection and dispatch of commodities in transit, as employed by our competitors elsewhere.

It became necessary to establish a cheap and certain transportation by river barges, the storage, transfer, and shelter of bulk grain and other products by elevator, with an organization of ocean steam line adequate to the dispatch of our staple crops, and other commerce. To each and all of these Mr. Oglesby has given the influence of his approbation and the aid of his capital. It is under such auspices that New Orleans bids fair to replace the commerce of which she has been despoiled, with an infinitely greater, for which she can never fear a rival. In enumerating the men who have contributed signally to maintain and advance the commercial destinies of our city, it is our duty to assign a most prominent position to Joseph H. Oglesby, Esq. With unimpaired health and energies, and enlarged capacity for continued usefulness, we may enjoy the benefit of his counsel and action until the crisis of commercial competition shall have passed from New Orleans, and the object of her restoration effected.

THOMAS H. KENNEDY, ESQ.

Judge Thomas H. Kennedy is an eminent jurist and a man of unblemished honor.

He was born in New Orleans, and is now nearly fifty years old. He is of slight but manly form, black haired, with high and broad forehead and eagle eyes.

He is thoroughly acquainted with the ancient and modern writers, and speaks several foreign languages fluently.

With culture, a keen intellect and much force of character, he is always prepared for a full discharge of his duties.

The genial current of his soul is not frozen by calculating policy. He loathes the cold and sordid propensity of clinging to power so epidemic in our day.

Endowed with the highest faculties of the understanding, despising all the surface accomplishments that dazzle the vulgar, he has an immovable fortitude in all those situations in which human weakness is most apt to yield.

His devotion to the maintenance of principle is embellished by modesty. These rare qualities are not only worthy of admiration, but of imitation in this degenerate age.

This true and worthy gentleman acts always so as to satisfy his own conscience. How very few like him !

Judge Kennedy is not only a man of firm mind and steadily fixed principles, but he is also a person of great accomplishments and excellent abilities as a lawyer.

Educated in the study of the civil law at one of our best colleges, he resided long enough in Europe to perfect his learning in all the ordinary branches of education.

Those of our readers who are personally acquainted with him will bear me witness that he is the most unpretending of men. His abilities and virtues make him an ornament of society.

He was for many years before our late war Judge of the Third District Court. At that time it was a high honor to occupy such a position, because the judicial ermine was then kept in all its purity. Since then how many changes !

LA. EQUITABLE LIFE INSURANCE COMPANY.

The business of Life Insurance in this country is of such recent growth that few people appreciate its importance and greatness. Beginning only about a quarter of a century ago from the most slender foundation it has grown into mammoth proportions. The combined assets of the various companies is estimated to exceed $250,000,000 with an amount of insurance at risk exceeding $3,000,000,000. The annual income exceeds a hundred millions of dollars. The influence of these corporations outside of the good they do to the widows and orphans of deceased policy holders, is paramount in every place that they are located. Their funds requiring prompt and speedy investment furnish means for commercial and industrial enterprises that otherwise might not have been initiated.

It was plainly seen after the war that one of the surest ways of rebuilding the prosperity of the South was the establishment of Home Life Insurance Cos. It was with this view that in the year 1868 a number of the most prominent gentlemen in New Orleans formed the Louisiana Equitable Life Insurance Co. under the management of Joseph Ellison Esq. an old time merchant of this city and one of its best known citizens as President, and Wm. P. Harper as Secretary, the Company began its career and notwithstanding the opposition it met with it steadily kept on its way, daily adding to its list of customers, and finding fresh favor in the eyes of the community and particularly of those who felt it their interest and duty to support Home Institutions. In the latter part of 1870 the official staff of the Company was increased by the appointment of Mr. Wm. C. Robbins as Manager of Agencies. Mr. Robbins' long experience in the business was of great value to the Company, and under his intelligent management its business grew rapidly and was extended into the adjacent states. In September 1872, owing to the resignation of Messrs. Ellison and Harper, Mr. James H. Low, formerly of the firm of Wood & Low, and Wm. Henderson, Esq., were respectively elected to the positions of President and Secretary. These gentlemen, in conjunction with Mr. Robbins have, by their earnest efforts, placed the Company in a position worthy of the city that gave it birth. The Board of Directors are composed of the first business men of the city. Their names are known throughout the whole country and give it a standing wherever it may be introduced. The Company has, by its promptness in settlement of claims, and the liberality of its plans earned a well-deserved reputation and it would be safe to prophesy that the day is not far distant when the Louisiana Equitable Life will stand among the foremost companies of the country.

TIVOLI CIRCLE is an unornamented public ground, circular in form and about 150 yards in diameter. It is surrounded by a wide pavement and is enclosed in an iron railing with four gate-ways. The circle is capable of such improvement as will add greatly to the attractiveness of the locality and to the comfort of citizens. From this point St. Charles street expands to double its width below the circle and becomes a broad and magnificent avenue. The New Masonic Temple, the Temple Sinai and the residence of Andrew Smith Esq overlook this Circle.

NEW ORLEANS GAS-LIGHT COMPANY.

In 1822, when Baltimore was the only American city lighted by gas, James H. Caldwell, Esq., an enterprising citizen of New Orleans, constructed works here for lighting his theatre, the old American. A gas company was formed in 1829, but failing in compliance with the terms of its charter, it was soon dissolved. In 1833 Mr. Caldwell obtained a charter, and in the face of many difficulties, and by his own resources, he established the Gas Works on a large scale and on a permanent basis. Mr. Caldwell also introduced gas in Cincinnati and Havana. He was long a member of the City Council, and foremost in measures of enterprise and public benefaction. The oddly sounding and usually mispronounced classical and mythological names of many of our streets above canal, were chiefly of Mr. Caldwell's suggestion while he was an alderman and our Fourth District a swamp.

The New Orleans Gaslight and Banking Company was chartered by the General Assembly in 1835, with a capital stock of six million dollars. By this charter it was provided that the Gas Works might be bought by the City after forty years. The charge for gas was at first regulated by the time of burning; afterwards meters were introduced. In 1860 an amendment to the charter limited the charge to $4 per thousand cubic feet of gas, required gas to be supplied to the Charity Hospital free, extended the term of the Company to 1895 and withdrew the exclusive privilege of furnishing gas. The capital of the Company is now about two millions. The works, a mile from the river, are bounded by Gravier, Pedido, Magnolia and Locust streets, the slate roofed brick buildings occupying the entire square. On the grounds are shops for blacksmiths, carpenters, and machinists, for the manufacture and repair of articles and implements used, except the clay retorts, which are brought from Belgium, of which there are 200 in operation. The interesting process of making gas, differs in no essential respect from the well-known method employed elsewhere, the coke and coal tar being utilized. To remove the carbonic acid and sulphuretted hydrogen gas, quicklime is used made entirely of oyster shells. The Pittsburgh coal employed produces 10,500 cubic feet of gas per ton. The reservoirs are six in number the largest being of more than half a million cubic feet.

The gas consumed in 1846 was 31,352,800 feet; in 1856, 85,421,000 feet; in 1866, 174,649,000 feet; in 1871, 249,417,000 feet. The present number of street lamps is 3476; of meters, over 10,000. The gas pipe in 1836, was eight miles in length; in 1846, 23 miles; in 1856, 61¾ miles; in 1866, 100 miles; and in 1872, 134½ miles.

The Presidents of the company were: in 1835 James H. Caldwell; in 1835-36, E. Yorke; in 1836, Samuel Heennan, Jr.; in 1836-37 and '38, Thomas Barrett; in 1838-39 and '40, Thomas C. Magoffin; from 1840 to 1856, James Robb; from 1856 to 1863, J. H. Wood; in 1863, W. H. Mercer; from 1863 to 1869, G. C. Duncan; from 1869 and present incumbent, James Jackson.

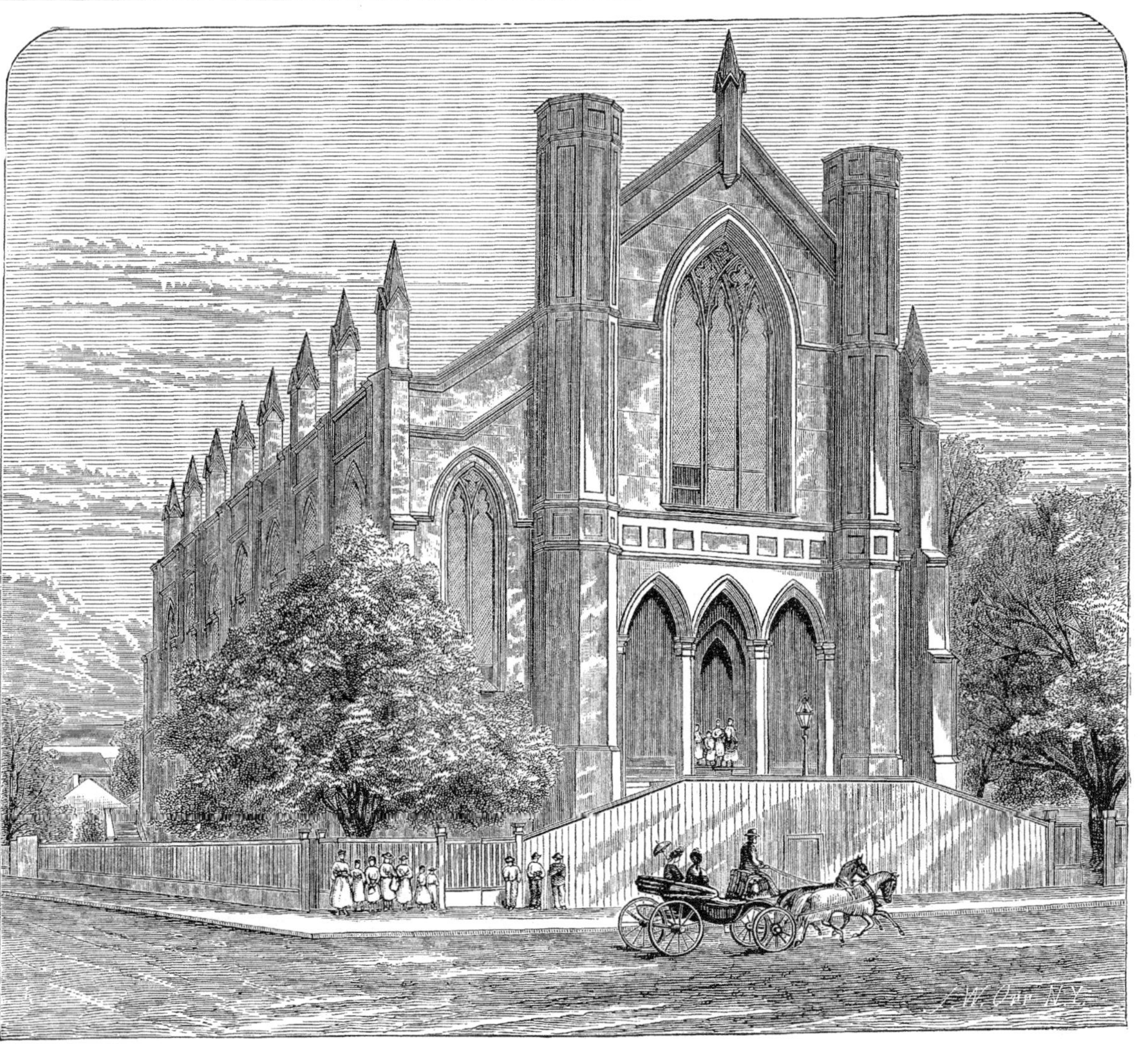

TRINITY CHURCH.

MAYOR JOHN R. CONWAY.

JOHN R. CONWAY was born in Alexandria, Virginia, August 24th 1825. His ancestors were from Wales, and emigrated to the State of his nativity in the reign of Charles the Second. Their exists now among their descendents, family portraits brought over from England at the time of their settlement on the Potomac, antique relics of the days of the Stuarts, and prized as mementoes of the men who, in common with all Virginia, repudiated Cromwell and his Roundheads, adhering under all circumstances to the fortunes and dynasty of Charles the First and Charles the Second, and the Cavaliers of the Restoration.

Mr. Conway came to New Orleans in December 1843, and actively engaged in a mercantile life, being connected with one of the largest Commission and Cotton firms in a position of great trust and responsibility to the time of the capture of the City, in April 1862, by the Federal forces. Business being thenceforth suspended in all of its legitimate branches, and in common with his Southern friends and neighbors, he made no effort to resume his own during the military occupation of the city.

At the close of hostilities in 1865 he again embarked in mercantile business as a Wholesale Grocer and Commission Merchant, which was successfully carried on up to 1867. During this time, and at all times since his residence in New Orleans, it was well known that he never considered it inconsistent with the business of a merchant to take an active part in public affairs, but on the other hand regarded it a duty to do so. Hence always acting in concert with the Democracy, he was selected Chairman of the Democratic Parish Committee on its first reorganization after the war. Cöoperating with the State Executive Committee the way was prepared for returning the State and City to the representatives of the people, the latter at least having been for more than four years wholly under Military rulers.

On the reorganization of the City Government, he was appointed by Governor Wells a member of the Police Board, presided over by the newly selected Mayor, John T. Monroe. He served in this capacity until removed by General Sheridan under the Reconstruction Act. Under the Supplemental Reconstruction Act of Congress an election was held for municipal officers on the 17th and 18th of April 1868. Mr. Conway having received the Democratic nomination for Mayor of New Orleans was elected by seven hundred majority.

Mr. Conway being the first Mayor elected by the people since the occupation of the city by the Federal authorities, necessarily found the affairs of the city in a complicated condition, and his administration of the city government was unavoidably attended by serious difficulties. The finances were in a deplorable condition and the credit of the city at a very low ebb. But with the substitution of the civil for military law, confidence was restored and gradually city securities improved in value, and fair promise was held out that the financial *status* of New Orleans would again reach that eminent standard it enjoyed before the war.

HON. JOHN A. CAMPBELL.

HON. JOHN A. CAMPBELL was born in the State of Georgia. He graduated at Athens, in that State, in 1830, when twenty years of age. He is now sixty-five. He is above the medium size, has blue eyes, light complexion, expansive forehead and classical features.

He was, before our late war for independence, one of the Judges of the Supreme Court of the United States, and in 1865 represented the Confederate States, together with Mr. Hunter, of Virginia, and Mr. Stephens, of Georgia, in the interview had by them with Mr. Lincoln and Secretary Seward, at Hampton Roads, in order to bring about a compromise between the North and the South.

He possesses a most extraordinary memory, and frequently refers, when consulted upon a decision or authority, to the number of volume and page in books he has not handled for years.

Judge Campbell is one of the greatest lawyers in the United States. He is certainly a most accomplished advocate. He confines himself to powerful argument and never indulges in declamation. His clearness of statement and the force and precision of his language are remarkable. His manner is above the common order of forensic delivery. His wit is not genial or playful, but sarcastic.

It is related of Judge Campbell that being asked by a young attorney of New Orleans, not distinguished for his talents, whether he (Judge C.) had any objection to the attorney joining in a great case at that time conducted by Judge Campbell and other eminent lawyers, he answered: "Most certainly not, my dear sir, provided you do not appear on m side."

His mind is eminently fertile in resources. He compresses his matter vigorously and reasons cogently.

He is known to be, in his personal character, of scrupulous integrity and unsullied honor.

EDWARD H. SUMMERS, ESQ.

IF enterprise, public spirit, liberality, firmness and devotion to the great interests of commerce, entitle any individual to respect and consideration in this community, no one is more richly deserving of them, than the unpretending but influential gentleman, whose name stands at the head of this notice.

Mr. Summers was born in Bullitt County, Kentucky, September 20th, 1827. We presume his father was in easy circumstances, able to give his son the advantages of a liberal education, for, after completing his preparatory studies, we find that he entered Bethany College, Virginia, where he graduated in July, 1848, at the early age of nineteen years.

His first intention was to pursue the law as a profession, for which he, accordingly, prepared himself, and graduated in the Law Department of Transylvania University, Lexington, Ky., in 1848.

On attaining majority, he abandoned the law, and, in 1850, devoted himself to mercantile business in Louisville.

In 1853, he removed to New Orleans, where he has remained ever since, engaged in the commission business.

In 1869, he was elected President of the Crescent City National Bank, which position he now holds.

In 1871 Mr. Summers was chiefly instrumental in organizing the New Orleans Cotton Exchange—the most important movement that has yet been made in this great court of commerce. In consequence of the energy which he displayed in originating this important association, Mr. Summers was elected its first President, and, at the annual election the second year, he was again elected. After two years service, he declined a reëlection. On which occasion he made a speech distinguished for its ability and eloquence, and which exhibits in glowing colors the important consequences which have resulted from this great movement of our merchants and which will be likely still further to flow from it in promoting our commercial prosperity.

We cannot better portray the traits which distinguish the character of this high-toned merchant than by giving some extracts from this admirable speech. The wretched condition to which New Orleans was reduced by the late unhappy war, and the necessity of resorting to some extraordinary measures for the extrication and the restoration of its commerce is thus eloquently referred to by him.

"When that long and devastating war," said Mr. Summers, "was ended, we found our beloved city crippled in her commerce on every side. The necessities of a mighty nation, battling against us, had greatly aided in tapping, at many points, the great artery of our commerce, the grand old Father of Waters, and our products were being taken from our very doors to the great Atlantic cities, where wealth, capital and prosperity all invited them, our cotton factors, at the same time, found themselves embarrassed by the indorsement of planters' paper, the main security having vanished by the fate of war.

"But we went to work with a will, settled our debts as best we could, and launched our little barks again into the great sea of commerce.

"Scarcely had we emerged into the open sea before the great storm of 1867 struck us with all its force. Our planters, with the pittance left them, had gone to work in good earnest, and with the brightest hopes of a good harvest. The disastrous results you all know. Suffice it to say that this unexpected and most lamentable failure of crops, together with the heels of Federal, State and Parish Collectors, was more than our poverty-stricken planters could endure, and the result was wide-spread demoralization, bad faith and diversion of crops on all sides ; but the cotton factors of this city had to breast this storm. We had to stand by our posts—to succumb was inevitable ruin. Our chief capital was our untarnished names, and I am proud to say that but few fell by the wayside.

"This year, however, gentlemen, taught us a wise but sad lesson, and that was, in the then disorganized and demoralized condition of our country, our main reliance was in the integrity, capacity, industry and good management of our constituents.

"It was absolutely necessary to separate the good from the bad ; and to accomplish this, *union* and good faith and harmony among ourselves were indispensable. And, this, gentlemen, was the main and direct cause of the establishment of this Exchange.

"I am proud to say we were nobly seconded in our efforts by many of our prominent cotton buyers and cotton brokers, who, realizing that they had an interest in common with the cotton factor in the prosperity of our city, and feeling moreover the necessity of proper rules and regulations for the government of the cotton trade, which could only be accomplished by union of all, most heartily aided us in our efforts. And though we were met at the threshold by difficulties which would have disheartened and deterred a less resolute set of men, we never faltered. Every previous effort towards establishing an Exchange in this city had been a failure.

*   *   *   *   *   *

"But nothing daunted, we worked faithfully, and manfully explained the necessity, and expatiated upon the advantages of union, and we finally succeeded in getting together a sufficient number to justify an organization.

"You honored me, at your first meeting, by electing me as your presiding officer ; and whilst appreciating your motives, I am free to say that I entered upon the discharge of my duties with many misgivings. But, gentlemen, you surrounded me with godfathers over this infant institution —merchants of large business experience and sagacity, all animated by the same zeal, and fully conscious of the charge intrusted to them.

"Then, gentlemen, after two years of service, I deliver back into your hands this predicted abortion, this weakly suckling, a two years old commercial giant.

"During less than two years back, with an empty treasury, and a limited membership, we have regularly, daily, and, I may say, almost by the minute, furnished you with telegraphic news, embracing every point of the habitable globe where cotton was a prominent article of commerce. And, besides this, we have furnished you daily a table of statistics unsurpassed, if not unequalled, by any Exchange either in Europe or America.

RESIDENCE OF W. B. SCHMIDT.

" And whilst we have accomplished this at a necessarily heavy outlay, we return you to-night, as shown by the report of the Finance Committee, a surplus in our treasury of $43,234,80.

" I proclaim it to-night, and with just grounds for the assertion, that, under the auspices of the Cotton Exchange, which now embraces almost every respectable dealer in cotton, that no city, on this or any other continent, can handle this great staple with the same economy, the same ease, the same impartial justice as can the city of New Orleans.

" I reiterate to-night what I said twelve months ago, that this Exchange presents an ' anomaly ' in the commercial history of the world, and to prove this, I have only to refer you to the report of our venerable Chief Justice of the Board of Errors and Appeals, read in your hearing this evening.

" Just think of it, gentlemen, receiving, storing and shipping one agricultural product, at our port, to the value annually of one hundred and twenty million dollars ; having control of this staple from the time the seed is assigned to mother earth, until the gathering of the harvest, and the final disposition of the product ; and yet, in all the various vicissitudes of this transposition, there is scarcely a ripple of contention or dispute among three hundred merchants handling and turning over the vast product.

" I defy the Exchanges of the world to produce such a record ; and this, gentlemen, with our great cosmopolitan trade, embracing every nation known to the category of civilization. I say the City of New Orleans can have no prouder escutcheon than the records of this Exchange.

" But, gentlemen, this Exchange has not confined the sphere of its usefulness to the cotton interest alone. It has ever had a watchful eye to the great general commercial interest of this city, which is inseparably connected with the cotton interest of this great Southern emporium.

" In evidence of this, need I point you to the great iron barge enterprise, which had its origin in this Exchange and though it now sleeps with a subscription of $300,000, is, just as sure as time rolls on, to be revived and culminate in a magnificent fleet of cheap and safe and prosperous public carriers, bringing to us from the Alleghanies on the East to the Rocky Mountains on the West, the untold and most inestimable wealth of this great valley.

" This grand enterprise had its origin, its support and its partial success under the auspices of this Exchange. Who, gentlemen, was it that set on foot the great iron highway that is destined to connect us with that vast domain of wealth, the State of Texas ? Was it not this Exchange that took Col. Scott, the great railroad king, by the hand, had him welcomed in our midst, and pledged ourselves, individually and collectively, that we would span the chasm that separated us from this great highway to the Pacific Ocean ?

" Was it not within the walls of this Exchange that the noted and efficient Rail Road Committee of Fifty had its birth ? And was it not through their unceasing labors that this great highway is guaranteed to us within the next twelve months ?

" I have thus, gentlemen, passed in review the origin, advantages, labors and fruits of this Exchange—the first example in this city of the effect of union and energy and self-reliance amongst ourselves.

" After a service of two years, I beg, this night, to bid you an affectionate adieu as your presiding officer, my business engagements, as also my ideas of rotation in office, rendering it necessary and proper."

Should the " Cotton Exchange," in its future results to our commerce, sustain the well-founded expectations of its public-spirited projector, (as it has done in its past brief career), he will be well entitled to the lasting gratitude of this community as a public benefactor. Though he has declined to act longer as its President, the same public considerations which, in the midst of doubt and discouragement, led him to embark fearlessly in the enterprise, will, we are assured, induce him still to watch over its interests with ceaseless vigilance, and will enable him and the large body of intelligent merchants associated with him to redeem New Orleans from the sad consequences of the late war, and make her what, from her position, the spirit that animates her, and the energy and ability of her merchants, she is well entitled to be, the great cotton market of the world. He has himself only just reached the meridian of life, and a long career of usefulness still lies open before him.

FATHER J. MOYNAHAN.

This distinguished ecclesiastic was born in the Parish of Konturk, County of Cork, Ireland, on January 1st 1815. He received his English and Clasical education at Missionary College, Youghal, County of Cork, Ireland.

In the year 1844, he emigrated to the United States of America, and finished his theological course of studies in the Diocese of New Orleans ; was ordained Priest on the 24th of November 1846 ; and spent four years as Curate of the Parish of St. Joseph. He was afterwards deputed by the most Reverend Arch Bishop Blanc to build a church in what now constitutes one of the most flourishing Parishes in New Orleans in a locality which was originally a swamp, but, at the present time, one of the most thronged portions of this great metropolis.

On the 1st of January 1851, he embarked on his arduous mission. People of every denomination rallied around him and contributed liberally to the sacred object which he had at heart. The result has been the erection of two churches, one of them a brick edifice, now nearly completed, which is one of the most substantial and beautiful in the South.

He has also established in the city two convents, and a parochial school for both sexes. Recently he has been clothed by Arch-Bishop Perché, with the functions of Canon, his duty as such, being to attend his Grace on all important occasions, be present at the Chapters of the Diocese, and act as one of his counsellors.

Father Moynahan, notwithstanding his intense devotion to the interests of the Roman Catholic Church, has, by his fine social qualities, the urbanity of his manners, the liberality of his opinions, and the deep interest he has exhibited in objects promotive of the public welfare, secured in a large degree, the homage as well as affections of his fellow citizens of all classes and denomination. His pulpit eloquence partakes of the controlling elements of his character, and is marked by boldness and intrepidity.

NEW MASONIC TEMPLE.

On the 15th February 1872, was laid the corner-stone of the new Masonic Temple by the Grand Master, officers and members of the Grand Lodge of Louisiana in the presence of many hundreds of visiting brethren and citizens. After the solemn and ancient ceremonies, eloquent addresses were delivered by the Rev. W. V. Tudor and Grand Master Todd. The Grand Lodge being in session, the imposing rites attracted a large assembly of Masons and a vast concourse of citizens. The corner-stone was a block of granite from one of the mountains of Georgia and a present from the Masonic Grand Lodge of that State. The foundation walls have been laid in brick, resting on a basis of blue clay.

The New Temple will be built according to the design and plans of S. B. Haggart, Esq., the architect selected to supervise its construction. It will front on St. Charles street, near the Tivoli Circle. Its dimensions will be as follows:—Front, 147 feet; depth, 92 feet; two wings 38 feet wide and 84 feet deep, extending back nearly to the rear of Temple Sinai; main portico, 30 feet wide, 9 feet projection, extending through a vestibule 24 feet wide, 12 feet deep and 20 feet high, having a beautiful tesselated floor and latticed doors. From these doors the passage, 24 feet wide and 20 feet high, extends to the staircase 42 feet, by which the second story is reached. On each side of the main entrance are to be two stores 70x27¼ feet. At the rear, on each side, are porticos leading by stairways to the corridor on the second floor and to the lodge rooms on the third floor, as well as to the ladies' parlor and ball-room, In the north wing will be the office of the Grand Secretary, 28x42, two library rooms 22x28 and 38x21 connected by arches, and in the rear the office of the Grand Master, 18 feet square. In the south wing will be a kitchen, supper room, lumber room, etc. On the second floor of the main building is the ball-room or hall, 140 feet long, 70 feet wide, 36 feet high, lighted by 19 windows, which extend from floor to ceiling and opening on broad balconies. By three vast doors the hall connects with the broad corridor across which, in the north wing, is the ladies' parlor, 28x42, which communicates with 3 large dressing rooms, a retiring room and a cloak room. From these, by brick walls, will be a gentlemen's 'parlor, 30x21 feet, a hat room and staircase extending to the saloon below. In the south wing, second story, is the supper room, 70x38, with butler's pantry and cook's pantry connecting with the kitchen below by dumb waiters and a staircase. Over the hall are 5 lodge rooms, each 27x50 and 16 feet high. The Grand Lodge room, 65x 38 and 20 feet high, is the third story of the south wing with a raised gallery for music. In the north wing, over the parlors, are the appropriate rooms of the Grand Commandery.

The Temple, when completed, will have an airy, graceful and elegant appearance, owing to the manner in which the walls are gathered up into columns and pilasters and to vast windows and balconies. It will thus become a lofty and conspicuous ornament to that part of the city, and a monument worthy of the ancient fraternity and the noble cause to which it is to be dedicated.

The details of structure may vary from the plans and dimensions as given above, according to the materials used and the funds available.

Under the jurisdiction of the Masonic Grand Lodge of Louisiana there are now 152 subordinate lodges, with an aggregate membership of 7,557. Thirty of these are located and working in New Orleans, named as follows:— Perfect Union, Polar Star, Concorde, Perseverance, St. André, Los Amigos del Orden, Silencio, Foyer Maçonique, Germania, Friends of Harmony, Mount Moriah, George Washington, Dudley, Marion, Hiram, Alpha Home, Quitman, Orleans, Hermitage, Louisiana, Ocean, Excelsior, Linnwood, Orus, Kosmos, Union, Orient, Dante, Perfect Harmony and Corinthian. The members of the city lodges number 2,700, or an average of 90 members to each lodge. The dates of the charters of the above-named city lodges are as follows:—Perfect Union, July 12, 1812; Polar Star, July 12, 1812; Concorde, July 12, 1812; Perseverance, July 12, 1812; St. André (originally Disciples du Senate Maçonique), chartered June 3, 1839; took its present name Feb. 14, 1865; Los Amigos del Orden, Sept. 24, 1842; Silencio, Feb. 12, 1861; Foyer Maçonique: Oct. 6, 1838; Germania, April 18, 1844; Friends of Harmony, April 22, 1848; Mount Moriah, March 24, 1849; George Washington, Dudley, Marion and Hiram, March 3, 1850; Alpha Home (a union of Alpha, organized in 1848 with Home, organized in 1855), chartered Feb. 14, 1860; Quitman and Orleans, March 4, 1850; Hermitage, Jan. 21, 1851; Louisiana, Jan. 23, 1851; Ocean, Feb. 10, 1857; Excelsior, Feb. 12, 1861; Linnwood, Feb. 13, 1861; Ours, Feb. 9, 1864; Kosmos, Feb. 9, 1864; Union and Orient, Feb. 17, 1865; Dante, Feb. 14, 1866; Perfect Harmony, Feb. 14, 1867 ; and Corinthian, Feb. 9, 1865.

The Grand Lodge was founded by Perfect Union, Polar Star, Charité (extinct), Concord and Perseverance, in 1812, since which the Grand Lodge granted charters to these original lodges and to 218 others. Twenty-three lodges, including Charité, have become extinct. Seventeen lodges have forfeited charters and 21 surrendered them. The oldest lodge in the State is Perfect Union, founded in 1793.

The Grand Masters of the Grand Lodge have been as follows:—P. Francis Du Bourg, 1812–13–14; J. Soulié, 1815–16–17; L. C. Moreau Lislet, 1818; J. B. Modeste, Lefebore, 1819; y. Lemounier, 1820; Aug. Macarty, 1821; J. F. Canonge, 1822–24–29; D. F. Burthe, 1823; John H. Holland, 1825–26–27–28–30–31–32–33–34–35–38–39; L. H. Férand, 1836–37; A. W. Pichot, 1840–41; Jean Lamathe, 1842; E. A. Canon, 1843–44; Robert Preaux, 1845; Felix Garcia, 1846–47–48; M. R. Dudley, Lucien Hermann, 1849; John Gedge and Lucien Hermann, 1850; Jno. Gedge, 1851; H. R. W. Hill, 1852–53; Wm. M. Perkins, 1854–55–56–57–66; Amos Adams, 1868; Samuel Manning Todd, 1859–69–70–71–72; A. J. Norwood, 1867; H. R. Swasey, 1868; J. Q. A. Fellows, 1860–1–2–3–4–5. Of the Past Grand Masters five only are living—Perkins, Fellows, Norwood, Swasey and Todd.

The Grand Secretaries of the Grand Lodge have been as follows:—J. B. Gregoire Veron, 1812–13–14; Auguste Guibert, 1815–16–17–18; N. Visinier (part of) 1819; F.

D. H. HOLMES,

155 Canal and 15 Bourbon Streets,

NEW ORLEANS.

FOUNDED APRIL 2d, 1842.

DIRECT IMPORTATION

OF

Dry Goods.

Dealer in

ALL KINDS OF

American Dry Goods,

AT

WHOLESALE & RETAIL.

41 RUE DE LE CHIQUIER,

PARIS.

91 CHURCH STREET,

NEW YORK.

Dissard, remainder of 1819 and until 1840 ; L. H. Ferand (part of) 1840 ; P. Dubayle, 1841–42 and part of 1843 ; F. J. Verrier, 1843–44–45–46–47 ; W. H. Howard, 1848 ; J. J. E. Massicott, 1850 and part of 1851 ; Edward Barrett, 1850–51–52–53 ; Samuel G. Risk, 1854–5–6–7–8–9–60–61 ; Samuel M. Todd, 1862–3–4–5–6 ; and Dr. Jas. C. Bachelor, 1867–8–9–70–1–2. Barrett, Todd and Bachelor are the only living Past Grand Secretaries.

The offices of Deputy Grand Masters, Senior and Junior Grand Warden and Grand Treasurer have been filled variously by the following :—L. C. Moreau Lislet, J. Blanque, Francis Pernot, Jean Baptiste Pinta, Jean B. Des Bais, Dominique Roquetté, G. Dubuzs, A. Peychand, G. W. Morgan, G. Leaumont, L. A. de Bodin, A. Longer, Charles Maurain, C. Miltenberger, M. Flertas, A. Morphy, D. F. Burthe, J. B. Fagot, M. Fouche Cougot, Seth W. Nye, Jean Lamathe, Aug. Douee, Thomas Blois, Alexander Phillips, J. B. F. Giquel, Charles Revoille, F. J. Verrier, Joaquin Viosca, Français Coquet, J. J. Mercic, J. B. Lambert, Zenon Colson, Perez Snell, Cotton Henry, G. A. Montmain, Ramon Vionnet, Fleury Generelly, A. D. Guesoun, Paul Bertus, Francis Calonge, H. Kidel, Joseph Lisbony, François Meilleur, Roman Brugier, Thomas B. Parten, Alexander Derbes, Thomas H. Lewis, W. P. Coleman, G. Gorin, Daniel Blair, Antoine Mondelli, Simon Meilleur, John W. Crockett, J. W. McNamara, George W. Catlett, R. F. McGuire, W. L. Knox, S. Herriman, S. M. Hart, H. W. Huntington, George D. Shadburn, D. Goodman, M. H. Dosson, Law P. Crain, Stephen C. Mitchell, Louis Texada, S. O. Scruggs, A. S. Washburn, Joseph Santini, A. G. Carter, John C. Gordy, Henry Regenburg, B. G. Thibodaux, S. J. Powell, Harmon Doane, George A. Pike, John Booth, John C. Jones, John A. Stevenson, Sy G. Parsons, William McDuff, Amos Kent, John L. Barrett, William Robson, John Sorapurn, Joseph P. Hornor, Michel E. Girard, Edwin Marks.

Fifty-two of those who have held elective offices in the Grand Lodge are dead, and forty were living in 1872.

COTTON SEED OIL WORKS.

THE manufacture of oil from cotton seed has been chiefly developed since the close of the war, and now every considerable Southern town has one or more factories, while New Orleans has six, employing a capital of a million and a half, and with capacity to use a hundred thousand tons a year. The largest of these (and the largest in the world) is in the Fifth District or Algiers (New Orleans Right Bank), owned by a company and controlled by a Board of Directors, of which Col. C. E. Girardey, Auctioneer, is President. The conspicuous buildings occupied formerly constituted Clark's Foundry. This factory will produce 500 barrels of oil and 400 tons of oil cake per week. The four brick buildings are connected and occupy a square of about four acres. Here the seed, which costs about $15 per ton, is re-ginned to divest it of lint, often in sufficient quantity to be worth as much as the seed cost. The seed is next passed through a simple huller, consisting of a grooved cylinder by which the seed is crushed, and a sieve by which the hulls are separated from the kernels. The kernels are mashed or ground, roasted, placed in vats and pressed by steam, the oil running off into tanks, whence it is pumped into vats for purifying. The oil cake is exported and is used for feeding cattle. The hulls are burned in the furnaces of the two 75 horse power engines or sold as fertilizers. The oil is purified by carbonate of soda and barrelled for shipment. What is precipitated by the process is reboiled and is used in the manufacture of soap. The oil finds a ready market in Great Britain at prices ranging about fifty cents per gallon, where it is variously employed for chemical, mechanical, medicinal and household purposes, no small quantity finding its way back to America in the form of Olive Oil for table use.

The only check to this lucrative industry is the difficulty of obtaining the cotton seed in sufficient quantity.

THE TOURO ALMS HOUSE.

ABOUT eighty thousand dollars were left by the late opulent and public-spirited Judah Touro, Esq., for the erection of an Alms House in this city. By judicious management this munificent bequest was increased, after the death of Mr. Touro, by R. D. Shepherd, Esq., to the amount of about $130,000, besides his making a donation of land worth about $45,000. The amount of cash in hand not being sufficient to meet the cost of the contemplated building (estimated at from $165,000 to $200,000), Mr. Shepherd proposed to make up the deficiency. War interrupted the work, and the edifice, as far as completed, was destroyed by fire on the last day of its occupation by negro troops. Some evidence existed to show that the disaster was attributable to the use of an intended ventilation flue as a chimney for a large bake oven, by which fire was communicated to the roof timbers.

The ground donated by Mr. Shepherd was about 318 feet wide from Piety to Desire street, Third District, and facing the river, extending about 746 feet. The main kitchen buildings, at the time of their destruction, were roofed in and floored, but not completed inside. They were three stories high, in the Gothic style, ranging from the pointed or early Gothic, in the centre, to square headed, or late Gothic, at the extreme wings, with the flattened arch or intermediate between, and stood 100 feet from the river road. The main building was 300 feet long by about 60 feet deep in the body of the structure, and 75 feet at the wings.

The centre pavillion contained the main entrance, parlors, offices, etc., between which and the extreme wings were three stories of iron galleries on the river front. The kitchen building contained the dependencies. The design further contemplated surrounding the ground with workshops for different industries, in which the inmates were to be kept occupied, while the intermediate space was laid off for orchards and vegetable gardens.

It was also contemplated to light the buildings with gas manufactured on the premises.

An unsuccessful effort has been made, since the war, to obtain an appropriation from the General Government for the restitution of this expensive structure, destroyed while in the occupancy of Federal colored troops.

GEN. RANDALL LEE GIBSON.

GEN. RANDALL LEE GIBSON was born on the 10th of September 1832, at the residence of his maternal grandfather, Spring Hill, Woodford County, Ky. He is descended from the Harts of Kentucky and the Prestons of Virginia, on his maternal side and from the McKinleys of Virginia, and Gibsons of Mississippi and South Carolina, on his paternal side. His father was the Honorable Tobias Gibson, of Terrebonne Parish, La., one of the largest planters of our State, and a gentleman of high character and intelligence. He was educated at Yale College, where he graduated in 1853, with the highest honors of his class—the valedictory.

After receiving his diploma from the law department of our State University, he travelled several years throughout Europe and remained nearly a year as an attaché of the American Legation at Madrid, where his personal accomplishments rendered him a welcome attendant. On his return his fondness for country life led him to become a planter, but he found time to contribute occasional articles to our leading reviews, characterized by fullness, accuracy and vigor, and he acquired a reputation as an effective and eloquent speaker, both in the English and French languages.

At the outbreak of the war between the States, he joined one of the first companies raised in his Parish, as a private soldier, and was elected captain. He afterwards, however, accepted the appointment of captain in the 1st Regiment Louisiana Artillery. He stood steadfastly by the colors of the Southern Confederacy until they were furled away, and rose successively through the various grades under such officers as Breckinridge, Hardee and Johnston, with whom he was an especial favorite, until he was assigned to the command of a division. He was the commander of the 13th Regiment Louisiana Infantry, and Gibbon's Louisiana Brigade, which became renowned as one of the *corps d'elite* of the army.

Much credit is due to General Gibson for the glorious reputation his brigade acquired. Unappreciated at first, because of his quiet reserve and shy isolation of manner, combined with rigid views of discipline as the true traits of his character were developed by events, he became one of the most beloved officers in the army—

> " Lofty and sour to those who love him not,
> But to such as seek him, sweet as summer. "

His firm hand gradually impressed upon his brigade that iron discipline and unyielding steadiness that no reverse could impair. His impartial justice enabled him to exact implicit obedience, for his orders were concieved in kindness, and founded upon necessity and reason. And it was his chivalric bearing and unselfish devotion to his troops and the service, and his uncommon energy and spirit, that, assisted by his meritorious subordinates, built up a command that became celebrated in an army of veterans, and by every title was fairly included in that incomparable and unconquerable infanty of the Confederacy, that though they might sometimes be compelled to recoil from ill-advised or impossible assaults were never driven from their positions by front attack, and were never surpassed in the history of war, in any age or country in all soldierly virtues. Gen. Gibson in his address of adieu, truthfully observed : " The old brigade has stood before the enemy for more than four years, and had never lowered its colors save over the bier of a comrade fallen." He was selected by General Lee to command the rear guard of Hood's Army, for the first day after Nashville, having command of his own, Holtzelaw's Alabama, and Stoval's Georgia brigades. No higher tribute could have been paid to his merits. He was warmly complimented and recommended to the Government, both by Generals Lee and Hood, for his services in this campaign. They regarded him as one of the best officers in the army.

He was assigned to the defences at Mobile and conducted the operations near the water battery of the Spanish Fort, with a Division of Infantry and about forty pieces of artillery ; Gibson's Louisiana, Holtzelaw's Alabama, Thomas' Alabama and Ector's Texas Brigades, with Col. Patton's 22nd Louisiana Artillery.

After the war he returned to his plantation, in Terrebonne Parish, but found it a wreck. In 1866 he came to this city and began the practice of that profession he had acquired years before, when young and prosperous. He has achieved an enviable position for exact methods of attending to business, and as a jurist and orator. He is admired and esteemed for his genuine goodness of heart, his perfect naturalness, his unfailing courtesy, his high sense of honor, his unflinching devotion to duty, and the wide range of his learning. Although a resident of this city, his tastes and sympathies are those of the country, and his plantation in Terrebonne parish, shows the evidences of his love and knowledge of agriculture. In all questions concerning the public welfare, without being a politician, he manifests a lively interest and takes an active and decided part. He is broad and liberal and non-partisan in his view.

In 1868 he was married to the eldest daughter of the late R. W. Montgomery, a prominent merchant of this city.

In June 1872, the name of General Gibson was prominently before the Democratic State Convention for nomination for the office of Governor of Louisiana, and but for the dissension in the party at that time, he would have been selected as its standard bearer.

THE Firemen's Charitable Association was incorporated in 1835, and managed by a board of directors chosen from each company, subject to certain restrictions. The officers, (a president, vice-president, secretary and treasurer,) are elected by the board from members of the association, on the first Monday of January, of each year. The object of this society is the relief of its members, who are incapacitated from attending to business from sickness or misfortunes not arising from improper causes. It makes provisions also for the benefit of their families—particularly widows and orphans. This is a very laudable association, and every way deserving of the excellent fire department from which it originated.

THE SUGAR SHEDS

MAYOR BENJAMIN FRANKLIN FLANDERS.

THE career of the late Mayor of New Orleans has been a very checkered one; but if office in the United States is indicative of merit, he is entitled to much praise. It is both interesting and instructive to trace his history up to the period when he became the chief executive officer of this city.

Mr. Flanders was born in New Hampshire in 1816, and, from the time of his arrival in New Orleans in 1842, he has been prominently before the public in situations which required ability, and which have served to test the extent of his powers. His first employment in New Orleans was that of a teacher in our public schools, and he appears to have been a principal teacher in what was then the First Municipality, but is now the Second District. How long precisely he remained connected with the schools we are unable to say, but it was not long, inasmuch as in 1844 we find him occupying the position of co-editor and proprietor of the Tropic newspaper. In 1848 and 1849 he began to be connected with municipal affairs, serving in the Council of the Third Municipality and again in 1851.

In 1852 he was elected Secretary and Treasurer of the Opelousas Rail Road, a position which he held till January, 1862. In July of the latter year, he was appointed City Treasurer by military authority, and was elected to Congress the following November. In 1863 he received from Mr. Chase the appointment of Supervising Special Agent of the Treasury Department, which he held, without interruption, till the year 1866. In 1864 he occupied for some time the post of President of the First National Bank of New Orleans.

In June 1867, he was appointed Governor of the State by General Sheridan, but resigned the office the following December.

In 1870 he became Mayor of the city, first by the appointment of the Governor, and subsequently, in November 1871, by election of the people.

GABRIEL DE FÉRIET.

Mr. Gabriel De Fériet is the oldest auctioneer and real estate agent now in the business in New Orleans, his connection as such dating as far back as 1836. Mr. De Fériet is the oldest son of Louis Claude, Baron of Fériet, a French nobleman who came here during the Colonial period, and attained the rank of Captain under the Spanish dominion. A native of Nancy, (Loraine,) he married Marcelite de St. Maxcent, a native of New Orleans, whose progenitors had settled here when Bienville laid the foundation of our city. Of this marriage Mr. G. de Fériet is the only surviving male issue. He received his education at the College of Father Martial, and subsequently went North in 1825, and completed his studies at the Lewisville Military Academy, in Lewis County, New York, then presided over by Col. Taylor. Returning to New Orleans in 1827, he went into the lumber business, and soon after received the appointment of Controller of the Treasury of the Third Municipality, which office he held with great satisfaction to his constituents, till 1836, when he was commissioned by Governor Roman, auctioneer for the City and Parish of New Orleans, a branch of business of which he is still one of the most prominent and successful members in this city. Although born in 1807, Mr. de Fériet retains all the ardor and energy of youth, and there is no one of a later generation who brings greater enthusiasm into all matters of public interest. His ardent temperament and patriotic impulses, got him iuto trouble during the Butler regime, and he had to pay the penalty of his unyielding integrity by a long imprisonment in the city, and was subsequently banished with many other estimable citizens, to the sand bank of Ship Island, by the "hero" of Fort Fisher. Mr. de Fériet is one of our most energetic, public spirited citizens, and deservedly enjoys the confidence and support of the old inhabitants of New Orleans, who understand and appreciate his many sterling qualities of head and heart.

MR. JULES TUYES,

President of the N. O. Mutual Insurance Co., was born in New Orleans in 1821, and after receiving his collegiate education in Paris, commenced business as a clerk in the commission house of Messrs. Blanchard, Eimer & Co., a position he afterwards exchanged for a more responsible one in the Banking House of F. de Lizardi & Co., from which last situation he was promoted in 1845 to the office of Secretary of the Company, to preside over which he was elected in 1854. Mr. Tuyes is a gentleman of cultivated mind and refined habits, in whom great suavity of manners and kindness of heart, unite with strict integrity, and a nice sense of honor. These qualities have endeared him to a large circle of friends and acquaintances, who look upon him as the genuine type of the Creole gentleman, ever courteous and straight forward in all his actions, and whose fair fame the breath of envy has never dared to touch. To his sterling qualities of heart and head much of the prosperity and success of the institution over which he so ably presides may be fairly attributed.

THE HOWARD ASSOCIATION OF NEW ORLEANS.

No PLEASANTER duty can be assumed than that of recording the organization and progress of the Howard Association of New Orleans, incontestably one of the noblest and worthiest of the philanthropic institutions of the civilized world. The name of the illustrious English philanthropist, Howard, has, in many instances, in his own native country and in the United States, been the leading title of various charitable and humane institutions, but it is doubtful whether as much honor has been conferred upon the memory of that great and good samaritan as by its adoption by the Howard Association of this city. Perhaps the field of labor has contributed largely in entitling the city of New Orleans to claim superiority in this matter ; but whatever the causes, we are none the less gratified at the belief that we possess an institution whose deeds by far surpass those of any other similar one.

Together with the Sisters of Charity—that exalted organization of the Catholic Church—the Howard Association shares the highest praise of our citizens and of many strangers whose lives have been saved or wants supplied through the ministrations of this body of self-sacrificing gentlemen. While the Sisters of Mercy have a vaster mission, it is nevertheless true that the Howard Association is a constant institution, the members of which are ready, at any moment, to answer the call of suffering humanity. Months, and, with the steadily improving wealth of New Orleans, years may come and pass, without even hearing the name of the Association referred to, until suddenly the dark cloud of disease lowers upon the city when the welcome Samaritans, forgetting self, rush forward to brave the tempest and pour forth sunshine from their glowing hearts.

It was in 1837, in the month of August, when the Yellow Fever of that year became epidemic, that Farquhar Mathewson, a young man, aged some twenty-two or three years, then a clerk in the establishment of Messrs Henderson & Gaines, a young man of active mind and ardent temperament, such as fitted him to be a leader among the young men with whom he associated, suggested to his associates the propriety of forming an association of young men, for the purpose of affording relief to the poor and distressed victims of the epidemic, who were without the means of procuring medicine or nurses. His suggestion was immediately acted upon, and a meeting of young men was held at the Planter's Hotel, on Canal street, for the purpose of organizing the proposed association. Among those participating at this meeting, and active members of the association in that memorable year (1837) were the following :

F. Mathewson, Virgil Boulement, Milton Boulmet, Wm. B. Rotta, Jno. C. Page, Jno. F. Dolan, Chas. H. Waldo, E. Hiestand, J. P. Breedlove, Simon Green, Ed. L. Nimmo, Jas. F. Rusha, J. D. Kenton, Theo. A. James, Thomas Y. James, L. C. Dillard, Alex. Levy, Almon Parsons, Thos. Love, Alex. Hazelett, P. W. Leslie and Jno. Leslie, Jr. Others were at the organization and active participants in the association, but owing to the destruction of the books of the Association by the burning of Odd Fellow's Hall in 1866, it is impossible to give their names.

Nearly if not all of those whose names are enumerated, were members of Protection Hose Fire Company, of which Mathewson was also a leading member. When the name of the society came up for consideration, that of " Howard," the great English Philanthropist, was suggested by Mathewson, who supported it by a few well chosen and pithy remarks, which led to its immediate adoption. Farquhar Mathewson was elected President, and Virgil Boulment, Vice President ; the other officers elected at the organization are not now recollected.

The operations of the Association were confined to searching out the poor and helpless victims of the epidemic, appointing Committees of members to set up with and nurse the sick, which duty was most cheerfully acquiesced in by each member when his time came, whilst the duty of the Stewards were to visit each Committee during the night with refreshments.

The first two weeks operation of the Association developed the fact, that the poor and helpless victims of the epidemic were vastly too numerous to be aided solely by the limited means of the Association, when it was resolved to appeal to the well known liberality of the citizens of New Orleans, and in every instance their appeals have been responded to in the most liberal manner.

The Association, during the epidemic of 1853 disbursed over $150,000 on some 11,000 sick and destitute. During the epidemic of 1867, over $78,000 were expended on some 5,000 sick and deslitute.

The number of members is limited to 30, but there are not that number at present.

The first President of the Association was F. Mathewson. At a subsequent date, Mr. D. I. Ricardo was elected Secretary, which office he continued to fill until his death in 1863.

The present officers are: E. F. Schmidt, President; W. S. Pike, Vice-President ; John F. Caldwell, Secretary ; R. S. Robertson, Treasurer.

CITY WATER WORKS.

An Act of the General Assembly, approved April 1 1833, incorporated the Commercial Water Works and Banking Co. of New Orleans, and among the conditions of their charter was the right and duty of supplying the city and its faubourgs with water at specific charges, except public institutions, which they were to supply with water free of charge. To the city was reserved the right to buy at the end of thirty-five years such Water Works as the company might construct, in accordance with which condition the city bought the Water Works in 1868 for thirteen hundred thousand dollars in city bonds, and the administration of the Water Works now forms a branch of the city government.

The engine buildings are in the First District one and one-half miles from Canal street, about two hundred yards from the Mississippi River. Two engines of 700 horse power each drive four double acting pumps of the united capacity of a million gallons per hour. The water, in consequence of the falling of a wall of one of the reservoirs, is pumped directly into the pipes during the day.

CRESCENT MUTUAL INSURANCE COMPANY.

CORNER OF CAMP STREET AND COMMERCIAL ALLEY.

Incorporated in 1849.

ASSETS, $732,129 40.

THOMAS A. ADAMS, President.   *SAMUEL B. NEWMAN,* Vice President.
HENRY N. OGDEN, Secretary.

There are 56 miles of main pipe, formerly of wood or cement, but now in process of replacement by iron. The pipe from the river to the reservoir is 48 inches in diameter, that extending from Calliope to Canal street is 30 inches. The rest are smaller. The hydrants number 11,000, many of which are now closed. For fires and street cleansing there are more than a thousand fire-plugs, which being frequently opened during hot weather add much to the health and comfort of citizens.

The water rate is, for one hydrant supplying a family of four persons, $12 per annum, and $1 more for each additional member. The supply to each hydrant is more than twice as much as it is in any other city. General Braxton Bragg, in his report for 1859, shows that the daily average to each person (allowing ten persons to each hydrant), was 95 gallons. The water of the Mississippi, when filtered or settled, is entirely pure and free from organic matter. Seamen find that it remains fresh longer than any other water taken on board their vessels.

When the Water Works Company was chartered all that region above Felicity road was swamp or plantations. What is now Melpomene street was a bayou, the delight of half the boys of the city for hunting and fishing. What were then frog ponds and almost impenetrable swamp thickets, are now the sites of elegant residences.

From 1845 to 1868, the Water Works were under the control of a Board of Directors, of which Felix Labatut was the honored, able and very efficient President. He was aided by Paulin Durel, A. Carriére, George A. Freret, Frank Perret and D. Lanata, members of the Board.

FIRST PRESBYTERIAN CHURCH.

This large and time-honored church, situated on Lafayette Street, opposite the fine square that bears the same name, is a brick edifice, 75 feet by 90 in length, and 42 feet in height. The main tower is 115 in height, the spire with pinnacle is 104 feet, and the entire height 219 feet.

The body of the church contains 1311 sittings, and is usually filled to its utmost capacity.

Attached to the church is a lecture room, 25 feet by 75 in length, and 18 feet in height, which has 218 sittings; also a school-room with the same number of sittings, and two session rooms and a library. The architect of this fine edifice was Henry Howard; the builder, G. Purvis; and the artist, P. Gualdi, Esquires.

The rostrum or pulpit, slightly elevated (in modern style) above the pews, is tastefully designed and elegantly furnished. The church, throughout, is richly, though not gorgeously, equipped. The orchestra, opposite the pulpit, accommodates a large choir, whose music, whether in hymns, psalms or anthems, always of a high order, is of the grave and noble style adapted to Protestant worship in the Presbyterian churches of America. Lofty and commodious galleries, on a level with the orchestra, and to the right and left of the minister, are, especially at the morning service, and in the Winter season, crowded with attentive listeners of all classes and colors

HANCOCK LITERARY ASSOCIATION.

This Association was chartered under the general laws of the State, June 1st 1872, to exist for a period of twenty-five years from the first Friday in March 1868, the date of its organization.

The objects of the Society are: the cultivation of polite literature, oratory and elocution, by discourses from history and the Belle-lettres and by recitations from the poets. It is an Association identical in its character and aims with the Raven Club of Washington city, which, composed of the *elite* of the National Capital, met weekly antecedent to the late war at the residence of D. K. Whitaker, Esq., on 11th street, and whose meetings were, by that gentleman, regularly reported for the press, he being historiographer and presiding officer of that well-known club.

Mr. Whitaker is President of the Hancock club, and J. J. Foley, Esq., Vice-President. Both these gentlemen have been accustomed to deliver weekly lectures on recondite subjects in the more elevated branches of literature, in which much learning is embodied. Distinguished visitors frequently take part in the discussions—always welcome and always appreciated. Since its commencement the Society has slowly but steadily advanced. *Recherche* in character, it is happily free from blatant demagogism in politics, and absurd bigotry in religion; indeed both these much-vexed and agitating subjects are excluded from its debates.

The President, drawing on his large and matured resources, is accustomed to open the meetings, handling at will, various epochs of the English literature, and dealing with them as familiar things.

Mr. Foley, Vice-President of the Association, has, during the years of his membership, dating from its organization, delivered discourses on the Lord Chancellors and Chief Justices of England, the Chief Justices of the United States —on epic poetry—the ancient and modern drama—on forensic eloquence, and the corrupt practices of the judicial tribunals of the past and present. These lectures have been marked by distinguished ability proving their author at once the able advocate and astute reasoner.

An agreeable feature of the Society consists in recitations, original and selected, by its lady members, who, though entirely ignoring the woman's rights dogma, as something unnatural and unbecoming, are still willing, in a quiet and modest way, to aid the cause of letters.

Mr. Overall, a much admired and highly esteemed poet and journalist, is critic of the Association and one of its most brilliant orators.

Weekly meetings take place at the residence of the President, and, on those occasions, as in the groves of Academus, leaving the work-day world behind, intellectuality may revel in its higher sphere, and mind and heart be alike cultivated.

It is the wish of its members to foster an especial *esprit de corps*, a love of letters in the Crescent City, which must always go hand in hand with refinement and civilization.

The original and interesting matter presented at different times, before this Association, would furnish volumes of valuable and useful information.

THE MISTICK KREWE OF COMUS.

HISTORY OF THE KREWE AND THEIR VARIOUS FESTIVALS
FROM 1857 TO 1873.

MARDI GRAS has ever been a memorable day in the social annals of New Orleans, and since the year 1857, its joys and festivities have been inseparably connected with the revels of the Mistick Krewe. Where they came from, what their history, and who compose the mysterious band, are as impenetrable mysteries now as they were fourteen years ago. This fact we do know, however, that the Krewe have become so much a part of Mardi Gras, that were they to drop out of the events of the day, the very life of that merry time would seem as dead.

The near approach of the time when they will " walk " again, and the general awakening of public interest and anticipation—which ever recurs when Mardi Gras draws nigh—prompts us to relate the history of the Mistick Krewe and their festivals from their inception to the present time.

In 1857, for some time before Mardi Gras, there were whispers that a fresh and novel entertainment would be offered to our people. Nobody at first knew what it would be, but by some means it leaked out that an organization calling itself the Mistick Krewe of Comus, would appear upon the streets on Mardi Gras night in all sorts of fanciful masks and costumes ; that they would form in procession, march through the principal streets, and then retire to the Varieties, (then called the Gaiety) Theatre, where certain tableaux of a mythological character would be exhibited, after which a grand ball would be given, to which only a certain select company would be invited. The affair created great interest and excitement, the greater from the profound secrecy and mystery which surrounded it, the beautiful cards of invitation which were issued to the ball, and the complete ignorance of each invited guest of the source from whence the invitation came.

After the first celebration of 1857, enough was known to satisfy the public that the Krewe were composed of precisely the right sort of persons to make the affair a complete success. Their identity was apparently known to no one, and to this day the impenetrable veil which has covered them so long has never been lifted. All sorts of speculations concerning them have been indulged in. Yet no one can say that he is positive of knowing a single individual connected with the Krewe. Thus far their incognito has been sacredly preserved. Without a doubt, however, they are all gentlemen of intelligence, wealth and social position, as the magnificent and select character of their entertainments fully testify.

It was decidedly noticeable that the interest in the forthcoming celebration shows itself long before the day arrives, and there is always an eager desire to procure tickets of admission to the tableaux and ball. In the year 1866, a gentleman of this city, in his eagerness, advertised for a ticket, offering to pay therefor a large sum of money—but no one has been known to procure a ticket through his own exertions, or to use one not intended for him—the lucky individual receiving his card of admission in a manner that leaves him in a most delighful state of uncertainty as to how it reached him.

The cards of admission and invitations to the annual balls of the Krewe are magnificent specimens of the engraver's art, and by the receivers are highly prized and preserved as treasures.

Having explained as much as we or any one knows about the M. K. C., we come to

THE FIRST FESTIVAL—1857.

Mardi Gras fell this year on the 24th of February, and the festival of the Krewe was described " as the great feature of the night." It can readily be conceived that curiosity concerning their appearing was at fever heat. They made their appearance in the streets—dressed in the most fantastic costumes accompanied by torchlights—which with the fearful looking masks they wore—made them as much resemble a deputation from the lower regions as the mind could well conceive. After marching through the principle thoroughfares to the intense gratification and astonishment of the throng gathered to see them, they repaired to the Gaiety Theatre, which was soon filled with invited guests.

In due time the Krewe appeared upon the stage in the tableaux, of which there were four. The first represented Tartarus. The characters in this scene were Pluto and Proserpine, presiding over the three Fates, Clotho, Lachesis and Atropos ; the three Fairies, Alecto, Tisiphone and Margaera ; the three Harpies, Aello, Oeyphete and Celeno ; the three Gorgons, Medusa, Sthreno and Euryale, with Ixion, Sisyphus, Tantalus, Minotaur, Cerberus, Charon and Chimera.

The second tableaux was the Expulsion. In this were represented Satan, Beelzebub, Moloch, Dagon, Belial, Isis, Osiris, Mammon, and a host of other infernals.

The third tableaux represented the conference of Satan and Beelzebub.

The fourth represented Pandemonium. This was described as a most magnificent spectacle, in which Gluttony, Drunkenness, Indolence, Avarice, Murder, Vanity, Theft, Discord, Licentiousness and Jealousy were personated, all being presided over by Satan, and flanked by Sin and Death.

The different tableaux were arranged in accordance with descriptions in Milton's Paradise Lost, and the truthful manner in which they were represented reflected the highest credit upon the poetic taste and judgment of the gentlemen composing the Krewe.

After the tableaux the ball commenced, being joined in by the mysterious hosts and their guests. Upon the stroke of midnight the Krewe silently disappeared, leaving their friends to continue the festivities. Thus commenced and ended the first festival of the M. K. C., which, from its brilliancy, gave promise of much in store for the future.

SECOND FESTIVAL—1858.

February 16th.

As may be imagined, the interest and pleasure excited by the first appearance of the Krewe, created a lively expectation as the time approached for their second appear-

U. S. CUSTOM HOUSE.

(FRONTING ON CANAL STREET,)

NEW ORLEANS.

ance. From the records, we learn that this festival exceeded in brilliancy and splendor anything which had until then ever been presented in New Orleans. The Krewe, upon this occasion, revived the mythology of the olden time in all its classic glory, presenting the pictures of the different deities which have for so many ages afforded material to the poet, the painter, and the sculptor.

The richness of the costumes and perfection of the appointments, were subjects alike for wonder and admiration. The characters represented in the procession were : Comus, Momus, Janus, Spring, Summer, Autumn, Winter, Flora, Pomona, Vertunus, Ceres, Pan, Fauns, Bacchus, Silenus, Satyr, Diana, The Muses, Vesta, Harpocrates, Hygeria, Esculapius, Fortune, Plutus, Destiny, Nemesis, Saturn, Cybele, Jupiter, Juno, Aurora, Phœbus, Apollo, Night, Æolus, Neptune, Amphritrite, Pluto, Proserpine, Hecate, The Furies.

As before, the procession wound its way to the theatre, which was crowded to its utmost with the beauty and fashion of the city.

The tableaux presented were, as on previous occasion, four in number.

The first represented Minerva's victory over Neptune, before an assemblage of the gods.

The second portrayed the flight of time, the characters represented being Castor, Pollux, the Hours, Time and Destiny.

The third tableaux shewed a Bacchanalian revel, represented by Bacchus, Silenus, Faunus, Fauns and Satyrs—Comus the Seasons, Flora and Momus.

Tableaux Fourth was a procession by the Krewe around the Theatre, by which the assembly was enabled to look closely upon the rich and beautiful costumes which had delighted them so much.

After the procession, the assemblage joined in the merry dance, and at midnight the Mistick Krewe " folded their tents and silently stole away."

THIRD FESTIVAL—1859.

This year, March 8, was Mardi Gras, and the two previous exhibitions having assured the people that the celebrations by the Mistick Krewe of Comus were firmly fixed as objects of the greatest interest, expectation was on tiptoe for a repetition of the glorious pageants which even now lingered like a sweet memory.

The procession this year represented the four old English holidays, May Day, Midsummer Eve, Christmas and Twelfth Night.

TWELFTH NIGHT was represented by two trumpeters, carrying trumpets of a most peculiar design. Herald and Ensign of the Lord of Misrule, followed by an enormous chicken cock. Page, bearing the crown ; Lord of Misrule, attended by his Jester, and the Abbott of Unreason as his chief adviser. Two Ushers and a group representing various games and sports.

IN MAY DAY—were Jack in green, Tom the piper, the Tabor man, Scarlet and Muck, May Queen, Robin Hood, Friar Tuck and Stokesley.

MIDSUMMER EVE—introduced most odd and startling characters. St. George, followed by the Dragon, Puck, the Bear, Moth, Mustard Seed, Pea Blossom, and the other fairies of Midsummer Eve, surrounding Queen Titania, with Bottom transformed into a donkey. The Lion and Unicorn. The great giants Gog and Magog.

CHRISTMAS presented Harlequin following a grotesque group of Christmas carollers performing upon silent instruments of most ridiculous design ; Bell man, Christmas tree, Santa Claus, boar's head, plum pudding, mince pie, wassail bowl, barrel of ale, bottle of champagne, bottle of port.

Arriving at the theatre, the tableaux were presented, and embraced the four seasons described, and in a manner most charming to behold.

The ball and disappearance of the mystical crew followed as before, and the Sons of Comus lived once more but in the memories of those who had·gazed upon their glory.

FOURTH FESTIVAL—1860.

By this time the Mistick Krewe of Comus had become a fixed institution, and their festival was looked forward to as a part of domestic history. It was expected that the Krewe having gone on from year to year, increasing in grandness of display, would this year present an exhibition superior to all their previous efforts, nor was the public disappointed. The procession eclipsed everything that had been attempted before. A tablet at the front expressed the design upon it the inscription of the display, bearing " Statues of the great men of our country."

Following were fifteen cars, each representing a block of granite, and containing groups of living statues of famous historic persons.

FIRST CAR—Christopher Columbus.

SECOND CAR—Sebastian Cabot, Vespucci and Carter.

THIRD CAR—Ponce De Leon, Narvaez and Alvaro, the early adventurers of Florida.

FOURTH CAR—Ferdinand De Soto, Vanzano Menendez, Vasquez and De Gourguez.

FIFTH CAR—De Bienville De La Salle, Father Hennepin, Landoinere, Jean Ribault, Lacaille and Nicolas Bone.

SIXTH CAR—Sir Walter Raleigh, Martin, Frobisher, Gerold, Archer, Greenville and Ratcliffe, early settlers in Virginia.

SEVENTH CAR—Captain John Smith and Pocahontas.

EIGHTH CAR—William Penn in the midst of a group of Indians.

NINTH CAR—Hendrick Hudson and Peter Stuyvesant, the Dutch discoverer of the Hudson River, and the Dutch Governor of New York.

TENTH CAR—Edward Winslow, John Carver, Miles Standish, John Alden, William Bradford, Edward Filly, Isaac Allerton and Roger Williams, the pilgrim founders of New England.

ELEVENTH CAR—Heroes of the American Revolution—George Washington, Lafayette, Marion, Putnam and Knox.

TWELFTH CAR—Gens. Lincoln, Wayne, Gates, Montgomery, Schuyler, Lee, and Green—Generals of the American Revolution.

THIRTEENTH CAR—The great statesmen of the American Revolution—Benjamin Franklin, John Adams, Robert Livingston, Thos. Jefferson, Patrick Henry, Roger Sherman, Richard Henry Lee, and John Hancock.

Fourteenth Car—General Andrew Jackson.

Fifteenth Car—Illustration of the compromise of 1833, Henry Clay, J. C. Calhoun and Daniel Webster. The Statues, while dressed to represent the various characters, were white as marble from top to toe.

As heretofore the Theatre was the scene of the crowning glories of the night, the tableaux were beautiful in design and faithful in execution.

"The historic sculpture of America," was the general design of the tableaux, represented by ten different groups, embracing "Landing of Christopher Columbus at San Salvador," Ferdinand De Soto discovering the Mississippi, Pocahontas saving the life of Capt. Smith, Landing of the Pilgrims at Plymouth Rock, William Penn's treaty with the Indians, Declaration of American Independence, Monument to the Generals of the American Revolution. The Compromise of 1833, The Hero of Chalmette—Andrew Jackson.

The tableaux concluded, Terpsichore reigned supreme. True to their faith, the Mistick Krewe vanished at the sound of the midnight bell, and were seen no more.

FIFTH FESTIVAL—1861.

The troubled state of the country, and the foreshadowing of civil war, led many to believe that the festivities of the Mistick Krewe would be held in abeyance; but, true as the needle to the pole, the revellers appeared on Madri Gras night, the date this year being February 14. The line of procession was on Camp, Julia, St. Charles, Royal, St. Louis, Chartres, Canal and Carondelet, to the theatré, the crowds on the street making the affair a complete ovation. The representation was "Scenes from Life," embracing the four divisions—childhood, youth, manhood and old age.

The costumes were gorgeous, and the characteristics of each age faithfully portrayed. Childhood was an infant in a cradle, followed by a nurse. Boyhood was surrounded by maskers, representing a kite, top, sweet cake, marbles and other boyish things, Youth was attended by the representations of virtues, aspirations, temptations and trials incident to that era. Manhood then came with the vices, follies and better qualities of mature life, all represented by maskers. Old Age was accompanied by a similar band, and following all came Death. As usual, the events of the night were the tableaux and ball; of the former there were five, as follows:

The Innocence of Childhood. The virtues and aspirations of Youth.

The vices and follies of Manhood,

Conflict between Virtue and Vice in Old Age.

The triumph of Virtue over Vice, in which was represented Childhood, Youth, Manhood and Old Age, leaving Vice and Folly behind and ascending toward fame.

The tableaux being concluded, the maskers joined in the merry dance which was continued far into the night; but after the witching hour of 12, the Krewe were no more seen, having faded away as they had done in every instance before.

AN INTERLUDE.

The war had now burst in all its fury, and in the contemplation of the bitter train of realities following in its wake, the Mistick Krewe dropped from out the local history of the city; their memory was dimmed by the terrible strife which ruled the land; for four years the Krewe roamed no more; where they went, or what they did, is known to none but themselves. However, with the return of peace, they once more appeared before the delighted gaze of assembled multitudes, and we chronicle the

SIXTH FESTIVAL—1866.

The announcement that the celebration of the Krewe would be revived, created the utmost enthusiasm, and kindled anew the happy recollections of the splendors which had always characterized their displays. The day (Feb. 13) was anxiously looked forward to, and when the night arrived the populace *en masse* thronged the streets to obtain a sight of the pageant which was about to resurrect itself from the ashes of the past. Their appearance was hailed with every demonstration of delight, and the people congratulated themselves upon the return of that spectacle which had come to be considered as an object of particular and peculiar pride.

The features of the procession were appropriately symbolical of the return of peace. At the theatre, as of old, was assembled the wealth and beauty of our city. The tableaux were four in number, as follows:

THE PAST—represented by the characteristic Strife, Destruction, Want, Grief and Terror.

THE PRESENT—Washington approving the blessings of peace, surrounded by Industry, Commerce, Science, Agriculture, History, Mechanism and Art.

THE FUTURE—Peace and Plenty.

THE COURT OF COMUS—represents the King of the Court entertaining his beasts in an unknown language.

The ball followed as of yore, and again did the Mistick Krewe vanish from the gaze of the world ere the new-born day was ushered in.

SEVENTH FESTIVAL—1867.

Mardi Gras came this year on the 5th of March, and as the grand firemen's celebration had taken place but the day before, the city was more than ever crowded with eager expectants for the forthcoming festivities of the Krewe. As suddenly and mysteriously as had ever been their custom, they appeared in procession, coming no one seemed to know from where.

The design of the display was the "FEAST OF EPICURUS," the costumes as gorgeous, their appointments as perfect as before, and their numbers somewhat increased. First came the Heralds of Appetite—Absynthe, Sherry and Bitters—followed by special aids, Oysters and Johannisberger; Lords of the Ladle, with soups, led on the Knights of the Shell, such as shrimps, crabs, etc. Pages of the household our codfish aristocracy, followed by the Hog. The Rulers of the Roast, King Comus leading the Boeuf Gras, surrounded by all the vegetables of the table; next came a basket of flowers, followed by the Salt Cellar, Maccaroni Italienne, Canard Grecque, Paté des Oiseaux, Grenoueille Francais, Snipe au Diable, Sausage *a la* bow-wow.

Then came the Knight and Lady of the Green Crests,

Merchants' Mutual Insurance Co.

104 CANAL STREET.

INCORPORATED 1854.

—:o:—

THIS is the oldest and undoubtedly one of the strongest, if not the first in point of capital and resources, of all the Insurance companies of New Orleans. It was founded in 1832, with Mathew Morgan as President and Mr. Relf as Secretary. Mr. Morgan having transferred his business to New York, Mr. Dupuy was elected in his place, and upon the death of the latter, Mr. John Pemberton, who had been acting for some years as Secretary, was called to the Presidency of the Company, an office which he held until his death in 1868. Mr. Pemberton was a kind-hearted, genial and well-educated gentleman, and under his management the Merchants' Mutual Insurance Co. acquired great popularity and influence. Of his successor, Mr. Paul Fourchy, we have already spoken in no exaggerated terms of praise, and the present highly flourishing condition of the company, as exhibited in its annual statement, as well as the large dividends paid during the past years to its patrons are the best evidence that could be produced of the faithful and able manner in which the affairs of the Company are now conducted. Whilst giving full credit to Mr. Fourchy and the Board of Directors presided over by him for the success of the Mutual Insurance Co., the services of its young and popular Secretary, Mr. G. W. Nott, should not be overlooked. Mr. Nott is the grandson of W. Nott, Esq., one of the merchant princes of New Orleans half a century ago, and on his mother's side of the late distinguished Judge Jean Francois Canonge, whose eminence as a jurist was only equalled by his accomplishments as a wit and a man of the world. Of these ancestors Mr. G. W. Nott is no unworthy scion, and his friends have every reason to anticipate for him a bright career.

CAPITAL STOCK,

$1,000,000.

—:o:—

Average Premiums Paid In,

$1,000,000.

—:o:—

Last Dividend, May, 1872,

30 PER CENT CASH.

—:o:—

OFFICERS:

PAUL FOURCHY, *President.*

G. W. NOTT, *Secretary.*

DIRECTORS:

PIERE MASPERO,	DAVID McCOARD,
J. M. ALLEN,	P. S. WILTZ,
D. A. CHAFFRAIX,	M. PUIG,
S. Z. RELF,	J. J. FERNANDEZ,
L. F. GENEREZ,	CHARLES LA FITTE.

followed by a Salad Fork, Lettuce and Castors. The Knight of the White Crest, attended by Cold Slaugh, Cauliflowers, Artichokes and Asparagus, were followed by the Stewards in waiting, flanked by Jelly and Plum Pudding.

Next in order were seen the Grand Equerry and Lady, supported by Ice Cream and Strawberries, Ushers of the Court, Maccaroon, Meringue and Champagne. The Fruits of Victory now appeared, aided by Apples, Peaches and Plums. The Gentlemen of Cultivation were represented by Bananas, Pineapples, Oranges, Grapes, Melons and Burgundy. The "Triflers of the Council" were Nuts, Confections, Omelettes, etc. The "Peacemakers"—Coffee and Cigars, Curacoa and Kirschwasser—concluded the Feast of Epicurus.

The affair was of the most magnificent character, and excited wonder and admiration, not only because of the elegance of the costumes, but for the very correct manner in which the many difficult characters were portrayed.

At the Theatre the crush was as great as ever, and expectation was at its highest for the presentation of the Tableau, on this occasion consisting of a single display— "The Gourmand's Vision of Two Courses and a Dessert." This tableaux was most elaborately gotten up, and embraced all of the members of the Mistick Krewe, who represented at the banquet the various dishes known to civilization. The press of the day pronounced it the most beautiful and appropriate of all the Tableaux which the Krewe had ever given.

Again did Terpsichore rule Queen of the night, and again did the Krewe melt into thin air, as they did on so many occasions before. Whether they remained there, or whether they reappeared in mortal form we cannot say, but we *do* know that they came again upon the occasion of the

EIGHTH FESTIVAL—1868.

February 26th ushered in Mardi Gras, and the return of the Krewe to the scenes of their former triumphs. The subject chosen for the display of this year was Moore's Lalla Rookh, one requiring a full appreciation of the poet's theme, and a particular attention to detail, and which, at the hands of its faithful expounders, met with such portrayal, that none could be at a loss to know and feel the perpetuation of the beautiful story.

The pageant was formed to represent the entrance of Lalla Rookh into Delhi—and she could not have been more thoroughly welcomed than was the Mistick Krewe by the thousands who thronged the streets upon this occasion. Leading the procession came a cavalcade of horsemen bearing aloft the blazing insignia of royalty, and blazing with jewels and gaudy colors.

In their train were the mighty Fadladeen, young Feramorz and the rest of the courtiers appointed to accompany "Tulip Cheek" to her bridal. Then came the elephants, bearing aloft in the palanquins the princess and her attendant houris. Interspersed in the procession were foot soldiers and attendants, bearing aloft many colored lanterns of strange and fanciful shape, and drooping garlands on their lances.

The line of horsemen was closed by a similar body, such as in the olden time galloped through the streets of Stamboul, and bore the banner of Islam to victory.

As the glorious vision passes from view, with its wealth of roses, light, fair women, and brave men, the spell was over all, that Comus was yet monarch of his own phantom realm, with all its dazzling glory and mystery.

The selections of Tableaux for this year exhibited the refined taste of the gentlemen composing the Krewe, and nothing which they had presented before was richer or rarer.

We give the list of tableaux as embodied in the immortal poem.

THE VEILED PROPHET OF KHORASSAN—His Court; The Oath; The Banquet.

PARADISE AND THE PERI—Gates of Heaven; Patriotism; Devotion; Contrition; The Gift Most Dear to Heaven.

THE FIRE WORSHIPPERS—Discovery; Death of Hafed.

THE LIGHT OF THE HAREM—Feast of Roses.

"At the end of the hall stood two thrones as precious as the Cerulean Throne Koolburga, on one of which sat Aliris, the youthful King of Bucharia, and on the other was in a few minutes to be placed the most beautiful princess in the world.

"Immediately upon the entrance of Lalla Rookh into the saloon, the monarch descended from his throne to meet her, but scarcely had he time to take her hand in his, when she screamed with surprise and fainted at his feet.

"It was Feramorz himself that stood before her. Feramorz was himself the sovereign of Bucharia, who, in this disguise had accompanied his young bride from Delhi, and having won her love as an humble minstrel, now amply deserved to enjoy it as a King."

The march by the Krewe, the ball and the flitting away of the mysterious shadows completed this most successful display of 1868.

NINTH FESTIVAL.—1869.

Mardi Gras came early this year falling on the 9th of February. The procession of the Mistick Krewe upon this occasion represented the Five Senses, or Sight, Sound, Smell, Taste and Touch.

Each sense was represented by a pallid antique statue in character. The first personated Phœbus in his car of light drawn by four coursers. Then followed Ceres as the Goddess of fruit, Orpheus as the Type of Music, Flora as the representative of Smell, and Venus as the personator of Touch. These emblematic representations gave the performers an opportunity of representing in a fantastic and amusing manner, various species of animals, insects, fruits and flowers.

During the procession a serious accident occurred, occasioned by the falling of a gallery on Camp street, precipitating many people into the street, resulting in serious injury to quite a number.

The usual route was passed through—the customary call upon the Mayor was made—and the pageant wended its way to the Opera House where the tableaux and ball were to crown the festivities of the night.

THE TABLEAUX were as follows:

Phœbus and his types of Light.

Orpheus and the types of Sound.

Flora, the Goddess of Flowers, with her types of Smell.

Ceres, daughter of Saturn, and Rhea, bursting like a ripe peach from her types of Taste.

Venus, the child of Jupiter and Dione, with her types of Touch.

The last scene, the Revel of the Passions, embodied a melange of all the characters, with the Genius of Decay in strong contrast.

Thus ended the Ninth Festival of the Mistick Krewe, which, like those which had preceeded it, furnished a source of delight and sweet remembrance to the multitude, and maintained the well-earned reputation of the merry King Comus.

TENTH FESTIVAL—1870.

Shrove Tuesday entered the year on the first of March, and found the eager and excited populace anxious to live over again the pleasant dreams which the revels of the Mistick Kerwe had now made a part of existence.

The subject chosen for the display this year was the HISTORY OF LOUISIANA, and was represented most beautifully and appropriately in statuary.

First came old "Mische-Sepe," the Father of Waters, mounted on a ghostly-looking horse, followed by sixteen cars, bearing the representatives of the different eras in the History of the State.

CAR No. 1—Louisiana, wearing as a crown a coat of arms, and in her hand a shield; standing near her New Orleans wearing a crown with a crescent. Next to these stood the personators of Sugar, Cotton and Rice.

CAR No. 2—YEAR 1539.—Ferdinand De Soto, surrounded by Juan D. Guzman, Pedro Calderon, Numo Tobar and Musco de Alvardo.

CAR No. 3—YEAR 1539.—Seven figures on this car: Vanconcellos De Silva, Gonzalo De Cordova and the five Spanish soldiers who made with De Soto that wondrous march from Florida to the Mississippi.

CAR No 4.—The central figure is the Indian Princess who made the gallant Fernando welcome to the country of Cofaciquis. She is surrounded by representations of the different tribes of Indians, upon whom fell the burden of the vindication of their race.

CAR No. 5—YEAR 1673.—Two priests are seen teaching to the Indians by whom they are surrounded, the truths of the Gospel.

CAR No. 6.—La Salle, on horseback, stands forward a representative of another phase of civilization. His faithful friends, Tontin and Father Hennipen, are with him.

CAR No. 7—YEAR 1700.—In this are Iberville and Joinville, Counts Pontchartrain, De Maurepas, Curate de la Vente and Marigny de Mandeville, honored names in the history of Louisiana.

CAR No. 8.—The central figure is Bienville—the true French chevalier. With him are the Sœur Denis and Dona Marie; around him is a trio of Governors, who represented, with varying credit, His Most Christian Majesty in Louisiana. Their names are Lamonth Cardilac, De L'Epinay and Pierier.

CAR No. 9—YEAR 1727.—Religion heads the list, with the figure of a Jesuit Priest and two nuns.

In striking contrast is the martial figure of General Groudel, a dashing French officer, flanked by the Marquis Vandrieul and Gov. Kerlerec.

CAR No. 10.—There is presented here Gen. O'Reilly and Don Juan Ualoa, first Spanish Governor of the Territory. At the side of Don Juan is the Marchioness D'Abrado, a beauty of the period. Next to them is La Frenier. Father Dagobert, a noted priest of the day, closes the picture.

CAR No. 11—YEAR 1772 to 1797.—The Governors of the Territory from 1792 to 1797. Don Luis Ungaso. Governor in 1772; Don Bernardo de Galvez, in 1777; Miro, in 1784; Baron Caromdelet, in 1790; and General Gayoso, in 1797.

CAR No. 12—1799 TO 1803.—Marquis Casacalvo, who ruled the State in 1799, and Don Manuel de Lalado, who governed in 1803. Next to them, Robert Livingston, Jas. Madison and James Monroe, the distinguished characters in the history of our country, who were charged by the Government with the purchasing of Louisiana from the French.

CAR No. 13, 1803.—This is a sequel to the last design. Napoleon has resolved to accept the $15,000,000 from the United States, and the group represents Gov. Claiborne and Gen. Wilkinson receiving the territory from the French Commissioner Laussat. The two remaining figures are Etienne Boré, first Mayor of New Orleans, and Girod, the second Mayor.

CAR No. 14, 1815.—General Jackson on horseback, surrounded by his staff, Major Latour, a gallant Frenchman, Major Thomas Butler and Generals Coffee and Carroll.

CAR No. 15, 1815.—In this are seen Pierre and John Lafitte famous in history as the Pirate Brothers, but who earned the names of patriots when they offered themselves with six hundred comrades to the service of Jackson. With them are seen Generals Thomas, Winchester, Labatut and Morgan. These men tell the story of the army of deliverance of Louisiana.

CAR No. 16.—This is the last, and contains General Villéré, a gallant looking man, representing worthily one of the highest and most ancient of creole families. With him are General Adair, of Kentucky, Major Plauché, Col. Edward Livingston and Commodore Patterson.

The design of this year's display was not only rich but it was historically valuable. It recalled to the people the deeds and names of those who for them fought with savage tribes, and hazarded life and comfort in a dream of empire, to result, in after years, to the benefit of their descendants.

The procession closed, the Theatre was the future scene of the closing revels, where the Tableaux and ball were to take place—which we give as follows:

TABLEAU FIRST—Louisiana; her Daughter, New Orleans; her Wealth, Cotton, Sugar, Rice; Miche-Sepe, the Father of Waters.

TABLEAU SECOND—Death of De Soto at the mouth of the Red River, in 1542.

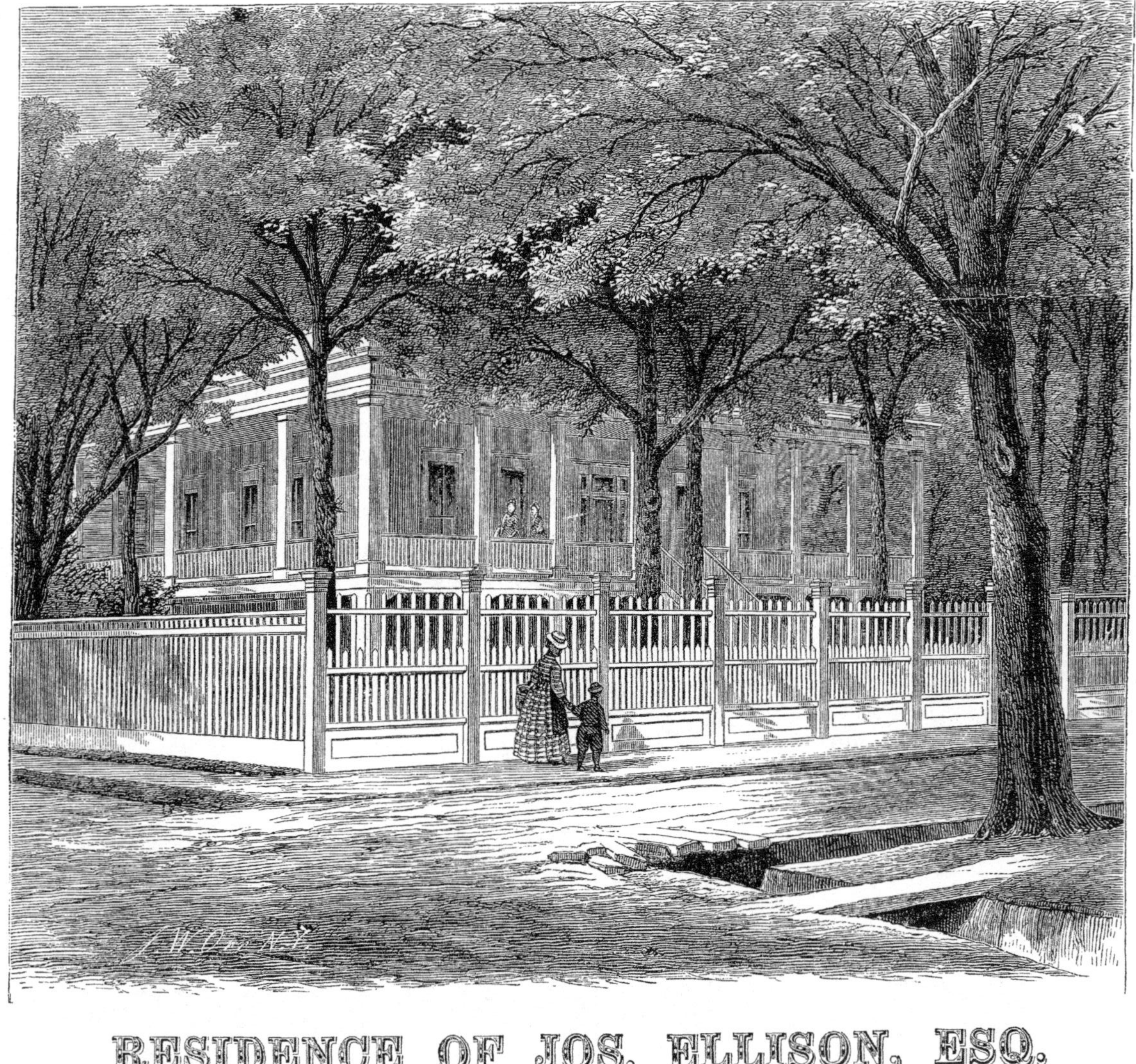

RESIDENCE OF JOS. ELLISON, ESQ.

NEW ORLEANS GRAIN ELEVATOR.

Tableau Third—Reception of Father Marquet and Joliet by the Indians, in 1678.

Tableau Fourth—La Salle taking possession of Louisiana in 1682, "In the name of the Most Puissant, Most High, Most Invincible, and Victorious Prince Louis, the Great King of France."

Tableau Fifth—Crowning the Hero.—On a raised platform the "man of iron will," glorious old Jackson, was seen standing, while the maiden Louisiana held out her hand over his head in the act of crowning him with the laurel wreath of victory, mingled with the olive leaves of devotion and love. Other figures were grouped around.

Tableau Sixth—Louisiana—Her Founders and Defenders—The grandest effort of the evening, and pronounced by all who saw it the most perfect, beautifully conceived, and handsomely grouped tableau ever beheld.

Words cannot convey the beauty and expression of the group. Louisiana appeared on a pedestal, with her daughter, New Orleans, and her friend Miche-Sepe on either hand, while in front stood the representatives of her wealth—Cotton, Sugar and Rice. Lower down were grouped the different characters who had appeared in the previous tableaux, while on her right and left, a little retired, mounted on their favorite horses, were those great heroes and our nation's idols, Washington and Jackson.

The tableaux concluded, the ball followed, and thus for the tenth time the Mistick Krewe flashed across the common-placed existence of mortality.

MECHANIC'S INSTITUTE AND NEW ORLEANS MECHANICS' SOCIETY.

The Mechanics' Institute is among the largest and most imposing of the public buildings of New Orleans. It is built of brick, painted and stuccoed in imitation of granite. It is well lighted on both sides and in front. The lower floor is occupied as the Library and Committee room of the New Orleans Mechanics' Society; two large rooms are occupied as the State Executive office; the Secretary of State has his office in another, and the Hall, intended as the lecture room of the Society, is appropriated to the State Senate. The second story, reached by two broard staircases, is lofty, light and airy. It contains besides, two large apartments, the vast assembly room now employed as the Hall of the Louisiana House of Representatives. The third story is used now as committee rooms, the windows of which command a view of a large part of the city, being higher than the roofs of houses in the vicinity.

This substantial and stately building was the work of the New Orleans Mechanics Society, and it occupies the site of the original institute, which was burned in 1854. The Society was instituted in 1806, the officers for the year 1807 being, H. M. Dobbs, President, Peter Craig, Vice-President, Nicholas Sinnot, Treasurer, and James Armitage, Secretary. The corporators announced in their Constitution, that their objects were: "to relieve the wants, comfort the sufferings and promote the happinsss of their fellow creatures," which they held to be essentially the duty of all. The Society was incorporated by an act of the legis lature of 1821, H. M. Dobbs, Nicholas Sinnott, Moses Duffy, Peter K. Wagner, Hugh Carr, W. Liddell, John Veasey and Martin Gordon being the first incorporators as named in the act.

The term, (20 years,) was extended by an act of 1838 for thirty years more. By an act of 1850, the State gave to the Society a lot, seventy feet front on Philippa, (now Dryades) Street, and one hundred and fifty feet deep, on condition of erecting a suitable Hall thereon. This is the site of the present Institute. In 1863 the Fisk Free Library, originally presented by Mr. Fisk to the City of New Orleans, was transferred to the care, possession and control of the Mechanic's Society, to be used as a Free Library according to the bequest of the philanthrophic donor, to be kept open to the public six hours each day. At the same time the Library Building at the corner of Custom House square and Bourbon streets, was transferred to the Society in order that its rents might be applied to the preservation and enlargement of the library.

This library was nearly destroyed by the fire of 1854, but the few thousand volumes which were saved have since grown into a respectable collection, enjoyed daily by many visitors.

In 1870 the Register of the Society bore 867 names of members, of whom 516 are dead and 71 resigned. Among these members have been some of the worthiest of the public-spirited men of the city who have contributed to its prosperity and honor by their intelligence, virtue, learning and high character. The charitable and useful works of the Society are beyond all estimate, while the scope and extent of its usefulness are continually increasing.

Among the adjunct institutions of the Society is a Savings Bank, authorised by an act of the Legislature of 1863. The Bank is under the management of a Board of twelve trustees.

The officers of the Society for the year 1872, were: John McIntyre, President; H. R. Swasey, Treasurer; Luther Homes, Secretary; and S. Jamison, E. M. Rusha, F. Wing W. McCulloch, Williamson Smith, John A. Shakespeare, Robert Roberts, Peter Ross, J. P. Coulon, James D. Edwards, E. Claren and Thomas O'Neil, the Executive Committee.

Coliseum Place.—This is a long, irregular triangle, having Race street for its base, and Camp and Coliseum streets for its sides, its apex being near Melpomene street. It is planted with shade trees, and is provided with seats. A drainage canal extends along the Camp street side and flows into the larger Melpomene canal. Many fine buildings surround this Park (usually called a "Square,") among which are the homes of Mrs. Stickney, and of Messrs. Peale, Wilson, Hendry, Seeds, Moore, Renshaw and Vincent. The square is overlooked by the new Baptist Church, remarkable for its substantial structure and the graceful spire which is one of the first seen by the traveler as he approaches the city by the river. The small "Church of the New Jerusalem" is on Coliseum street just below the "square."

MAYOR L. A. WILTZ.

MR. LOUIS ALFRED WILTZ is a native of New Orleans, and, we believe, enjoys the distinction of being the youngest man ever elected in this country to the chief magistracy of a city of the size and importance of the Southern Metropolis. Mr. Wiltz was born in 1843, and is therefore under thirty years of age. He received his education in the Public Schools of this city at a time when they were much better organized and conducted than they have been since. When the State of Louisiana seceded from the Union in 1861, Mr. Wiltz, although not yet of age, entered the Confederate service and was elected captain of a company of infantry, and after the fall of New Orleans, he went into the Trans-Mississippi Department, where he remained on active duty during the war, performing every obligation imposed upon him with characteristic intelligence and conspicuous gallantry.

In 1868, Mr. Wiltz was elected to the House of Representatives from the ninth ward of New Orleans, and the next year he was also elected to the Board of Aldermen, of which body he was made the President by a unanimous vote. Mr. Wiltz's course as a legislator and a city administrator was marked by strict integrity and great vigilance in guarding the interests and vindicating the rights of his constituents, and the Democratic Parish Convention which met in 1869 acknowledged the value of his services by tendering to him the unanimous nomination for the Mayoralty. The municipal election which was to have been held that year having been postponed by an act of the Legislature, Mr. Wiltz was again unanimously chosen for the same position in 1870, and although he did not receive his certificate of election, it was generally believed at the time that he had obtained a majority of the votes cast, and that he was unfairly " counted out."

In 1872, Mr. Wiltz was again nominated for the Mayor-

alty by the Democratic, Liberal and Reform parties, and was elected by a very large majority over Mr. Fish, the radical candidate.

Although he has always taken a lively interest in public affairs, Mr. Wiltz is not a politician, in the vulgar sense of the word, and in his case it may truly be said that the office sought the man, not the man the office. Since the war he has been engaged in commercial pursuits, and is a member of the well-known and highly respected firm of P. S. Wiltz & Co., commission merchants on Carondelet street.

Mr. Wiltz has also devoted much time to the Public Schools of his section of the city, and is also an active and zealous member of our Volunteer Fire Department. This intelligence, knowledge of the wants of the people and thorough acquaintance with the affairs of the city, admirably qualify him for the task of introducing order and economy into every branch of the municipal administration, and his well known integrity and firmness of character are guaranties that the supervisory powers of the office shall be wielded by the new Mayor in such a manner as to hold every member of the city government to a faithful performance of their duty.

E. B. BENTON,

The President of the Accommodation Bank, was born in Vermont in the year 1832. His early occupation was that of a farmer, a pursuit he continued to follow in his native State until 1858, when he removed to Tennessee, and purchased the site now known as Fort Pillow. Here, through indomitable energy and unceasing labor, he succeeded in establishing a trading point, and attracting thither a number of settlers to locate with a view of building up a town. Wishing to enlarge his sphere of business, Mr. Benton visited Europe for the purpose of making contracts for the delivery of oak staves. Whilst absent the war broke out, and all kinds of business being suspended, he returned to New York, and there engaged in the practice of the law in Albany. After the occupation of Tennessee by the Federal authorities, he returned to Fort Pillow, and there re-established the trading post. Enjoying the confidence of the military commanders, he was enabled thereby to render many and valuable services to the Southern people in the vicinity, whom he knew by a previous residence in their midst, and whose respect and esteem he had secured by uniform kindness and correct deportment. After the capture of Fort Pillow by Gen. Forrest, Mr. Benton, who lost all of his property by the fall of the place, went to St. Louis, and there resumed the practice of his profession. He, however, did not remain there long, before finding an opportunity to make an investment of a large amount of capital in the town of Shreveport, La.

Having secured the confidence and assistance of a wealthy gentleman in St. Louis, Mr. Benton established one of the largest and most successful business houses in Shreveport, and conducted it until 1867, when he came to New Orleans, where he has since resided. By industry, frugality and discreet judgment, Mr. Benton has succeeded in accu-

S. T. BLESSING,

No. 87 CANAL STREET, (near Chartres,)

Opposite the Fountain.

DEALER IN

ALBUMS,	STEREOSCOPES,
PICTURES,	FRAMES, ETC., ETC.

PHOTOGRAPHIC GOODS OF EVERY DESCRIPTION.

mulating an independent position, and his sagacity displayed in the purchase of stocks has secured for him the directorship of several companies, and the Presidency of the Accommodation Bank, a position to which he has been twice elected. His management of this institution has been eminently successful, profitable to the stockholders and satisfactory to its patrons. This bank is established upon a firm basis, and its dividends will compare favorably with any similar institution in the country. As Cashier, President Benton has the valuable assistance and services of Mr. Richard Wood, an experienced accountant and business man, whose devotion to the affairs of the Company has contributed not a little to its success. Although a Northern man by birth, Mr. Benton has become thoroughly identified with the South, and is as devoted to its welfare and prosperity as the most ultra Southerner. He married the daughter of the late Barton Lee of Mississippi, and since his residence in this State has become a large land owner. Never having been a politician or a partisan, he has avoided making enemies and he now enjoys the satisfaction of feeling and knowing that the community in which he lives cherishes no bitter animosities against him. On the contrary, those who know him recognize and appreciate his sterling qualities, whilst his general reputation is that of an honest, upright, and enterprising citizen, and a generous and benevolent man. Though comparatively just embarking in business in this city, a bright and prosperous future is in store for all who possess the industry, perseverance and integrity of Mr. E. B. Benton.

BENJAMIN MORGAN PALMER, D. D. LL. D.

Rev. Dr. Palmer, one of the most distinguished divines of this city and of the age in which he lives, was born January 25th, 1818, in the City of Charleston, S. C., where his ancestors were settled prior to the Revolution, and where his father before him was born.

The family was well known in that city, the grandfather living to the advanced age of 98 years, and one of the last links connecting with the Colonial History of South Carolina. The uncle, whose full name was transmitted to the nephew, was, for a quarter of a century, a leading pastor in one of its churches. The father, Rev. Edward Palmer, survives, at the age of 84 years, and is still a laborious pastor in the town of Walterboro, S. C., having always maintained the character of an accomplished divine and most urbane gentleman. It is not too much to say that he has transmitted to his still more eminent son, as an invaluable inheritance, much of the grace which marked the character of the beloved disciple of the Great Founder of the Christian Faith.

Dr. Palmer graduated, with the highest distinction, at the University of Georgia, August, 1838; entered upon the study of Divinity in the Theological Seminary at Columbia, S. C., and was licensed to preach the gospel by the Presbytery of Charleston, April, 1841.

He was married in October of the same year, to Miss Mary A. McConnell, a native of Liberty County, Georgia, and was, soon after, ordained and installed pastor of the First Presbyterian Church in Savannah, Ga.

His ecclesiastical relation was dissolved a year after, by transfer to the pastoral charge of the church in Columbia, S. C. In this connection he remained fourteen years, 1842–1856, during the last three of which, 1853–1856, he filled the chair of Church History and Government in the Theological School at Columbia, in connection with his pastoral duties.

A visit to the South West, in the interest of this Divinity School, during the Winter of 1855, brought him into acquaintance with the First Presbyterian Church, New Orleans, then vacant by the removal to California of its former pastor, Rev. W. A. Scott, D. D., and resulted, after negotiations protracted through a portion of two years, in his settlement in this important church, in December, 1856. Here his labors have been continued to the present time.

In the year 1847, in connection with the Rev. Drs. Thornwell, Howe, Smythe, and other distinguished men, he became one of the projectors and editors of *"The Southern Presbyterian Review,"* an able religious quarterly, published at Columbia, S. C., and which has maintained an almost uninterrupted existence, being now in its 23d volume.

The Honorary Degree of Doctor of Divinity was conferred on him, in 1852, by Oglethorpe University in the State of Georgia, and that of Doctor of Laws, in 1870, by Westminster College, in the State of Missouri.

At the formation of the General Assembly of the Southern Presbyterian Church, in 1861, he was called to preside over that venerable Court at its first sessions in the city of Augusta, Ga.

Few American divines, North, South, East or West, have obtained a reputation for eloquence equal to that of Dr. Palmer, none surpass him in theological or secular lore. To intellectual powers of a high order, admirably trained and disciplined, he unites an amount and variety of learning seldom attained. Literary associations and even Universities receive, rather than confer, honor, by his acceptance of their appointments to address them on important occasions. Envy and jealousy are silenced and overcome by the singular modesty and thorough absence of all assumption, which are characteristic traits of this distinguished scholar. In the respect that is entertained for him, in the secret and overt influence he exerts, no divine belonging to the great Presbyterian Church of the United States stands in advance of Dr. Palmer. Even those sects, denominations and churches in New Orleans, which occupy other platforms of religious faith, acknowledge his rare genius, his profound learning, his wondrous eloquence, his possession of all those fine qualities of mind and heart, and his manifestation of all those christian virtues and sympathies, which constitute the model diqine. The Crescent City is proud of his reputation, and his own numerous, intelligent and wealthy congregation regards him with enthusiastic devotion.

PAUL FOURCHY.

Mr. P. Fourchy, President of the Merchant's Mutual Insurance Co., and of the Mutual National Bank of New Orleans, is the youngest of our Bank Presidents, having been born in 1832. Mr. Fourchy is a native of New Orleans, and an excellent home education was the only inheritance he received from his father, a distinguished French officer, who commanded a cavalry regiment under the first Napoleon. Commencing life without any of the adventitious influences which usually lead to success, Mr. P. Fourchy owes his present high position to his own industry and good conduct, united with a remarkably clear and well disciplined intellect. In addition to his fine business abilities, Mr. Fourchy is a man of liberal and enlarged views, always ready to take the initiative in all improvements and to lend his assisstance to every enterprise calculated to promote the public good; nor is he to be turned aside from what he deems the right course, by outside pressure or popular clamor, his rule of conduct being, "*Fais ce que dois advienne que pourra.*" Mr. P. Fourchy commenced life as clerk in the well known banking house of Messrs. Jeannet, Quertier & Co., and was subsequently connected in the same capacity with that of Mr. Pierre Poutz, of this city. In 1857, he received the appointment of general accountant of the Merchants's Mutual Insurauce Co., was promoted in 1864 to the position of Secretary, and finally on death of the esteemed President of that company, the late John Pemberton, he was unanimously selected as his successor. During the few leisure hours allowed to him, by his laborious duties, Mr. Fourchy found time to qualify himself for admission to the bar, and received his diploma in 1854; and although the engrossing nature of his avocations never permitted him to engage into active practice he is generally admitted by competent judges to be very accurate in all questions relating to the laws of Insurance.

THOMAS A. ADAMS, ESQ.

This gentleman, a native of Boston, Mass., came to New Orleans in the winter of 1842–3, as the representative of the Mutual Safety Insurance Company of New York, and introduced here the Mutual Scrip System of Insurance.

At the time of the arrival of Mr. Adams, five local stock companies were doing the entire insurance business of the city.

The Fireman's Insurance Company soon failed. *The Western* and the *Ocean*, in a few years, went into liquidation. The *Merchants'* and the *New Orleans*, which completed the list, continued with greatly impaired capitals, and with limited business, mostly fire; but they continue to this day, with amended charters, converted into mutual companies, and with enlarged capitals, and greatly increased business.

Soon, other agencies followed, and they so multiplied that they controlled the principal business of the city.

On reviewing the history of insurance in New Orleans, Mr. Adams discovered the important fact that ultimate success had never attended any local insurance company, or any agency. Pursuing his research, another fact was developed, viz: that there had never been any bond of union with the underwriters; and believing this to be the true cause of failure in connection with the leading insurers, he sought, and, in 1846, obtained, the formation of a Board of Underwriters, and to that association he attributes the large and general success that has attended the Isurance interest of New Orleans. Aug. Martin, Esq., the highly respectable President of the New Orleans Insurance Company, was its first President. On his removal to France, Leonard Mathews, Esq., was his successor; and on his death in 1854, Mr. Adams was elected President, and has annually been unanimously reëlected during the eighteen following years.

The Crescent Mutual Insurance Company was incorporated in 1849, Mr. Adams as its Vice-President. In 1850, he was unanimously elected its President, which position he still holds.

Other local companies, chartered under the Mutual Insurance system, succeeded each other, all important agencies gradually retiring; and the insurances which, for a series of years, had been transacted by agencies, were now again in the hands of the local companies, who have since controlled them to a large extent.

Before the war, Mr. Adams was, for a number of years, President of the New England Society, composed of many of our leading citizens, a society purely social and charitable, and, we may add, doing great good in its day, aiding the poor, visiting the sick, and relieving the distressed.

Mr. Adams was an active member and trustee, for many years, of the Church of the Messiah, and was one of the largest contributors to the building of the new and beautiful church which bears that name.

In the establishment of a savings bank for the laboring poor, upon a strong and sure basis, Mr. Adams worked assiduously—was an original Trustee in the New Orleans Savings Institution, the leading association of the kind in

E. A. TYLER,

115 CANAL STREET,

Has on hand, and is constantly receiving from the best manufactories in the world, a large and well=selected stock of

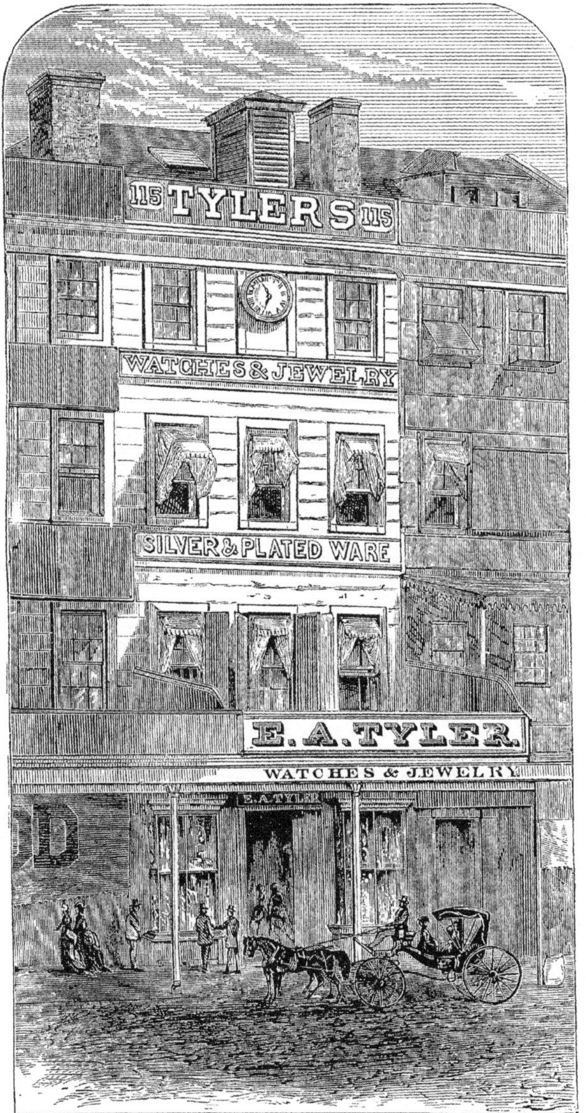

Watches, Clocks, Jewelry,

—:o:—

Silver and Plated Ware,

—:o:—

Masonic and Odd Fellows' Jewels,

———AND———

Fancy Goods.

—:o:—

All of which are offered at reduced prices.

—:o:—

Sole Agent for the celebrated Watches of Thos. Russell & Son, Chas. E. Jacot, Alfred Gerard, David J. Magnin, and Henry Hoffman.

Southern Agent for the celebrated **Whiting Manufacturing Company,** *Manufacturers of Sterling Silver Ware only.*

Our stock of Silver Ware is very large, and our prices defy competition.

the South. He is, now, its first Vice President—also Vice President of the Printing Institution of the Blind.

With most of the various charitable institutions of the city, the name of Mr. Adams is associated.

Quiet and retired in his habits and tastes, he has uniformly declined any proposition of a political or public nature—shrinking always from attracting any kind of publicity. With a large and well selected library, a devotee to his profession, he may be said to seek his happiness with his books, and in the refined domestic intercourse which awaits him, at his elegant mansion of Prytannia street. Here he is the earnest and sincere friend, the courtly host, and the frank, genial companion, fully informed on all subjects.

An ardent and unpretending student, his compeers readily esteem him authority in questions of Insurance Law, and he is never happier than when giving them the advantage of his experience. It is not too much to name him among the leading financiers of New Orleans, yet one who seldom volunteers an opinion in monetary matters, until summoned from his privacy, and then pronounces a judgment which is accepted as law, and remains unreversed.

Thirty years have nearly passed since Mr. Adams became a citizen of New Orleans. His life has been an open book, read of all men. Its pages have been stainless, and its records, in which manliness, virtue and integrity are predominant, have gone forth to eternity. Of him, we may say, in sincerity, what was said of the acts of Addison: "His logic fed his morality, and the uprightness of his mind carried out the justice of his heart!"

COL. JAMES T. TUCKER,

Was born in Salem, Massachusetts, March 16 1839, educated in the public schools, and at the age of sixteen was taken into the service of the Illinois Central R. R. Co., at the principal office in Chicago, then under the administration of President J. M. Douglas. At the opening of the war, he entered the federal army as aid-de-camp on the staff of Major-General Banks, U. S. A., with the rank of Colonel in which capacity he served until the close of the war. He was acting Chief of Staff and private secretary to the same general officers during the Louisiana campaign. After the war he settled in New Orleans, as the general agent of the Illinois Central Railroad Company. In this capacity he has brought to bear an unusual degree of energy and business training. The particular commercial problem which he has undertaken to solve, is the establishment of a direct trade between the Lakes and the Atlantic States, with an extension to the Spanish America or Tropical trade. He has exercised his influence with the Presidents of the Company who have visited New Orleans to inspect personally the feasibility of his views. As a result it has been determined to connect with the Illinois Central Steamboat and Barge navigation at Cairo; and second to extend the Mississipi Central, or the Mobile and Ohio R. R. from Columbus, Kentucky, along the river to a crossing of the Ohio at or near Cairo. This will make a through rail from New Orleans to Chicago without break of grade or change of car. These connections completed, the Illinois Central can now bill freights through between Chicago and New York, Havana, Vera Cruz and Rio Janeiro, or other points having connection with New Orleans. It is undoubtedly the establishment of a longitudinal commerce which will connect the ever-expanding north-west with the American Continent, and its islands. Mr. Tucker is a representative man who brings the enterprise and capital of the northwest to develop the commercial future of the South. He has chosen the South as a permanent residence, and has united himself in marriage with a young lady of one of our oldest and most respected Creole families. As a young man he has a biography to make, but with his character, energy and the confidence of one of the largest and most influential Railroad Corporations in the West he may achieve much honor to himself and usefulness to the section whose interests he has done so much to harmonize.

PIERRE SEVÈRE WILTZ.

Mr. P. S. Wiltz was born in 1818, and is undeniably one of the most influential men of the race to which he belongs, particularly in the Third District of New Orleans, where he has resided uninterruptedly for the last forty-five years. Mr. P. S. Wiltz was born in the Parish of St. Charles, his father and mother being also Louisianians by birth, but tracing their respective ancestry to Germany and France. Leaving school when he was only thirteen years old, Mr. Wiltz went at once into the hardware business, which he subsequently left for the Cotton and Sugar Factorage, completing his studies by his own unaided exertions, during his leisure moments at home. The rudiments of the strong, sturdy, self-reliant character of the man, were thus laid down in early life, and the subsequent career of Mr. Wiltz has shown that the seed was not sown in barren soil. In 1844, Mr. Wiltz first entered public life, being elected to the City Council as a Democrat from a hitherto strong Whig district, nor was it possible for his political opponents to unseat him at subsequent elections, although they carried the district by large majorities for all their other candidates. When the city was consolidated in 1854, Mr. Wiltz was also four times elected to the Common Council, by an almost unanimous vote. He was also sent to the House of Representatives, and was one of the leading members of the Secession Convention in 1861. In 1855, Mr. Wiltz was elected Clerk of the Second Court, over a very formidable competitor, and was again reëlected to the same office in 1859. Mr. Wiltz is now engaged in the Factorage business, and is also a director in two of the most flourishing Insurance Companies in New Orleans, the Merchant's Insurance Co., and the New Orleans Insurance Co. One of his partners in business, is his nephew, Mr. L. A. Wiltz, a rising young Creole, who, after gallantly serving his country in the field, received the high compliment of a nomination for the Mayoralty of New Orleans, in 1870, and who is generally believed to have received a large majority of the legal votes, although his opponent was *counted in* by the returning officers.

THE KING OF THE CARNIVAL'S STORY.

His Royal Highness, the King of the Carnival, sprang into existence like Minerva, from the brain of Jove, full armed, on January 31st, 1872. The project was at first a novel one, lacking both men and means to carry it to a successful issue, and, as usual in such cases, a little ruse was employed to secure these two necessary adjuncts for its triumph. The first public intimation given of the project appeared in an editorial in the New Orleans *Times* of that date, as follows:

According to Mr. Greeley and all other great public lights, the raw material should never be wasted, and so think a few respectable and public spirited young citizens in regard to the annual display of Mardi Gras. Heretofore the maskers, who are generally out in goodly numbers upon that day, have wandered round in small bands loosely all over the city. These they propose to collect together on Canal street, at 3 o'clock in the afternoon, and arrange into a procession. Bands of music will be provided, and at the specified hour the Chief Marshal and his aids propose to be in waiting at the Clay Statue to take charge of all arrangements. Orders will be issued in time for more direct guidance, and it is expected that the officers holding their commissions from the shadowy King of the Carnival will be obeyed in all respects with cheerfulness and alacrity.

No doubt the announcement will stimulate the young people to greater efforts, and New Orleans will, this year, revel in a day procession almost equal to the gorgeous night display of the Mystic Krew of Comus.

The services of several gentlemen were now privately enlisted, and with such good prospects, that the same evening appeared the following advertisement:

Notice.—The King of the Carnival herewith notifies all parties desirous of taking part in the Carnival Celebration to report to him immediately through their Marshals, stating character of display, probable number, and whether with or without music.

In due time, positions will be assigned, and such arrangements completed as best calculated to make the contemplated procession a complete success.

For the present. his Majesty's address will be "King of the Carnival," New Orleans postoffice. REX.

New Orleans, January 31, 1872.

Meanwhile, friends had been at work with subscription lists, encouraged by the liberality of a gentleman thus referred to in the *Times* of the following day:

Col. Charles T. Howard, having read in yesterday's *Times* of the laudable intention entertained by a band of enterprising young men to organize the wandering maskers of Mardi Gras "into an army with music and banners," has placed in our hands one hundred dollars to further the merry purpose. This sum now awaits the personal order of the "King of the Carnival." Mr. Howard's prompt and liberal action, while creditable to him as a citizen, gives assurance that the enterprise will be accepted and encouraged in a proper spirit by the public, for whose benefit and amusement it has been improvised.

The project was already on the high road to success; subscriptions flowed in liberally, and on February 1st the campaign was opened with the following publication:

MARDI GRAS.

As will be seen by the following correspondence, "The King of the Carnival" allows no grass to grow beneath his royal feet, and by proceeding in a systematic manner has already established his usurping authority in the cause of fun and frolic.

All our people will be delighted at the prospect of thus having one of our olden glories revived, and what has heretofore been a day of vagrant mummery turned into one of grandeur and magnificent display, in which the fanciful tastes of the people will be allowed full license.

His Majesty, though a king, is yet the most liberal one alive, and welcomes all to his revel, whether on foot or horseback, in carriage or in cart, though they come in numbers like organized armies, or singly as spies, all are his subjects, and can share his glory. Let them beware, however, how they disobey his orders, as he is said to be a very choleric, though a very good old party. And so "Long live the King," and may his reign be a merry one.

New Orleans, Jan. 31, 1872.

To the Hon, B. F. Flanders, Mayor :

His Royal Highness the "King of the Carnival," believing that both the peace and prosperity of the city could be better secured by organizing the wandering maskers of Mardi Gras into a procession on Canal street, respectfully requests your permission to carry out his views, and the co-operation of the police in enforcing his "self-assumed" authority. An early answer is respectfully requested. REX.

To A. S. Badger, Superintendent of Police :

The permission asked for above is granted, and I would respectfully request that the police assist and protect the procession.
BENJ. F. FLANDERS, Mayor.

New Orleans, January 31, 1872.

To His Royal Highness the " King of the Carnival " :

The request referred to me (as above) by his Honor Mayor Flanders, is cheerfully acquiesced in. I will do all in my power, and that of the force under my command (as far as consistent with public duty), to make your Majesty's fleeting reign as powerful and pleasant as it no doubt deserves to be.

In accordance therewith, I hereby order all maskers of Mardi Gras to join in the procession under your Majesty's direction.
Respectfully yours, A. S. BAGER, Sup't of Police.

The only difficulty remaining was a serious one. An unknown, yet efficient, authority had to be established over the people to which all would yield unquestioned obedience, while yet in ignorance of its character or personality. To achieve this, it was decided to issue a series of "edicts," the first of which appeared on February 2d, in the New Orleans *Times*, as follows:

THE KING OF THE CARNIVAL.

In the language of Louis Napoleon, if there are men who do not comprehend their epoch, the royal personage whose title heads this article, is evidently not of them. His steps at usurpation betray as much daring as enterprise, and from the meek manner in which his encroachments on supreme power are met, it is very plain that he will reign monarch of all he surveys on Mardi Gras. By the annexed correspondence, it will be observed that the military arm of the State yields without question to his shadowy authority, and will do all in its power to add to the glory of his evanescent reign:

EDICT I.

To Whom it may Concern, Greeting:—Our beloved subject, Charles W. Squire. Colonel Commanding Louisiana Field Artillery, is hereby ordered to hold himself in readiness with a battery of artillery at the foot of Canal street, on Mardi Gras, February 13, 1872.

Then and there to fire such salutes as may be deemed by his

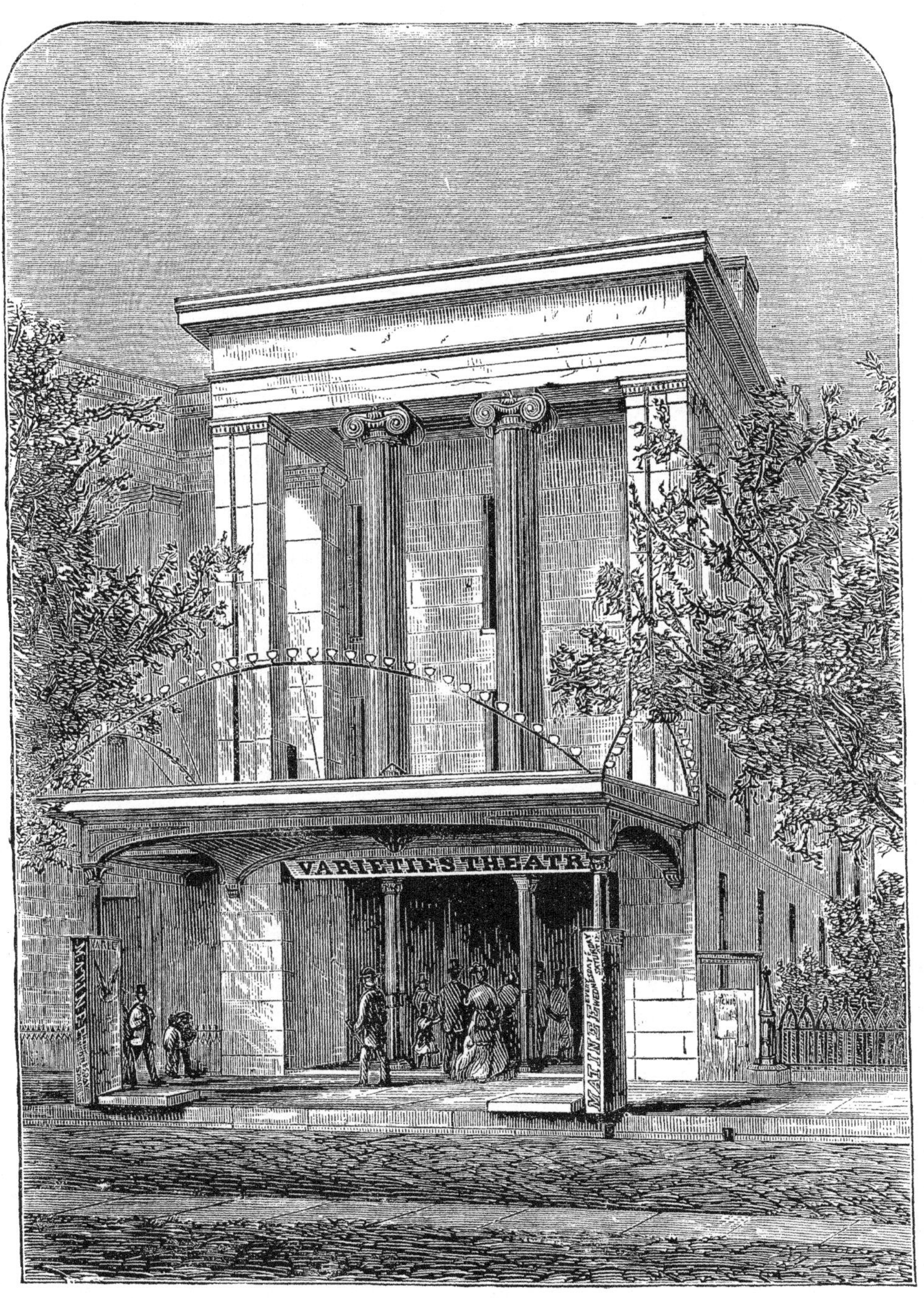

VARIETIES THEATRE.

JEWELL'S CRESCENT CITY ILLUSTRATED.

Royal Highness, the "King of the Carnival," necessary to the proper maintenance of his state and dignity.

Given under our hand and seal at Carnival Palace, February 1, 1872. REX.

HEADQUARTERS REGIMENT LOUISIANA VOLUNTEER
FIELD ARTILLERY,
NEW ORLEANS, Feb. 1, 1872.

To His Royal Highness the King of the Carnival:

Fully recognizing the supreme power and glory of your Majesty's authority, I respectfully submit to its mandate, and will forthwith take the necessary measures to station a battery of Napoleons at the foot of Canal street on Mardi Gras, February 13, and there await your Majesty's orders.

Kissing your royal hand, I remain with much respect your obedient servant, CHAS. W. SQUIRES,
Colonel Commanding La. Artillery.

In addition to the above information, it has pleased his Mightiness to request from us a public notification to the following effect :

That large or distinct organizations need only communicate with him officially, previous to Mardi Gras. Small parties, or single maskers, in whatever guise they choose to appear, will find themselves provided for, and their positions assigned in the general edict, containing the programme of the procession, which will be issued in good time. All are welcome. God save the King.

This was speedily followed by other edicts, as will be seen by the following extract from the *Times* of Feb. 3 :

"VIVE LE ROI !"

As an usurper the "King of the Carnival" is evidently a success, since history furnishes but rare examples in which ambition has met with so few obstacles in the pathway to power.

If His Majesty possesses one shining qualification superior to all others, it certainly consists in what vulgar people would denominate "cheek." By a few well directed movements and judicious orders he has achieved a successful *coup d' etat* and will reign on Mardi Gras, with a title none dare dispute.

With the example of obedience thus set in high places, it is expected that the people, who are more directly interested, will yield an equally prompt and willing submission to all His Majesty's orders.

The following edicts were yesterday promulgated by His Royal Highness :

EDICT II.

To His Excellency the Governor of the State of Louisiana:

In order to avoid any unpleasant complications which might arise through conflict of authority, you are hereby directed to close your office on Mardi Gras, and during that period to refrain from the exercise, or attempt to exercise, any gubernatorial privileges or duties whatsoever.

Further—In order to better preserve the peace and maintain the dignity of the realm, you are also directed to disperse that riotous body known as the Louisiana State Legislature, and close their halls of meeting during the same period of time.

A prompt acknowledgment of your Excellency's submission will be esteemed a favor.

Given under our hand and seal, at Carnival Palace, on this, the 2d day of February, 1872. REX.

STATE OF LOUISIANA, EXECUTIVE DEPARTMENT,
NEW ORLEANS, Feb. 2, 1872.

To His Royal Highness the King of the Carnival :

The Governor of the State of Louisiana, entertaining the highest regard for your Majesty's person and authority, will feel honored in obeying your Royal mandates as far as lies in his power.

He regrets that his influence with the State Legislature is not sufficient to control their action to the extent demanded, but will cheerfully transmit to that body your Majesty's gracious communication.

With a high sense of the honor conferred, he remains obediently, H. C. WARMOTH,
Governor of Louisiana.

Subsequent to the occurrence of the above important correspondence, His Majesty was pleased to order the promulgation of the following :

EDICT III.

To all whom it may Concern, Greeting :

In view of numerous petitions laid at the foot of the throne—all to the following tenor :

NEW ORLEANS, Feb. 1, 1872.

Your Majesty would confer a great favor on a large number of employees, if you could succeed in having business suspended on the evening when your dictum will be the acknowledged law of the city. Wishing you abundance of fun, and hoping through your aid to be able to assist in the frolic, I remain your subject, EMPLOYEE.

Now, therefore, we, the "King of the Carnival," do hereby order and ordain, That *all private places of business in this city* BE CLOSED AT ONE O'CLOCK, P. M. ON TUESDAY, February 13, 1872, (Old Probabilities permitting,) so that none of our beloved subjects may be debarred from participating in the honors to be accorded their liege Sovereign.

Given under our hand and seal, at Carnival Palace, this, the 2d day of February, 1872. REX.

In addition to the above we learn from one of the King's Chamberlains that the procession promises to be not only a complete success, but perhaps one of the grandest affairs that ever occurred in New Orleans. Masking parties are everywhere forming, among which are some composed of the wealthiest and most respectable young men in the city. All seem to have caught the spirit of the thing, and are reporting as directed to headquarters. The system thus introduced cannot fail to add greatly to the enjoyment of all parties concerned, including the public, and Mardi Gras promises to be this year an "upside down" day of the most comical yet orderly character.

Next day the following notice appeared :

"AYE, EVERY INCH A KING !"

Is His Majesty of the Carnival. All day yesterday his cabinet was crowded with secretaries answering communications and completing preparations for the grand organization of Mardi Gras, his Majesty personally superintending the duties of his ministers. Two edicts were issued during the day, which have not yet been promulgated. It was rumored however, around the court yard of the Palace, that one was aimed at suppressing an important judicial body, and that the other was issued in behalf of the school children.

The cheerful alacrity with which his Majesty's edicts have been obeyed has not been without a beneficial effect upon his health and spirits. He properly regards this as not only flattering to his dignity, but as attesting a mark of approval on the part of his beloved subjects promising well for his reign.

The Keeper of the Royal Boot-jack reported to his Majesty at a late hour last night holding a Council of State upon the subject of the Committee of Fifty-one, which he is inclined to view as an insurrectionary body, he being overheard to say that they reminded him of an old flintlock musket that would never " report and go off" when it was wanted to.

It was officially announced during the day that five bands of music have already been engaged, and that organizations are daily reporting in greater numbers. Everything is now in train for a happy and successful issue. God save the King.

Excitement had now been fired, and all the necessary preparations for the display were under way in competent hands. His Majesty's coffers were full to plethora, and nothing remained but to keep public attention aroused. With this design, the following appeared in the *Times* of the 6th:

H. R. H. THE KING OF THE CARNIVAL.

ANOTHER EDICT.

The following edict, issued by His Majesty on Saturday, now for the first time officially promulgated:

EDICT IV.

To the Hon. Chairman of the Congressional Investigating Committee, Greeting:

His Royal Highness, the " King of the Carnival," having a firm belief in the doctrine "Pleasure first and business afterward," hereby interdicts any session of your honorable body being held on Mardi Gras, February 13, 1872, and respectfully invites its members to witness the glory of his regal state during his reign upon that day.

He now awaits a signification of your acquiescence in this Royal mandate.

Given under our hand and seal, at Carnival Palace, February 3, 1872. REX.

NEW ORLEANS, Feb. 3, 1872.

To His Royal Highness the King of the Carnival:

Bowing to your royal will the members of the Congressional Investigating Committee will obediently comply with your command.

With many wishes for a successful reign, we remain your Majesty's grateful servants.

By order JAS. R. YOUNG,
Secretary of Congressional Investigating Committee.

COURT JOURNAL.

His Majesty was in session nearly all day yesterday with his Council, and was pleased to signify his approbation of the conduct of the Recorders in deciding to adjourn their courts on Mardi Gras, without waiting for a royal edict to that effect. He expresse himself so warmly in consideration of this delicate recognition of authority, that he was obliged to be vigorously fanned by the Lord of the Meerschaum in waiting. His Majesty also completed the appointments of his royal household, assigning the new officials their final duties in providing for his reign. He subsequently, during the afternoon, retired to the Divan, where he passed the evening in meditation, puffing vigorously at one of Don Jose Domingo's cigars.

His Majesty, it was rumored, is somewhat perplexed in regard to the precise and proper relations to be established between himself and his royal cousin, the Grand Duke Alexis, who will be in the city during his reign. Upon this subject he is profoundly reticent, his silence being almost Grant-like in its grandeur, but as His Majesty has already proven himself a poor hand at making mistakes, no doubt the problem will be solved to the mutual satisfaction of both distinguished personages.

In the course of the afternoon, many of his principal subjects called and earnestly solicited an audience with the King; among them Col. J. B. Walton, Judge Cooley, D. F. Kenner, Judge Howe, Dr. Mercer, John Burnside, Chas. Cavaroc, Robert Moore, Mayor Flanders, Pat. Irwin, C. A. Weed, T. A. Adams, Jno. G. Gaines, W. S. Pike, E. Salomon, and many others. All these gentlemen were respectfully but firmly denied an audience, His Majesty having fully determined to hold no public levee until Mardi Gras. Of course the reception of this determination was received with profound regret by the applicants, all of whom desired to have their compliments conveyed to His Royal Highness, by the Groom of the Royal Velocipedes, who was in attendance.

Toward 10 o'clock P. M., His Majesty, as always his custom of an afternoon, commanded the attendance of one of his Under Secretaries, who proceeded, as usual, to read him to sleep with the proceedings of the City Council. He was noticed to yawn repeatedly under the infliction, and at 11 P. M. fell off into a gentle slumber.

At 11.30, a peaceful smile stole like an exhalation over his childlike and bland features, and the Royal Bootjack signified to his brother of the Dressing-gown, that " an Angel whispered to the King." This the latter, who is not much given to the melting mood, refused to " see," saying " Morelike he vas dreamin' he'd drorn a prize in the State Lotterree."

At midnight the gates of the Palace were closed, when the sentinel's watchword went echoing from battlement to battlement, " Long live the King."

Next morning the following short biography of His Majesty was laid before the public:

H. R. H.

SOMETHING ABOUT HIM.

The King of the Carnival is the offspring of Old King Cole and the Goddess Terpsichore, whom, in imitation of Jove, he wooed and carried off, in the form of an Irish Bull. He is, therefore, gifted with immortality by virtue of his Olympian origin on his mother's side. He was born somewhere upon the shores of the Mediterranean, about the eighth century, and in consequence is now, though hale and hearty, somewhat advanced in years. Upon arriving at man's estate he speedily conquered the whole of Southern Europe, which he held under dominion for a long period of time. About two centuries ago he declared war against his cousin, King Gambrinus, who at that time held all Northern Europe under sway, and after fighting that monarch desperately a long time was finally conquered and driven into obscurity. During these dark days of misfortune, he sought refuge in England, where he assumed the

New Odd Fellows' Hall.

NEW ORLEANS,

Natchez AND Vicksburg Packet.

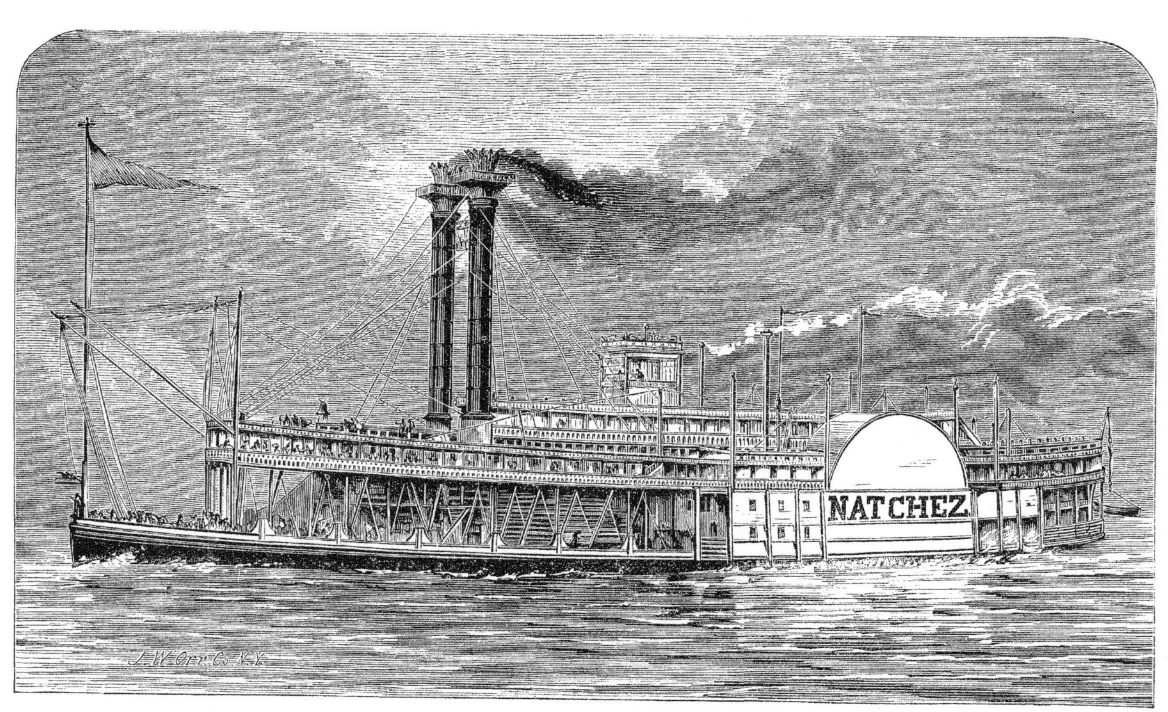

STEAMER NATCHEZ,

CAPTAIN T. P. LEATHERS, MASTER.

Length of Hull,	307 Feet.	Eight Boilers, 34 feet long---
Width of Beam,	44 "	40 inches diameter and 2 Flues.
Depth of Hold,	10 "	Two 34 inch Cylinders, 10 feet Stroke.
Diameter of Wheel,	44 "	Extreme Height, 119 feet, 6 inches.
Length of Bucket	16 "	Capacity for 5,500 bales cotton.

JEWELL'S CRESCENT CITY ILLUSTRATED.

name of Joseph Miller, familiarly known as "Old Joe Miller," and devoted himself to politics, in which he subsequently achieved some fame as the author of the Junius Letters and the founder of the London *Punch*. A few years since he returned to Rome, where he established a race course on the Corso, and made a desperate attempt to reclaim his dynasty. Failing in this, through the machinations of Count Cavour and Victor Emmanuel, he set sail for the United States, where he landed in 1866, and has since been living in seclusion at the South, managing the political affairs of its people. The prince of mischief-makers and jokers, he is credited with having inspired the queer governments and social relations existing in this benighted section. Only a few days have elapsed since his successful attempt at overthrowing the government of Louisiana, one of the most remarkable occurrences on record—in a cheeky point of view.

His Majesty, in personal appearance, is more interesting than commanding. Rather below the medium height, an erect form surmounted with a well set head, covered with a profusion of snow white hair, and a long patriarchal beard, his aspect is at once venerable and imposing. His brow is wide and expansive, his eyes dark and glittering, always fixed, as it were, on a dreamy futurity. His mouth firm set and stamped with a perpetual smile. His face bronzed with the exposure of centuries, and his entire appearance and bearing are calculated to inspire the most profound awe and respect.

His Majesty has never married, giving as an excuse that this state should not be entered into until experience has sobered the liveliness of youth and all the wild oats have been sown. We give this latter piece of information for the benefit of the ladies who are already overwhelming His Majesty with billet-doux.

It is well to note in the latter connection that the national air or anthem of the Carnival Dynasty, for many centuries past, has been, as is at present, "If ever I cease to love."

A bold stroke was now resolved upon, no less than a general edict closing the District Courts on Mardi Gras. In every instance the order was acquiesced in, eliciting in some instances letters in reply. We quote from the *Times* of the sixth instant:

"REX."

THE KING OF THE CARNIVAL ISSUES HIS EDICTS TO THE DISTRICT JUDGES.

This (Monday) morning, the Judges of our several District Courts were served with a royal edict emanating from His Highness the King of the Carnival, by which it will be seen that "Rex," with an assumption of sovereignty as sweeping as that of the most elevated monarch, has but to command his faithful subjects, even to the dignified Judiciary, fall down and obey. Annexed is a copy of the edict, a *fac-simile* of which was received by each Judge:

EDICT V.

To our Beloved Brother, Judge ———:

Greeting—His Royal Highness the King of the Carnival, by virtue of authority in him vested, does hereby ordain and decree:

1. That the ——— District Court stand adjourned on or before the hour of 12 M., on Tuesday, February 13, 1872.

2. That the Honorable Judge thereof immediately notify the officers thereof, and the bar practitioners of this royal mandate.

All for the glory and state of their sovereign liege, whom God preserves.

Given under our hand and seal at Carnival Palace, this the fifth day of February, 1872. REX.

In response thereunto the judges have signified their cheerful willingness to obey the royal commands, and have addressed His Royal Highness, by hand, as follows:

FROM JUDGE ABELL.

FIRST DISTRICT COURT, Parish of Orleans.

To His Majesty the King of the Carnival:

Your royal authority is fully recognized, and will be cheerfully obeyed. Respectfully,

EDMUND ABELL, Judge.

FROM JUDGE COOLEY

To His Royal Highness, the "King of the Carnival:"

Your Majesty—I have received your communication, enclosing your Majesty's edicts, to the effect that the Sixth District Court be closed on Tuesday, the 13th instant, from the hour of 12 M., and also that I, as Judge of that court, notify the officers thereof, and the members of the Bar, of your royal mandate.

I beg to assure your Majesty that I am anxious to comply with your desires; that instead of adjourning my courts as you order, at 12 M., on the 13th, I shall have it hermetically closed at 3 o'clock P. M., the day preceding, and shall so advise the officers and members of the Bar.

Tendering to your Majesty my best wishes for a prosperous and jovial reign, I remain your Royal Highness' most obedient servant,

W. H. COOLEY,

Judge Sixth District Court.

FROM JUDGE DUVIGNEAUD.

To His Majesty the King of the Carnival:

Sire—I cheerfully acknowledge the receipt of your royal mandate, and beg leave to inform your amiable Majesty that I will faithfully, as a loyal subject, comply with your request. Praying Almighty God that you may live thousands of years in our beloved city, I have the honor to be, of your Majesty, the most humble and obedient servant, LS. DUVIGNEAUD,

Judge of the Second District Court, by the grace of your Majesty and the true people of this city.

FROM JUDGE LEAUMONT.

To His Royal Highness, King of the Carnival:

Sire—A significant nod of the judicial cranium has just brought me near—nearer to the somewhat antique bench of his Honor, Don Cæsar Leaumont, holding forth as Major Domo, sole Judge of the Fifth District Court for the parish of Orleans.

That functionary now affectionately hands me your peremptory order and decree, directing the closing of his infirmary on Tuesday, February 13, 1872, and begs me to assure you that—

He deems it not only a duty, but a pleasure to strictly comply with your Royal behests, feeling as he does that "the Court is in full accord with Mercadel," and that this case "presents no difficulty."

I am further enjoined by Don Cæsar to renew the assurance of his eternal loyalty.

Thrice saluting, oh! King, I am thine.

LOUIS POWER,

Clerk Fifth District Court, parish of Orleans.

FROM JUDGE DIBBLE.

PALACE OF JUSTICE,
Department of Prerogative Writs.

To His Royal Highness, King of the Carnival:

I am directed by his Honor the Judge of this our Court, to inform your Highness that in obedience to your royal command, our court will be adjourned on the occasion of the entrance of

JEWELL'S CRESCENT CITY ILLUSTRATED.

your Majesty into this city, and that all of your Majesty's commands thereunto will be strictly obeyed.

I am further directed by his Honor the Judge, to make his pledges of fealty to your Majesty.

I have the honor to be your Majesty's most obedient servant,
O. M. TENNISON,
Register of Decrees.

In addition to above, Judges Theard and Collens have given the bearer of His Majesty's edicts personal assurance of their compliance.

———

Another batch of edicts appeared the following morning, and it was now very plain that His Majesty's authority was established beyond all cavil or dispute. We quote from the daily papers of the seventh:

IMPORTANT EDICTS.

FROM H. R. H. THE KING OF THE CARNIVAL.

Now, by St. Paul, the work goes bravely on, and all the realm is alive with preparation. Never before was a conqueror more thoroughly successful. He has but to speak, and lo! all hasten to obey. Below we publish the four last edicts of the King of the Carnival, which give holiday to a vast number of public employees, and all the public school children:

EDICT VI.

To J. B. Carter, Esq., Superintendent Public Schools, Parish of Orleans:

Greeting—His Royal Highness the King of the Carnival, being desirous that the children of the realm should be afforded an opportunity of participating in the honors to their liege Sovereign on Mardi Gras, February 13, 1872, hereby ordains and decrees, that all the schools under your jurisdiction be closed upon that day, and that you immediately take the necessary steps to secure the enforcement of this royal mandate.

A prompt acknowledgment of your acquiescence in this order will be esteemed a favor.

Given under our hand and seal, at Carnival Palace, this, the third day of February, 1872. REX.

———

OFFICE OF DIVISION SUPERINTENDENT PUBLIC SCHOOLS,
Sixth Division, 20 City Hall,
NEW ORLEANS, February 6, 1872.

To His Royal Highness, the King of the Carnival:

The kingly decree of your Majesty, as to the public schools of this division, has been received, and in due submission to the illustrious mandate the schools will be closed on the thirteenth instant—Mardi Gras.

I crave permission to add that your Majesty has no more faithful subjects than the "children of the realm" in the schools, albeit they themselves are, to a degree, sovereigns and rulers with undoubted, if not constitutional sway, in the home dominion.

Wealth, prosperity and great wit, and wisdom to your Majesty.
J. B. CARTER, Superintendent.
WM. ROLLINSON, Secretary Board Directors.

———

EDICT VII.

To the Hon. C. W. Lowell, Posmaster, New Orleans:

Greeting—His Royal Highness, King of the Carnival, by virtue of authority in him vested, and in consideration of communications received to the following tenor:

To His Royal Highness the King of the Carnival:

Wishing to take an active part in the festivities on the thirteenth instant, I trust Your Majesty will request the Postmaster to ease his employees from slinging literature on that day. I am very respectfully, etc., yours, EMPLOYEE.

It is hereby ordained and decreed that you conform as closely to the above request as consistent with your public duties. This for the honor and glory of the King, who awaits a signification of your obedience.

Given under our hand and seal, at Carnival Palace, this, the fifth day of February, 1872. REX.

———

POST OFFICE,
Corner Canal and Old Levee streets,
NEW ORLEANS, February 6, 1872.

His Royal Highness, the "King of the Carnival:"

Sire—Your decree of the fifth instant has been duly communicated to me, and I have the honor to inform you, that in obedience to your command, this office will be closed on Tuesday, the 13th instant, at 12 o'clock M.

Your Majesty's most loyal subject,
C. W. LOWELL, Postmaster,
New Orleans, La.

———

EDICT VIII.

To James F. Casey, Esq., Collector of the Port of New Orleans:

Greeting—His Royal Highness, King of the Carnival, having been informed that a large number of his well beloved subjects are under your authority and control, hereby ordains and decrees—

First—That they be released from duty at noon, on Mardi Gras, under penalty of our Royal displeasure.

Second—That the revenue cutter "Wilderness" remain in port during the entire day.

His Majesty now awaits notification of your compliance with this Royal mandate.

Given under our hand and seal at Carnival Palace, the fifth day of February, 1872. REX.

———

CUSTOM HOUSE, NEW ORLEANS,
Collector's Office, February 6, 1872.

To His Majesty, the "King of the Carnival:"

I am instructed by Collector Casey to acknowledge the receipt of your royal command, directing the suspension of the collection of customs and the detention of the United States revenue steamer "Wilderness" in port during the Mardi Gras festivities, and to assure you that it will be his pleasure for to faithfully execute the decerees of your Majesty. Your loyal subject,
E. P. CHAMPLIN, Deputy Collector.

———

EDICT IX

To Charles T. Howard, President Louisiana State Lottery:

Greeting—It having come to the knowledge of his Royal Highness, the King of the Carnival, that some three hundred of his loyal subjects are temporarily under your control, therefore,

Know ye, that this mandate hereby interdicts the transaction of any business whatever, connected with the Louisiana State Lottery, on the day, (February 13, 1872) consecrated to His Majesty's reign.

Given under our hand and seal at Carnival Palace, this, the sixth day of February, 1872. REX.

———

NEW ORLEANS, Feb. 6, 1872.

To His Royal Highness, King of the Carnival:

Sire—Bowing in mute allegiance to your royal authority, I hereby notify the public and all employees connected with the Louisiana State Lottery, that the regular day drawing of the same will be omitted on February 13, 1872, (Mardi Gras), and at the same time entreat them to do everything in their power to contribute to your Majesty's state and glory on that occasion. With the best wishes for the health, power and prosperity of your Royal Highness, I remain your humble servant,
CHARLES T. HOWARD,
President L. S. L.

His Majesty desires us to state that in consequence of his secretaries and attendants being overwhelmed with preparations for Mardi Gras, he will issue no more special edicts.

JEWELL'S CRESCENT CITY ILLUSTRATED.

GRAND STATE PAGEANT.

His Royal Highness, the King of the Carnival, will command in person, assisted by the Grand Marshal of the Empire, and the Lords of the Horse, Carriages, Vans, Yeomanry and the Unattached—all of whom, with their Aids, will appear at Clay Statue at 2 o'clock P. M.

Upon arrival, the Lords herein named will immediately take position at the points assigned for the rights of their respective Divisions, in the manner laid down in this our Royal mandate, taking care to place and hold in line their several bodies, subject to the orders of the Chief Marshal of the Empire.

HOW IT WILL FORM.

The pageant will be divided in Five Grand Dvisions, which will form as follows:

THE FIRST DIVISION—Will comprise all foot maskers, (in ranks of four), and will form on the South side of Canal street, their right resting on St. Charles street, extending toward the swamp.

THE SECOND DIVISION—Comprising all maskers in open or private carriages, will form on St. Charles street, the right resting on Canal street.

THE THIRD DIVISION—Comprising all maskers in vans, floats, milk-carts and other public vehicles, will form on Camp street, their right resting upon Canal street.

THE FOURTH DIVISION—Comprising all masked horsemen (in sections of four), will form on the south side of Canal street, their right resting upon Camp street, and rear extending toward the river.

THE FIFTH DIVISION—Comprising all stragglers, late comers and subjects not elsewhere provided for, will form on the North side of Canal street, their right resting upon Chartres street, and rear extending toward the river.

All the above are required to be in line by 2 o'clock P. M.

HOW IT WILL MOVE.

At precisely three o'clock P. M. a Royal Salute of thirteen guns will be fired from the foot of Canal street, by Col. C. W. Squires, Commander-in-Chief of his Majesty's forces, when the King and Court will immediately move from the Clay Statue, taking up the line of march, followed by the First Division, down the north side of Canal street to the intersection of Camp and Chartres streets, up the south side of Canal street to Royal, and down Royal street.

When the left of the First Division passes St. Charles street, the Second Division will move into line; when *its* rear passes Camp street, the Third Division will move into line; the Fourth Division following next in order, and the Fifth Division last.

Each Division will be provided with a Band of Music, and its and its Lord Marshal attended by a Standard Bearer.

ORDER OF PROCESSION.

Squadron of Mounted Police.

Grand Marshal of the Empire.

H R. H., THE KING OF THE CARNIVAL, with attendants.

Music.

Lord of the Yeomanry.

Bœuf Gras.

FIRST DIVISION—Music; Lord of the Carriages.
SECOND DIVISION—Music; Lord of the Vans.
THIRD DIVISION—Music; Lord of the Horse.
FOURTH DIVISION—Music; Lord of the Unattached.
FIFTH DIVISION—Platoon of Police.

THE ROUTE OF MARCH.

Down Royal street to Esplanade street; down Esplanade street to Rampart street; up Rampart street, north side, to Canal street; up Canal street, south side, to St. Charles street; up St. Charles street to St. Joseph street, to Camp street; down Camp street to Canal, to Clay Statue, where His Royal Highness will graciously review his subjects, and dismiss the pageant to their own enjoyment—a Band of Music being placed in each square between Rampart and Camp, to better secure this end.

GENERAL ORDERS.

1. All organizations and subjects intending to participate must report to the Lords Marshal of Division, at 2 o'clock P. M.

2. All places of business, public and private, are hereby ordered to be closed at 12 o'clock M.

3. Owners and drivers of public and private vehicles, are required to keep out of the highways in which the Divisions of the Royal pageant will form and through which it will pass.

4. Owners and masters of vessels and steamboats in port, the proprietors of public buildings, the Consuls of all foreign nations at peace with His Majesty, are directed to display their colors during the entire day.

5. The City Authorities are hereby ordered, under penalty of Royal displeasure, to remove all obstructions from the highways on which the pageant is to form or pass.

6. All malicious mischief upon the part of his loyal subjects, such as throwing flour, is interdicted and forbidden under the severest penalty.

7. The Lords Marshal will be distinguished as follows: Grand Marshal of the Empire, purple and gold rosette and baton; Division Lords Marshal, red and gold ditto; Aids, to correspond.

At Sunset another Royal Salute will be fired by the Commander-in-Chief of His Majesty's forces, when all his subjects will immediately disperse, in order to give place, and do appropriate honor to, our Cousin COMUS, who visits His Majesty after that time.

And now, enjoining strict obedience upon the part of his beloved subjects, His Royal Highness trusts his honor and glory to their loyal hands.

Given under our hand and seal, at Carnival Palace, this, the 9th day of February, in the year of our Lord, 1872.　　　REX.

———

Preparations had now advanced to such a point, that nearly everything was in readiness; and, on the 12th, the following preclamation was issued by the Lord Grand Marshal:

PROCLAMATION

By the Grand Marshal of the Empire.

CARNIVAL PALACE, FEBRUARY THE TWELFTH, }
Anno Domini, 1872.　　　　　　　　　　}

I. In obedience to H. R. Highness' Edict No. X, and to carry out its provisions and commands promptly and harmoniously, the Grand Marshal of the Empire, call upon all loyal and obedient subjects, to form at their respective places of rendezvous, precisely at one o'clock, on Tuesday, (Mardi Gras,) 1872, in order that they may report to the Lord Division Marshal, to whose division the character of the organization belongs.

The prompt carrying out of this command alone will prevent confusion and unnecessary delay. As the Royal State Pageant will move punctually at 3 o'clock, all organizations and subjects will have to be in line at 2 P. M.

II. The Lords of Yeomanry, of Carriages, of Vans, of the Horse and of the Unattached, together with their Aids, are commanded to report in person to the Lord Grand Marshal, at his department of State, at 12 M.

III. Col. A. S. BADGER, commanding His Majesty's Household Guard, is commanded to report to the Grand Marshal of the Empire at the same hour and place.

　　　　　　BY THE LORD GRAND MARSHAL.
Approved, REX.

On the same day the following notices appeared in the *Times:*

THE KING OF THE CARNIVAL.

COURT JOURNAL.

The calm which invariably precedes the storm, prevailed at the palace yesterday, and but little work was done. The guards lounged around the galleries and ante-chambers in a listless manner, occasionally gathering into knots listening to the jovial yarns of Col. Jack Wharton, Chief Equerry in waiting to His Majesty, or exciting stories of the chase as related by Billy Connor, Lord Groom of the

JEWELL'S CRESCENT CITY ILLUSTRATED.

Royal Stables. During the entire morning His Majesty remained in seclusion, only granting an audience to a deputation of loyal ladies, who desired some information concerning the Royal colors, with a view to using them in the decorations of Tuesday. His Majesty received them graciously, and summoned Garter King-at-Arms, to his presence. The latter explained that the Royal colors were Green, Gold and Purple; regretting that the subjugation of the State had been too recent to prepare a Royal Standard, but that upon all His Majesty's future fete days it would invariably be displayed. An hour was subsequently spent in completing additional arrangements for the reception of the Grand Duke; His Majesty, who of course understands all languages, inditing the following autograph letter, to be handed to his Royal cousin upon arrival. We give it in the vernacular;

His Royalovitch Highnessoff The King of the Carnival, Officia llywelc omest one worle ansh isroy alcous inth emostp uiss ant Duke Alexis Alexandrovitch Romanoff andwi llh o ldaspe ciala udie ncef orh Isrece pti on atsu nse ton *Mardi Gras.*
REX.

In the evening a grand State banquet was given. Among the guests attending which were to be found Gen. H. S. McComb, Gen. Beauregard, Col. Sam Boyd, Norbert Trepagnier, P. O. Hebert, Samuel Smith, J. W. Burbridge, I. N. Marks, C. A. Whitney, and C. H. Slocomb, Esquires. The approaching festivities were here discussed at length with the viands and wines until 9 o'clock, when His Majesty, attended by his Lords in waiting and Gentlemen of the Bed Chamber, retired, leaving the guests to their own enjoyment. His Majesty was subsequently read to sleep by one of the Under Secretaries, but with some difficulty. The proceedings of the City Council usually productive of somnolency being found upon this occasion ineffectual, through their unusual brevity of late; resort was then had to the minutes of the Academy of Natural Sciences, under the soothing influence of which nature shortly succumbed.

Many additional applications for position were filed during the day at the office of the Grand Marshal of the Empire, and another heavy batch of correspondence was being opened up to a late hour of night, all testifying greater promise of gorgeous magnificence of the Royal State Pageant. God save the King

---

A CARD.

More Honors to H. R. H.

New Orleans, Feb. 10, 1872.

To His Royal Highness, the King of the Carnival:

Sire—Hearing that some three hundred employees of the New Orleans, Jackson & Great Northern Railroad have addressed a petition to your throne, praying a special edict releasing them from duty upon the occasion of your reign, February 13, 1872, I hasten to forestall that necessity.

Proud of being ranked among your Majesty's most loyal subjects, and fully appreciating the wisdom and profound judgment which characterizes your rule, I herewith announce the intention of the New Orleans, Jackson and Great Northern Railroad to release all employees from duty upon your *fete* day, except those actually necessary to bring the throngs of subjects daily arriving to do honor to your Royal Highness.

I hope that all said employees may join in the pageant, and thereby publicly testify the high and loving estimation in which you are held by your honored and submissive subject.
H. S. McCOMB,
President New Orleans, Jackson & Great Northern Railroad.

On the 13th dawned the memorable day of His Majesty's first triumph, on the morning of which he issued his last edict, through his official journal, as follows:

THE KING RIDES FORTH TO-DAY.

Yesterday at Carnival Palace.—Another Edict.—

Preparations for the Display Being

Actively Pushed Forward.

''VIVE LE ROI!''

His Majesty remained in his private apartments throughout the entire day yesterday, absorbed in meditation and the inevitable Gonzales cigar. Having been apprised the evening previous of the arrival of his royal cousin, the Grand Duke Alexis, at 10 A. M., he ordered the State carriage, with outriders and chasseurs, and dispatched it with the Lord Chamberlain, Chief Equerry in waiting, and his Honor the Lord Mayor of the Corporation, to conduct His Highness to the apartments arranged for him in the north wing of the Imperial Palace of St. Charles.

To-day having been set aside for the official reception of the Grand Duke, of course great quiet and seclusion prevailed around His Majesty's apartments. The offices of the Grand Marshal, the Grand Almoner, and the Secretaries were, however, very busy all day making preparation for to-day's celebration, and from what we could glean, everything promised a happy consummation.

The following letter from a prominent firm in the railroad and steamship interests was handed to His Majesty's Secretary while just upon the point of issuing a special edict in the premises:

New Orleans, Feb. 12, 1872.

To His Royal Highness, the King of the Carnival:

Sire: In obedience to your Royal mandate, contained in Edict X, we beg leave to announce our intention of releasing all employees from duty, on February 13th, 1872, who may wish to participate in the honors to be accorded your Royal Highness, and who can be consistently spared from the exigencies of business.

With highest esteem, we remain, your obedient servants,
C. A. WHITNEY & CO.

As night wore on, the gates of the Palace were closed, the portcullis lowered and the draw-bridge raised. All strangers and newspaper reporters were exiled beyond the moat, but long into the silent watches of the night, the flickering lights waving to and fro, and clink of hammers closing rivets up, gave evidence that the work of preparation was being pushed on with unabated ardor.

During the course of the day, the following edict was ordered promulgated by His Royal Highness the King:

EDICT No. XI.

To all Whom it may Concern:

His Royal Highness, the King of the Carnival, being deeply impressed with the enthusiastic loyalty manifested by his beloved subjects of all degrees and conditions, upon this, his most blessed *fete* day, has resolved—

That a proper consideration for the glory of his regal state and sovereign care for his loyal subjects, demands the abrogation of all laws, and the removal of all impediment of whatsoever kind or nature, that may impair or interfere with public enjoyment.

In pursuance of this determination, he, therefore, solemnly enacts the following decrees to rule the law of the land during the entire reign of his illustrious and glorious Majesty:

First—Whereas, It having come to our Royal knowledge that one Stockdale, Collector of Internal Revenue, intends taking advantage of His Majesty's preoccupation in affairs of State connected with the Royal Pageant, to collect all the taxes of the Realm, his office is hereby abolished.

Second—The following laws enacted by a previous government having been found to weigh greviously upon his Majesty's subjects—The Registration Law, Constabulary Law, Election Law, Printing Law, Taxes and Judge H. C. Dibble—all of the same are hereby abrogated and abolished.

Third—The credit of the Realm is hereby re-established on a specie

CHURCH OF THE IMMACULATE CONCEPTION.

basis, and all securities, of whatever nature, are declared to rule at par value. Any person, subject or foreign, detected at any attempt at their depreciation will be immediately incarcerated in the lowest dungeon of the Donjonkeep.

Fourth—All subjects guilty of any breach of the peace, working all and any description of disorder or offence against good taste and delicacy, in the display of *outre* or improper costumes, will be immediately conveyed to the barracks of the household troops: and our well beloved servant, Col. A. S. Badger, Captain of the Guard, near to the person of his Majesty, is hereby charged with the strict enforcement of this order under penalty in default thereof of being forced to attend the meeting of the Academy of Natural Sciences for the entire year.

Fifth—The market rate of cotton is hereby established for this day at fifty cents per pound, low middling grade, and for sugar at 25 cents per pound, other products of the realm to grade in proportion. Any subject violating this edict will, upon trial and conviction be sentenced to serve not more than one term at hard labor in the Louisiana State Legislature.

Sixth—All punishments incurred by the children of the realm for any offences of whatever nature, committed anterior to this date, are hereby cancelled in honor of the fete of His Royal Highness. Parents or guardians disregarding the provisions of this edict are hereby sentenced to a perpetual deprivation of their night-latch keys.

Seventh—All quarrels, hatreds, jealousies and vendettas heretofore existing between any of His Majesty's subjects are hereby cancelled, as nothing but the most unalloyed good humor and jollity will be allowed to prevail throughout the realm during the glorious reign of His Majesty.

Eighth—All persons residing along the route of the royal pageant, are ordered to provide proper extra supports for their galleries, to festoon and decorate the same with the royal colors, [green, gold and purple,] and to pay due obeisance to his Royal Highness, in passing, under penalty in default thereof of perpetual exile to the Balize.

Lastly—Sir Warren A. Stone, the Right Hon. D. C. Holliday, the Hon. J. T. Scott, and Sir Howard Smith, Physicians in Ordinary to His Majesty's household, having recommended a change of air and scene, the King of the Carnival will therefore be under the unpleasant and regretful necessity of bidding his loyal subjects adieu at sunset to-day, for a brief period of time; promising to return again when his health, in the opinion of the Royal Physicians, shall have been fully re-established.

In doing so, it is with a profound and gratifying sense of the loyalty displayed by his subjects, of the cheerful and prompt alacrity with which his orders have been obeyed, and with the promise that on the occasion of his re-entry into his capital, the splendors of to-day's pageant shall be far outshone in magnificence and gorgeous state.

And now, with the best wishes for their health, prosperity and happiness, he bids them, in anticipation of his rather sudden departure, an affectionate adieu. Enjoining upon them during his absence, unswerving loyalty in their allegiance to the Royal House of Carnival, and an unimpaired continuance of that loving affection already manifest for its reigning head, which is above all price. God save the King.

Given under our hand and seal, at Carnival Palace, this, the 12th day of February, in the year of our Lord, 1872.

REX.

The unprecedented success of the Procession is yet too fresh in the recollection of our readers, to need elaboration in this short story; it can, however, be readily referred to if desired, in all, or any of the New Orleans daily papers of February 14, 1872; from which the following short comments are extracted:

It is with pleasure that the chronicler reflects that the work of this article was to record the dawning of a new era in the long history of Mardi Gras festivities, and that the advent has been not only brilliant but successful, the thousands of delighted people who were not slow to express their enthusiasm, can fully testify. It is no easy matter to conduct such a spectacle satisfactorily, and it is therefore a cause for much gratification that in every respect the Procession of Rex, his court and kingdom, will be looked forward to as one, if not as the great event of Mardi Gras, and when he again "rides forth" the King of the Carnival, his loyal subjects will greet him with a welcome made stronger and heartier by reason of his achieved success, and the assurance of additional pleasure, which have by his means entered into the glorious and festal time.

*   *   *   *   *   *   *   *   *

It has opened a new era to New Orleans; one we trust to see cultivated, and the little plant of only ten day's growth which yielded so bountifully of blossoms, we trust to see expand, in the future, to a lusty tree, hung with the golden fruit, that all will be glad without exception to pluck and enjoy. In the old language of the sectional unpleasantness, the association of gentlemen who managed this affair, "covered themselves with glory."

The benign yet firm reign of His Majesty on this occasion, developed one remarkable result. Although 5,000 maskers were assembled in Procession, yet the police statistics of disorder and arrests were notably smaller on that occasion than any preceding Mardi Gras; while the jollity and enthusiasm was immensely augmented. Not the slightest break or delay occurred in the programme, and at sunset, His Majesty and escort left the city, *via* Carrollton, en route for Assyria.

Previous to leaving, His Majesty ordered the Legislature of Louisiana to constitute his fete day a legal holiday. Which order was promptly complied with, as will be seen by the following extract from the daily press of April 4th, at which point the King of the Carnival story closes for the present.

MARDI GRAS.

H. R. H. HEARD FROM.

Yesterday the bill passed by the last Legislature, making Mardi Gras a legal holiday, was signed by Governor Warmoth and has now become a law; in compliance with the last strict orders issued by his Majesty of the Carnival before leaving our city on the 13th of February last. Notice of this act of submission and homage to his supreme domination was immediately dispatched by the Governor of the State, after affixing his signature, to the office of the Lord High Chamberlain at Carnival Palace. Upon its reception the guard was immediately turned out, the Royal standard was displayed upon the battlements, and the guns of the Citadel fired a Royal salvo in honor of the act of obeisance.

In the evening, a bearer of dispatches, duly attended, left the city with the notification for His Majesty, who is now on his way to Assyria, where he proposes to spend the summer in travelling for the benefit of his health.

The last information received at the Palace, was to the effect that his majesty was then at Malta, recuperating for his further journey. He was at the time engaged in the preparation and perfection of many Patents of Nobility; it being his royal intention to create a Peerage in his newly conquered dominions, in order to add still further to the magnificence of his reign and state. The commission bearing these graceful evidences of royal condescension were expected to leave for New Orleans in the course of three or four weeks, and pending their arrival, his ambitious subjects who aspire to share their honors, must restrain impatience.

It was also given out at Malta, that his Majesty's army was now actively recruiting in Assyria, with a view to immediately placing his realm upon a war footing, impelled thereto by the warlike preparations going on throughout Europe, and the threatening attitude of the United States army towards the South under the operation of the Kuklux law.

His Majesty, at last accounts, was reported much improved in health, but somewhat jaded by the fatigues of travel. Although in his 1025th year, he is said to have grown both in statue and weight since leaving New Orleans, and now presents a most imposing appearance. His Majesty's leisure moments are constantly occupied with making plans for his next *fête*, to which he looks forward to with pride and satisfaction. Having definitely settled upon the final transfer of his seat of government from the shores of the Mediterranean to those of the Mississippi, it is to be expected that his entry on the ensuing Mardi Gras in 1873, will far surpass in splendor and ceremony, anything ever witnessed in any country during the present age. The preparations are certainly upon a stupendous scale, and with the active co-operation of his loyal, loving subjects, so freely and cordially extended, he feels that nothing is impossible.

GOD SAVE THE KING !

[NOTE.—In excellent and responsible hands, embracing a large number of our most highly esteemed and responsible citizens, The King of the Carnival, whose origin is herein related, has now become a permanent institution of New Orleans. Its design and object while pleasurable and æsthetic have still a practical and ulterior object in benefitting the City of New Orleans, commercially and socially. It not only offers increased attractions to visitors from abroad, but in all the festivities arranged, or consequent thereupon, the entertainment and accommodation of the *Mardi Gras visitors*, are primarily considered in the true spirit of hospitality. It is to be hoped that it will ever meet with the good wishes and encouragement which have so far marked every step of its progress.

THE EXPOSITION BUILDING.

THIS beautiful and imposing structure has lately been added to the ornaments of our city by the South Western Exposition Association.

The purpose for which it was erected was to establish a PERMANENT and attractive place for the exhibition and sale of all manufactured articles used in the South.

The fact that New Orleans is the commercial centre of the Southwest, and that through her is supplied a vast agricultural population, requiring the manufactures of other sections, pointed out the great advantage to the consumers of the articles, as well as to the manufacturers, of the establishment of the permanent Exposition and manufacturers salesroom in the Exposition building. The Planter or the Merchant here sees collected under one immense roof every article he can need, from the steam engine, cotton gin or sugar mill, down to the smallest article needed in his household, all of the latest and most improved style.

The manufacturer here has an opportunity for bringing the article *itself* which he makes directly before the attention of the consumer, a far more effective plan of introducing and selling than by trusting only to descriptive circulars and engravings. In short the manufacturer is thus brought face to face with the consumer, and the latter is enabled to decide satisfactorily upon the merits of any article he may need, because he has an opportunity of personally examining and testing it before purchasing. It will thus be seen that the enterprise is one of great importance to the trade of this section.

The association was incorporated in October 1871. Early in the Spring of that year the originator of the enterprise, Mr. Henry Shaw, first suggested its advantages to some of our leading capitalists. The first to take an active part in it, was the late John Davidson, Esq., a gentleman always ready to use his large means and influence in the futherance of any enterprize promising public benefit. Amongst the other incorporators were Messrs. Richard Lloyd, Charles J. Leeds, Jas. D. Hill, Geo. Purves, Samuel H. Kennedy, Harmon Doane, L. F. Generes, John G. Fleming, all prominent and well known gentlemen of this city.

Immediately after the organization of the association a large property on St. Charles and Carondelet, between Julia and Girod Street, was purchased, and the services of Mr. Albert Dietiel, architect, were engaged to prepare plans for the Exposition Building.

The contract was awarded on the 21st of December, 1871, and by the 1st of May 1872, the association was able to give their inaugurating exposition of the manufacture of the country, the building being by that time sufficiently finished for their purpose. The inaugurating exhibition was continued until June 1st, at which time the permanent exposition opened under most favorable auspices and is now an assured success.

The following dimensions will give an idea of the scale upon which the Exposition building is constructed.

Occupying a front of 85 feet on both St. Charles and Carondelet streets, it runs through the Square by straight lines 341 feet. The entire building is built of brick, with a slate roof, and in its exterior appearance as well as its interior arrrangement and adornment, is an ornament to the City of New Orleans, of which her people may well be proud. The whole of the first floor, a hall of 341 feet by 85, is devoted to the exhibition and sale of heavy machinery and agricultural implements, a line of shafting, driven by a powerful engine, traverses this hall from end to end, furnishing facilities for showing machinery in motion. In the second story, Carondelet street end, is located the Fine Arts and Miscellaneous Departments, a hall 170 feet long by 81 feet wide, filled with all kinds of useful and ornamental articles. In addition to these two large and elegant exhibition rooms for the display of manufacturers articles, a Concert Hall 170 feet long by 81 in width, with a 40 foot ceiling was constructed. Decidedly the handsomest room of the kind in the South. And over the Fine Arts Hall on Carondelet street are two Halls, one 60x60 feet for use in connection with the Grand Concert Hall, and the other 90 feet by 60 feet, to be used as a Lecture Room, etc.

The beautiful fresco work and interior adornment of these Halls is done under the direction of Mr. F. Hang, and reflects great credit upon his artistic skill and taste.

This entire enterprise has been carried forward from the beginning with an energy and determination on the part of the managers of the Association, which was worthy of the success which it has already attained, and which is a sure augury of its future stability.

OFFICE OF THE

LOUISIANA STATE LOTTERY COMPANY,

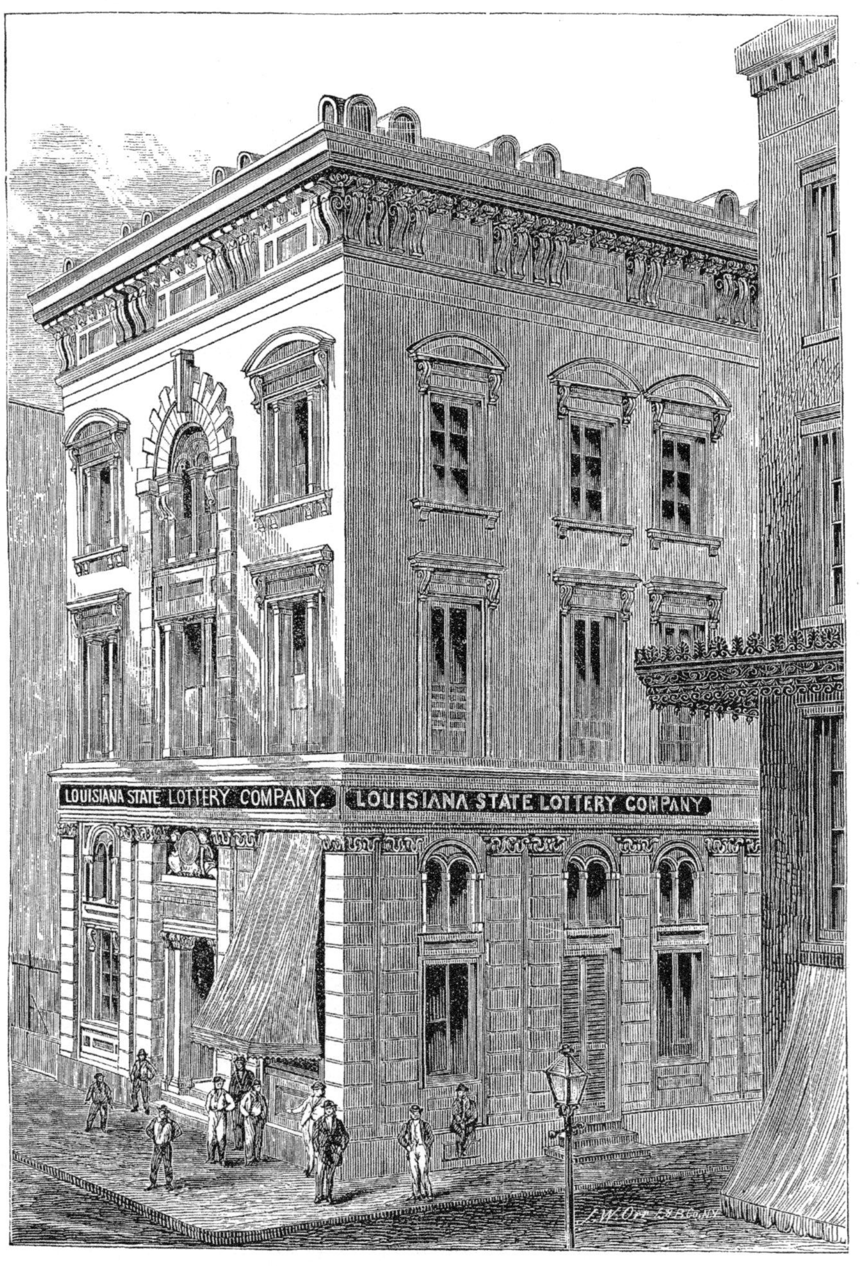

CORNER OF ST. CHARLES AND UNION STREETS,

NEW ORLEANS.

E. A. TYLER, ESQ.

THE life of this gentleman, who has been the architect of his own fortune, has been marked by adventure and a spirit of enterprise peculiar to the natives of New England, and been crowned by remarkable success. Few citizens of New Orleans have been more distinguished for devotion to business, in his particular department of Art, for reliability, intelligence and public spirit. By the steadfastness, manliness and energy, which have constituted leading traits of his character, by the loftiness of his aims, and the purity of his motives, he has acquired a multitude of friends and admirers, and has left the impress of his history on that of the great metropolis with whose fortunes his own have blended for more than a quarter of a century.

Mr. Tyler was born in Boston, Mass., on the 22nd of April 1815, commencing life at the date of the declaration of peace after the second war with Great Britain. His early education was pursued in the Boston schools, always remarkable for the advantages they offered for moral and mental culture—if not superior than of any other American city. From the age of twelve years, he earned his own living. When he reached fourteen, he became apprenticed to the watch-making and jewelry business, which has ever since been his vocation. In 1834, he went to Belfast, Maine, where he remained four years in the same occupation. At the expiration of that period, he determined to remove to New Orleans, where fortunes, he understood, were readily made by young men of intelligence, enterprise and steady habits. The journey before him was an expensive one, and he had but little money ; but nothing daunted by the fact, he resolved, by obtaining business on the route, as he had opportunity, to work his way hither.

It was the commencement of his great life struggles, but he was animated by youthful hope and a courage fitted to the emergency. He accordingly, in April 1838, left Belfast, and started from Boston, his native city, early the following May, with only forty-two dollars in his pocket. After remaining a few days in New York and Philadelphia, he left for the West by the way of Pittsburg, thence to Cincinnati. Here he lingered a few days, looking around for business, but, not obtaining any, paid his hotel bill, and found he had only eighteen cents left for the prosecution of his journey ; whereupon he packed his tools in his valise, left his trunk with an old schoolmate, and, with valise in his hand, crossed the Ohio river to Covington. Here he struck the turnpike road to Lexington—walked twelve miles to the first village, stopped there a few days, repaired watches, clocks and jewelry, and in a week made seventeen dollars beyond expenses. He then went to the next village, Crittenden, where he made sixteen dollars over expenses ; thence to Williamsburgh, where he only paid his expenses. There he took the stage to Lexington, where, after remaining several days and finding nothing to do, he gratified his curiosity by visiting Henry Clay, the servant of the nation, with whom every citizen had a right to be acquainted. He also went to see the celebrated Irving Estates. Thence he proceeded to Nicholasville, where he did not do much that increased his resources, but received a letter from a gentleman in Cynthiana, holding out some promises to him if he would visit that place. He returned to Lexington, and, after making friends, and spending most of his money in sight-seeing, went to Paris by stage, and thence walked, a distance of twelve miles, to Cynthiana, got a ducking in a stream which he had to ford, besides being thoroughly soaked in a shower—arrived late in the day at the hotel kept by a gentleman named Boyd, and knowing, from certain premonitions, that he was going to be sick, frankly told his host of the fact, informing him at the same time of his inability to defray his expenses. The latter assured him with true Kentucky liberality, that he need give himself no uneasiness about the matter, and that he was quite welcome to the best that could be done for him under the circumstances.

A comfortable room was assigned him in the hotel, and a doctor immediately sent for to whom he was equally frank in making known his circumstances. This Kentucky Doctor told him that he never asked people if they had money ; all that he had to do was to take the medicine he gave him, and obey orders ; if he did not recover, it would be no fault of his. Mr. Tyler, in referring to this part of his history, testifies that he never knew a nobler or better hearted man than Dr. Deshea, (son of ex-Governor Deshea) and Mr. Boyd, the hotel keeper. On his recovery, he commenced business in earnest. It accummulated on his hands. His friends increased in number—among others—A. Broadwell, Esq., one of the wealthiest citizens in Kentucky.

Early in October he left Cynthiana for the South. The Ohio river being so low that no boats could be run upon it, he returned to Lexington ; thence he went, by stage, to Nashville, Tenn., where he met with a friend who accompanied him to Mill's Point, Ky., the nearest point at which to take a boat for New Orleans. This little town was crowded with parties waiting to obtain a passage. Among them were those whole souled planters, Duncan F. Kenner, Alexander Barrow, and several others, with their families. After waiting four days, two boats came down the river, when all embarked, late in the evening, on board the Somerville, except himself and friend, who took passage in the Prairie, (Capt. Freligh,) which, encountering a fog, was obliged to lay up during the night. Next morning, coming up with the Somerville, found she had run on a snag—worked with all hands, all day, to get her off. Finally, the passengers on the Somerville came on board the Prairie, and on the ninth day of their embarkation, reached New Orleans.

On his arrival in the Crescent City, Mr. Tyler was so fortunate as to find an old friend and acquaintance, a jeweler at 18 Chartres street. He induced this artisan to rent him his window fronting on the street, and immediately commenced business, retaining the locality four years, when he removed to 37 Camp street, with better accommodations, and where he remained with varying fortunes, the good however attaining the ascendancy, when, through the influence of Rev Father Mullen, he was so fortunate as to secure his present elegant and extensive establishment on Canal street, in the most thronged and fashionable part of the city—certainly an excellent stand for his business, and where, by his enterprise, he has succeeded in amassing a large fortune.

Mr. Tyler is a model American, who, like most of our people engaged in various branches of commerce, is doubtless fond of accumulation, but who eschews avarice and employs his wealth to noble ends, the advancement of all our social interests, including all public and private charities, relieving distress whenever brought to his notice, lending a helping hand to the unfortunate, and always anxious to recognize and reward merit. No object of great public utility is started in the community that does not find in him a zealous and liberal supporter. He was one of the original projectors and proprietors of the Fair Grounds, whose annual exhibitions have done so much to the advancement of our agricultural, mechanical, commercial and manufacturing interests.

During the inundation of the city which occurred somewhat upwards of a year ago, he proved himself equal to the crisis, being one of the largest contributors for the relief of the houseless sufferers. He has been, for many years, one of the most prominent leaders in the Church of the Messiah, on St. Charles street, and an influential individual in commercial circles as Director of the Bank of Lafayette. During the late war, he acted earnestly with the State of his adoption, to which his allegiance was due. He was guilty of no offense, but, being one of our most prominent citizens, General Butler regarded his opinions dangerous, and accordingly applied the gag of imprisonment, and had him sent to Fort Jackson, where he was confined four months. His friends, who were permitted to have no communication with him, and hearing nothing from him, supposed that he was dead, and when it was supposed that he actually would die, he was released on a bond for ten thousand dollars. His arrest took place on the same day with that of the late Dr. Warren Stone.

On the 22nd of September 1840, he married Miss Julia A. Barnes, of Cambridge, Mass. The ceremony was performed by Rev. Dr. Charles Lowell, of Boston, at Lynde street church. He has had five children, of whom three are still living.

Without pride or ostentation, he has yet surrounded himself with all the comforts and elegancies of life. His residence on St. Charles street, is one of the most beautiful in the city. Its garden, filled with the choicest flowers and shrubbery, and all its appointments, bespeak the man of taste and refinement. His energy, his public virtues, the wealth acquired by his own skill and industry, and the uses to which he employs it, entitle him in fine, to be regarded one of the merchant princes of this great emporium.

CHARLES CAVAROC, ESQ.

Mr. C. Cavaroc, President of the New Orleans National Banking Association, of the New Orleans Mutual Insurance Association, and of several other companies organized for industrial or commercial purposes, is one of the representasive men of the Latin race in Louisana.

Mr. Cavaroc was born in New Orleans in 1828, of French parents, and received his education in the mother country of his progenitors. He first entered into business as clerk in the general wine importing house of T. M. Lucas on Royal street, and upon the death of Mr. Lucas, which occurred in 1851, he took charge of the business in which his success was both steady and rapid. This was owing no less to the strict integrity than to the thorough knowledge of this branch of trade posesssed by the able merchant who is the subject of this sketch. In 1868, Mr. Cavaroc was called to the Presidency of the Bank of New Orleans at a very critical period of the career of that bank, whose stock was then much depressed owing to heavy losses consequent upon the late civil war. Under the skillful management of its new President, this institution soon recovered from its disasters, and the stock rose in a few months from $16 to $30. A year ago the New Orleans Bank was reorganized as a National Bank, with a capital of $600,000, and under its present title of the New Orleans National Banking Association, and it now stands in the front rank of our financial institutions. In 1870, the New Orleans Mutual Insurance Association was organized by Mr. Cavaroc upon an entirely new plan, the particulars of which are given elsewhere, and its success has been such as to realize the most sanguine anticipations of its founder and stockholders.

Mr. Cavaroc is not only one of the most successful and enterprising merchants of New Orleans, but also one of its most public spirited and liberal citizens. There is hardly an undertaking calculated to enhance the prosperity of our city or State in which he has not taken a prominent part, and in private life his charities have all been munificent as well as judiciously bestowed.

He is emphatically a pushing, *go ahead*, live merchant, a useful citizen, and an honorable, high-toned gentleman. There are few men whose loss would be more universally felt in this community than Charles Cavaroc.

THE STORY BUILDING.

CITIZENS' BANK.

THE ACADEMY OF SCIENCES.

THE New Orleans Academy of Sciences was founded in 1853 by a number of gentlemen belonging exclusively to the medical profes.ion. The first meeting, held on the 21st of March of that year, was presided over by D. Bennet Dowler, whose devotion to scientific pursuits is well known. On the 25th of April following, Dr. Josiah Hale was elected President and a constitution was adopted. In May, correspondence with the Smithsonian Institute at Washington was opened, and a promise of its co-operation obtained. That promise, commencing with contributions in the following October, has been constantly and liberally fulfilled, and now the Academy is in communication with most of the great scientific institutions of various parts of this continent and Europe. At first the meetings of the Academy were held at the private residences of members. Subsequently, the gratuitous use of a room was obtained in the City Hall, then the hall of the Mechanic's Institute was rented, and on the 21st of November of the same year, a hall at the southeast corner of Poydras and Carondelet streets, rented for the purpose, became the place of meeting. On the 5th of December, the Academy subscribed for fourteen scientific publications, the members assessing themselves for this expense, as they had for all others. On the 6th of March following, the Academy ordered the publication of its proceedings, and on the same day Dr. E. H. Barton was elected President.

The object of the Academy is the promotion of science by lectures, papers, and discussions on scientific subjects, and by the collection of a library and museum. The year 1853, it will be recollected, was one in which fearful havoc was made by an epidemic; but the Academy, nevertheless, perserved in its prescribed course, and progressed to a firm establishment, without any material aid or sympathy or aid from either the authorities or the general public. The first paper was read by Dr. B. Dowler, on the 30th of May. On the 27th March 1854, the late Professor J. L. Riddell exhibited before the Academy one of the most interesting and useful improvements yet achieved in aid of scientific research. This was a binocular microscope which he had constructed, and the honor of inventing which is universally conceded to him. As since improved and simplified, under the designs of Mr. Wenhom, and the manufacture of the famous Beck, this instrument has now become the great microscope of the world. On the same day the Academy earnestly discussed the necessity for a geological survey of the State, and adopted a resolution to present to the Legislature a recommendation that it should be made. Although this has not been done, Professor Hilgard has, under the auspices of the Academy, made some surveys of parts of the State, the results of which have been given to the public through the newspapers.

On November 6th 1854, the Academy again changed its place of meeting to a room in the City Hall, which the Council had appropriated for the purpose, this room being subsequently changed for another. On the 5th of March 1855, Dr. Riddell was elected President. A few days afterward the Academy was incorporated, and made a branch of the University of Louisiana, subject, in a great measure, to the discretion of the administrators of the University. On the 26th of May, with this status, the Academy met in the east wing of the University buildings, although it was not till 1860 that the administrators formally acknowledged the Academy as a branch of the University, and then with a condition that they might disconnect it by giving a year's written notice.

During the war, the buildings were taken possession of by the military, and much of the property of the Academy was lost, destroyed and injured; that it was not all sacrificed was due to the exertions and influence of Dr. Riddell. After the war, the Academy, not without much struggling, however, soon re-established itself in its efforts and regained its former position without any outside aid whatever. On the death of Dr. Riddle, in 1866, Dr. Copes was elected President, as he still remains.

The Academy gives weekly lectures, except during the summer, besides holding general discussions on scientific subjects, politics and religion being excluded. These are open to the public gratuitously, under invitation from members, which, however, is all but nominal, and the hall of the Academy is open to visitors daily in the same manner. The records of the Academy contain a great deal of very interesting and instructive information upon a great variety of subjects, many of them of the highest importance in connection with the welfare and progress of the city and State. The library contains very valuable contributions from leading scientific societies in various parts of the world. The Museum, though comparatively small, contains conchological, geological, palæontological and other collections well worthy of examination.

Election to membership, under the rules, requires recognized scientific acquirements, nomination and recommendation by two or more Fellows, posting for one month and ballot.

The institution is one which needs and deserves much more consideration from the authorities and the public of the city and State than it has yet received, and we hope yet to see it recognized as worthy of liberal countenance and support.

THE SYNAGOGUE ON CARONDELET STREET.

THIS beautiful house of worship is owned and used by the Hebrew Congregation, "Dispersed of Judah," whose charter of incorporation dates from 4th June 1847, though its organization had taken place some years previously. Its present vitality and prosperity are, however, mainly due to the benevolence of the late Judah Touro, who made the congregation a free gift of the church edifice which stood on Canal and Bourbon streets, and at his own cost fitted it up and converted it into a synagogue.

A few years later, this building requiring extensive repairs, it was decided to pull it down and build another place of worship located further up-town. Accordingly, the present edifice was erected on Carondelet street, on six lots of ground which had, at one time, formed a portion of the Poydras Estate.

The mode of service is according to the Sephardic ritual, known commonly as that of the Spanish and Portuguese Jews, though with some modernization.

The present minister is the Rev. Henry S. Jacobs.

GEORGE A FOSDICK, ESQ.

This enterprising merchant, largely identified with the shipping interests of New Orleans, affords in his career a striking illustration of the influence exerted by talent, energy and perseverance, in a country like ours, in overcoming difficulties, and of attaining, in the end, to success, fortune and independence. From childhood up to manhood, he wasted no golden moments in frivolous occupations and idle amusements, but regarding labor as the great law of life, first with a view to subsistence and next to comfort and elegance, exerted all his physical and intellectual powers in order to the attainment of these ends. Exemplary success has crowned his well-directed efforts.

He was the son of Capt. W. R. Fosdick, who, for a series of years, commanded one of the first packet ships running between New York and New Orleans, and was born at the former city, May 3, 1820. At the early age of twelve years, he had the misfortune to lose his father, and was thus suddenly thrown on his own resources. Of a respectable family, active and intelligent, and with no indisposition to labor for a living, he found little difficulty in obtaining employment in the commission house of James Hamilton & Son, of New York city, who paid him a salary of fifty dollars for the first year; and the American boy, who could command fifty dollars a year, when he was not yet in his teens, was somebody, and he felt that he was. So he went to work with a will, looking to the future. Here he remained for five years, until the crisis of 1837, which swept off most of the mercantile houses of the country—during which period he worked in the daytime and continued his educational studies at night, his salary being increased from year to year, as he grew older and more capable of being of service to his employers. He was not yet in the way of making a fortune, but certainly—which was far better—was passing through the preliminary stages necessary to make him a man of business and a thorough merchant.

In 1837, the calamitous year referred to, he left New York and came South, first stopping for a while at Mobile, seeking business in vain, and then coming to New Orleans, where he was equally unsuccessful. He now embarked on the Tombigbee, which seemed to invite the adventurer, sailing up as high as Westport, Miss., a small town situated about two miles above Columbus, on the other side of the river. Here he was employed, for the space of eighteen months, by Dunstan Banks, doing a supply business.

In the meantime, his brother had established himself at New Orleans in the shipping and commission business, and, knowing his industrious habits, at once took him into the concern in the capacity of a clerk. This was in 1839. In 1840, he became associated with him as a partner in the business, which he has prosecuted with singular energy and success ever since. Taught in the school of hard experience, making the most of his opportunities, taking no step forward without being sure of his footing, he has attained the enviable position he occupies, and the fame he has achieved of an accomplished and prosperous merchant, by relying mainly on his own exertions, and depending but little on the uncertain, however well meant, advice and fluctuating assistance of others. In other words, he furnishes a fine example of the self-made man, who thinks for himself and acts for himself, and who entertains opinions and prosecutes enterprises which reflect credit on the age and country in which he lives.

Such men, in a community of high-toned merchants like New Orleans, are advanced to places of honor and responsibility, and may command almost any position that they please. For two years Mr. Fosdick occupied the high post of President of the Chamber of Commerce, to which no individual could have been appointed who was not at once a thorough merchant and a perfect gentleman. The pressure of his business, after his service in that capacity for the term mentioned, led him to decline a re-election; but he is still an influential member of the Chamber, and a perspicuity and forethought that lead him to investigate the past and anticipate the future, he seizes on every occasion calculated to advance the interests of this great mart of commerce.

Again, he was the first delegate elected to the National Board of Trade at Philadelphia, where he exerted a decided influence in securing the passage of a resolution of that body, calling on Congress to grant immediate aid to improve the mouth of the Mississippi river.

He has always taken a lively interest in politics, having acted as Chairman of the Democratic Committee since the war, and Chairman of the Douglas State Democratic Committee and Co-operative Committee before the war.

He has never held any public office except that of State Registrar on the First Board of Registration, a position which he accepted solely at the request of the State and Parish Democratic Committees, in the hope of accomplishing some good for our people, though at a sacrifice to his personal interests. He was nominated for Congress by the Second District Convention in 1870, but withdrew at the request of the Democratic State Committee, to enable them to carry out a fusion which they contemplated.

B. T. WALSHE,

Importer of and Dealer in

Men's Furnishing Goods,

Men's Shirts,

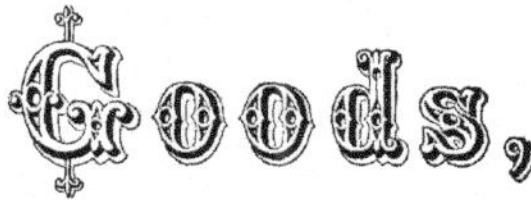

Boys' Shirts,

Underwear,

Underwear.

Gloves,

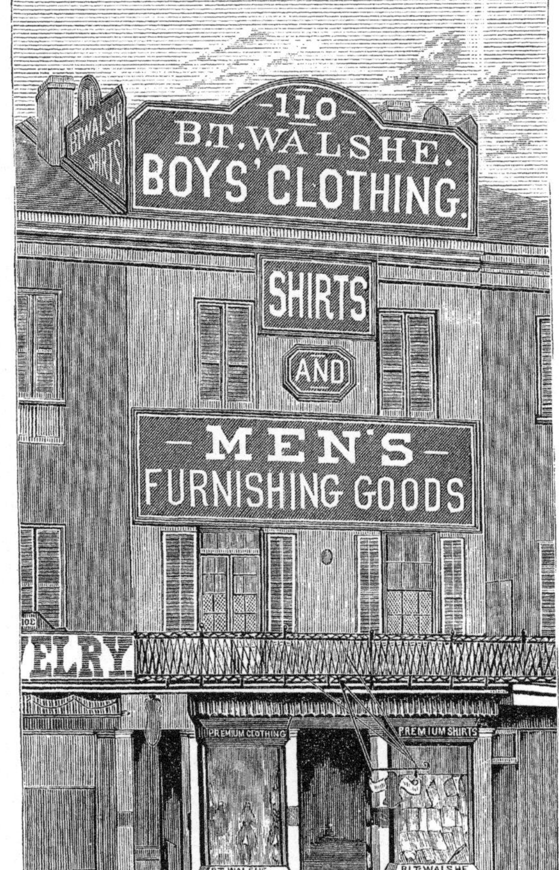

For all ages.

AND

Hosiery,

Umbrellas &c.

—and—

BOYS' AND CHILDREN'S CLOTHING.

110 CANAL STREET,

NEW ORLEANS.

THE SLAUGHTER HOUSES.

ABOUT four miles below Canal street, immediately above the dividing line of the parishes of Orleans and St. Bernard, and about two hundred yards below the United States Barracks, stands the aggregation of buildings of which a partial view is herewith exhibited. This is the spot where the law prescribes that all animals intended for our markets must be slaughtered, under the supervision of officials appointed, some by the State and others by the "Crescent City Live Stock Landing and Slaughter House Company,"

The arrangements for carrying out the objects contemplated by the law creating the Slaughter Houses are very complete. There are two wharves for landing the stock, with pens for receiving them upon the Levee. Immediately adjoining the wharves, and also upon the Levee, is a building containing a pumping apparatus worked by steam and capable of supplying 150,000 gallons of water daily to the entire establishment. Fronting the public road, a row of one-story buildings contains the telegraph, the company's offices and also the private offices of Messrs. C. Mehle & Co., Inbau, Aycock & Co., and L. B. Collins, live stock dealers.

In the rear of these offices at 200 feet from the public road, there are twelve large covered cattle pens, 67 by 15 feet each, where the live stock are first placed for inspection and sold to the various stock dealers who are always in attendance. Adjoining these are the main pens for cattle, twenty-eight in number, and each one having the dimensions of 75 feet by 17, and also eighteen hog pens for sheep and other cattle. After these you come to the large hog and sheep slaughter house, 265 by 80 feet. which is constantly supplied with hot and cold water, pulleys, etc. On the right hand as you look toward the river, is another immense building containing twenty-two divisions 32 by 25 feet for slaughtering beeves and calves, each division having in its rear two large pens 60 by 10 feet for receiving the cattle previous to slaughtering. Fronting the above building from which they are separated by a broad paved alley for carts are twenty-two stables for the horses of the butchers, and next to these, nearer to the river, are covered vats for salting and curing the hides. Some fifty feet in the rear of the whole is another steam engine, and a little further back of this stands the Blood Fertilizer Manufactory, occupying a space of 200 feet square, lodging horses for the employées etc. The outhouses are all new and in perfect order, and in another part of the grounds there is an apparatus for curing hides by acids in two hours, and Esteban's large sheep-skin tannery. The other buildings are rented by the company to various parties, who are principally coffee-house and tavern keepers. The charges for slaughtering are as follows :

Beeves	.	.	.	.	$1 00 per head.
Calves	.	.	.	.	50 "
Hogs	.	.	.	.	50 "
Sheep	.	.	.	.	30 "

The average number of cattle slaughtered daily is about 700 during the summer, and from 900 to 1,100 in the winter. With the present arrangements there is ample accommodation for the slaughter of 1,500 head of cattle daily, and these facilities can be increased to any extent, the company owning 240 acres of land. All the buildings, pens and slaughter houses are lighted by Barbarin's apparatus, at the charge of the company.

The Slaughter House company was incorporated in the summer of 1869, and at its inception met with much opposition from the butchers and live stock dealers, but a compromise having been effected on the 15th March 1871, between the contending parties, a new Board was elected, composed almost entirely of stock dealers and butchers, under whose administration the present location of the Slaughter House was purchased from the Butcher's Association and the operations transferred from the right bank to this side of the river. The officers of the company for the present year (elected March 15, 1872,) are as follows:

President . . . . . C. Cavaroc.
Secretary . . . . . J. N. Augustin.
Superintendent . . . . John Dolhonde.

Directors: L. E. Lemarié, C. De Ruyter, P. Sarthon, L. Ruch, E. F. Mioton, C. A. Weed, J. Donaldson, J. N. Avegno.

THE CITY PARK.

Between the old and new canals fronting for about one mile, on the Metairie Road lies the property bequeathed to the city for a Public Park by the late John McDonough. Being about half a mile in depth it contains an area of about half of a square mile. The Park is crossed in one direction by the Orleans Canal, and in another by the bed of the Metaire Bayou, recently dried by drainage. In front the Park is high and it was not overflowed by the flood of 1871, when the city was submerged from the swamp up to Rampart street and when 20,000 inhabitants for several days could only move from their houses by means of boats and rafts. In the rear the once marshy land has been rendered solid and dry in consequence of the opening of the Orleans canal and Taylor's canal but the thick undergrowth of palmetto weeds and grass still obstruct passages by any but hunters.

The Park is abundantly supplied with enormous Live Oak shade trees some of which measure twenty feet in circumference and spread their massive branches fifty feet in all directions from their gigantic trunks. These will be retained for ornament and shelter when the city government begins to make improvements. No attempts have yet been made to lay out or adorn the Park although the donor has been dead more than twenty years. The extension of the city in the direction of the Lake will in a few years render the adornment and protection of the Park more important. When the time arrives the productive soil of the Park will give a quick response to the labor of those who may plant it with trees, flowers and shrubbery.

ANNUNCIATION SQUARE, in the First District, is the largest, and, consequently, may some day become the most elegant in the city. Orange and Race streets are on its front and rear—and facing are some very tasteful private residences—the handsomest of which is that of Mr. E. J. Hart.

THE NEW ORLEANS ST. ANDREW'S SOCIETY.

THE commendable friendship which Scotchmen entertain for each other, when worthy of their respect, and the pride and fondness with which they recall the valor and glory of their Fatherland, and the fame of their distinguished men, acquired in war, letters or civil life, are proverbial all the world over. It is with a view to cement, vitalize and perpetuate sentiments so honorable to them as men and patriots, that in several cities of the American Union to which they have emigrated from the Old World, they have formed themselves into associations bearing the above characteristics and time-honored titles. Another and leading object of the society is the encouragement and promotion (not by words only of sympathy, which they do not withhold, but by positive acts,) of the greatest of the virtues, charity. The objects of the association are succinctly stated in the preamble to its constitution as follows:

" Whereas, A number of the citizens of New Orleans, Scotchmen by birth, desirous of cultivating the friendship and promoting the welfare of each other and of assisting their countrymen in sickness and distress, have banded themselves together for these philanthropic and charitable purposes, they cordially and earnestly invite all respectable Scotchmen, residing in New Orleans and suburbs, to join them in the above good works; that, by their cordiality and good-will to each other, they may show to the world that the countrymen of Wallace, Burns and Scott still love their country."

The New Orleans St. Andrew's Society was incorporated March 11, A. D. 1837, and reorganized October 27, 1868. During the late war its meetings were suspended. The officers of the society consist of a President, Vice-President, Secretary, Treasurer and nine Directors, chosen by a majority of the members present, by ballot, at the meeting immediately preceding St. Andrew's Day. Any native of Scotland, or person of Scotch descent, who has attained the age of eighteen years, and bears a good moral character, may be admitted a member of the society; and the society may, at any time, confer honorary membership on any person of whatever nation he may be, whenever they may deem it proper. Application for membership is to be addressed in writing to the President and members of the society, inclosing the initiation fee of $5. At the next regular meeting, a committee of three reports on the qualification of the applicant, and if the report be favorable he is elected by a two-thirds ballot. In case of rejection, the initiation fee is returned. By Article 13th of the Constitution, every member is required to contribute and pay to the funds of the society $1 each month into the hands of the Treasurer.

St. Andrew's Day and the anniversaries of the birth of Robert Burns and Sir Walter Scott are usually celebrated by the society with appropriate ceremonies and festivities.

The present officers of the society are Alexander Hay, Esq., President; Duncan Sinclair, Esq., Vice-President; Alexander McIntosh, Esq., Treasurer; and W. R. Russell, Esq., Secretary.

RESIDENCE OF E. A. TYLER, ESQ.,

565 St. Charles Street, New Orleans.

JACOB C. VAN WICKLE.

THE subject of this sketch was born in Middlesex County, New Jersey, on the 20th of October 1805. At an early age he left his native State with a view of making for himself both a fortune and a name. He came to Louisiana and settled in the Parish of Point Coupee, in December 1827. His temperate and industrious habits, favorably impressed the people among whom he had cast his lot, and it was not long before he received the appointment of Deputy Sheriff of the Parish, in which capacity he served from 1828 to 1833. He was then appointed Sheriff by Gov. White and subsequently re-appointed by Gov. Roman, retaining this office from 1833 to 1842. In 1845, Mr. Van Wickle was elected to the Lower House of the Legislature, on the Whig ticket and served his constituents with zeal and fidelity. His political affiliations have always been with the Whig Party, of which he was a consistent and devoted member, but political prejudices could never induce him to ignore or neglect the interests of his opponents or make him intolerant, and the reputation he acquired as a politician was that of an honorable, just and liberal gentleman. By prudence and economy, Mr. Van Wickle had succeeded in amassing a sufficient amount of money to purchase a sugar plantation in 1846, and from that time until 1869, he devoted himself entirely to the cultivation of sugar-cane. A series of successful crops soon made him a rich man. Surrounded by all the comforts and luxuries of life, he dispensed the hospitalities of his house with a liberal hand. Naturally of a very kind and generous disposition, he was never deaf to appeals for assistance from those in distress ; and in all the relations of life he was an exemplary citizen and highly esteemed by all who know him. In 1836, he married Miss Elezar Ledoux, the daughter of Mr. Valerién Ledoux, one of the most respectable and wealthy planters in the State, and

became the father of two lovely daughters, one only of whom lived to womanhood, the elder, Julia, having died at the age of thirteen years, whilst at school at Nazareth, Ky. The younger, Miss Amanda, an interesting and handsome lady, married Mr. Ogden K. Dunning, of the house of J. B. Burnside & Co., of this city, but soon became a widow by the death of her husband, about three years after her marriage. In 1841, Mrs. Van Wickle died, and Mr. Van Wickle married the widow Dayries, also a member of the Ledoux family, and who is now in the full vigor of health, a devoted wife, and a most excellent and charitable lady. Like most of the Southern planters, Mr. Van Wickle sustained heavy losses by the ravages of war, and after its close, finding the labor system so demoralized and uncertain that he concluded to abandon the cultivation of his plantation, and finding a purchaser for it, he removed to New Orleans to reside permanently. In 1868, his name was prominently before the Democratic Convention of this city for Mayor, and was defeated in the Convention by only two votes by his successful opponent, Mayor Conway. Subsequently, his friends presented him as a candidate before the Legislature 'for the position of United States Senator, but it was withdrawn when it was ascertained that a sufficient Republican majority had been obtained to elect Hon. W. P. Kellogg. His large experience as a successful planter, and his thorough knowledge of the Levee system of the State, eminently qualified him for a position on the Board of Public Works, and in 1869, Gov. Warmoth appointed him to represent the Second Levee District, extending from the Balize to the Atchafalaya river. During his administration, and under his supervision, the largest levee in the State, known as the Grand Levee, was substantially built, and through his energy and perseverance, other public levees were constructed and a large area of country saved from overflow. To these works he can point with pride and satisfaction to himself, feeling conscious that his official career has ever been without reproach and universally commended. For the last twenty years Mr. Van Wickle has been the lessee of Wood's Cotton Press, one of the largest institutions of the kind in the city, an illustration of which will be found on another page of this book. The press is the property of his sister, Mrs. Wood, and under his management has averaged, per annum, about seventy-five thousand bales of cotton compressed for shipment to New York and Europe. Besides being a real estate owner in this city, Mr. Van Wickle is now the proprietor of the old homestead at " Old Bridge," New Jersey, where he was born, and where for many years past he has spent his summers in quiet retirement and in the peaceful contemplation of a long life of usefulness and exemplary character.

LAFAYETTE SQUARE is decidedly the handsomest in the city. It is in the First District, and has St. Charles and Camp streets in front and rear, and several public buildings in its immediate neighborhood. It has a handsome and substantial iron railing around it, based upon well laid blocks of granite ; is well laid off in regular walks, and is ornamented with beautiful trees and a statue of Franklin, presented to the city by Mr. Charles A. Weed, proprietor of the N. O. *Times.*

ALFRED PHILIPS, ESQ.

THE gentleman whose name heads these lines was born in 1832. He was partly educated in this city and at St. Mary's College, in Baltimore, Md.

He began the study of the law with Mr. Christian Roselius, and after attending three courses of lectures in the Law Department of the University of Louisiana, graduated from the same in 1853 ; but not being of age, he did not commence the practice of his profession until 1858.

In 1865 he was elected a professor in the Law Department of the University, to fill the chair made vacant by the death of the lamented Judge Theo. H. McCaleb. He continued to act as professor down to 1870, when he resigned.

Mr. Philips was a member of the House of Representatives of the State Legislature in 1866 and 1867, which was distinguished as an upright and very able body.

He was, of course, carried away by the patriotic ardor which filled the heart of every young man in the South during the late war for independence, and rendered valuable services to the Confederacy as a Captain in one of the Louisiana regiments.

Mr. Philips is an unfortunate bachelor, but has been most happy in all his relations in life. He has been peculiarly fortunate in his profession, and his exertions have been rewarded by a fortune of respectable dimensions.

In 1864 he became Mr. Roselius's partner, and has continued to practice law, associated with him, ever since.

As a lawyer, Mr. Philips is one of the most accomplished in this city, being thoroughly learned in jurisprudence and literature. He is an elegant speaker, and his arguments reveal his vigorous and logical mind.

Those who are well acquainted with him will bear witness to the fact that it has ever been his aim since he was first admitted to the bar to endeavor to cultivate friendly relations with his brother lawyers and to look accordingly with warm approval upon all their exertions to elevate themselves in the ranks of the profession ; never to envy or detract, but always to encourage and applaud. He has always by liberality and frankness sought to encourage an *esprit de corps* among the members of the bar, never taking improper advantage of the weakness or want of preparation of his adversary, but on all occasions granting and very rarely asking favors.

He has never failed to recognize that the vocation of the lawyer is to assist, instruct and guide courts of justice in arriving at truth and administering right, and that he should never undertake to mislead a judge or jury ; that he is an officer of justice and should faithfully exert all his talent and energies in aid of justice.

The lawyer should be a gentleman ; that is, no man can be a lawyer, in the proper acceptation of the term, unless he is a gentleman, which implies, necessarily, high integrity, unsullied honor, charity of heart and mind, sensibility and regard for all animated nature, polished address and polite demeanor to all, as well as the possession and exercise of all those elevated mental faculties which stamp humanity as the master animal. All these qualities mark the gentleman and should be recognized in the lawyer, and his efforts should be directed to the cultivation of all these graces and qualities.

In personal appearance Mr. Philips is of the medium height, with brown hair and light blue eyes. He is very social and genial in his feelings, aspiring to no praise except that of being regarded as an honest, upright man, all of which he deserves, as he is remarkable for his candor and truthfulness.

W. M. RANDOLPH, ESQ.

NO LAWYER in this or any State more fully commands the respect and confidence of the members of the bar, and the public, than Judge W. M. Randolph. He is a native of Virginia, about fifty years old, and a near relative of the great defender of State Rights, John Randolph of Roanoke.

A learned and upright man, no worldly consideration can turn him from the strict path of honor and duty. He is amiable, courteous, gentlemanly and chivalrous.

Descended from a noble line, he commanded from his birth all that wealth and family influence could give, with the best opportunities for education.

In his youth he resided in one of the mountain districts of Virginia, and his constant application to the study of the law impaired seriously his health. His grandmother, who was devotedly attached to him, requested him to take a horse and travel, for exercise and recreation, in the neighborhood of the place where they resided.

Randolph, who was an excellent rider, did as he was instructed. A few miles from his residence there was a circus with an excellent equestrian company. He joined them, and after traveling with them seven days, returned, home much improved in health. Upon being asked what he had done during his absence, he frankly stated the truth. His grandmother, who was an aristocratic lady and a strict Presbyterian, confessed that the young acrobat had done more than she had bargained for.

It has been said that to genius irregularity is incident, and great men are often marked by eccentricity, as if they disdained to move in the vulgar orbit. Judge Randolph does not seem to pay much attention to appearances. His flowing beard resembles that of a Capuchin friar, and his hair, uncommonly long, hangs down over his coat collar, after the old cavalier fashion.

He is tall and well-formed, his features are regular and his eyes grey and brilliant.

His familiarity with the principles of jurisprudence is as ample as his application of them is masterly. He has great intensity and directness of purpose and meets difficulties boldly. Accomplished as a scholar, he is unhesitating in his conduct, although polite in demeanor. His powers as an advocate are great. He is one of our best speakers. He has a refined classical wit and loves harmless pleasantry.

Unlike his great relative, John Randolph, of Roanoke, his spirit is cheerful and his temper mild.

NEW TEMPLE SINAI.

THE FAIR GROUNDS.

THE entrances to the Fair Grounds about three miles from the Clay Statue are reached by the street cars which pass down Canal to Rampart, down Rampart to Esplanade, and down Esplanade towards and near Bayou St. John, being the pleasantest railroad ride afforded by the city cars, as well as a delightful drive for carriages. By the Gentilly gate, or the Mystery entrance, the visitor is introduced to a park of 120 acres, (formerly the old Creole Race Course,) studded with magnificent oaks, thickly overgrown with grass, containing a fine tract in complete order, and all the buildings required for fairs, fetes, and exhibitions of all kinds. The race course is an ellipse exactly one mile in measurement, and from the nature and elevation of the ground is usually in good condition. Within the ellipse are the Club House of the Fair Grounds, a platform for music and dancing, and a base ball park. The Public Stand, built by the Jockey Club on the south side of the course, is considered the best stand on the continent, being an enormous three story pile of graceful and substantial carpentry, two stories high, with comfortable seats for more than five thousand people, with ample promenades, broad and easy staircases, roomy saloons, and commanding a view of the whole course and enclosure. The view from the ample and lofty cupola takes in the whole city and its suburbs, a lovely mingling of rivers, bayous, lakes, swamps, forests, gardens, streets, shipping, spires, and railroad trains.

The main building is appropriated to the exhibition of fine and delicate manufactures, paintings, statuary drawings, musical instruments, machinery for household uses, needle work, furniture &c. It is of brick, 200x95 feet, two stories high, amply supplied with light and ventilation from large doors, lofty windows, and numerous skylights through its slate roof. The cost of the building was $70,000.

At each side of the main building at a distance of fifty yards, is a wooden building 206x80 feet, used for agricultural products, and implements, machines and mechanical inventions, often in full operation, and competing articles of produce or manufacture. The largest engines and machines are stored and exhibited under a shed near the principal buildings which covers an area of nearly nine hundred square yards. Extensive stables on the north side will accommodate more than a hundred horses, and on the same side adjoining the grounds is the live-stock farm of Mr. Slocomb, containing many specimens of thorough-bred and imported animals. The deer park is on the east side and was improved by Mr. Slocomb at his own personal expense.

Six acres in the south east corner are appropriated to the Flower Gardens and Nurseries, under the charge of Mr. Joseph Muller, by whose care and judicious management, the garden has become a special attraction. This garden now affords to visitors an exhibition of vigorous tropical shrubs, flowers, plants and trees not to be found elsewhere north of the Gulf of Mexico. The walks are shelled and the grounds symetrically laid out The number of specimens is increasing and the whole garden is undergoing constant improvement.

Attached to the garden and furnished from it is the Floral Hall, a walled circular arena, 60 feet in diameter, sheltered by canvass and cooled by numerous fountains. Here during the regular public exhibitions are seen banks and pyramids of the rarest and most beautiful flowers and vines that grow in the garden, field or forest.

The Fair Grounds reflect credit upon the Association, for their enterprize, zeal and public spirit. They are seconded in their laudable and industrious efforts by a generous public. Such coöperation will accelerate the attainment of the great objects which all should have in view, the maintenance of the dignity of labor, the vindication of the worth of brains, and the practical promotion of the prosperity of our State.

MECHANIC'S AND AGRICULTURAL FAIR ASSOCIATION.

This body was incorporated in April 1860, " to promote and foster improvements in all the various departments of agriculture" and for "the promotion and development of the mechanical arts and home manufactures in all branches; the rearing, development, and improvement of the races of useful animals ; the general advancement of rural economy ; the encouragement of household manufactures and the dissemination of useful knowledge upon such subjects by offering inducements and premiums therefor."

The first officers of the Association were: G. W. Race, Esq., President ; Messrs. C. H. Slocomb, P. A. Rost, and H. R. Swasey, Vice-Presidents; T. D. Harper, Secretary and Treasurer ; and I. G. Seymour, C. Patthoff, J. O. Nixon, Luther Homes, Charles Pride, L. Folger, T. N. Blake, G. W. Sizer, L. W. Pilié, David H. Fowler, John Pemberton, J. W. Tilton, Isaac N. Marks, Thomas O. Moore, E. E. Kittridge, J. H. Overton and J. Hardesty, Directors.

The first fair was held on the New Fair Grounds in the Fall of 1866, the second in January 1868, the third and fourth early in 1869 and 1870. The buildings of the Association were burnt in the Spring of 1871 and the Fair, necessarily postponed, was held in the Fall of that year. The Fair of April 1872 was eminently successful, giving renewed promise of a brilliant future. Besides diplomas and other rewards, premiums to the value of more than twenty thousand dollars were distributed.

The Association is to continue twenty five-years. There is no room to doubt that its success and marked influence will secure a renewal of its term.

Its officers for 1872, (chosen May 1st) were I. N. Marks, President ; C. H. Slocomb, N. E. Bailey, and James Jackson, Vice-Presidents ; Luther Homes, Secretary and Treasurer ; and Williamson Smith, L. Folger, J. A. Blaffer G. W. Dunbar, A. W. Merriam, Joseph L. Harris, C. A. Miltenberger, John Geddes, G. A. Breaux, A. Fortier, E. A. Tyler, G. G. Garner, W. B. Schmidt, E. M. Rusha and Frederick Wing, Directors.

CRESCENT CITY SUGAR REFINERY,

On Tchoupitoulas street, between Julia and St. Joseph streets, occupying about half a square, is the enormous eight story brick building, which, with several subsidiary brick structures adjoining, constitute the Crescent City Steam Sugar Refinery, the most substantial, best managed and perhaps the largest manufactory of refined sugars in the world. Steam power is ingeniously applied wherever manual labor can be saved, so that with no more than one hundred laborers, results are accomplished, which, with less ingenuity, might require five times as many. The crude sugar as it comes from the plantation is hoisted by steam to the eighth story, and the molasses is pumped by steam from a tank or resevoir in the basement. From the top the sugar passes downward through the "blow ups," the bag filters, coolers, vacuum kettle, mixer, drainers, cutters and mill, by a succession of automatic processes, some of which are the invention of Adam Thompson, Esq., the enterprising sole proprietor, whose earnest study has long been to improve upon every mechanical contrivance by which time and labor can be saved. His establishment has thereby become the model refinery and the special admiration of all practical engineers.

No chemicals are used here in the process of refining, the sugar being whitened and purified entirely by filtration through charcoal. Of these charcoal filters Mr. Thompson has twenty-eight in operation, and intends soon to add twenty-three more. They are cylinders sixteen feet high, and four feet in diameter, compactly filled with bone black through which the liquid filters in about thirty-six hours. The charcoal, after having been used for several charges of liquid, is washed and revivified by burning in a furnace, which renews its purifying properties as often as may be required. Fifty tons of charcoal are in constant use. When in full operation four hundred and fifty barrels of sugar or five hundred barrels of molasses are used, the most of which is imported from Cuba.

The Louisiana molasses cannot be refined by charcoal filtration, as it contains sulphur, which prevents the whitening action of the bone black. Mr. Thompson has therefore provided eight centrifugal mills through which it is passed for refining and deoderizing.

Water is supplied by eight "drove wells," one of which is 140 feet deep. From these are filled very large tanks and cisterns in all parts of the establishment, extending to the eighth story and roofs. Pipes descend from these in all directions, so that in case of fire, the whole can be flooded in a few seconds. An extensive cooperage supplies the manufactory with barrels, &c. for refined sugars and syrups, besides making large numbers for the outside market.

The products of this establishment have become noted in American and foreign markets and the demand for them has so increased as to make an enlargement necessary. For his enterprize, energy and talents, the liberal and public-spirited proprietor merits the gratitude of all our citizens, and he is held in especial esteem by all who seek the development of Southern resources.

J. LEVOIS & JAMISON,

126 CANAL STREET,

NEW ORLEANS.

Importers of

Foreign Dry Goods

and

GENERAL DEALERS IN

American Dry Goods

AND

NOTIONS,

AT

WHOLESALE AND RETAIL.

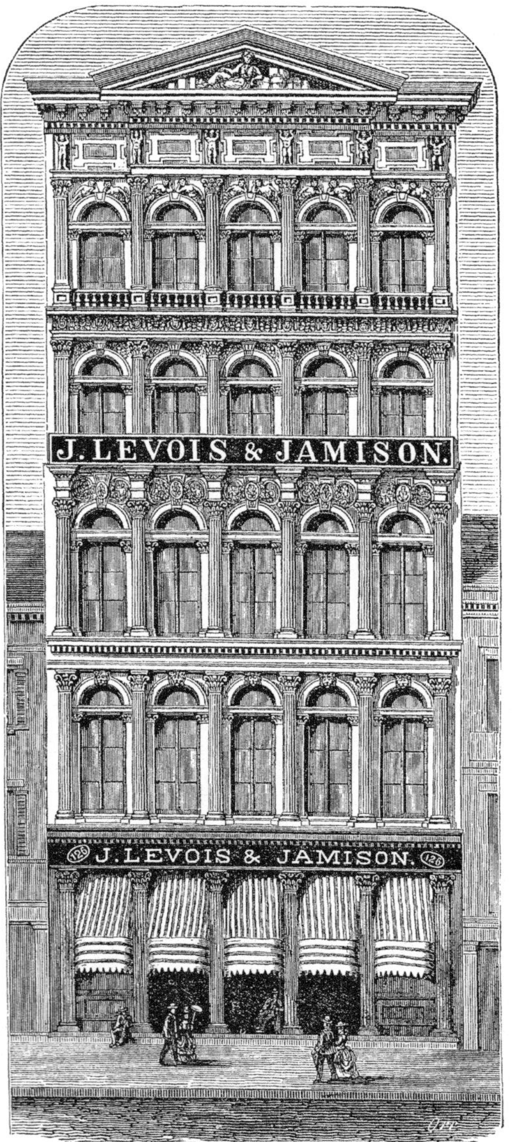

J. LEVOIS,

Commission Merchant,

3 Rue de Chateaudun,

PARIS.

THE ONLY HOME COMPANY.

LOUISIANA EQUITABLE LIFE INSURANCE CO.,

ORGANIZED MAY, 1868.

Corner CARONDELET AND GRAVIER STREETS,
New Orleans.

DIRECTORS.

CHARLES CAVAROC,	GEO. A. FOSDICK,	JOHN I. ADAMS,	JAMES I, DAY,	B. T. WALSHE,	C. E. GIRARDEY,
C. H. SLOCOMB,	EDWARD RIGNEY,	A. THOMSON,	D. B. PENN,	WM. CREEVY,	JOSEPH ELLISON,
DAVID WALLACE,	E. J. HART,	SAM'L M. TODD,	E. B. BRIGGS	J. W. STONE,	WM, HENDERSON,
W. B. SCHMIDT,	JOHN HENDERSON,	S. CAMBON,	E. H. FAIRCHILD,	E. A. TYLER,	

MEDICAL EXAMINERS.

DR. B. H. MOSS,   DR. HENRY SMITH,   DR. SAM CHOPPIN,   DR. J. H. LEWIS,   DR. J. DICKSON BRUNS.

THOMAS J. SEMMES, ESQ.

Hon. Thomas J. Semmes was born at Georgetown, D. C., in 1824. He springs from one of the oldest families in Maryland, his ancestors having emigrated to that State with Lord Baltimore.

He graduated with the highest honors at Georgetown College in 1842. He read law in the office of Clement Coxe, of that city, and entered the law school of Harvard University, where Judge Story and Simon Greenleaf were professors. He graduated in 1845, and was admitted to the bar of Washington the same year.

In 1850, he removed to New Orleans. Five years after he was appointed a member of the Democratic State Central Committee of the State Convention. During the gubernatorial canvas of '55 he had a controversy with a committee of the American party as to the right of naturalized citizens to vote. He distinguished himself at that time for his strong intellect and firmness of character.

In the same year he was elected a member of the Legislature, and in this body he became Chairman of the Judiciary Committee.

In July, 1857, he was appointed U. S. District Attorney, and in November, 1859, elected Attorney General of Louisiana.

In 1862, he was elected Confederate States Senator, and in this body he was made a member of the Judiciary and Finance Committee. He prepared the tax bill in conjunction Hon. R. M. T. Hunter, of Virginia, and wrote the report on retaliation and the resolutions from the Judiciary Committee on martial law.

His palatial residence on Annunciation street, in this city, was, after the capture of New Orleans, confiscated, together with its fine furniture, paintings, mirrors, carpets, etc., which amounted to a considerable sum of money. His law library was stolen by soldiers under Gen. Butler, and at the end of the war, when he returned home and resumed the practice of his profession, he was quite poor.

Since that time Mr. Semmes, by close application to business, has been accumulating property, and he is now on the road to fortune. It is generally believed that he and his partner, Mr. Robert Mott, have an excellent practice in the city.

In person, Mr. Semmes is of the middle size; he has eyes of the color of the waters of the sea, that grow with promethean fire, regular features, and moustache and goatee, in which assiduous labor and long nights of study have interspersed not a few silver threads. His bald head is a capital one—unrivaled; still, he scorns to wear a wig.

His exterior is apparently cold, probably from the fact that he is not demonstrative. Yet he is a true and reliable friend. His countenance is serious, but when excited in speech it grows articulate with the emotions that thrill his soul. His voice is musical and fits every intonation and cadence.

His penetrative intellect possesses a perspicuity, as quick as it is vivid, and his conclusions do not wait upon labored induction. He darts at once upon the core of the subject, and starts where most reasoners end.

He is familiar with the Latin and Greek classes. Tacitus is his favorite author.

Disciplined by such an education his taste is always correct.

In the subtle game of law he is adroit as a practiced general in the field. When he gets into his subject and is warmed with it, he utters words of fire that carry the listener captive along with him. If his argument is close to the point, it is at the same time full of expositions of the adversary's inconsistency. Mr. Semmes is renowned for his ability to sway courts by a logic, almost irresistible, and juries by a fascinating eloquence. He is, no doubt, a man of positive character, of pure reputation, and of untiring energies. He is called by some of our lawyers, " The incarnation of logic." At home he is quite amiable and his spirit buoyant and even playful.

JUDGE THOMAS WHARTON COLLENS.

Hon. Thos. Wharton Collens, who presides over the Seventh District Court for the Parish of Orleans, is a gentleman of unimpeachable integrity and a Judge of great capacity and learning.

He was born in Covington, La., and is fifty-nine years old. He was educated in this city, and has been thirty-nine years at the bar, discharging, at different periods, the offices of District Attorney and Judge of the Criminal Court with great ability. He is acquainted with the ancient and modern languages, and has written several philosophical works, which have been highly praised by the best critics.

In order that the reader may see Judge Wharton Collens in the mind's eye, a brief outline of his outer man is necessary.

In person he is slight and of the middle size. His face is pale, but often kindles up with the light and brilliancy of his dark eye. He has regular features, and iron-gray hair and beard. With fibres and nerves delicately toned, and not enjoying good health, his nervous system is some times irritable.

Judge Wharton Collens has a metaphysical turn of mind. Like all men of such bent, he is a stickler for technicalities. If he were a soldier he would be a martinet.

His style is that of the severest reasoning. The language is choice, perfectly clear, and admirably suited to the matters which the words clothe.

His decisions are based upon clear and rational grounds, evincing learning and showing a legal structure of understanding, felicitous statement and profound knowledge.

Over the Seventh District Court he has presided for several years, and his administration of its functions has shed a lustre alike upon that tribunal and the Judge.

It may be said, without fear of contradiction, that a long time will elapse before there shall arise in this State such another legal luminary, to adorn the bench, as the worthy gentleman I have briefly portrayed.

FRANCIS H. HATCH.

THE subject of this sketch, although he has lived in Louisiana for nearly forty years, is a native of New England, his ancestors being among the early settlers of that colony, and having taken part in the Revolutionary struggle inaugurated by Adams, Franklin, and Washington. Mr. Hatch was born in 1815, and came to New Orleans when a mere youth, commencing life as a clerk in the then prominent wholesale grocery house of McLeod & Campbell, in which position he gave so much satisfaction to his employers that, before he was of age, he became a partner of the firm on the withdrawal of McLeod from business. The failing health of the remaining partner, Mr. Campbell, threw the entire management of the business into the hands of Mr. Hatch, and thus, at the early age of twenty-one, he found himself in a position of great responsibility, in which he proved himself equal to the occasion, and became well prepared for the vastly more arduous and responsible public offices he was to be called upon to occupy. In 1848, the failing health of his wife induced him to retire from business and to settle into the Parish of St. Helena, where he soon entered into the arena of politics, being first elected to represent that piney-wood region to the Constitutional Convention of 1852, a body which achieved the very unusual feat of preparing, discussing and adopting a Constitution for the State in the short space of twenty-five days. From 1854 to 1857 Mr. Hatch represented his parish in the Legislature, and in 1857, he received from President Buchanan the appointment of Collector of the Port of New Orleans, an office which he filled to the entire satisfaction of the mercantile community, and with much honor to himself, as well as credit to the general government. Mr. Hatch's long identification with Louisiana led him to embark warmly in the cause of Secession, which he served with devoted fidelity throughout the late struggle, to the great detriment of his private

interests. Returning from the war impoverished, but not disheartened, Mr. Hatch again reverted to his old business pursuits, and is now the President of the New Orleans Branch of the Mound City Life Insurance Company, one of the best known and most flourishing institutions of that kind in the South. Mr. Hatch is one of the best specimens of the hardy New England stock grafted upon the Southern stock. For his energy and industry, combined with great prudence, a clear head, and a high sense of honor, he owes the enviable distinction of having passed through the most trying vicissitudes, commercial and political, without ever failing to meet all his obligations, both private and public, and to retain to the fullest extent the esteem and confidence of the population among which he has spent the last forty years of a useful life.

SAMUEL H. KENNEDY, ESQ.

THIS gentleman was born in Massachusetts, in the year 1816, and brought up as a farmer's boy in a family of eight children. His education was confined to those advantages which most farmers' sons were compelled to accept, who were obliged to till the sterile soil of New England—that is, to go to school in the winter months and work on the farm during the summer. His ambition as a youth was to go to Harvard College, at Cambridge, where his oldest brother graduated in 1826, and his position in all his classes, while at the town school and at the academy, induced his father to promise to send him to that institution. But the death first of his mother and then of his father, while he was yet a boy, prevented the execution of that plan, which was a favorite one with him, and he was taken from his classes at the early age of sixteen, forthwith launched into the world and fitted for American life in the rigid but not profitable school of experience.

He soon obtained a situation in a wholesale grocery store in Boston, where he remained till 1835, when influenced by the attractions of the Western country, which exerted a wondrous spell upon many young men of that region, he turned his steps thitherward. In December of that year he arrived at Alton, Ill., with only a trifle in his pocket, but after looking around him found a situation at fifty dollars a month as book-keeper in a dry goods store. After two years service he embarked in the wholesale grocery business, in which he remained till impaired health compelled him to seek a warmer latitude, in order to avoid a threatened pulmonary disease.

In 1843 he commenced business in New Orleans, under the firm of Kennedy & Foster, as Western commission and produce merchants. The death of Mr. Foster, in 1850, caused a change of the firm to S. H. Kennedy & Co., which name has remained unchanged up to the present time, and he is the only merchant now living in New Orleans, who has continued twenty-nine successive years in the Western business.

Mr. Kennedy has always been devoted to his profession, and by economy and close application has been rewarded with success. His rule has been—and he has found it a good one—to confine expenses in his own private affairs to a sum within his income.

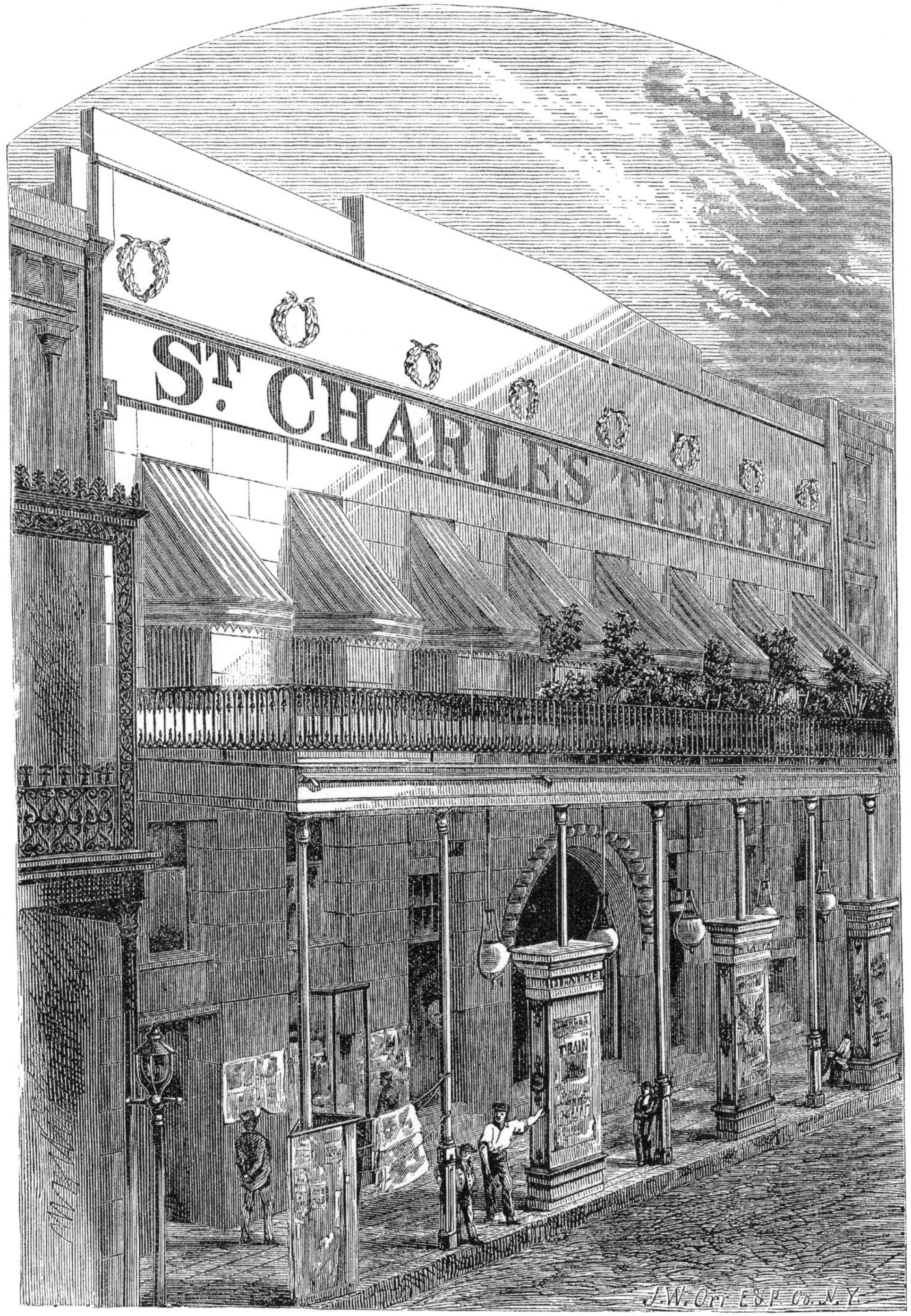

ST. CHARLES THEATRE.

Mr. Kennedy has been one of the most active members of the Chamber of Commerce of New Orleans, and for several years was elected its President.

He was for many years before the war a Director in the Louisiana State Bank, when that institution was the leading bank in the city. It had a capital of $2,000,000, and a deposit of over $5,000,000. Its stock was $190 in gold. The disaster of the war caused the bank to lose over $3,000,000. But under able management it paid all its liabilities. The result, however, was a condition so crippled that it was in 1870 about to go into liquidation when, at the request of a large number of stockholders, Mr. Kennedy was induced to take charge of the institution and resuscitate it. This has been done under his skillful administration of its affairs, and it is now, under the National Bank system, one of the leading banks of the city.

Mr. Kennedy is now in the prime of life and full of business energy. He is distinguished for public spirit, and takes a lively interest in all matters connected with the progress and welfare of the community.

On the corner of First and Camp streets, in the Fourth District, can be seen one of the most elegant houses in this city, surrounded with lovely grounds, laid out in the English lawn style, with a large variety of trees and shrubbery. Here Mr. Kennedy has resided for twenty years, surrounding himself and his family with those comforts and elegancies (the result of a well-earned prosperity) which a refined and cultivated taste can so well appreciate.

THOMAS ALLEN CLARKE, ESQ.

THIS respected and successful lawyer was born at Albany, in the State of New York, in 1814. His father was in the United States army, and at the close of the second war with Great Britain he moved to Utica. His grandfather was Lieut. Allen, who, not suspecting the treason of Arnold, announced to him the capture of André.

The youth of Mr. Clarke was spent at Utica. One of the oldest boys at school with him was Gov. Horatio Seymour. Among his companions were Professor Dana, of Yale College, the most distinguished living geologist in the United States; Dr. S. Wells Williams, the eminent Orientalist; the late Gen. Morris S. Miller, of the United States army; Capt. Lathrop, of the Texas navy, prepared for College at Utica and Canandaigua.

Mr. Clarke graduated at Hamilton College in 1834. He studied law at Utica, with Judges Kirkland and Bacon.

He came to New Orleans in 1835, and (like Benjamin and other eminent lawyers, whose modesty makes them diffident and distrustful as to their immediate success), engaged in mercantile pursuits. He resumed the study of the law with Judge Slidell, at the same time that he was paying teller in the Canal Bank of this city.

In 1842 he was admitted to the bar, and since that time he has been one of our prominent lawyers.

Mr. Clarke is a gentleman of fine personal appearance, with fair complexion, blue eyes and light hair. He has a striking air and dignified bearing, and is admired both for his talents and sterling integrity.

CHARLES T. HOWARD.

AMONG the many instances of men in this city who have, by their own exertions, industry and strict attention to their business, elevated themselves from comparative obscurity to positions of influence, wealth and character in the community, there is a no more striking instance of this fact than that represented by the subject of this sketch.

Mr. Howard was born in Baltimore in 1832. It was not his good fortune to enjoy the benefits of a thorough education but such as circumstances permitted, he readily availed himself of every opportunity. At an early age he left school in Philadelphia, after having qualified himself for the ordinary avocations of life. He then engaged in commercial pursuits in that city until 1852, when he came to New Orleans.

His first business connection here was with the steamboat interests of the South and West, with which he was identified until 1854. At this time having demonstrated business qualities of a high degree by an assiduous attention to his duties, he was recommended for and received the appointment of agent in this city for the Alabama State Lottery Company. His management of the affairs of this company, which was highly successful and satisfactory, was terminated by the breaking out of the war, in which Mr. Howard was one of the first to enlist under the banner of the Confederate States.

He first served in the navy and afterward joined the Crescent Regiment, then under command of Col. Marshal J. Smith. In this regiment he was made Orderly Sergeant of Co. G, and served in that capacity until he was discharged on account of sickness. He afterward entered the cavalry service, where he remained on active duty around Mobile until the termination of the war.

Upon returning to this city in 1865, Mr. Howard, like many others who had risked their all upon the issue of the great struggle for State Rights, found himself again upon the threshold of life. Nothing daunted, however, by the reverses of fortune or the loss of time, he again resumed work with the determination to recover all that had been lost. About this time the agency of the Kentucky State Lottery was tendered to and accepted by him. This position he filled with remarkable success until 1868.

Mr. Howard's connection with the Alabama and Kentucky State Lotteries familiarized him thoroughly with the operations of those companies and demonstrated the immense profits accruing to these States under the patronage of which these institutions were conducted. Mr. Howard conceived the idea that Louisiana, too, might be made the beneficiary of a similar corporation and the thousands of dollars annually paid as a tribute to the lottery companies of Alabama, Georgia, Kentucky and Havana might be poured into the coffers of his own State. With this object in view he secured the co-operation of a number of capitalists and citizens and obtained a charter from the State Legislature in 1868, for the incorporation of the Louisiana State Lottery Company. Of this company Mr. Howard was elected President, a position he has filled from 1868 to the present time with marked ability and efficiency. The Louisiana Lottery Company, under his control, has become one of the most substantial and lucrative institutions of the city, the dividends on its stock exceeding those of any of the banks.

Besides the business tact of Mr. Howard, which has made him so successful in life, he is a liberal-minded, generous and public-spirited citizen.

His name will be found connected with many of those public institutions which contribute so largely to the attraction of the city and which, but for the patronage, energy and liberality of a few such active and live men as Mr. Howard, would languish and finally pass away. To him is due in a great degree the establishment of the finest race course and Jockey Club House in the United States, and the success of the "Crescent City Yacht Club" is in like manner attributable to his lively interest in its welfare. Of the La-Jockey Club Mr. Howard is the Vice-President, and is also Vice-Commander of the "Crescent City Yacht Club," and is the owner of the famous yachts "Protos" and "Xiphias," whose fame as fast-sailing crafts is national as well as local.

To all subscriptions for works of public improvement, charitable purposes and all schemes for the welfare of the city, Mr. Howard is always a liberal contributor.

The institution of which he is President pays a tribute annually of $40,000 to the Public School Fund of the State, whilst personally the generous nature of Mr. Howard is evidenced by his many acts of kindness and charity unostentatiously bestowed and hence unknown to any but the grateful recipients.

Mr. Howard is an exempt member of the Fire Department. For a number of years he was Treasurer of the La-Hose Company, and as a testimonial of the high appreciation in which he was held by the members, their elegant steamer is called the "Annie Howard," in honor of the charming little-daughter of Mr. Howard.

In 1854, Mr. Howard was married to Miss Floristelle Boulemet, a member of one of the oldest and most respected creole families of New Orleans, and is now the father of four children. His residence (an engraving of which is on another page of this book) is pleasantly situated in the most delightful portion of the city, and is surrounded by all the elegance, luxury and comfort wealth can afford. And here Mr. Howard enjoys life and the fruits of his labor without ostentation, but with liberality in dispensing the hospitalities of his elegant home.

THOMAS L. BAYNE, ESQ.

THOMAS LIVINGSTON BAYNE, a distinguished lawyer of this city, was born in Jones county, Ga., but moved at an early age to Butler county, Ala., and resided there until his education was completed. He is about 45 years of age. I am told by one of his intimate friends that Mr. Bayne entered Yale College in 1843, and graduated with distinction in 1847.

He came to New Orleans in 1848, and studied law with his friend, Mr. Thomas Allen Clarke.

He was admitted to the bar in 1850. Three years afterwards he entered into a partnership with Mr. Clarke, which continues to the present time.

When our late war for the independence of the Southern States broke out, Mr. Bayne entered the 5th Company of the Washington Artillery as a private. He was one of the foremost in the battle of Shiloh, where he was shot through the right arm whilst serving one of the guns of his company. He recovered in a few weeks, and subsequently was appointed captain of artillery for gallant conduct in the field. Soon after he was promoted the rank of Lieutenant Colonel.

At the close of the war, Mr. Bayne returned to New Orleans and resumed the practice of the law with his former partner, Mr. Thos. Allen Clarke.

A few years before the war, he married in Selma, Alabama, the fair and accomplished daughter of Hon. John Gayle, ex-Governor of that State, ex-member of Congress of the Mobile District, and ex-Judge of the United States First District Court.

Mr. Bayne is a gentleman not only highly esteemed in this State for his honesty and profound knowledge of the law, but for his amiability and courtesy towards his fellow members of the bar. This gentleman, together with his partners, Mr. Clarke and Mr. Ren haw, has an excellent and deserved practice in this city.

Mr. Bayne is of the middle size, of slight frame, and with fair complexion.

WASHINGTON SQUARE is in the Third District; is bounded by the Elysian Fields, Great Men's, Casa Calvo and Frenchmen streets. Though admirably situated, owing to the distance it stands from the denser portion of the city, it has not yet received those attentions which, at some future day, will render it a beautiful promenade.

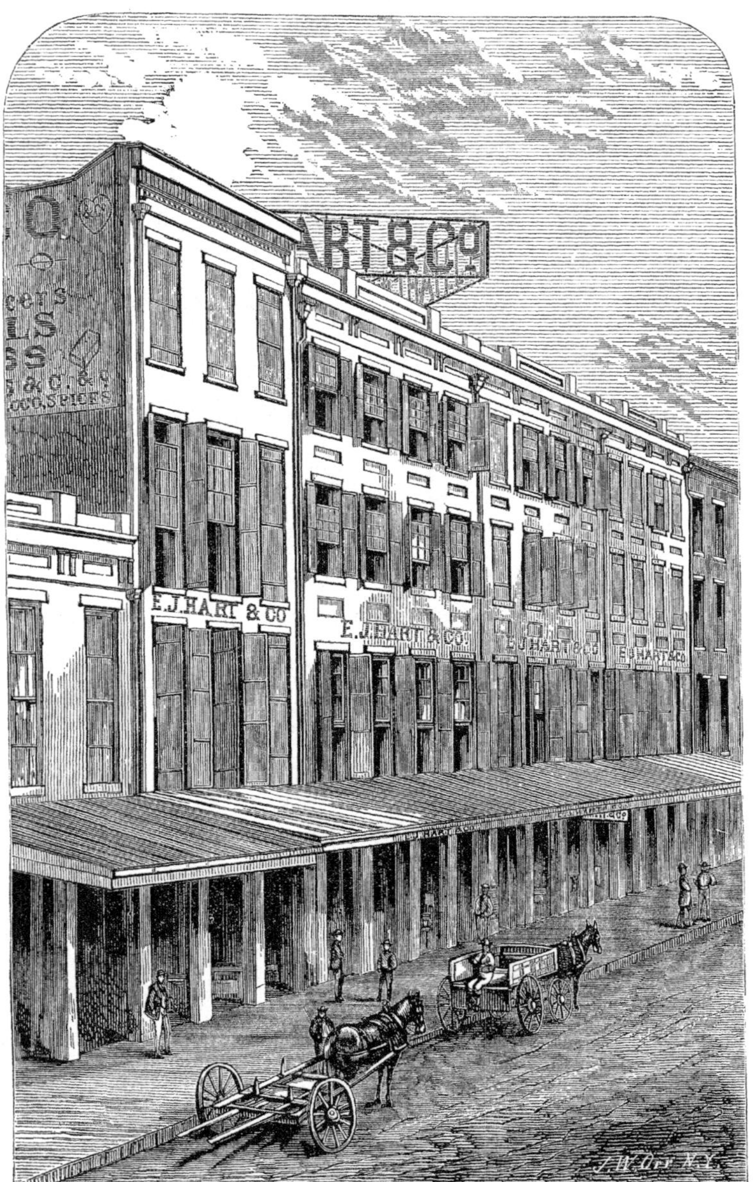

E. J. HART & CO.

WHOLESALE DEALERS, IMPORTERS AND COMMISSION MERCHANTS,

IN

GROCERIES AND DRUGS,

Nos. 73, 75 & 77 TCHOUPITOULAS ST.

E. J. HART,
B. B. HART

New Orleans, La.

CAPTAIN W. I. HODGSON.

WASHINGTON IRVING HODGSON was born in Louisville, Kentucky, on the 27th day of November, 1833, and after receiving a very limited education in that State, and at the "Eaton Seminary" in Murfresboro, Tenn., removed to the City of New Orleans, during the Fall of 1847, (then only about fourteen years of age), and began his business career as an under clerk in the well remembered hardware establishment of J. Waterman & Co., corner of Common and Magazine Sts., remaining there some years; he changed to the house of Samuel Locke, as entry clerk, in the same line of business, and afterwards as bookkeeper and cashier with Messrs. Alex. Norton & Macaulay, grocers, and C. C. Bier & Co., stove dealers. We find him in 1858, and up to the breaking out of the war in 1861, occupying the same position with Col. Jas. B. Walton, the well known auctioneer, and after many years service with that distinguished gentleman, in March, 1869, we find him associated with Mr. Charles T. Nash, as the junior partner in the firm of Nash & Hodgson, Auctioneers and Real Estate Agents.

Mr. Hodgson is the youngest son of Captain Henry Hodgson, favorably known from 1815 to 1834, as the commander of some of the largest and finest ships then plying the Atlantic, between New Orleans and the ports of Europe, and it was on one of these, the "Parker & Sons," under his command, that some of our most worthy, enterprising and public-spirited citizens of foreign birth made their first trip to this country. Among whom may be mentioned Robert Stark, John Watt, John D. Bein, Dr. Richard Bein, William and Samuel Bell, and hosts of others, the most of whom, with their old friend, now fill honored graves, Captain Hodgson dying in England at an advanced age, during the recent war.

Mr. Hodgson's mother, Jane Josephine Howard, was born in Dublin, Ireland, of American parents, and was returned to Dublin and educated, and on her final return to America, was married at an early age, while a guest at the hospitable residence of a Louisville gentleman. She was very popular in Washington and Philadelphia society, along from 1825 to 1830, and was noted far and wide for her beauty and accomplishments, speaking fluently five or more languages, and numbered among her particular friends the families of Washington Irving, Henry Clay, Daniel Webster and others.

This esteemed lady died suddenly of cholera in this city in 1853, deeply mourned and regretted by a large circle of friends.

Mr. Hodgson is a direct descendent, on his maternal side, from some of England's great personages, and is a great great grand nephew of Robert Elliott, who so successfully commanded the defences of the "Gibralta," during a seven years seige, by all the combined forces of Europe, and for which His Royal Master knighted him "Lord Elliot Heathfield."

His maternal grandfather was an officer in the U. S. Army during the English war of 1812, and while gallantly leading his troops at the battle of Bladonsburg, in the defense of Washington City, received wounds from which he suffered for many years, and which finally resulted in his death.

The subject of our sketch, imbibing somewhat the spirit of excitement and adventure, as it were, of his ancestors, joined the renowned corps, the Battalion Washington Artillery, (then a single company) as far back as the 3rd of April, 1851, and during a series of years, passing through the various grades from private onward. He entered the Confederate service in March, 1862, as captain of the Fifth Company of that famous corps, which office he subsequently resigned, to accept service with his good friend, the late Henry W. Allen, then Governor of Louisiana, as the commander of the State Artillery (doing outpost duty with the Confederate troops and under Confederate authority), and rendered eminent and conspicuous services to the state and government throughout the entire war, remaining in the service until after the last gun was fired, receiving his parole from the U. S. forces, on the surrender of Gen. E. Kirby Smith's army, in the Trans-Mississippi Department, in June, 1865.

Through his checkered and varied life, either as clerk, merchant, soldier, citizen or friend, Captain Hodgson has ever proven himself honorable, just and charitable to his fellow man, with a gay and happy disposition and cheerful pleasant manner with all, he has, through his indomitable energy, capacity and sterling entegrity (in connection with his partner), built up a large and prosperous business, second to none in their line, and they enjoy the esteem and confidence of the entire community.

A PECULIARITY in our city railroads is that there are no conductors. Passengers on entering the cars walk up to the fare-box, and deposit five cents—this being the price for a ride to any portion of the city. The amount saved by the Companies, by salaries for conductors and their perquisites add largely to the increase of dividends on the stock.

HENRY ABRAHAM, ESQ.

THIS gentleman, of Israelitish extraction, was born in Germany in 1836. Having finished his academic course at home, he, at an early age, emigrated to the United States, and the first place where he fixed his residence was the beautiful city of Montgomery, Alabama, where, in 1851, he entered into trade with his brother, who had also left his fatherland for the New World, and where he remained ten years advantageously and prosperously occupied.

In 1862, he removed to New Orleans, the great mart of Southern and South-western commerce. Here he first entered into the wholesale business on a large scale, with F. Goldsmith, Esq., under the firm name of Abraham & Goldsmith, which continued until 1866, when he formed a co-partnership with other parties in the cotton commission business, under the firm name of Lehman, Newgass & Co., New Orleans. He subsequently became partner in the firms of Lehman Brothers, New York, under the name of Lehman, Newgass & Co.; also of Lehman, Durr & Co., Montgomery, Ala., and of B. Newgass & Co., Liverpool, England.

The business of this firm has been prosperous from the start, owing to the mercantile skill, high integrity and general intelligence of the principal at the head of it, and of the gentlemen associated with him in the management of its affairs. It has experienced no reverses, and has rapidly risen to occupy the rank of one of our first commercial houses. It has also extended its branches to other commercial centres.

Mr. Abraham has settled the question, which has provoked skepticism at the North, and been regarded doubtful at the South, of the perfect feasibility of establishing cotton manufactures successfully in this section of the country. Indeed with the staple, machinery, water power and steam power necessary for manufacturing purposes, at our own door, it is surprising that our large capitalists and enterprising citizens have not embarked in this profitable enterprise at an earlier period. His Lane Cotton Mills, beautiful and commodious structures, situated on Tchoupitoulas Street, near Napoleon Avenue, in which yarns, ropes, osnaburgs, sheetings, shirtings and blankets, of the finest texture, are manufactured, equal to any produced in Europe or America, and for which the demand is large, and being continually extended, have introduced an era in this great industrial interest, for which not only New Orleans, but the whole Southern country is greatly indebted to this public-spirited citizen. We have regarded these mills as furnishing so marked a feature in the history of the times and of the *renaissance* of this metropolis, that we have had an accurate engraving of them made for this work. In prosecuting the noble enterprise (a novelty in our midst) with a species of enthusiasm that has been attended with the most encouraging results, the subject of this notice has had a special eye to the condition of a large class of persons among us who have been reduced to poverty and destitution by the late unhappy war. With a humanity that does honor to him, and to the persecuted and distinguished race from which he has descended, he has sought out, in the thoroughfares of the city, this class of persons, by the hundred, and given them a home and occupation. Not only men, but indigent boys and girls, clamoring for bread but willing to work, have been employed by him and rewarded for their labor. The number of operatives daily employed in and about the factory, in various tasks, ranges at from sixty-five to seventy. It forms the nucleus around which similar institutions will, in process of time, spring up, by means of which, as the example spreads, far and wide, from city to city, and from town to country, the South will, at length, become as well known and as noteworthy, for its manufactures, as it now is for its agriculture and its commerce.

In addition to the cotton mills, Mr. Abraham, under the firm of Smith & Goldsmith, started the Commercial Cotton Press, which, with the buildings attached to it, occupies four blocks on Tchoupitoulas street, where cotton is received in large quantities, stored, handled, pressed, prepared for market, and shipped on its destination. This is a great advantage to our planters and to purchasers and shippers of cotton. The Press itself is the most complete piece of workmanship of the kind ever imported into this city, and furnishes occupation, in various ways, for a large number of operatives.

Mr. Abraham is a Director in the Germania National Bank, and also a Director in three of our Insurance Companies, viz: the Crescent Mutual, the Hope, and the Teutonia. When not at his office, where he is generally to be found "from early morn to dewy eve," he is usually to be met with at the Bank, or some of the Insurance offices, or on "'Change, where merchants "most do congregate," receiving or imparting information as to the rise or fall of stocks, and the condition of the market at home and abroad. To politics, such as it has been for the last ten years in this community, he has an extreme aversion and never meddles with it.

This prosperous merchant takes a deep interest in the progress and completion of the new Jewish Temple "Sinai," on Carondelet street, now nearly finished, and has been a liberal contributor to it, as well as an ardent supporter of the cause of the Reformed Israelites, for whose special benefit that elegant structure was originally designed. One of the features which distinguishes their worship from that of the old time Israelites is, that, in accommodation to the spirit of the age, and the requirements of modern civilization, their service, in part at least, is conducted in the English language.

WASHINGTON SQUARE.—This fronts on Elysian Fields street and the line of the Pontchartrain and the New Orleans, Mobile and Texas Railways. The square is otherwise bounded by Frenchmen, Dauphine and Casacalvo streets. From the river side it is overlooked by the Third Presbyterian Church a fine brick building, whose front and steeple are now green with clambering vines. The square is enclosed with an iron fence, is copiously shaded upon the borders and is open for parades in the centre. It is the favorite resort for the children of the vicinage.

SLOCOMB, BALDWIN & CO.

HARDWARE IMPORTERS.

Dealers in

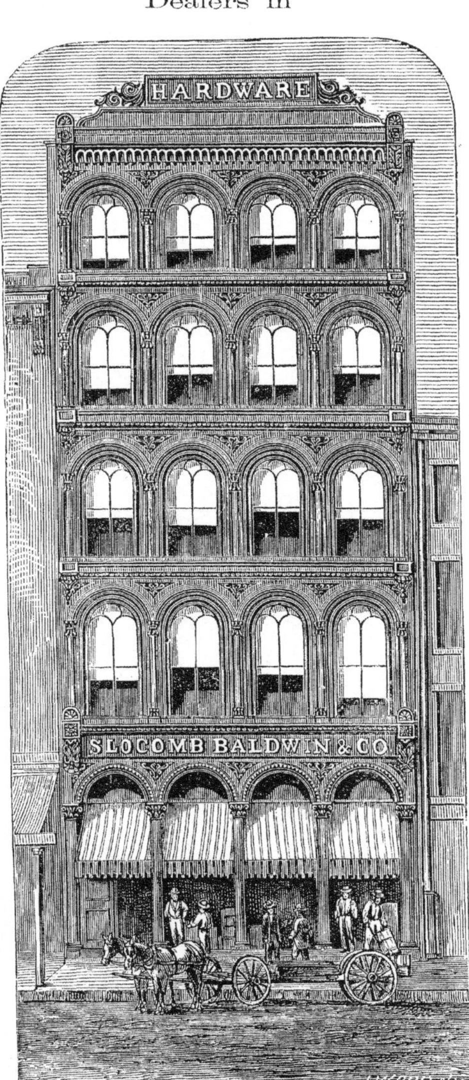

Agricultural Implements,

Iron, Steel,

Nails, Castings,

Tin Ware,

Paints, Oils,

Metals, &c., &c.

Rail Road Supplies,

Blacksmiths' and

Carpenters' Tools,

Carriage Hardware,

Cutlery,

Guns, &c., &c.

74 CANAL AND 91 TO 95 COMMON STREETS,

Adjoining the City Hotel.

WAREHOUSES:----PETERS and CROSSMAN Streets, NEW ORLEANS.

Our Importations are all direct and prices guaranteed as low as any market North or South.

JAMES W. ZACHARIE.

The subject of this sketch was one of the oldest and most respected merchants of this city. He was a native of the city of Baltimore and at the time of his death was in the seventy-fourth year of his age. He arrived in this city on the 1st of January 1803, about the period of the transfer of Louisiana from the French Republic to the United States, and was one of the few survivors who witnessed the event.

Mr. Stephen Zacharie, the father of the present subject, was Cashier of the Bank of Louisiana, the first institution of the kind established in the States, and his family soon became closely connected with the business interests of the newly acquired territory. At the period of the British invasion, James Zacharie, in common with the youths of his age, threw aside his books, to participate in the effort to expel the invaders. He was wounded in the battle of the 23d of December 1814, and was also in the celebrated battle of the 8th of January 1815.

Shortly after his father's death he was summoned from school to take charge of his business affairs, and by his industry and capacity soon became one of the most prominent merchants of this city. He supported with untiring energy every effort to advance the mercantile interests of New Orleans, and during his long and prosperous career, was very active in maintaining the commercial relations with the Spanish West Indies, the Spanish Main, and with Mexico. He was made President of the Chamber of Commerce, and was frequently the director of Banking institutions. Like most men of sterling and positive character he possessed many eccentricities, but withal was exceedingly kind hearted, liberal and honorable. Being one of the most prominent and successful merchants he soon acquired a large fortune and was enabled to retire to private life and enjoy the fruits of his labors. At his death New Orleans lost a most useful and enterprising citizen, and his family a kind, generous and indulgent parent.

LOUIS JANIN, ESQ.

The subject of this sketch is a living example of a man retaining his physical and mental powers in perfection past seventy years.

He was born in France. In spite of his reticence concerning his origin, his contemporaries know that on his mother's side he belongs to one of the noblest families of the Kingdom of Portugal. His grandmother married one of the generals of Frederick II, of Prussia. The King of Portugal, who admired the genius of this eminent soldier, employed him to instruct his troops in the new military tactics.

The mother of Louis Janin was the issue of that marriage. Mr. Janin became an orphan in his infancy, and was sent to Germany and reared on the estate of his grandfather. After the death of the latter, his tutor settled his accounts and succeeded in getting young Janin to travel through Western Europe.

He saw military service for some time, and at last felt a desire of coming to the United States.

He arrived in 1826 or '27 and visited the West, where he learned the English language, which he now speaks with rare perfection, as well as the German, French, Italian and Spanish.

In 1828 or '29 Janin came to New Orleans and was much pleased with the country and the manners of the people.

He was, a few years afterward, admitted to practice as a lawyer, and has since had no superior competitors in his profession.

He has great professional energy, and his numerous successes in the most complicated cases, mark him as a great lawyer.

Mr. Janin is a cultured gentleman, frank and straightforward, and always ready to assist others.

In 1845 he established a sugar refinery in the neighborhood of New Orleans, in association with Mr. J. P. Benjamin, at that time a famous lawyer in this city. He lost in this undertaking a large capital, which he had accumulated by his untiring industry at the bar.

In 1830 or 1831 he married Miss Covington, one of the daughters of Governor Covington, of Kentucky. He had from that marriage four sons, who have distinguished themselves by their acquirements and honorable character.

Edward, the eldest, died in the field of honor, during our late civil war, whilst in command of a Confederate company. The other three sons are at present practicing law in California, Nevada and Washington City.

Mr. Janin is of small stature and rather stout, with piercing dark eyes.

All those who know him can testify to his amiable disposition and suavity of manner.

It is generally conceded that as a land lawyer he has no superior in the United States.

HON. RANDELL HUNT, ESQ.

Hon. Randell Hunt was born in Charleston, South Carolina. He is about fifty years of age, and above the middle size.

He has been United States Senator, and is one of the Professors of our University.

He firmly opposed secession and showed at all times his attachment and devotion to the Union; but when the war broke out, he did not hesitate to partake of the destiny of the South, and was true to her cause and interests.

If we have an orator in the highest sense of eloquence—the lofty, the impassioned, not being among us common qualities—it is he. No lawyer ever advanced greater claims to the personal confidence and respect of the bar.

He possesses great depth of voice, speaks with fluency, and displays a confidence both of assertion and tone which seldom fails to take his hearers' judgment captive.

Mr. Hunt is distinguished for a most honorable character in private life, moderate opinions in politics, extensive information upon all subjects in his profession, and talents of a high order.

He is a great constitutional lawyer. The efforts of his genius combine with majestic declamation the deepest pathos, the most lively imagination and the closest reasoning.

When addressing a jury his strength lies in the lofty appeals he makes to the nobler qualities of the heart and in his withering scorn of the sordid and base.

Mr. Hunt is generally admired not only for his high talents, but loved for his generous, charitable, magnanimous and social disposition, frank and direct, with no mean qualities or littleness of mind.

ISAAC N. MARKS, ESQ.

THIS gentleman, of Hebrew descent (as his name indicates) and universally regarded as a distinguished representative of his ancient and highly favored race (in all respects save his adoption of Christianity as constituting a positive fulfilment of Hebrew predictions), was born at Charleston, South Carolina, May 5th, 1817. At the age of nineteen he removed to New Orleans and has resided here ever since, greatly esteemed by all classes of citizens of all creeds, both for his private and his public virtues. None of our merchants have maintained a higher character for integrity than he, none have reached the acme of wealth and prosperity by the exercise of superior skill. Nor does he appear at any time to have been more solicitous for his own advancement than for the public interests.

Soon after his arrival here, the mercantile firm of E. J. Hart & Company was established, of which Mr. Marks was an influential member. The credit, financial ability, and extensive resources of that firm are as well understood at New York, Chicago and St. Louis, as they are at New Orleans, and whenever and wherever the name of Isaac N. Marks is mentioned in connection with it, it has always been considered a synonym for honor, promptitude and efficiency.

Mr. Marks has identified himself very creditably with our public institutions. Officially, he stands in a most responsible position, at the head of the Fire Department of the city—an essential part of our city organization, and probably no city in the Union is more adequately provided with men and means for the prompt extinguishment of destructive fires, and for relief to the sufferers by them, not merely by Insurance Companies, but by the Fire Companies themselves, than the city of New Orleans. In 1840, four years after his arrival here, he was elected President of Perseverance Fire Company No. 13, and, from year to year, continued to be reëlected to that office. In 1850 he was chosen President of the Firemen's Charitable Association, representing all the Fire Companies of New Orleans, a kind of Masonic brotherhood, whose province it is to minister to the wants of the families of its deceased members. For seventeen years Mr. Marks has been elected to fill this delicate and difficult post by acclamation—an evidence of the fidelity with which he has dispensed the charities of this noble association. During all that time he has also been Chairman of the Board of Commissioners of the Fire Department, and, in that capacity, been often required to settle nice questions, referred to him, growing out of their contract with the City Government.

The thirty-fifth anniversary of the Firemen's Charitable Association will ever be a memorable day in the history of New Orleans, and in the life of the subject of this brief notice. The whole population of the Crescent City took a deep interest in the celebration of this anniversary. The sentiment which pervaded the entire community was one of deep gratitude to the brave and heroic men who were in the habit of exposing their lives to save from destruction the lives and property of their fellow citizens and to their distinguished President. As the Fire Companies moved on through our great thoroughfares, arrayed each in its own uniform, with their glittering engines gaily dressed with flowers, to the sound of martial music, they, by previous arrangement, paused opposite the City Hall, in order to pay their respects to his Honor, the Mayor, and the City Council. The address made by the President of the Fire Department, and the response of the Mayor on this occasion, were equally creditable to the good taste of both those distinguished individuals, and the subsequent presentation to Mr. Marks, at the Varieties Theatre, with imposing ceremonies, of a magnificent silver punch bowl, goblets and salver, testified to the high respect and esteem entertained for him by the Fire Companies, and was recognized as well merited by the approving acclamations of thousands of gentlemen and ladies who were present to witness it.

Soon after his establishment in New Orleans, the interest which he took in public affairs caused him to be elected an Alderman of the Second Municipality, which brought him into association with such men as Samuel J. Peters, James H. Caldwell and Henry Renshaw, who are, to the present day, justly regarded as fathers of the city, and projectors of some of the most important reforms, particularly in the department of education, that have occurred since the foundation of it. In all these interprises Mr. Marks took a decided and prominent part.

As President of the Louisiana Fair Association for a series of years, he has furnished evidence of an interest in the Agriculture, Mechanic Arts, and Manufactures of the State, such as has probably been displayed by no other individual in our midst. He is President also of the New Orleans, Florida & Havana Steamship Company, President of the New Jerusalem Church Society, Director of the Sun Mutual Insurance Company and President of the Mutual Aid and Benevolent Life Association.

Mr. Marks was always, in politics, an old Line Whig, belonging to a party that embraced many of the purest patriots and ablest statesmen in the Union. In our late troubles he adhered steadfastly to the cause of the South. Two of his sons were in the Confederate army. One of them (Henry Clay) died at Malvern Hill, fighting valiantly at the head of his own company. The other, Rev. Alexanders Marks, is a highly esteemed Episcopal clergyman of this city. Mr. Marks is one of nine brothers, all of them still living, save one. He is said to have been iminently fortunate in all the relations of domestic life.

NEW ORLEANS ROW BOAT CLUB.

CAPT. BLAYNEY T. WALSHE.

AMONG the young and rising merchants of New Orleans there is none whose success has been so marked and so rapid as that of Mr. B. T. Walshe, nor is there any one more highly esteemed in the community than he is for high social character and sterling integrity. Born in New Ross, Co., Wexford, Ireland in 1840, Mr. Walshe, with his parents, came to New Orleans at the early age of thirteen years, and soon after his arrival here found employment in the house of Lagay & Lecanu, then the leading boys' and children's clothing establishment of the city. Here he remained for a series of years, and by diligence, industry and close application prepared himself for the discharge of more responsible duties and for a wider field of labor. At the opening of the war Mr. Walshe was engaged in the well-known clothing house of Norris, Maull & Co., but like hosts of his countrymen, when his adopted State claimed his services in the army, he promptly responded to the appeal, and in 1861 joined the famous Washington Artillery. In May of the same year he was elected Lieutenant of Company A, of the Irish Brigade, subsequently incorporated in the Sixth La-Regiment, commanded by Colonel I. G. Seymour. In the record of this regiment, made famous by its bravery and efficiency and by its proud position in Hay's Brigade and Stonewall Jackson's Corps, he fully participated in all of its glories until, at Gaines's Mills, Captain Walshe was severely wounded in the ankle during the seven days' fight before Richmond. Thus being made unfit for active duty in the field, he was assigned to duty in Richmond as Chief of the Passport Office of the Department of Henrico. About a year after, when able to dispense with the use of crutches, he was assigned to staff duty as Chief Provost Marshal of South Mississippi and East Louisiana, and served until the termination of the war.

Having discharged well and faithfully his duties as a soldier he returned to New Orleans poor in pocket, but full of hope, and with a determination to begin anew as it were the battle of life, but not upon such blood-stained fields as those he had so recently abandoned. Peace once more blessed the land ; the avenues of trade and commerce were once more opened. For these avocations the early training of Mr. Walshe had cultivated a taste and developed a talent that subsequently crowned his efforts with abundant success. In October 1868, by industry and economy, Mr. Walshe was enabled to embark in business on his own account. His knowledge of the business of gentlemen's furnishing goods and boys' and children's clothing prompted him to make this line a specialty, and to say that he has been eminently successful would only be to re-echo the public verdict. As one thoroughly identified with all of the interests of New Orleans, coming from a foreign country and adopting this as his home, there is no better specimen of a stranger possessing all of the attributes of an exemplary and valuable citizen than Mr. Walshe. In 1863, he married a most estimable lady of New Orleans, and is now the father of five interesting children, three boys and two girls. In his pleasant but unostentatious home he is surrounded by all the comforts and pleasures a devoted family and the fruits of an industrious life can alone procure. In the various relations of life Mr. Walshe is by every one recognized as worthy of confidence, respect and esteem. As a citizen he is public-spirited, enterprising and liberal. The improvement of the city, public works, and private enterprises for the general good all meet with his hearty support and substantial assistance, whilst his social character is that of an upright and honorable man, a true friend and a generous benefactor.

AMILCAR FORTIER.

The President of the Bank of America has filled the position up to the present time with great honor to himself and great acceptability to the Stockholders, having already declared during the last three years of his administration, dividends exceeding *ninety per cent* on the original capital of the Bank, after paying all its cash balances since the war in gold. Mr. Fortier is a native Louisianian and traces his ancestry to two of the oldest, best-known, and most esteemed families in the State. Although still in the prime of life, (he was born in 1826), Mr. Fortier has the reputation of being one of the most prudent, cautious and conservative of our Bank Presidents, and his judgement, being guided by a very accurate as well an extensive knowledge of the business men of New Orleans, the Bank of America, under his administration, has suffered fewer losses than it ever did before, whilst its deposits have gradually increased, until they now surpass in amount those of every other Banikng Institution in the city.

PLACE D'ARMES.—This is an open parade ground commonly known as "Congo Square," fronting on Rampart street, between St. Peter and St. Anne streets, with St. Claude street in the rear. It differs in no essential respect from the other public squares of the city.

JOSEPH A. MAYBIN, ESQ.

THIS eminent citizen and able lawyer came to New Orleans from Philadelphia, his native city, in the year 1817, and has resided here ever since, greatly respected by all classes of citizens among us. Learned, faithful, conscientious, judicious, no member of the profession has commanded more of the confidence of the community, and he has enjoyed an uniform and respectable practice.

He has been forty-four years a ruling elder in the First Presbyterian Church of this city, over which the Rev. Dr. Palmer is now pastor. This office is one of great trust and importance in the Presbyterian denomination,—the duties being to assist the pastor in visiting the sick, dying and bereaved members of the church, and in other most important spiritual matters, and, on account of his want of legal practice for a number of years past, Mr. Maybin has been enabled to execute this trust with great assiduity and fidelity.

He prefers the Presbyterian Church from education, and the conviction that its doctrines are most accordant with, and sustained by, the truths of the Bible and by sound philosophy.

Although not a minister of the gospel, he is permitted to officiate every Sunday morning in the Presbyterian church at Carrollton.

Regarding the intelligence of the people, as well as religion, essential to the maintenance and prosperity of free institutions, he was among the foremost of those who sought to promote the interests of education in our midst. He accordingly united with the late Samuel J. Peters, Joshua Baldwin, Leonard Mathews, Dr. Picton, and other high-toned and patriotic men in the great educational reform which was introduced here in 1841, and which secured for the inhabitants of this city and State, and ultimately (as the light of example spread) for the inhabitants of the whole Mississippi Valley, the advantages of a course of popular education, which united all the best traits of the New England and Prussian systems. To the promotion of this cause, Mr. Maybin, " in season and out of season," devoted all the energies of a benevolent heart and of an acute and powerful intellect.

He was, for nine consecutive years, chairman of the Committee on Teachers for the Schools of the Second Municipality,—a difficult, delicate and responsible trust, in the discharge of which (however attached to his own religious opinions) he endeavored not to be influenced by any theological bias. Whether the applicant for a place were a Catholic, a Protestant or an Israelite, it mattered not to this truly liberal man, provided he or she (as the case might be) possessed the necessary qualifications for teaching. On the latter point, he was inflexible.

During the same period, he also acted as a member of the different committees for visiting the schools in the same municipality.

After a high-school for boys was established in the second municipality, he did not regard the system complete till a similar institution was introduced for the benefit of the other sex. The paternity, so to speak, of the Young Ladies' High-School, in this city, it is believed, is to be attributed to Mr. Maybin, who, for the space of five years, watched over its interests and progress with enlightened and ceaseless vigilance.

Mr. Maybin, if not the founder of the Houses of Refuge in this city, was one of the first of our philanthropic citizens who took effectual steps for their establishment and organization ; and, with a view to the reformation of the juvenile inmates, the commissioners procured the erection of and rented different buildings for the two sexes.

Mr. Maybin was appointed by the Council of the Second Municipality a commissioner of those houses for eight consecutive years ; and, during the nine years last past, he has, every Sunday afternoon, instructed the inmates of the Girl's House of Refuge, in the Holy Scriptures.

In 1837, Governor Edward White offered to appoint him one of the Judges of the Supreme Court of the State, but he declined.

In the year 1841, his friends requested him to apply for the appointment of District Judge of the United States for the District of Louisiana, which application would probably have been successful. He declined this also.

For the space of twenty years, commencing from 1841, and extending down to the secession of the State from the Federal Union, he was in the habit, as opportunity offered, of giving oral religious instructions on Sunday afternoons to colored people, in the Lecture Room of the First Presbyterian Church.

When the question of secession was agitated, Mr. Maybin was opposed to the measure. He delivered his first public speech against it in the theatre on Poydras street, and other public speeches in opposition to it at different places, and wrote three articles on the subject, which were published in the *Picayune* with his name attached.

He did not discuss the constitutionality of secession, admitting that there were great authorities in its favor, but he denied its expediency, considering it a bold and dangerous remedy, and recommended the co-operation of the several slave States for the adoption of such measures as would most fully protect their interests and rights.

But, when the State of Louisiana adopted its ordinance of Secession, on the 26th day of January, 1861, Mr. Maybin could not unite with men, who, for a quarter of a century, had assailed our institutions in violation of the Constitution of the United States, who were strangers to him, and for whom he had no sympathy ; and he determined to unite with his fellow-citizens, with whom he had resided forty years, to whom he was attached by strong associations, and with whom he was identified by pecuniary interest. He accordingly laid aside the obstruse question of the propriety of secession, and heartily united with his fellow-citizens in favor of the Confederate cause.

He was a member of a company of one hundred men, too aged to perform military duty, but who were organized to maintain order and preserve peace in the city, in imitation of a corps of citizens formed for the same purpose during the invasion of Louisiana by the British in 1814 and 1815 ; which company of one hundred men were called

THE MECHANIC'S INSTITUTE.

" The Fossils," and, during the whole year of 1861, paraded the streets with their double-barreled shot guns, and were called, by Mr. Maybin, " Old Fogies."

Governor Moore appointed him Chaplain in the Louisiana Militia, which office he accepted, in order to be with the sick, wounded and dying soldiers, and administer to them those comforts and consolations which humanity and religion prescribe. He, however, had no opportunity to perform the duties of the office, as the city was soon afterwards captured.

Mr. Maybin has nearly lost the sight of his eyes, but his intellectual vision is bright as ever. He is still professionally consulted, but, in preparing law documents, employs an amanuensis. He may be seen, nearly every day of the week, at the Sun Mutual Insurance Company's office, whose law concerns are committed to his management, in which, however, he is ably and faithfully assisted by Henry J, Leovy, Esq., of this city.

No citizen of the living generation, in New Orleans, has devoted himself, for half a century, with more singleness of purpose, with a clearer and more comprehensive intelligence, or more sustained perseverance, to the great interests of law, religion and the education of the people, than the venerable citizen, to whose active and able career we have, in these brief remarks, only done partial justice.

JAMES I. DAY, ESQ.

THIS distinguished gentleman, descended from one of the oldest families of New England, was born at New London, Conn., in 1812. No incidents connected with his childhood and early education have come to our knowledge, but his career as a man of business is well understood. In 1827, at the age of fifteen years, he became connected with a hardware establishment in New York city, in the capacity of a clerk. Five years afterwards, viz: in the Fall of 1832, he came to New Orleans, and connected himself in the same way with a mercantile concern of like character, the old and respectable firm of Whiting & Slark, of which firm he became a partner in the year 1837, and in which he continued, under the respective firms of Whiting & Slark; Slark, Day, Stauffer & Co.; and Slark, Day & Stauffer, until the year 1853, when he retired and removed to Connecticut, his health having been considerably impaired by his long and close application to business.

In 1836 Mr. Day formed a matrimonial connection with Miss Armitage, of Baltimore, sister of Mrs. Robert Slark, of this city, an alliance which contributed greatly to his domestic felicity.

Upon the death of Mr. Benjamin Story, in consideration of his financial abilities and influence, he was elected to supply his place as President of the Bank of Louisiana, which position, however, he resigned in favor of Mr. Wm. W. Montgomery, his own avocations not permitting him to give as much attention to the Bank as he thought necessary.

After taking up his residence in Connecticut, he became partner in the house of Bruff, Brother & Scarer, in New York, who, at the commencement of the war, were doing the largest hardware business in that city, and that almost entirely with the South, and which, in consequence of the war, became utterly ruined, involving him (being the capitalist in the concern), in very large losses.

Mr. Day was for many years President of the New York, Providence & Boston Railroad Company, and of several other Corporations in Connecticut and New York.

In consequence of his sympathies with the South in the early part of the war, he was threatened with arrest and imprisonment, and other hostile demonstrations. An order was at one time issued in New York for the seizure of his papers and effects, and only deferred through personal influence of Republican friends. The pressure on him was so great that he at length felt compelled to leave the country for a time. He accordingly went to Europe, where he spent about a year, till matters were quieted at home. He then returned to New York, where he remained until the close of the war, which stripped him of all his property.

In 1868 he returned to the Crescent City, where he associated himself with his son-in-law, C. H. Slocomb, Esq., and where he remained until his election recently to the office of President of the Sun Mutual Insurance Company.

During his long residence in New Orleans, he has been associated with most of the public enterprises of the day, always acknowledging the obligations which every successful man of business owes to the community in which he lives, and consequently co-operating with a cheerful spirit with all patriotic men, and contributing substantial aid to every meritorious object that claimed his attention. A Northern man, trained in Southern principles—the principles of the Federal Constitution—he loved with ardor the land of his birth, but has always adhered to his political faith with inflexible firmness. Exposed to the vicissitudes of fortune, he has never succumbed to them, but with every reverse that has befallen him has reasserted his independence, and addressing himself with renewed energy to the task of triumphing over difficulties and achieving the success which, for the most part, crowns the labors of courageous men.

THOMAS SLOO, ESQ.

THIS venerable gentleman, now in the eighty-third year of his age, but with intellect unimpaired, and a cheerfulness of temper which promises a prolongation of his active and useful life, was born in Washington, Mason County, Kentucky, April 5th, 1790. At sixteen years of age, he removed from his native State to Cincinnati, Ohio, and the first position in which we find him, is that of Assistant to General Findlay, Receiver of Public Moneys at Cincinnati, and which he appears to have occupied till the year 1820, when he removed to Illinois, and devoted himself to agriculture.

The interest which he took in public affairs led to his election several times to the Legislature of that enterprising and prosperous State. On one occasion he was nominated as its Whig candidate for Governor, when he canvassed the entire State, in opposition to the celebrated Ninian Edwards.

In 1828 Mr. Sloo removed to New Orleans, and established himself as a Commission Merchant, maintaining a high reputation for gentlemanly demeanor, honor and integrity. For several years he occupied the responsible post of City Treasurer.

Upon the organization of the City Schools, about the year 1840, the deep interest he had always taken in the cause of popular education, led to his appointment as one of their Directors, in connection with Leonard Mathews, Esq., Hon. Joshua Baldwin (then Recorder of the Second Municipality), Dr. Picton and J. A. Maybin, Esq.—all men of great respectability and among the leading citizens of New Orleans, at a period when it was the custom of the city to appoint only such men to stations of trust and honor.

From the time of the incorparation of the Sun Mutual Insurance Company of New Orleans, he has filled, with marked ability, the office of President of that flourishing institution ; but, in consequence of advancing years, has recently retired from its arduous labors. He still takes a lively interest in its affairs, is provided with a seat at its office, which he frequents daily, and retains for life, through the courtesy and liberality of the company, his annual salary.

Trained in the old school of politeness, no gentleman is more remarkable for the urbanity of his manners, the equanimity of his temper and the eminent purity of his character ; none is ever more ready to find some apology for any one whom he may hear accused of wrong. So scrupulous is he as to injuring the virtue of others, that he was never heard to speak ill of any one, or repeat a rumor to his injury. In his friendships he is as reliable as he is slow and deliberate in forming them.

In politics Mr. Sloo used to belong to the Old Line Whigs, when that party was in the ascendency, and his memory still lingers with fondness over its history. In religion he is a quiet, steadfast devotee of Episcopacy. In opinions and practice he is a conservative, holding the golden mean that lies between objectionable extremes.

THE CITY PRISONS.—These edifices are built of brick, and plastered to imitate granite, they are three stories in height, occupying one hundred and twenty three feet on Orleans and St. Ann streets, by one hundred and thirty-eight feet nine inches between them. They are two in number, and divided by a passage way that is closed to the public. The principal building has its main entrance from Orleans street, through a circular vestibule, closed by strong iron doors. The lower story contains the offices and apartments of the jailor. The second story is divided into large halls for such prisoners as require to be less strictly guarded. The plan of the third story is similar. The whole is surmounted by a belvidere, with an alarm bell. The cost is estimated at $200,000.

MRS. MARY S. WHITAKER.

THIS well known poet, essayist and novelist, is a daughter of Rev. Prof. Samuel Furman, one of the most eminent, eloquent and learned divines of South Carolina, and granddaughter of Rev. Richard Furman, D. D., of Charleston, S. C., *charum et venerabile nomen*, connected with the annals of the American Revolution, and the early history of South Carolina, of whose Constitution, such as it was before the commencement of the late war, he was one of the original framers. So powerful was the influence exerted by this celebrated divine in spreading, among the masses of the people, the flame of liberty and independence, during the revolutionary era, that Lord Cornwallis set a price upon his head. He was greatly beloved by all classes and denominations of people while he lived, and his funeral, upon the interment of his remains, was the largest ever seen in Charleston, except that of the late John C. Calhoun.

On the mother's side, Mrs. W. is of Scottish lineage, of the family of Scrymzeour, famous in Scottish history, and including among its celebrated names, those of Montook and Dundee, immortalized by their heroism, and by the pens of S r Walter Scott and the late lamented Aytoun.

She received her earliest instructions under the domestic roof, from her now venerable father, always a ripe scholar, an acute logician, and imbued not less with the love of letters than philosophy. She early exhibited a sensitive genius, and displayed much poetic power, devoted herself assiduously to the study of history on an extended scale, and of English classics, particularly the poets of Great Britain. To an amount of leaning, rarely attained by the women of America, she unites a cultivated taste and a high order of intellect. Probably there is no English prose writer, of either sex, who has attained to greater vigor and purity of style. She particularly excels in the delineation of scenery and character. Her Poems, published in 1850, elicited the highest praise from William Cullen Bryant and other American critics. In Europe, her poetical effusions attracted attention, and the celebrated Thomas Campbell, at a literary reunion at the house of the late Robert Chambers, on hearing one of her pieces recited, clapped his hands, exclaiming: " That belongs to the school of Pope and Campbell, which is the best of all schools, and I claim this young lady as my spiritual daughter."

While in Scotland with her parents, she married John Miller, Advocate, of Edinburgh, brother of the present Member of Parliament for Leith and the adjacent boroughs. Mr. Miller was at that time Assessor for Leith, and, subsequently, her Britannic Majesty's Attorney-General for the British West Indies. This distinguished official died at Nassau, New Providence, three months after their marriage.

Mrs. Whitaker is still actively engaged in writing, and, if her life is spared, will, in all probability, be better known to the public hereafter than she now is; although, by her voluminous communications to the press, and her published pieces, prose and poetical, she has already acquired the reputation of being one of the most finished and elegant authors of this century.

She is wife of Prof. D. K. Whitaker, of this city.

BANK OF AMERICA.

INCORPORATED 1857.

Capital, $507,800.

OFFICERS:

AM. FORTIER, President,

J. E. PASCAL, Cashier.

DIRECTORS:

Am. Fortier,
C. J. Leeds,
J. J. Fernandez,
J. I. Adams,
J. Scherck,
D. Bouligny,
W. B. Schmidt,
D. Fatjo,
F. W. Tilton,
M. Puig,
Ant. Giraud,
Gus. Miltenberger,
A. C. Hutchinson.

Corner of Canal Street and Exchange Alley.

THIS well-known and excellent Banking Institution is located in the fine building fronting on Canal street, and of which an engraving is given above, the rear of the premises (which belong to the Bank) being occupied by the wholesale wine and liquor store of Messrs. Cavaroc & Son. The Bank of America was established in 1857, with a capital of half a million of dollars and was originally located in one of the Pontalba Buildings on the corner of St. Peter and Old Levee streets, and where the People's Bank now stands. Mr. W. G. Hewes, an old and highly-esteemed merchant of New Orleans, was its first President. Mr. Amilcar Fortier, the present very able and popular President of the Bank, receiving the appointment of cashier. Upon the death of Mr. Hewes in 1862, the Presidency of the Bank was successively held by Messrs. Wm. Whann and Charles Cavaroc, when, upon the resignation of the last-named gentleman in 1866, the office was unanimously tendered to the present incumbent. Mr. J. E. Pascal, the present Cashier of the bank of America, is also a native Louisianian, and is held in very high esteem by all those who have been in contact with him either officially or personally.

CHURCH OF ST. JOHN THE BAPTIST.

This noble edifice, built in the Renaissance style of ar chitecture, measures, on the outside, 172 feet in length by 75 in width. Its ceiling, groined and arched, is fifty-five feet in height from the floors, and the groins supported by columns. The pews, 186 in number, are made of black walnut with mohogany trimmings. The Organ Gallery is of elliptic shape. The impressions made on the mind of the beholder on entering this sacred edifice are those of simple grandeur, accuracy of proportion and beauty of finish. The senses are charmed, the tastes gratified, the sensibility touched, and the imagination exalted. All the surroudings are calculated to awaken emotions at once august and tender—in a word—to lift the soul from earth to heaven. Over the alter of St Joseph, (in fresco) you see a representation of one of the earliest and most touching incidents in Christian History, the Flight of the Savior of Mankind into Egypt, a picture, and, over the Virgin Mary's altar, another picture of the Assumption of the Blessed Virgin.

All the decorations of the Church were in the beautiful Renaissance style, but they are not yet completed. An organ is being built, in that style by Henry Eben, Esq., of New York city, the fourth of the kind built in the United States, and the most powerful ever introduced into this city. Altars are being built for the Church at Cork, Ireland, of pure white Italian marble, the shafts of the columns and pilasters of Irish Green and Gold marble. A statue of St. John, is to be on one side of the altar, and one of St. Patrick on the other, the altar itself to be surmounted by the Angel of Hope holding a Chalice. The sanctuary floor will be in Mosaic, with different light-colored Irish marble, and the floor of the Transept and Sanctuary steps, of Italian marble. The estimated cost of St. John's Church, when completed, is set down at $200,000. The grand structure reflects infinite credit on the skill of Thomas Mulligan, Esq., the architect, as well as from the indefatigable zeal and enterprize of Father Moynahan, (who prosecuted the arduous labor to its completion with the spirit of another Solomon), and upon the citizens of all classes and creeds, who contributed to its erection with unbounded liberality.

The dedication of this church took place on the 9th of January 1872, under the auspices of his Grace, the Most Rev. Arch-Bishop Perché, (all the Catholic clergy attending) with the imposing magnificence that belongs to the ceremonials of the Roman Catholic church on such occasions, and in the presence of a vast concourse of citizens. The well known poet-priest and orator, Father Ryan, of Mobile, officiated on the occasion, and rendered it more memorable by his eloquence.

THE NEW ORLEANS MUTUAL INSURANCE CO.

The New Orleans Insurance Company was incorporated in 1835, a fact which confers upon it the distinction of being the oldest Insurance Company in New Orleans, and the oldest but one in the United States. Its first officers were M. M. P. De Buys and Thos. Urquhardt, Mr. A. Saint Martin succeeding the latter as President in 1845, in which year Mr. Jules Tuyes took Mr. Saint Martin's place as Secretary. On the retirement of Mr. St. Martin in 1854, Mr. Jules Tuyes was promoted to the Presidency of this company—a position still filled by him with credit and ability. In 1859, the mutual system being much in vogue, the stockholders of the company reorganized it in accordance with that system and under its present title of the New Orleans Mutual Insurance Company, its capital being then $500,000, and its assets amounting to $750,000. The New Orleans Mutual Insurance Company is justly looked upon as one of the safest and best managed public institutions of this city. It is distinguished from the other companies by a feature which originated with Mr. Tuyes, and has proved generally acceptable as well as eminently successful. Instead of being merged together, the dividends earned in each of the three departments (Fire, Marine and River,) are paid out to each insurer in proportion to the premiums he has paid in the particular department in which the profit was made thereby securing to him *in practice* the lowest rate of insurance attainable under the mutual system, as he receives the full share of the profits realized in the department to which his insurance belongs without being called upon to make, from his earned dividends, any deficiency that might occur in another department. Mr. J. W. Hincks, the present efficient Secretary of the New Orleans Mutual Insurance Company, was for more than twenty years Deputy Collector of the Port of New Orleans. Like Mr. Tuyes, he is a native of this city, where he has always stood deservedly high.

THE FERRIES.

The Third District Ferry plies every half hour from the head of Elysian Fields Street, Left Bank, and Olivier Street, Algiers, from 5 A. M. to 8 P. M., and is owned and conducted by Jose Carreras, Esq.

Morgan's Railroad Ferry plies between the head of St. Anne Street and the landing in front of his depot in Algiers. The arrivals and departures of his boats are regulated to correspond with the time of the passengers and freight trains to and from Algiers. Cars from Brashear over the Morgan road are crossed to the Left Bank and sent east over the New Orleans, Mobile & Texas Road without change or breaking bulk, the gauge of the former having been lately changed, to correspond with the entire line from New Orleans to New York.

The Second District Ferry plies every half hour between St. Anne Street and Bouny Street, Algiers, from $4\frac{1}{2}$ A. M. until $8\frac{1}{2}$ P. M. under the direction of Messrs. Drum and Hanley.

Canal Street Ferry plies from the head of Canal Street to Villeré Street, Right Bank, two, three or four times each hour, from $4\frac{1}{2}$ A. M. to 9 P. M., and each half hour during the night. This ferry employs two boats, the " Louisa," with capacity for 25 carriages or vehicles, with ample accommodations for passengers. The cabins and decks of the boats and the ferry passages and platforms are kept in scrupulous order and the officers are noted for urbanity. The Tug propeller, Little Jerry, performs the night service for foot passengers and at times alternates with the Louisa. In warm summer, by invitation of the liberal proprietors, the boats are thronged with citizens who remain on board for hours enjoying the breezes of the river, making several trips for a single fare.

The Ferry is owned and conducted by Capt. John Kouns and Capt. Wm. T. Scovell, under the firm of John Kouns & Co.

The Fourth District Ferry plies between the head of Jackson Street and the village of Gretna, making twelve or fifteen trips per day, between 5 A. M. and 7 or 8 P. M.

The Sixth District (or Bobb's) Ferry plies from the head of Louisiana Avenue, Sixth District, to Bobb's Mills from dawn until dark.

THE ACADEMY OF MUSIC.

Although the Academy of Music is of more recent establishment than its competitors, it can boast of being the oldest building after the St. Charles' Theatre, devoted to theatrical entertainments. It was constructed in 1853 by George C. Lawrason, Esq., of this city, for its present lessee and manager, Mr. D. Bidwell, and opened the same year as an amphitheatre, with a portable stage, by the renowned circus man, Dan Rice. Its character as an amphitheatre was retained until the next year, 1854, when the "Varieties Theatre —where Mr. and Mrs. Dion Boucicault were then to perform—was destroyed by fire for the first time. The opportunity of supplying the deficiency was seized upon by Mr. Bidwell, who immediately transformed the amphitheatre into a regular theatre. Mr. John Calder, who had been the treasurer of the Varieties, opened the institution with the unemployed members of the Varieties company, and the "Pelican Theatre," was thus inaugurated. From this time until the year 1856 the Pelican Theatre was rented by Mr. Bidwell to combination companies, until that gentleman was joined by Messrs. Spaulding and Rogers in the proprietorship and management of the theatre, and it assumed its present popular name, "The Academy of Music." The attractions to the Academy were increased by the addition of a museum, in which was gathered a large collection of natural and other curiosities. In 1866 Mr. Rogers' connection with the firm ceased, and Dr. Spaulding, in 1870, leaving Mr. Bidwell, the original manager, sole proprietor. Every year the Academy, under its intelligent and energetic administration, has received new improvements which make it now one of the most complete of modern theatres. The museum has been discontinued, and the space allotted to that department, in the front portion of the building, has been converted into neat and elegant reception and dressing rooms for the use of ladies and children, who so liberally patronize the Academy. The seasons at the Academy commence earlier and end later than at any of our other theatres, and its administration presents besides several important and noteworthy features, an elaborate steam apparatus supplies the auditorium with hot or cold air, according to the season, and ample provision is made for a copious supply of water in case of fire ; an admirable arrangement exists about its stage, consisting of the entire absence of scenery, except that which is needed for the evening's performance. All surplus scenery is carefully stored away in an adjoining fire-proof room, to which it is easily shifted by means of a simple contrivance. This is an excellent arrangement (which, we believe is not adopted by any other theatre in this country,) not only as an additional precaution against fire but because of the facilities it affords in the stage operations. The Academy is the original matinée theatre in New Orleans, and the success and popularity resulting from these noon performances have led the other theatres to follow Mr. Bidwell's example. The Academy was also the first theatre in New Orleans to be provided with the patent iron settees now so generally popular in the North. To say that the Academy is one of the cosiest and most elegant places of amusement in the country is but to confirm the public opinion. The uninitiated would be surprised, in fact, at the first glance to conceive that its seating capacity is nearly 1,800, and that very few theatres in the country have achieved the pecuniary success which has attended its management—the clear profits of one season, since the war, being estimated at a figure approximating sixty thousand dollars. During the career of this theatre most of the distinguished actors, actresses, and combination ocmpanies, varying from negro ministrelsy and the burlesque to the most refined comedy, and the lightest order of the drama, have appeared on its boards, and entitled it a patronage rivaling the most successful enterprises of its kind. In Mr. Jake Kittredge, who has been connected with the Academy in the capacity of Treasurer, for many years Mr. Bidwell has found a valuable assistant in the management of his theatre. Combining, as he does, strict business qualifications, and a peculiar tact to make himself the favorite of the patrons and the employées of the institution, his services have been as invaluable as his popularity is extensive.

THE MORESQUE BUILDING.

This magnificent iron edifice, which occupies an entire square at the corner of Camp and Poydras streets, was commenced by J. C. Barelli, Esq., in the Winter of 1859—1860. It was originally to have contained six stores, and a ball room 68 feet by 147. One-half of the building was roofed, when its further progress was interrupted by the war, during which all the copper was stolen, and the timbers of the unstated ball room rotted. About $249,000 had then been expended on it.

Subsequently, the building was purchased by John Gauche, Esq., for $160,000, who received an offer equivalent to about $87,000 per year for it, to be converted into a hotel. He refused taking the risk of the additional cost, about $215,000, including furniture, and expended about $110,000 in putting it in its present condition.

The building covers a small square of 150 feet on each side, between Poydras, Camp, North, and St. Mary streets. It is three stories and an attic in height. The four fronts are of iron in the Moorish style, or style of the Alhambra, and were executed at Holly Springs, (Miss.,) by Messrs. Jones, McElvain & Co. This foundry was used for an ordnance foundry in the early part of the war, but was afterwards destroyed.

ST. ANN'S ASYLUM.

HON. DUNCAN F. KENNER.

This gentleman, whose name was so familiar to the people of Louisiana before the late war, as a Sugar Planter and leading turfman, was born in New Orleans in the early part of the present century. The best portions of his life have been devoted to agricultural pursuits and the cognate matter of rearing and improving the thorough-bred horse. Few persons of the present day have been more successful in either pursuit. As a planter he was active, energetic and devotedly attached to his vocation, for he was a strong believer in the good old maxim, that

> " He, who by the plough would thrive,
> Himself must either hold or drive."

As a turfman, his career was brilliant, as all who recollect the glories of the old Metarie, Eclipse, Louisiana and Bingaman course, will testify. In the days of the glories of the American turf, Mr. Kenner's name ever ranked among the first.

Like many planters, he devoted much of his time to reading and to study. The taste and habits of his collegiate education was not allowed to rust from neglect. He possessed one of the finest private libraries in the State, and devoted hours, each day, to literary pursuits. A man of enterprise and progress, he never hesitated to adopt the most scientific methods of perfecting the development of the cane and manufacture of sugar.

It is not to be supposed that a gentleman of his fortune and attainments should not have been frequently called upon by his fellow-citizens to take an active part in the political affairs of his native State. He first took his seat in the House of Representatives of the State Legislature in 1836, and continued, almost without intermission, a member of the House, or State Senate, from that time till 1860. He was elected to the State Constitutional Convention called, in 1844, to remodel the Constitution of 1812, and again, in 1852, when he was elected to a Convention called to amend the Constitution. Over this Convention, which embraced among its members many of the ablest jurists and leading politicians of that day, Mr. Kenner presided, having been elected its Président by a most flattering majority.

In 1860, Mr. Kenner was a candidate for what is known as the Secession Convention, and, for the first time in twenty-four years, was defeated by his old constituents of Ascension Parish, the people of Ascension having strong Union sentiments, and Mr. Kenner equally decided Secession proclivities. After the adoption by the Convention of the Secession Resolutions, Mr. Kenner was elected by the Convention as one of the six Representatives to the Congress called at Montgomery, Alabama, to frame a Confederate Constitution and Government. He continued a member of the Confederate Congress, from its first formation to the final disruption of that Government and the surrender of General Lee. Probably the best estimate of the appreciation in which Mr. Kenner was held by his colleagues is found in the fact, that, after one year's service in the Provisional Congress, he was appointed Chairman of the Committee on Ways and Means of the House of Representatives, the most important Committee of that body, whose Chairman is the acknowledged leader of the House. This position was not attained by the power of speech nor by the graces of oratory, for to these Mr. Kenner never pretended (though no member, when he rose to address it, ever commanded the more undivided attention of the House), but to the exhibition in the Committee Room, where the real business of legislation is usually done, of practical good common sense, and a thorough knowledge of the adaptation of the means to the ends to be accomplished.

In 1863 and '64, Mr. Kenner became convinced that the great difficulty in the way of the recognition of the Independence of the Confederate States by the European powers was *the institution of Slavery*, and that, without such recognition, the question of Confederate Independence was probably destined to defeat, in fact, that the institution of slavery had to be given up, or the hopes of Confederate Independence would, more than probably, be lost forever.

Under this conviction he urged upon the Richmond Government to assume, in the face of the world, the obligation to abolish slavery in the event of the success of the Independence of the Confederate States. Though the views entertained by him were assented to, more or less, by many of the leaders at Richmond, it was thought that the public sentiment of the Southern States was not ripe for so bold a movement at that time. These views, however, were strengthened by the progress of events, and, in October or November 1864 Mr. Davis determined to adopt the policy of Emancipation as an extreme means to secure recognition by England and France, and, as he then thought, the consequent Independence of the Confederate States.

A trusty and confidential agent, fully possessed of the wishes of the Richmond Government, and, at the same time, a discreet and judicious person was required to go to Europe and communicate this change of policy on the subject of slavery to the Emperor Napoleon and to Lord Palmerston, the then recognized controllers of the French and English foreign policy. Mr. Kenner was eelected by Mr. Davis and the Richmond Cabinet as that agent. To pass through the Federal lines, which were then being gradually drawn closer and closer around Richmond, was no easy or altogether safe trip for a Confederate Congressman. Provided with the proper credentials and documents, all in cypher, concealed on his person, Mr. Kenner accepted the mission with all its chances of discovery, imprisonment, and, probably, death, and left Richmond to go *via* New York, in December 1864. He arrived in New York in some three weeks from the time of his departure from Richmond, walking nearly across Maryland, hid for days, occasionally, in farm houses, where the owners avowed themselves as " Southern sympathizers;" he often made narrow escapes of detection, under an assumed name and for an assumed purpose. He arrived in England in January or February 1865. Steps were immediately taken to bring to the notice of Louis Napoleon and Lord Palmerston the intentions and purposes of the Richmond Government. How unsuccessful the effort was need not now be dilated on. The constant advance of the Federal armies on to Richmond, and the evident weakening of the Confederate defences, destroyed all possibility of foreign recognition.

Immediately on Mr. Kenner's return to Louisiana, after the war, he was elected to the State Senate by his old constituents. He served in this capacity in the sessions of 1866 and 1867; and, since the adoption of the Reconstruction measures of 1868, he has confined his attention to his private affairs, and returned to his former occupation of cultivating the sugar cane, which, we learn, he is doing on a very extensive scale, being, with one exception, probably, more largely interested in that cultivation than any person in this State.

FATHER CORNELIUS MOYNAHAN.

Father Cornelius Moynahan emigrated to the United States at the same time, and in the same ship, with his distinguished brother, Father J. Moynahan; and so similar has been the career of these two brothers, the influence they have exerted in Catholic circles, the energy they have displayed in building churches, founding schools and convents, the ecclesiastical offices they have filled, and the esteem in which they have been held by all classes among us, that they have acquired in this community, the title to be regarded and to be called, *par nobile fratrum.*

Father C. Moynahan received his classical education in Ireland, finished his theological course in the Diocese of New Orleans, and was invested with the functions and dignity of the priesthood by the Most Reverend Archbishop Blanc, in the year 1848. The sphere of his operations lay in the Third District of New Orleans, which, at the time of his investiture, was without any proper ecclesiastical organization for the Roman Catholics. He was accordingly commissioned by the Archbishop of the Diocese, to build a church for the English speaking population of that district, and first erected a framed edifice for the purpose; but the congregation increased so rapidly under his administration, that a more commodious and substantial building for its accommodation became necessary, and the result was, the erection of what is now St. Peter's Church,—a fine brick edifice of sufficient dimensions to meet the requirements of that portion of the metropolis. The frame church, first erected, was converted into a Parochial School, largely attended by the children of that and the neighboring parishes, the department of female instruction being presided over by the Sisters of the Holy Cross, and the male department by lay teachers.

No naturalized citizen has ever identified himself more entirely with our national institutions than Father C. Moynahan,—none is more universally respected and beloved; none more influential in social, theological, and educational circles; none a more decided champion of Roman Catholic schools to be placed exclusively under Roman Catholic influences. His pulpit eloquence is classical, pathetic, earnest, persuasive and impressive, deeply imbued with what the French call *onction*, and the Latins *suaviter in modo.* The latter trait is conspicuous in his general intercourse with society, whether lay or clerical. Like his older brother, he has been raised to the dignity of Canon, and is one of the Counsellors of his Grace, the Archbishop.

PROFESSOR EUGENE PRÉVOST.

Mr. Eugene Prévost, the distinguished musical composer, professor and orchestra leader, was for ten years a pupil of the Paris "Conservatoire de Musique," where he obtained in 1829 two prizes for composition, and in 1831 received the unanimous vote of the jury (composed of the most eminent musicians of that period) for the "Grand Prix de Rome," the highest honor bestowed by the Conservatory of Music. In 1835 Mr. Prévost's first opera, *Cosimo*, was produced at the "Opera Comique," where it was performed for more than two hundred nights in succession, and at once gave him a reputation as one of the most promising musical writers of the day. This charming *opera bouffe*, which still retains its place upon the stage, was followed in quick succession by "Les Pontons de Cadiz," one act, and "Le Bon Garçon," both of which were also performed at the Opera Comique with great success, the latter especially, as well as "L'Illustre Gaspad," another comic opera produced upon the same boards in 1837. The next year Mr. Prévost came to New Orleans, having been engaged by Mr. P. Davis as leader of the orchestra of the French Opera—a post he has filled almost uninterruptedly for over twenty years with immense credit to himself and great benefit to the management, the artists, and the musical amateurs of New Orleans. During that period Mr. Prévost composed "La Esmeralda," a four act opera; "La Chaste Suzanne," four acts; "Alice et Clair," three acts; "Josué," an oratrio in three parts; "L'Orléanaise," a patriotic overture; several cantatas with full orchestral and choral accompaniments; a "Solemn Mass," a "Te Deum," dedicated to the Queen of Spain, and for which the author received the grand cross of Charles the Third; a "Requiem Mass," and other compositions too numerous to mention, all of which were performed here with great success. In 1862 Mr. Prévost returned to Europe, where, after filling for two seasons the post of leader of the orchestra in several first-class theatres, he was engaged by the celebrated composer, Offenbach, as leader of his theatre, "Les Bouffes Parisiens," which position he subsequently relinquished for the leadership of the grand concerts of the "Champs Elysées," in Paris. Since his return to New Orleans, Mr. Eugene Prévost has devoted himself almost exclusively to teaching, and the eagerness with which his lessons are sought after is the best evidence of the excellence of his method, and of the gratifying results he has obtained. It may safely be asserted that to no single individual is our community more deeply indebted for the excellent musical taste and the general cultivation of that most fascinating of the fine arts than to Mr. Eugene Prévost. Should Mr. Placide Canonge succeed in engaging an operatic company for the season of 1872–'3, it is gratifying to know that the orchestra will be under the experienced leadership of the learned and accomplished musician whose career we have briefly sketched, and whose pre-eminent claims to the distinction are universally acknowledged by all competent judges.

Since the foregoing sketch was written, Mr. Prévost has died. His illness was brief and his demise was as unexpected, as it was sincerely regretted.

LAKE PROTECTION LEVEE.

CHRIST'S CHURCH,

CANAL STREET, NEW ORLEANS.

DR. DANIEL WARREN BRICKELL,

Was born in Columbia, S. C., in 1824. His ancestry, of mixed Irish, French and English blood, were among the earlier settlers of the State, and his maternal grandfather, Daniel Faush, was the founder of the first newspaper in Columbia, which became the official organ, when that town was made the Capitol of South Carolina.

Dr. Brickell received a careful classical education at the best schools, and graduated as a physician in the University of Pennsylvania in 1847.

In the fall of the same year he was passed second, in a list of some forty applicants, before the Naval Examining Board at Philadelphia, and received his Commission as an Assistant Surgeon in the U. S. Navy. His orders, however, assigned him to duty at the Naval Station of Pensacola, in the place of active service afloat, which he strongly desired, and throwing up his Commission, he began his career as a practising physician in the City of New Orleans, in January, 1848.

The reputation which he soon acquired as a thoughtful, earnest, and indefatigable student, gave him early admittance to the Charity Hospital, as one of its attending physicians, and in the winter of 1859 he established a private class, and begun his distinguished career as a teacher of medicine.

The success of himself and colleagues was immediate and marked, and in 1856 he, together with Drs. Fenner, Choppin, Beard, A. & F. Penniston, J. M. Picton and Howard Smith, organized the NEW ORLEANS SCHOOL OF MEDICINE, which opened with a class of 76 students. In 1860 the class aggregated 270, with the promise of larger numbers thereafter. These hopes were disappointed by the war; but at its close in 1865, the college was re-opened, and at the death of Dr. Fenner in 1866, Dr. Brickell was chosen the Dean of the school he had helped to found, and of

which he always was one of the chief ornaments and supports.

The Chair of Obstetrics and Diseases of Women, which he so long and brilliantly filled, gave him a steadily increasing reputation in the South and West, and at his resignation from it, in 1870, he occupied the foremost rank as a Gynacologist in his state and section.

For many years Dr. Brickell was connected with the *N. O. Medical News and Hospital Gazette,* and with the *Southern Journal of Medicine,* as editor-in-chief, and exhibited, during a long career and in an eminent degree, all the high qualifications of a successful journalist.

As a citizen Dr. Brickell's deep interest in and capacity for public affairs, have won him the largest esteem and confidence of his fellow townsmen, who have more than once called him to their head in cases of the most trying and delicate nature. And in every relation of life, his lofty character, his earnest manhoood, his spotless integrity, his strong love of justice, his truthfulness, fidelity and generous temper have ensured him the regard and friendship of all classes.

In stature Br. Brickell is tall and spare; of a delicate frame, and nervous temperament; but capable of unusual energy and endurance. His features are classically regular, almost stern in their faultless outline, but luminous with an active and overflowing sensibility. A high-bred self-repose, a marked dignity of manner, mingled with much grace and sweetness, and his surpassing tact, have given him a sure passport to general and continued favor. Nor is it overpraise to add that nature has adorned him, in a conspicuous degree, with those rare accomplishments of mind and heart which go to make up the enviable *ensemble* of a successful and beloved physician.

Dr. Brickell has been twice married and has a large family.

PATRICK IRWIN. ESQ.

THIS opulent and public-spirited citizen was born in the county of Cork, Ireland, in the year 1810. In 1829 he emigrated to the United States. In 1832 he came to New Orleans, with the progress and prosperity of which he has since been largely identified. In 1853, he was elected an Alderman of the city, and, in 1854, appointed to fill a vacancy created in the Louisiana Legislature by the death of Hon. Preston W. Farrar.

In 1840, Mr. Irwin built, at his own expense, the Dryades Street Market, in a part of the city which was then little better than a wilderness, but which has since become one of its most populous thoroughfares. This market alone would be an enduring monument of his wealth, enterprise and municipal ambition, had he conferred no other benefits on the city; but he has added many to the list, which will cause his name often to be repeated with esteem and gratitude.

In 1850, he established two lines of omnibuses, one on Rampart, the other on Carondelet street, which were kept up for the space of from twelve to fifteen years, and were not only a great comfort and convenience to our citizens in this warm climate, but the source of a princely income. When city railroads superceded the omnibus, he invested capital in them, and became one of their largest stockholders. As an evidence of his abundant means, when the city, a few years since, proposed to dispose of its entire interest in the markets, he offered to purchase it, at a cost of two millions, two hundred thousand dollars, but the offer was declined. No capitalist, in New Orleans, enjoys more unlimited credit.

Without making any pretensions to religion, Mr. Irwin has always, in fact, been one of the most ardent friends and supporters of the Roman Catholic Church in the Crescent City, and one of the most liberal contributors to its progress. Had it not been for his efficient aid, it is not perhaps too much to say, that the elegant church of St. John the Baptist, the Parochial School House, the Convent, and other edifices connected with the church, which occupy an entire square on Dryades Street, would never have been built.

Mr. Irwin had not only been a purchaser, to a large extent, of real estate in the city, but has built many stores and houses on Tchoupitaulas, Natchez and Dryades streets, (near the Market,) and is now erecting a building on Gravier street, (next to Lum's Carriage Ware Room,) all of which edifices have added to the beauty and wealth of the city and the convenience of the inhabitants.

In 1870, he was elected President of the Hibernia Bank, which situation he still occupies with the reputation of a skilful financier and an energetic executive officer. The confidence reposed in him is such that he has recently also been elected President of the Hibernia Insurance Company.

ACHILLE CHIAPELLA.

Mr. Achille Chiapella, President of the Union Insurance Company, is of Italian descent, his grandfather, Geronimo Chiapella, having come here from Geneva towards the middle of the last century. Of his two sons, Celestin and Stephen Chiapella, the former, after realizing a handsome fortune on his fine Sugar estate in the Parish of Plaquemine, went to live in France, where he purchrsed in the vicinity of Bordeaux, the celebrated vineyard of "Haut Brion, La Mission," better known to every Louisiana *gourmet* of the *Ante Bellum* period, as the place where was produced the superb "C C" claret, so called because every bottle came here lablcd with the initials of the proprietor. Stephen Chiapella, the father of the subject of this sketch, preferring the life of a sailor, took command of a merchant ship plying between New Orleans and Europe, where his son, Achille Chiapella, received his education. Returning here, after completing his studies, Mr. Chiapella embraced the Notarial profession, in which he was very sucessful, and which he relinquished to assume the Presidency of the Union Insurance Company, which office he still continues to fill with much credit to himself and great advantage of the shareholders of that well managed corporation. Besides the above positions Mr. Chiapella was twice elected to the City Council at a period

when that body was composed of many of our best and most intelligect citizens, and in which his knowledge of business, strict integrity and a thorough acquaintance with the wants of the city enabled him to render valuable service to the community.

He was one of the originators of the Opelousas Railroad and acted for a short period as its President. He was also the founder and presiding officer of the first Oddfellow's lodge established below Canal street.

Mr. Chiapella is yet in the full vigor of manhood, having been born in 1813. In addition to his laborious duties as President of the Union Insurance Company, he also fills the position of Director of our most important Banking Institution—the Citizen's Bank.

Affable in his manners, and generous in his hospitality, he is a gentleman of cultivated taste, a lover of the Fine Arts, and a liberal patron of artists and musicians. When the Opera Company was formed, Mr. Chiapella was selected as one of the Directors, and was retained in that position until 1871, when he declined a reëlection.

If the Union Insurance Company owes much to its accomplished President, the latter has been fortunate in securing the services of its intelligent and popular Secretary, Mr. J. M. Crawford, a son of the late John Crawford, formerly Her B. Majesty's Consul in New Orleans, where he left a large circle of attached friends, and gave unlimited satisfaction to the mercantile community.

PROF. G. COLLIGNON.

Mr. Gustave Collignon, was born in Rennes, Brittany, in 1818, and entered the "Conservatoire de Musique" —the most celebrated musical school in the world—in 1824. His teachers were: Zimmerman for the piano, and Barbereau for hormony and composition ; the last named professor, (whose daughter M. Collignon afterwards married,) being the author of the best and most complete treatise on musical composition ever published. In 1837. Mr. Collignon lef the Conservatoire after receiving the first prize in his class, and in 1848, he was induced by Mr. Davis, then manager of the French Opera, to come to New Orleans, where he soon became known as an accomplished musical instructor, and when he established in 1857 the Classical Musical Society, which has been lately revived, and of which M. Collignan is still the leader, and the moving spirit.

In addition to his numerous professional engagements, M. Collignan is the Musical Director and Organist of the Church of the Immaculate Conception on Barronne street, where many ladies and gentlemen, constituting the *elite* of our musical amateurs may be heard every Sunday. One of the greatest attractions of these religious concerts, it is proper to add, is the magnificent voice, faultless style and impressive singing of Madame Comes, M. Collignan's daughter and pupil—a young lady who possesses a soprano voice, ranging with ease from the lower B flat to E flat above the line, and whose musical attainments are worthy of the splendid vocal gifts bestowed upon her.

Having lived in New Orleans for nearly a quarter of a century, M. Collignan justly considers himself a Louisianian. As a gentleman and as an artist, there is no one who stands higher, or who enjoys a larger share of the esteem of the community

N. O. Insurance Association Building,

102 CANAL STREET.

NEW ORLEANS
MUT'L INSURANCE
ASSOCIATION.

—o—

CHARTERED MAY 7th, 1869.

—o—

Capital, $1,000,000

—o—

C. Cavaroc, *President,*

G. Lanaux, *Secretary.*

DIRECTORS:

C. Cavaroc,	S. Cambon,
Chas. DeRuyter,	A. Poincy,
Leon Haas, Jr.,	J. Egli,
E. F. Mioton,	P. S. Wiltz,
W. Agar,	L. Queyrouze
	A. Thibaut.

—o—

This Insurance Company, although one of the youngest, is already numbered among the most prosperous and popular associations of the same character in New Orleans. It was established in August '69, under the auspices of Mr. C. Cavaroc and a number of well known capitalists and merchants, and in December 1870, the act of incorporation was amended by the adoption of the mutual principal, under which no stockholder can participate in the profit of the company unless he has effected insurance therein and paid premiums accordingly, and then only in the proportion of the earned so paid, and by which also the capital of the Association was fixed at one million of dollars [1,000,000.] The last quarterly statement of the New Orleans Mutual Insurance Association, published Sept. 30th, 1872, shows that during that quarter the Fire, Marine and River premiums received amounted to $316,492,08, the net earned premiums to $150,287,90, from which amount, after deducting losses, expenses, interest on capital paid, etc., there still remained the sum of $70,922,09 as the net profits of the quarter ending Sept. 30th, 1872.

The assets of the Association at the same date amounted to $1,092,438,35. The above figures show a most flourishing condition of the Association, so ably conducted by Mr. C. Caravoe, with the efficient aid of Mr. George Lanaux, the accomplished and highly esteemed Secretary of the company. It is proper to add that the magnificent marble front three story building just erected by Mr. H. Howard, architect, on the site formerly occupied in Canal Street by the Mechanics' and Traders' Bank, is the property of the New Orleans Mutual Insurance Association, whose office occupies the front part of the ground floor. The rear part is occupied by the New Orleans National Banking Association, and on the first story is the office of the Cresent City Live Stock Landing and Slaughter House Co., all of which are also presided over by Mr. Cavaroc.

NEW ORLEANS
NATIONAL BANKING
ASSOCIATION.

—o—

Chartered as Bank of New Orleans, MAY 14th, 1853.

—o—

Converted into the

N. O. National Banking Association, JULY 1st, 1871.

—o—

Capital, $600,000.

—o—

Chas. Cavaroc, *President,*

Numa Augustin, *Cashier.*

DIRECTORS:

E. F. Mioton,	P. S. Wiltz,
S. Cambon,	Leon Haas, Jr.,
A. Thibaut,	E. K. Converse,
J. Aldige.	C. DeRuyter,
	A. Tertrou.

—o—

This Bank, formerly called the Bank of New Orleans, was about to go into liquidation at the end of the war, when a few of the stockholders had the happy idea of calling Mr. C. Cavaroc to the helm. Under his auspices a vigorous and altogether successful effort was made to revive this institution, the result of which was soon felt in the highly increased value of its stock, which in 1868 was quoted at $17, and is now [1872] worth 32.50. Under its new title, the New Orleans National Banking Association is now organized as a National Bank, with a capital of $600,000, divided into 20,000 shares of $30 each. The last official report made according to law on the 3d of Oct. 1872, shows the large sum of one million one hundred and ninety-eight thousand five hundred and twenty-eight dollars and twenty cents [$1,198,528,20], as amount of individual deposits at the close of business on that day, from which an accurate conception of the popularity and success of this bank may be formed. To Mr. C. Cavaroc, the able and energetic President, this flourishing condition of the New Orleans National Banking Association is mainly due, nor should we forget to add that he is very efficiently supported by an excellent Board of Directors, and by the gentlemanly cashier of the Association, Col. Numa Augustin, an intelligent merchant who, having left the counting-house for the tented-field during the late war, returned to his former peaceful avocations in 1865, and is now doing good service to the community in his present capacity. The New Orleans Banking Association is one of those financial institutions of which any city might feel justly proud, and it stands second to none in the estimation of the public.

D. K. WHITAKER, ESQ.

THE following embraces some of the principal events, and all that are important to be known in the life of this gentleman. He was born at Sharon, County of Norfolk, and State of Massachusetts, on the 10th day of April, A. D., 1801, being the second son and child in a family of ten children, of Rev. Jonathan and Mrs. Mary Whitaker, his father being minister of the Congregational Church and Society of that town. He received his education, preparatory to entering Cambridge College, first at home, from his father (a son of Harvard of the class of 1798; next at Bradford academy, on the Merrimac River—place of nativity of his mother); subsequently at Derby academy, Hingham, then under the direction of his uncle, Rev. Daniel Kimball, also a graduate of Harvard College, and for some time its Latin Tutor, after whom he received his baptismal name); and, finally, at Andrew Phillips' academy. Upon leaving the last named institution, where he spent three years, he delivered, at the anniversary exhibition, by appointment of the principal, the Latin Salutatory Oration, the first time such an honor had ever been conferred on any pupil of that seminary

At sixteen years of age he entered Cambridge College, where he received the degree of Bachelor of Arts in 1820, and that of Master in 1823. His favorite studies, in college, were the Latin and Greek Languages, Moral and Intellectual Philosophy, Politics, Logic, Rhetoric, and the Belles Lettres, in all which he is said to have excelled. In 1819 he obtained a Boylston Gold Medal for a dissertation on "The Literary Character of Dr. Samuel Johnson," for which all the undergraduates of the four classes, as well as resident graduates, were at liberty to contend; and, in 1820, a Bowdoin Gold Medal for Oratory, open for competition to undergraduates and the graduate class. John Quincy Adams and Daniel Webster were among the judges who awarded the latter prize.

Inheriting a partiality for the clerical profession both from his paternal and maternal ancestors, he, shortly after leaving the university, placed himself under the theological tuition of the Rev. Dr. Richmond, an eminent clergyman of Dorchester (in the environs of Boston), and upon the completion of his studies, having been pronounced morally and intellectually fitted for the sacred office, received, from the Bridgewater Association of Divines, a license to preach the Gospel.

About this time he suffered severely from the condition of his health, which had been frail from his childhood. He had had alarming attacks of illness while prosecuting his studies both at Andover and Cambridge, which led to his temporary abandonment of them; and, upon his recovery on this occasion, his family physician and friends recommended, as indispensable to the complete establishment of his health, his temporary, if not permanent, removal to a Southern and more genial climate. His parents consenting this course was adopted; and towards the close of the year 1823, he, in company with his venerable father who had recently dissolved his pastoral connection with his church and his congregation in New Bedford, Massachusetts, (pre-

viously presided over by the celebrated Dr. Samuel West, and subsequently by the equally celebrated Dr. Orville Dewey), left that place for the South. He had previously elaborately prepared a few discourses with a view to make a favorable impression on any audience he might be called on to address, and some of which he soon had occasion to deliver to large audiences in New York City, in Philadelphia, Penn.; in Washington, D. C.; Baltimore, Md.; Richmond and Petersburg, Va.; Raleigh and Fayetteville, N. C.; Cheraw, Camden and Charleston, S. C., and Savannah, Milledgeville and Augusta, Ga. These discourses were said to be very eloquent and effective, and, as a youthful preacher, he started on his career with no inconsiderable reputation. While in Charleston, S. C., he was invited by the Rev. Dr. Gilman to supply his pulpit during the Summer months on the occasion of his exit North, and the congregation of that eminent divine and scholar paid him the compliment of publishing two of his sermons. At the beautiful town of Augusta he succeeded in organizing a society, of which he was invited to take the charge, and, for his accommodation, a neat and commodious church edifice was erected. There he continued to officiate for nearly a year, when his health, in consequence of his constant and novel labors, was completely broken down. He now, as a measure of duty and prudence, determined to abandon the ministry altogether.

Removing to South Carolina where his parents and family had now arrived and settled themselves, he remained with them till his health was recuperated. He shortly afterwards married a lady residing in St. Paul's Parish, Comton District, of that State, widow of an eminent physician and planter, and devoted himself for about ten years to the culture of the great staples of the South—rice and cotton. The daily exercise his new avocation required him to take in the open air, proved highly beneficial to his health, while the associations he formed with educated planters, presented to him an entirely new and favorable phase of Southern society. Having been invited to become a member of the State Agricultural Society of South Carolina, he delivered by appointment before that body, an anniversary discourse on "The claims of Agriculture to be regarded as a distinct Science," which was published by the society and republished in "the *Southern Agriculturist*," edited by Dr. Bachman, our great Southern Naturalist. The subject of making the science of agriculture a distinct branch of education for Southern young gentlemen was much discussed about that time, and the plan of making it a part of the college curriculum was actually adopted by the States of South Carolina and Georgia.

The quiet and monotonous pursuits of a country life were not, however, altogether adapted to the peculiar tastes of the subject of this notice. He desired to be an active participator in more exciting scenes. He had determined, for the reasons already assigned, not to resume the ministerial profession, but the law had its attractions, and, as his health was now established, he had ample time and opportunities for the purpose, he resolved to enter upon its study; and placing himself under the direction of James L. Petigru, Esq., the leading lawyer of South Carolina, he prepared himself for the bar, in due time passed a successful examination before the judges of the Supreme Court, and was admitted to practice in the Courts of Law and Equity in South Carolina. He had scarcely opened a law office in Charleston when he was solicited by the Hon. John Lyde Wilson, ex-Governor of the State, and an eminent practitioner at the Charleston bar, to enter into co-partnership with him. Governor Wilson placed in his hands the trial of several important causes, both in the lower and higher courts, in which he was successful.

In 1832, he was appointed Chairman of the Committee of the citizens of St. Paul's Parish (consisting chiefly of planters,) to draft a series of resolutions on the subject of Nullification, which were unanimously adopted. Those resolutions he supported in a speech which was published in the Charleston *Mercury*. He spoke occasionally at public meetings, and, in the midst of the crisis, delivered, by invitation, the Fourth of July Oration before the " '76 Association" of Charleston, availing himself of the occasion to express the views he entertained on the important questions of the day.

He was a member of "the Literary and Philosophical Society of South Carolina," of which the Hon. Joel R. Poinsett was, at that time, President, composed of the most distinguished scholars of all professions in Charleston, a city second to none other in America for its high literary tone. On one occasion he had the honor to be appointed the anniversary orator of this association, and selected for his subject, " The Habits, Customs, Genius, and Languages of the Indian Tribes of North America."

Under the auspices of this learned body, in the year 1835, he issued proposals for the publication of a Southern monthly magazine at Charleston, S. C. The proposition was received very favorably throughout the whole South. After the demise of the old Southern Review, brilliantly edited, first by the Messrs. Elliott (father and son), and subsequently by the celebrated Hugh S. Legare ; some such medium for communicating to the Southern public the opinions of distinguished Southern writers on literary topics was deemed highly desirable. This work, under the editorial conduct of Mr. Whitaker, was for some years well sustained by himself and the same corps of writers.

A work of a graver character than the monthly journal just referred to, was now demanded by the necessities of the times, in which the prominent interests of the country, political as well as literary, should be fully and elaborately discussed, with a view to the creation of a sound public sentiment, at the instance, once more, and upon the recommendation of " The Literary and Philosophical Society of South Carolina," Mr. Whitaker issued proposals, in 1840, for the publication of the " *Southern Quarterly Review.*" It was thought best, this time, to transfer the place of publication from Charleston to New Orleans, as likely to command a more extensive circulation throughout the whole South and Southwest. By the energy of Mr. Whitaker, a subscription list amounting to $16,000 was procured, and the publication was commenced in this city in January of the following year.

Its contributors were numerous, embracing the ablest writers and scholars in the Southern States. After conducting it for a series of years with marked ability Mr. Whitaker sold the *Review* to a company of gentlemen, who were aware of the difficulties in which he was involved by the heavy outlay he had incurred at the beginning of the enterprise and afterwards. The proceeds enabled him to meet honorably all the liabilities occasioned by the publication of the work, which then passed into the hands of other able editors who continued it for twenty-one years from the date of its announcement up to the time of the breaking out of the late war. It was very influential, and continued to maintain a reputation fully equal to that of any quarterly published either in the United States or in Great Britain.

Having had the misfortune to lose his wife, Mr. Whitaker, in 1848, formed a matrimonial alliance with Mrs. M. S. Miller, of the High Hills of Santee, South Carolina, widow of the Hon. John Miller, advocate of Edinburgh, Scotland, and subsequently Queen's Attorney General for the British West Indies, a lady equally celebrated for her personal and literary accomplishments, and by whom he has had six children, a son and four daughters, of whom only two daughters survive, having lost their son, a promising child of five years on a visit of a year spent in the bleak latitude of Canada. Of two sons by his former wife, one survives, who now resides on his own homestead near Greenville, S. C.

During the administration of Mr. Buchanan, Mr. Whittaker held an official position under the United States Government, until the secession of South Carolina, when he removed to Richmond, where through the kind instrumentality of the Hon. Alexander H. Stephens, he obtained a post first in the General Post-office Department of the Confederate Government, and subsequently in the War Office. He left Richmond on the day of its evacuation by the Confederate troops, came to New Orleans early in January, 1866, was for a year and a half, associate editor of the New Orleans *Times*, and has since been engaged in various literary avocations.

The writer of this sketch, who is intimately acquainted with Mr. Whitaker's literary character and entire career, feels fully authorized to say in conclusion, that, as a writer, he is distinguished by a style critically correct, and in argumentative powers is rarely surpassed. A total absence of affectation assists in establishing the cogency of his reasoning and the logical accuracy of his deductions. Few care to measure swords with him in a fairly conducted argument. His blows fall with persevering force, and, even when diffuse, as he sometimes is, he seldom fails in establishing any point for which he contends.

A sketch of Mr. Whitaker was written many years since by Edgar A. Poe, and published in a periodical edited by that great American poet, in which he makes the following assertion : " Mr. Whitaker is one of the best essayists in North America, and stands in the foremost rank of elegant writers." His habits are those of a man devoted to letters, and the want of a publishing house at the South, and his own modesty, though operating against his celebrity, have not been sufficient impediments to seriously cloud his well earned reputation.

RESIDENCE OF C. H. SLOCOMB. ESQ.,

Corner of Esplanade and St. Claude Sts., New Orleans.

THE SAINT LOUIS HOTEL.

Thirty-seven years ago, the spot where now stands the Saint Louis was selected for the purpose of building a hotel, on a scale commensurate with the growing importance of New Orleans. At that time the only hotels in the city were the Stranger's Hotel, kept by Marty, and the Orleans Hotel, kept by the beautiful Mrs. Page, both houses being still used for the same purpose on Chartres street. The space now occupied by the St. Louis Hotel and the surrounding structures, was, thirty-seven years ago, a conglomeration of stores, shops, and private dwellings. On the side fronting St. Louis street, where the rotunda now stands, was the residence and pharmacy of Mr. Germain Ducatel, flanked by the residences an l offices of Dr. Fabre Fourciszy, a collecting agent and broker; Antoine Abat, the well-known capitalist and banker; Leroy, an individual so named because he sold the then celebrated patent medicine known as Leroy's specific; a barber's saloon, and a cooper's shop. An importer of foreign goods named Bellanger, occupied the corner of Royal and St. Louis streets, while at the corner of Chartres and St. Louis streets stood Hewlett's Exchange, consisting of a coffee house and auction mart, with billiard tables and a " cock pit " in the rear. On the opposite of Chartres street were the original ice house (La Glaciére), now located on Bienville street, and the residence of Judah Touro. On Royal street, going towards Toulouse, were the well-known stores of Larue and Seignouret. On the northeast corner of Royal and St. Louis stood the drug store of Grand Champs, now kept by Dr. DeCasteluan, which enjoys the distinction of being the oldest establishment of the kind in the city, having preserved its well-earned reputation for over sixty years. Diagonally across the street was, above, the residence of Mr. Le Carpentier, the grandfather of Paul Morphy, the great chess player, and underneath was the dwelling of Mr. Brumage. Over the way, at the northwest corner, stood the fashionable jewelry store of Hyde & Goodrich, which still maintains its place in the front rank under its title of A. B. Griswold, on the corner of Canal and Royal streets. Among the well known citizens residing around the hotel were D. Ambrosio, Lucien Carriére, Mioton and Girod, the first Mayor of New Orleans, and the founder of the Girod Asylum, who kept an importer's store on the northwest corner of St. Louis and Chartres streets. The Improvement Bank, by whom the old St. Louis Hotel was built, was presided over by Judge Jean Francois Canonge, and numbered the late Pierre Soulé among its directors. The edifice was commenced by Mr. Depouilly, a distinguished architect still living; in 1836, and at about the same time the stately building in the rear of the hotel on Toulouse street, subsequently occupied for many years by the Citizen's Bank, was also erected by the Improvement Bank for its own use. The total cost of the hotel, and the annexed buildings, was nearly a million and a half of dollars. It was at first contemplated to take up the entire block, but the commercial crisis of 1837 interfered with the plan, and in 1841 the whole structure, which was even more stately than the present one, was accidentally destroyed by fire. The present edifice soon rose from the ashes of its predecessor, and under the skilful management of the well known James Hewlett, the St. Louis Hotel became the most celebrated house of entertainment in the South. One of the most pleasing reminiscences of the palmy days of the St. Louis Hotel is the annual series of " Bals de Société," or Subscription Balls, that took place every Winter in its magnificent ball room, then fronting St. Louis street. Nowhere else could a better idea of Creole beauty and elegance be realized so well as in those delightful gatherings, in which none but the representatives of the most refined circles of our city were invited to participate, although a generous welcome was also given to visitors from the other States, and to distinguished foreigners. Some of the most pleasing recollections of former days are identified with the gay scenes of which the St. Louis ball room was the theatre between twenty and thirty years ago. Particularly vivid among the survivors of that period is the remembrance of a magnificent " Bal Traveste" given in the Winter of 1842—'43, and above all of the splendid entertainment gotten up the same Winter in honor of Henry Clay's visit, by his New Orleans friends and admirers. The subscription price was one hundred dollars, and there were two hundred subscribers—the ball and supper costing twenty thousand dollars, an enormous sum for that period. Over six hundred ladies and gentlemen sat down to a feast of regal magnificence in the spacious dining hall of the hotel where the famed orchestra of the French Opera discoursed sweet music, and a most felicitous and graceful tribute was paid by the " old man eloquent " to the ladies of New Orleans, " beautiful, accomplished, and patriotic." This was the only time the Demosthenes of the American Senate ever spoke in public in Louisiana. Mr. Mioton, the present able and popular manager of the St. Louis Hotel, has just inaugurated a series of subscription balls, under the patronage and direction of the ladies of this city, which, judging from the success with which the first one was attended cannot fail to revive the pristine terpsichorean glories of the house. The Convention of 1843 to form a new State Constitution, and which embraced almost every man of talent and influence in Louisiana, such as John R. Grymes, Soulé, Roselius, Mazureau, Roman, Downs, Conrad, Marigny, Brent, Eustis, and other distinguished men was held in the old St. Louis ball room.

The St. Louis Exchange, under the management of the universally popular Alvarez, and his genial assistant, Santini, was, for a long period, the favorite resort of all the leading politicians, planters, and merchants of the city and State. From twelve o'clock, meridian, till three in the afternoon the splendid rotunda was occupied by the auctioneers, whose resounding appeals in the English, French, and Spanish languages made it a modern counterpart of the Tower of Babel. This rotunda, with its beautiful frescoes (now used as a restaurant, attached to the hotel,) served the purposes of a Chamber of Commerce, Board of Brokers, and Cotton Exchange. Meetings for political, charitable, or patriotic purposes were frequently held there, as were also the Conventions of the Old Whig and Democratic parties.

More than a year ago, Mr. E. F. Mioton, aided by a few other enterprising and public spirited citizens of the Second and Third Districts of New Orleans, succeeded, after much labor and trouble, in organizing a joint stock company for the purpose of purchasing, renovating, and re-opening of the St. Louis Hotel on a scale consummate with the present wants of the community. Of the association Mr. Mioton was made the President, and Messrs. A. Chaffraix, Charles Cavaroc, M. Puig, Charles Lafitte, and A. Rochereau, were elected directors. The remodelling and improvements of the building were made by Mr. A. Suari, architect, under the supervision of Mr. L. U. Pilié, late City Surveyor. A magnificent verandah, new in pattern, elegant and unique in design and consisting of a series of arches supported by a colonade of Corinthian pilasters ornamented in the highest style of art now surrounds the building on every side, with the exception of the grand entrance on St. Louis street, where the fine marble perystile is covered with a terrace or balcony, above which a superb illuminated clock has been placed. The entire verandah is lighted at night by a great number of beautifully ornamented lamps, and the whole structure now presents a most beautiful and imposing appearance. Elaborate as the improvement has been in the outside, equal labor and skill has been brought into requisition inside to render the hotel one of the most commodious and comfortable in the world. There are 237 sleeping rooms besides the offices, parlors, drawing and reception rooms, dining halls and parlor suits on the first floor, affording ample accommodation for five or six hundred guests. The papering, carpeting, and furnishing of these rooms and parlors is of the best modern style and pattern. The hotel is kept on the European and American style combined, there being a restaurant where meals are furnished to the guests of the hotel as well as to the public generally, at fixed prices, and a magnificent dining room for the exclusive use of the boarders who prefer to live in the American style. This dining room, which is brilliantly lighted by eleven splendid chandeliers, is also used as a ball room in connection with the spacious and magnificently furnished parlor on Royal street. The hotel kitchen is 40 feet by 60, is probably the largest and best appointed in America; the ranges, cooking, and roasting apparatus, ovens, etc., being of the best and most modern patterns, and the arrangements for ventilation, and the removal of every offensive smell being altogether perfect. On the Chartres street side are numerous parlors, reception rooms, a nursery, dining room, a gentlemen's reading and smoking room, with a small bar and lunch room attached. There are thirty bath rooms in the main building, and it is contemplated to convert the old Bank building, on Toulouse street, into a Roman *aquarium*, or swimming bath.

The hotel is divided by iron sliding doors into three distinct fire-proof compartments, and the iron tanks on the top of the building contain 30,000 gallons of water, so that in case of a fire, the means of putting it out would be instantaneous. One of the most pleasing features of the St. Louis is the fact that owing to the great space covered by the building, the bed rooms are either on the first or second floor, thereby saving the fatigue and inconvenience of going up a great many flights of steps.

The hotel is now under the management of Mr. E. F. Mioton, the energetic President of the St. Louis Hotel Association, aided by able and courteous assistants; and since he took charge of the house it has become a favorite and fashionable resort for the planters and their families, as well as for that already large and daily enlarging class of persons who prefer the comfort of a well kept hotel to the trouble and expense of house-keeping.

REV. WILLIAM T. LEACOCK, D. D

THIS eminent divine was born at Barbadoes, A. D. 1800, commencing life with the day dawn of the present eventful century. He went to England in the year 1818, and received his education at the renowned University of Oxford. He was ordained in 1824, by the Right Rev. Dr. Howley, Lord Bishop of London. In 1825, he went to Jamaica, where, for the space of ten years, he labored as a popular and successful clergyman of the Protestant Episcopal Church. In 1835, in consequence of the state of his health, which had been effected by the unpropitious climate of the West Indies, he removed to the state of Kentucky in this country, and subsequently became Rector of Williamsport Church in Tennessee, in the diocese of the Reverend Bishop Otey. He thence removed to Natchez, Missisippi, and, in 1852, became Rector of Christ Church in this city, over which, in that capacity, he has since presided. He is assisted by the very estimable, Rev. Campbell Fair.

The family of Dr. Leacok, consists of his wife and three children, two daughters and one son, Rev. William Leacok, of the Diocese of California. He lost one son by yellow fever.

The Rector of Christ Church is physically of large proportions and unusual height, reaching probably to fully six feet. His aspect is venerable and commanding, his manner fatherly, affectionate and guileless, his style logical, terse and suggestive. His sermons contain a happy combination of the intellectual and the pathetic, appealing, in adequate proportions, both to the head and to the heart. He is a man of large experience and shining virtues, whose influence is deeply felt in the circles in which he moves. As a clergyman, his principles are both liberal and evangelical.

ANNUNCIATION SQUARE.—This is situated on the four squares bounded by Annunciation, Orange, Chippewa and Race streets. It is protected by a substantial iron fence, and has been otherwise partially improved. St. Michael's Church (Catholic) overlooks the square from the east. Fronting upon the square are several elegant residences surrounded by choice varied and luxuriant shrubbery. At at cost of a few thousand dollars the square itself might be converted into a miniature forest if desirable.

MORESQUE BUILDING,

Corner of Camp and Poydras Streets, New Orleans.

MAYOR JOHN T. MONROE.

THE capture of New Orleans in April 1862, by Farragut and Butler, brought the name of Mayor Monroe before the country, and the people, both of the United States and the then Confederate States. Nor was this prominency confined to the belligerent powers. It pervaded all British journalism, and even made its way into Parliament. Mayor Monroe's refusal to surrender the city, although under the guns of the Federal fleet, his subsequent refusal to lower the Confederate flag floating from the City Hall after the enemy was in full possession, resulted in his deposition from the Mayoralty (when near the expiration of his term) by General Butler, and his incarceration in Fort St. Philip, and afterward in Fort Pickens. Refusing to take the new oath of allegiance imposed by the Federal Government he endured, until the summer of the succeeding year, all the rigors of prison life, consigned at one time to solitary confinement and doomed at another time to wear ball and chain. Regarded at last as one possessed of a spirit untameable by any process known to jailors, he was released on condition that he should immediately go within the lines of the Confederates. This he did, going first to Mobile and from thence to Richmond, where he was received by Mr. Davis with unusual cordiality and finally fixing his residence in the former city, where he was when captured by General Canby. Returning to New Orleans after the close of the war, Mr. Monroe was arrested and kept under surveillance for several months. No reason was assigned by the Federal Provost Marshal for his extraordinary proceeding. Shortly after the reorganization of Louisiana under what is commonly known as the Johnsonian policy, Mr. Monroe was re-elected Mayor of New Orleans. He took his seat in March 1866, and was deposed by General Sheridan under the Reconstruction Act of Congress, the pretext being complicity in the celebrated riot of the 30th of July of the same year.

The second deposition of Mayor Monroe took place in March 1867, after much *ex parte* testimony taken against him at the instance of General Sheridan. This act was followed by the appointment of a Radical Mayor, and an Americo-African Common Council, the genesis of the humiliation and misrule which has since befallen Louisiana. In April following, Mr. Monroe visited Washington and and was kindly and sympathetically received by President Johnson and Attorney-General Stanbury. Nor did he leave the capital until his restoration was clearly intimated and the removal of General Sheridan made certain. There can be no doubt that the deposed Mayor would again have been seated but for the second batch of Reconstruction measures which overthrew the opinion of the Attorney-General defining and limiting the provisions of the first Act.

John T. Monroe, a blood relation of President Monroe, was born in Dinwiddie County, Va., and was carried to Missouri when quite young. His father, Daniel Monroe, represented at an early period the latter State in Congress. Coming to New Orleans before his majority, the future Mayor learned the business of a stevedore, which made him familiar with the men who form and control what is popularly known as the "masses." Over the working classes he possessed a power which was not broken at any time. He was of the people and with the people, and they looked upon him as their representative and champion. They made him an Assistant-Alderman and the lower Board seated him as its President. He served as Assistant-Recorder and was twice elected Mayor. His mind was eminently practical, his integrity unquestionable, and his proverbial fearlessness, the sequence of the practicability and integrity of character. He knew men so well that it was difficult to impose upon him, and he discharged his duties with a conscientiousness which made him disregard clamor or criticism. Mr. Monroe removed to Savannah, Ga., and died there in February 1871, when about forty-eight years of age. The rigors of imprisonment and of official vicissitudes told severely upon him. He looked old while yet in his prime of years. He had ascended the Masonic ladder to its topmost round, and hence was buried in Savannah with distinguished Masonic honors. The year succeeding his death his remains were brought to New Orleans, where they were deposited in the family tomb by his Masonic brethren beside the body of his favorite son. When this son lay upon his deathbed, the father was a prisoner in Fort St. Philip. General Butler sent word that if the Mayor would take the new oath of allegiance he might come to the city and see his dying child. The offer was promptly and firmly declined, and father and son never met in life. Of such Roman mettle was the subject of this brief biographical sketch.

DOUGLAS SQUARE.—This is bounded by Washington, St. George, Second and Freret streets, and was inclosed in 1864. It is notable for an irregular and luxuriant growth of indigenous and tropical trees, shrubs, flowers and grasses, and for its numerous birds of bright plumage.

ALFRED HENNEN, ESQ.

This truly estimable and learned jurist, who has recently passed off the stage of life, at the advanced age of eighty-five years, is deserving of the highest tribute of respect that can be paid to his memory by the living generation. His name is a connecting link between two centuries, of which the eighteenth claimed his boyhood, and the nineteenth his youth, manhood and old age. Around both epochs his numerous virtues have shed an undying charm. Louisiana will never forget one who was a denizen of her territory five years before she became a State, and who, through all the mutations of politics, was an unflinching advocate of her sovereignty and her honor. New Orleans, with whose interests his own were identified, from the time it was a village till it became the great and flourishing city it now is, where he acquired solid and enduring fame and an ample fortune, in his capacity of an able advocate and a learned counsellor, has equal cause to remember the venerable sage, who, by his wisdom, energy and lofty example, has shed lustre on her history.

This distinguished personage was born in Maryland, A. D. 1786. He pursued his collegiate course of studies at Yale College, where he graduated with distinction in the twentieth year of his age. Piously trained by excellent parents, the religious element of his nature was fully developed at the early age of sixteen years, when he became, by open profession, a member of the Presbyterian Church, to which he was ardently attached and of which he was a Ruling Elder for nearly half a century, having been raised to that influential position by regular ordination in the year 1828, according to the forms of that church. "His name," says Dr. Palmer, in the eloquent discourse of that distinguished divine, delivered on the occasion of his death, "heads the list of the original twenty-four, who, in the month of November, 1823, were organized, according to our ecclesiastical canons, into the First Presbyterian Church of New Orleans."

In his youth he was inclined to adopt the ministry as his profession, but subsequently shrank from its lofty responsibilities, and, on his graduation, determined on the study of the law, which he commenced and prosecuted for a couple of years at New Haven under the direction of Judge Chauncey.

To the noble profession he adopted he was always passionately devoted, especially to the Department of the Civil Law, emphatically the law of Louisiana, the fountain, as well as crown, of the Common Law of England. It would be invidious to compare him with other great civil law lawyers with whom the New Orleans bar has been graced from time immemorial. Suffice it to say, that he was among the most prominent of its expounders and among the most successful of its practitioners. To great legal lore he added a taste for literature, which served to elevate the tone of his profession. He had no mean acquaintance with the Oriental tongues, especially the Hebrew. To great dignity of manners he added a grace and affability that were truly attractive; and to very decided views a spirit of conciliation, that secured respect and prompted affection. Few individuals who have adorned the municipal, ecclesiastical, and legal annals of the Cresent City, have passed off the stage with a nobler and more stainless record than the late venerable Alfred Hennen.

For about twenty years he was an able and efficient Director of the old Bank of Louisiana, during its days of prosperity.

JAMES FRERET, ESQ.

James Freret, Esq., descended, on the mother's side, from the Chevalier D'Arensbourg, of Swedish stock, and, on the paternal, from the Frerets, of England, belongs to one of the oldest families in Louisiana. His maternal ancestor, the Chevalier D'Arensbourg, emigrated to this country in the early part of the last century, and was invested with the government of the "German coast." According to Gayarré, about 1721, three years after the foundation of the city. His name appears in the roster of the garrison, as Captain, in 1740.

His paternal grandfather, James Freret, emigrated from England some time previous to 1790. It is worthy of mention that he started the first cotton press ever used in this city, (a hand-power press,) on Royal street, in the first decade of the present century. His example was shortly after followed by his brother-in-law, V. Rillieux, who also had a hydraulic hide press.

The subject of this notice was born at New Orleans, April 26, 1838. He commenced his studies as an architect, the profession for which he had an early predilection, in 1856, at the age of eighteen years, remaining for a few months in the sash factory of Mr. George Purves, then in the office of that architect, who was then erecting the First Presbyterian Church. One year afterwards, he entered the office of W. A. Freret, Esq., one of our most highly esteemed architects, where he remained till the month of June, 1860, during which he drew the plans for the Touro Alms House, unfortunately consumed by fire before the edifice was completed; the celebrated Moresque Building, corner of Camp and Poydras streets, three iron buildings on Canal street, &c., &c.

In June, 1860, Mr. Freret visited Europe with a view to perfect himself in his profession, where, for the space of thirteen months, he prosecuted with diligence the course of studies prescribed by *L'Ecole des Beaux Arts.* He then travelled in Italy, Switzerland, France and England, sketching notable buildings.

In August, 1862, he returned home through the blockade at Charleston, S. C., entered the engineer service of the Confederate States Army; was disabled at Port Hudson; began business again after the war; completed the Moresque Buildings; designed the first Fair buildings, the Louisiana Savings Bank; the four-story building at the corner of Common and Magazine streets, the new office (shortly to be built) for the New Orleans Gas Light Company; also, the new Spring Hill College, the extension of the Convent of Visitation, and the new front of the Cathedral, at Mobile, Ala.

Mr. Freret is highly esteemed by his brother architects, and his fellow citizens, for his skill in his profession, and for the honor and integrity which have always marked his career in life.

INTERIOR VIEW OF B. T. WALSHE'S

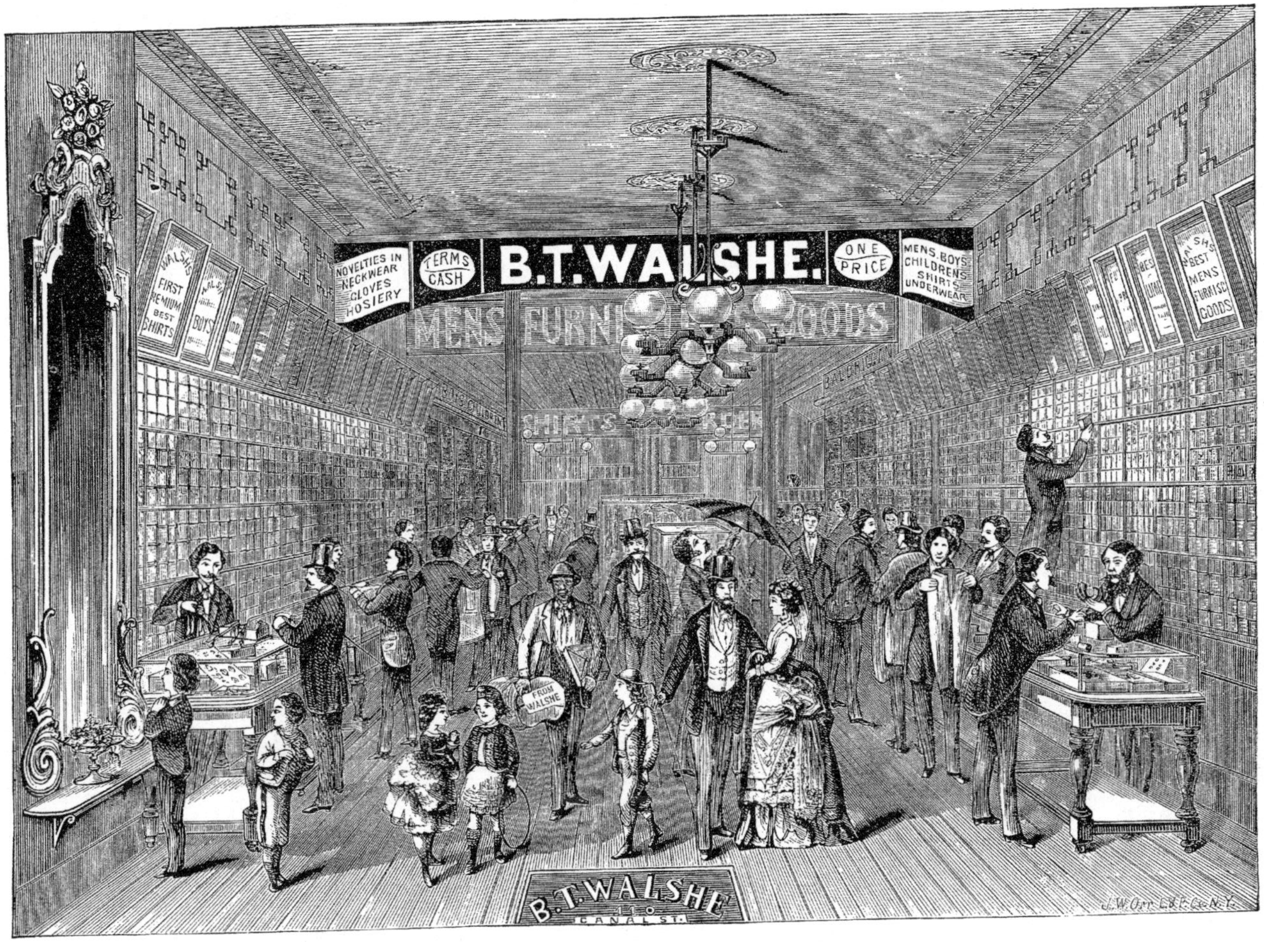

Well known Shirt, Mens' Furnishing Goods and Boy's and Childrens' Clothing Establishment,

NO. 110 CANAL, NEAR ST. CHARLES STREET,

NEW ORLEANS.

THE KNIGHTS OF MOMUS.

THIS is a new organization, having made its initial appearance on New Year's eve, last.

When it became known towards the end of the year 1872 that another organization was in process of being formed, and that the night of December 31st would witness its first appearance, the curiosity which has always attended such affairs was at once aroused.

In a community where the spectacular appetite is so strong, and yet so epicurean, and where such gorgeous and elaborate efforts have already been successfully made, it was certainly no slight undertaking in the Knights of Momus to enter the arena, and promise an event worthy of addition to the memories of past pageants, and of comparison with those which are to follow.

Yet all this was confidently promised, and, as a consequence, New Orleans turned out in force, and the known route of he procession was, at an early hour, lined with expectant crowds.

Need we say to any true lover of traditions that no happier selection of a subject could have been made than that which distinguished this event? In that dim age which the masters of romance and poetry have peopled with grand figures, and to the beautifying of which the immortal Scott has lent his genius, are to be found the most majestic subjects of pageantry. The stark old days of Richard Cœur de Leon and of Godfrey de Bouillon, and the countless other personages who animate our legends and our songs, make a rich field from which to cull the very fairest flowers of pageantry, and in this field our knights have roamed with unhindered feet, and culled a lavish wealth of beauties for our enjoyment.

The sireless deity of raillery, who, in the dim old days of mirth, make gods the victims of his ridicule, and but hardly spared the matchless Aphrodite, daughter of the Foam, descends through the generous shadows of the centuries with a kindlier spirit, with a touch whose magic only beautifies, and the grim old motto " *dum vivimus vivamus*" takes a better significance through the interpretation which his latter-day votaries have given it, and gives us the right to welcome his advent with every sincerity and pleasure.

THE PROCESSION

Was of the gorgeous fashion peculiar to our festival pageants, and represented the principle figures in the grand tableau of the " Talisman."

First came

MOMUS—1873.

On either side of him ride his attendant knights, and so, with all appropriate surroundings, the pageant of Momus comes into full view, hemmed in by the rippling sea of eager faces, and shimmering in the radiance of a thousand lights.

Then came the English Division headed by Devereux, the Lord of Giesland, bearing the standard of the Plantagenets. The Hermit of Engaddi and the Earl of Salisbury follow.

Here is Blondel, the faithful troubadour, whom Richard loved, and who, in the dark days when wily John turned traitor, and friends forgot their benefactor, showed that the devotion of the minstrel was a sweeter thing than the fearful friendship of the warrior. He holds the lyre which many a time soothed the fierce king's wayward heart, and near him sit Iloise and Calistra, Maids of Honor to the Queen.

Upon the throne reclines

RICHARD CŒUR DE LEON

beneath a royal conopy, on which blaze the leopards and the crown of England. He never greatly loved the glory of the court, nor the sweet flavors of ladies' hands and eyes, and yet the

ROYAL BERENGARIA

who stands beside him now, was the loveliest woman of her day. The mellow sun of fair Navarre never shown on a statelier crest, nor did the love-lights ever dwell in deeper blue eyes.

The French Division was composed of a cavalcade of knights and priests, noblemen and pages, in the midst of whom sits upon a dais

PHILIP OF FRANCE,

robed and crowned, magnificently attired in armor silken draped. On his right stands that famous prelate,

THE ARCHBISHOP OF TYRE,

who in the days of handsome men, was noted for his splendid beauty, and in a court where magnificence of dress was the rule, was distinguished by his matchless costume.

On the left the

EARL OF CHAMPAIGNE,

dressed in a complete armor.

The Austrian Division was headed by

LEOPOLD OF AUSTRIA,

who, tall and strong and handsome, fair of face and hair, and brave as the lion whose effigy he wore, was yet an awkward and ungainly man, save when the *gaudium certaminis* infused his stalwarth frame and the fierce light of battle in his eye burnt only on his prey.

Conrad of Montserrat stood by him here as he used to stand in war, and about him were the knights and pages and jesters of the Ducal household.

Here comes the gigantic Wallenrode, of Hungary, with vizor drawn and the lion of his house upon his shield.

And then, after the splendid christian cortege had passed, it was only fitting that our friends of Momus should give us some pictures of the nation against whom the crusade was directed. So it happened that the fourth platform was preceded by horsemen of another race from those who had gone before. Here were the representatives of that nation which, in those wild days, had drawn its myriads around the shrines and sepulchres of Palestine and made the hot sands of Syria sodden with the Christian's blood.

Trooping down the streets of an American city, between rows of stately modern edifices came the dusky battalions of the Saracen-representatives of the race who could not be conquered, and who fought with blind savagery for things they only prized because the hated Christian desired it. Their swarthy faces and the barbaric splendor of their trappings recalled the vanished centuries and re-peopled the arid plains of Acre with Paynim and Crusader.

To complete the picture here cames the dais of

SALADIN.

About his royal couch the semi-savage creatures of his household group themselves, the hideous deformed eunuch and voluptuous Odalisque making vivid contrasts with their matchless ugliness and beauty. And in the midst was Saladin himself, the splendid barbarian who divided with the lion-hearted king the crowns of history; in whom Richard owned his equal in prowess as in generosity.

It was a splendid pageant, and did fair justice to the gorgeous epoch from which its figures have been drawn. Our brethren of Momus have cast no flimsy gage into the lists, and they of Comus and Revelers must take heed of their laurels, for henceforth they will be more hardly won.

The usual Ball and Tableau at the Opera House completed the affair, and as a matter of course, the tableaux were a reproduction of the procession.

TABLEAU FIRST.
The Defiance.

King Richard trampling the Austrian Banner,
at St. George's Mount.

———:o:———

TABLEAU SECOND.
The Council of the Crusade.

Richard's Reconciliation with Leopold.

———:o:———

TABLEAU THIRD.
The Victory.

Defeat of Conrade of Montserrat by Sir Kenneth
of the Leopard.

———:o:———

TABLEAU FOURTH.
Honoring the Victor.

" High place to thee in the Royal Court;
High place in battle line :
Where Beauty sees the brave resort,
The honored meed be thine."

———:o:———

FINAL.
A Happy New Year.

The Ball was such as they have always been on similar occasions. The most select company of our city was present, and ignorance as to who were the hosts had no power to lessen the enjoyment.

Thus terminated their first entertainment. The ability and energy displayed by our Knights of Momus, their happy choice of subject, and the felicitous manner in which their ideal has been realized, gave us good reason to welcome them in the present and anticipate their reappearance in the future with every expectation of pleasure.

HON. JOHN McENERY.

THIS distinguished civilian and gallant soldier was born at Petersburg, Va., March 31st, 1833, the fifth child of Col. Henry O'Neal McEnery, a native of Limerick, Ireland. In early life his father emigrated from the old country to Virginia, where he formed a matrimonial alliance with Miss Caroline H. Douglas of James River, by whom he had eight children, only three of whom survive. He had a decided genius for military affairs, which soon developed itself in the chivalrous state of his adoption, where he held the rank of Colonel of the Virginia militia for several years. In the year 1835, he removed to Monroe, Louisiana, became a planter, and, at the same time, filled, with reputation to himself and advantage to the community, the position of Register of the Land Office for a period of eight years. His superior knowledge of land matters contributed largely to the settlement of North Louisiana by emigrants from other states, enabling him to furnish them with valuable information as to localities for settlement, &c. A practical man of business, distinguished for his intellectual activity and knowledge of public affairs, few individuals, in that section of the state, exerted a more wide-spread influence than Colonel McEnery.

His son, the subject of this notice, received the rudiments of his education in the common schools of Monroe. In 1848, at the age of fifteen, he went to Hanover College, South Hanover, Indiana, and remained there till the fall of the year 1849. He then returned home, wrote for his father in the Land Office, and continued to prosecute his studies, and extend his information by assiduous and varied reading. In 1850, he entered the law office of Isaiah Garrett, Esq., of Monroe, La., a prominent and able lawyer read with him till 1852, attended the lectures of the Law University of New Orleans during the sessions of 1852 and 1853, and graduated in due course. He immediately went into partnership with his brother, (J. D. McEnery, Esq., recently deceased) at Monroe, where he obtained a very fair practice in a short time.

In 1856, Governor McEnery married Miss Mary Thomson, daughter of the late Dr. Thomson, of Caldwell Parish, by whom he has had eight children, four of whom only are living. In 1857, he was, without solicitation, appointed Register of the Land Office at Monroe, La., a lucrative and responsible office, (previously held by his father,) and in the administration of which he gave general satisfaction. He occupied this important post till the year 1861, when Mr Buchanan removed him from it in consequence of his advocacy of Mr. Douglas's election to the Presidency, and his championship, on the stump, throughout the state, of the claims of that distinguished senator to the first office in the gift of the people. Had Mr. Douglas succeeded in that canvass, little doubt is now entertained by any party that the secession of the Southern states would never have taken place, or, if it had, that the war, inaugurated by Mr. Lincoln, would never have occurred.

He now resumed the practice of the law, but, immediately upon the commencement of the war, waged by the Federal executive, by and with the consent of his cabinet, and

LOUISIANA JOCKEY CLUB.

THIS Club was chartered May 15 1871, for the purpose of establishing a race course for the advancement of racing and improving the breed of horses, and the erection or the purchase and equipment of a club house for the social enjoyment of the members. The stock of the Association is $100,000 in 1,000 shares, which may be increased to $250-000. By agreement with the Fair Grounds Association, the club has the exclusive use of the race course, for four weeks before and during each Spring and Fall meeting, for the period of twenty years, upon condition of erecting upon the grounds a Public Stand of the value of $20,000, which is to revert to the Association at the end of the period of the lease, without incumbrance. The Club has, accordingly erected the splendid stand noticed in the account of the Fair Grounds.

The Club bought the property adjoining the Fair Grounds, which was once the residence of Mr. Luling, for $60,000. It has a front of 500 feet on Esplanade street, by 2,500 deep, with an area of nearly 30 acres, situated on the Metaire Ridge and exempt from overflow. The grounds are well arranged and thickly set with choice shrubbery. The family mansion has been converted into a club house. It is a substantial and handsome three story brick edifice, with a gallery extending entirely around it at each story.

The lofty, wide and airy rooms are employed for Reception and Dining rooms, Parlors, Library, Reading and Billiard rooms, Restaurants, &c, all very handsomely and liberally furnished, most of the oaken furniture being elaborately carved by hand. The other buildings on the premises are in keeping with the main house, consisting of bowling alley, Pavillion, Kitchen and ten costly stables, with ample room for a hundred horses.

The flower garden contains an extensive collection of indigenuous and exotic plants and flowers comprising all the rarer varieties to be found in the temperate zone or within the tropics. The adjoining Park has a great number of forest trees of every kind, and orchards of orange, peach and apple trees, and grapevines, all bearing plentifully in their proper seasons. In the centre of the Park is a lake of pure fresh water surrounding a small island.

Thus the members of the club have the benefits of a princely private establishment, adorned with all that taste or comfort could suggest or wealth command. This they obtained already prepared, and at a cost less by many thousands than its real value, which can be little if any short of $100,000. The club is under judicious, energetic and liberal administration, and its perfect prosperity and progress, give high hopes of its future career.

CATHEDRAL AND COURT HOUSES.

THE CATHEDRAL AND COURT HOUSES front on Jackson Square—which is bounded by St. Anne street on the North, St. Peter street on the South, Chartres street on the West, and the Levee, open to the river, on the East. The splendid rows of the Pontalba Buildings, with their lofty gables and broad verandahs, overlook the square from the upper and lower sides. A massive paling of iron, set in a foot-wall of granite, encloses one of the most interesting and peculiar of public squares, which is European in character, and reminds the foreigner of the gardens atttached to palaces in the old world. Flowers in great variety bloom here in the open air at all seasons, and there is no month in the year when the rose, the indigenuous and favorite flower of Louisiana, is not found here in profusion in all stages of development. The walks are bordered with orange trees, which show their golden wealth throughout the Autumn and Winter; the glassy green leaves of the magnolia reflect the sun back upon its vast snowy and green-like bowers; the clustering bananas hang in luxuriant bunches under their canopy of gigantic leaves; and birds of rich plumage and choice notes, unmolested by their familiar human companions, mingle their music with the voices of children, the tread of passengers, the panting of steamers, the rattle of cars and carriages, and the solemn echoes of the cathedral clock marking the hours of joy or care for young and old.

The most interesting and conspicuous object in the Square is the colossal equestrian statue of Andrew Jackson standing in the centre on ground slightly elevated, enclosed in an iron fence, and based on an enormous block of granite containing about thirty cubic yards. The statue represents the grim warrior in the full dress uniform of 1815, in the act of raising his military chapeau in salute, his ponderous sword hanging from his belt, his left hand griped firmly to the reins of his horse. The latter is represented in the act of rearing, and stands balanced upon his hind feet. It is a spirited copy from life, and so well has the artist succeeded in this minor part of his great study, that one almost looks to see the bronze counterfeit spring from his granite footing.

the military aid supplied by the governors of seven Northern states, he entered the Confederate army as captain of a company of infantry, was soon promoted to a majority, and, subsequently, to the grade of lieutenant-colonel, commanding the 4th Louisiana Battalion. He served, with gallantry and distinction, in the campaign of 1861, in West Virginia, in Kanawa, under General Floyd—was ordered to Richmond, and, in the winter of 1862, was sent with his battalion to Savannah, Ga.,—that place, as well as Charleston, S. C., being then threathened. In front of Savannah, he held the advanced posts. General Lee then commanded there. He has now in his possession a friendly note, (which he highly prizes) under the hand of that illustrious personage, complimenting him for his dispositions, entrenchments, &c.

In 1863, he was ordered to Charleston, and participated with his command in the celebrated battle of *Secessionville*, on James Island, January 16th, 1863. His battalion arrived at the fort in time to save the day, and, consequently, to save the City of Charleston. The Southern troops were driven out of the fort. The battalion under his command recovered it, and drove back the enemy, who were ten times their number. He was complimented in the General Orders, and the citizens of Charleston, always alive to feats of chivalry and bold daring, showered honors on him and his command.

Governor McEnery also figured in the battles of Jackson, Miss., of Chicamauga, of Dalton, Resaca, &c., &c., and was wounded twice, which disabled him for nearly a year.

At the conclusion of the war, he resumed the practice of the law, in which he was successful. In 1866, he was elected a member of the popular branch of the state legislature, and served till 1867, when he was disfranchised by the *soi disant* 14th Constitutional Amendment of the Reconstruction committee of the Federal Congress. He now devoted himself, with renewed and increased energy, to his chosen profession; and the law, in his case, as with many statesmen, proved for him the stepping-stone to political eminence. Probably his firm adherence to principle, and the gallantry he had so often displayed on the battle-fields of the Southern Confederacy, were in a still higher degree, elements of his popularity with the high-toned and true-hearted masses of his fellow citizens. Suffice it to say, that, in June, 1871, he was nominated, almost with acclamation, by the Democratic convention, and, in July, by the Democratic and Reform parties, and, in August, by the Democratic and Liberal party, for the office of governor of Louisiana, then reduced to the lowest stage of political degradation by Federal speculators and spendthrifts. The state, in consequence of the nearly universal apathy that prevailed among its friends after the war, and its total indifference to politics, had, without due reflection—without "looking before and after"—surrendered all its great interests, State and Federal, into the hands of a set of desperate sharpers and adventurers, y'clept "carpet-baggers," who flocked hither in large numbers, after the Southern cause was lost, in order to share the spoils of an ill-gotten victory; and who, by seizing on the reins of government, and using their power only to enrich themselves, have reduced this once opulent state and flourishing city to the very brink of bankruptcy and ruin. In the year 1871, the friends of civil liberty and state rights made a bold and united effort to throw off the incubus of this disgraceful and pernicious misgovernment. Governor McEnery advanced gallantly into the breach, as the trusted file-leader of the large party which advocated reform in state and municipal affairs, and the restoration of the original principles of the Federal constitution, and, with heavy odds against him, will, we trust, come off victor in the contest as he did in the famed battle of Secessionville, during the late war. Louisiana has again unfurled the state rights banner to the breeze, and other states, North as well as South, who were once independent, look to the result of her present political controversy with "the powers that be" with intense and trembling interest, knowing that their own fate will, in all probability, be involved in that of down-trodden Louisiana, if she does not, at an early date, extricate herself from the dangers which now threathen her very existence as an independent member of the Federal union.

Governor McEnery unites a naturally strong and vigorous intellect with great sweetness of temper and extraordinary firmness and singleness of purpose. He is a man of action, and, having once adopted a plan that meets the approval of his judgment, suffers nothing to divert him from its accomplishment, and is subject to none of those outside influences which have degraded the American character in this age of political corruption. A thorough conviction of his honesty, of his steadfast adherence to principle under all circumstances, of the transparency and simplicity of his character, and his lion-like courage, has made him, wherever he is known, a universal favorite. No individual, in the midst of times of high party excitement, was ever more remarkable for the equanimity of his temper, nor for the self-possession and cool deliberation with which he addresses himself to the discussion of subjects and the adoption of measures. The style of his proclamations and public speeches, is equally marked by strength and terseness, while it exhibits no vicious fondness for rhetorical ornament. He is certainly an impressive speaker. In social life, he is rather reticent than loquacious, and never obtrudes his opinions unasked.

Governor McEnery is a conservative politician, opposed to everything like proscription. He is a friend to immigration from all lands and all sections that can supply the state with good citizens, and is disposed to do equal justice to all parties and all classes of men among us.

THE ORLEANS COTTON PRESS.

This vast establishment fronts on the Mississippi, running back on Roufignac and New Levee streets. The ground occupied is six hundred and thirty-two by three hundred and eight feet; and is nearly covered by the buildings. The whole was built according to designs made by Charles F. Zimpel, begun in 1833, and completed in 1835, at a cost, including the site, of $753,558. The front on the river, although having no pretensions to architectural effect, is still, from its location and extent, quite impressive. This press can store twenty-five thousand bales of cotton; and compresses on an average, one hundred and fifty thousand bales per annum; but its capacity is much greater.

The statue was conceived and modeled by Clark Mills of Washington, and was cast under his supervision at Bladensburg. It weighs more than twenty thousand pounds, and cost to the city more than fifteen thousand dollars. Critics are not agreed as to the artistic merits of the figure of the heroic rider, whose costume is not claimed to be historically correct.

This monument was raised as a tribute of gratitude and honor by the descendants of those who were saved from insult, plunder and depredation by the hero of Chalmette, the best friend that New Orleans ever knew. Nearly fifty years afterwards, the basest, most cruel and most ignoble enemy of this city, regardless of the purport of the monument, caused to be engraved upon its pedestal a memorable, but wholly inappropriate sentiment of Jackson—"The Union—it must and shall be preserved."

The Square is a favorite playground, and upon any fair Sunday evening it is thronged with flocks of happy children of all nations, of various colors, speaking many languages, the French predominating. The curious student of Southern character, as he sits upon one of the iron benches, under the shade of an orange grove, will remark an utter absence of social distinctions and pretensions among these merry actors in the busy drama of fun and frolic, as well as their cordial and unvarying good nature, for which the native children of New Orleans are justly noted. The observer will be equally charmed with the musical voices and graceful movements of the little creole *demoiselles*, who exhibit choral and rythmic instincts as soon as they can talk or walk.

HISTORY OF CHRIST CHURCH.

At a meeting held 2d of January, 1805, composed of the Protestant citizens of New Orleans, at the residence of a lady (Madame Fourage,) with a view of taking preliminary steps to procure a Protestant clergyman, and to secure a lot of ground on which to erect a suitable building for the performance of Divine worship, a committee was appointed to procure subscriptions, etc.

Meetings were held on the 9th and 16th of June, following, at which a report was received from the committee appointed to obtain subscriptions. At the meeting of June 16th, it was determined to go into an election of a denomination of the clergyman, and the ballot resulted as follows: Episcopalian, 45 votes; Presbyterian, 7 votes; Methodist, 1 vote. Total, 53 votes.

At a meeting held 16th November, 1805, the Rev. Philander Chase was reported as having arrived, bringing letters of recommendation from the Right Rev. Bishop Moore, and the Rev. J. H. Hobart. At the meeting, an election of two wardens and thirteen vestrymen was made. A salary of two thousand dollars yearly was voted to the Rev. Mr. Chase.

At a meeting held April 2d, 1806, the rector was, by resolution, placed under the ecclesiastical government of the Bishop and convention of New York, until a Diocese should be organized in the Territory of Louisiana.

By the records it appears that Rev. Mr. Chase resigned and returned to New York in 1811.

At a meeting held June 17th, 1814, Rev. J. F. Hull was invited to officiate in Christ Church. Salary two thousand dollars from January 1st, 1815.

In May, 1815, a lot of ground was purchased on which to erect the church, and the church edifice was commenced, which appears to have been completed by the 7th of April 1816.

Rev. Mr. Hull, when he first commenced officiating in Christ Church was not an ordained minister of the Episcopal Church. It would seem that he took orders in the church in 1815, or easily as 1816.

In the year 1830, the building of a new church was determined on.

In December 1832, the office of Rector of Christ Church was declared vacant, but a stipend of twelve hundred dollars per annum was settled upon Mr. Hull during his life.

On the 2d of June, 1833, the wardens were authorized to arrange with the Rev. Mr. Barlow to perform the duties of rector for the time being—also, to procure a suitable person to fill the position of rector permanently.

It would appear that the Rev. Mr. Hull died about 10th of June, 1833, having been pastor of the church about nineteen years.

During the Winter of 1834, Bishop Brownell, of Connecticut, officiated in Christ Church.

At a meeting held 18th January, 1835, it was determined to build a new church at the corner of Bourbon and Canal streets, north side of Canal street. The style of architecture was precisely (in exterior) like the Jew's Synagoge, on Carondelet street, between Julia and St. Joseph streets.

Bishop Brownell again officiated during the Winters of 1836 and 1837.

Christ Church was consecrated by Bishop Brownell on the 26th of March, 1837.

On April 20th, 1838, Rev. Dr. Wheaton entered upon his duties as Rector of Christ Church.

May 13th, 1844, Dr. Wheaton resigned the Rectorship of Christ Church.

Rev. Mr. Ramsey was invited to perform pastoral duty in July, 1844.

In 1845, Dr. Francis L. Hawkes was invited to the rectorship. He arrived in New Orleans 7th January, 1845, and entered upon his duties.

In March, 1845, preliminary steps were taken for building the present church edifice, corner of Canal and Dauphine streets. In May, 1846, it was determined to go on with the work under a contract with Mr. James Galier to cost fifty thousand dollars.

In December, 1847, a beautiful Baptismal Fount was presented to the church by James Grimshaw, Esq.

April 13th, 1849, Rev. Dr. Hawkes tendered his resignation as rector, which was accepted. Arrangements were made with Dr. Camp to officiate in the church temporarily.

In September, 1849, the Rev. Dr. Neville was invited to the Rectorship of the Church, and, in November, 1849, he had entered upon duty. The Rev. Dr. Neville resigned the rectorship in April, 1852.

In June, 1852, the Rev. Dr. Leacock was invited to the rectorship, and entered upon his duties during the Fall of 1852. At present, (January, 1873,) he still fills the position very acceptably.

Christ Church is one of the most elegant church structures in New Orleans, and is frequented by very large numbers of intellectual, refined, and appreciative hearers.

HUGH McCLOSKEY, ESQ.

Since the publication of this work was begun the people of New Orleans have lost one of their noblest citizens, Hugh McCloskey, who died in his residence, on St. Charles Street, on the 28th January last, in the fifty-eighth year of his age.

Mr. McCloskey was a native of Dungiven, in the county Derry, Ireland, the same village in which the distinguished Irish patriot and exile, John Mitchell, was born. Mr. McCloskey's father was a shoemaker, who, in Dungiven and the country about, was universally known as "Honest George McCloskey," a title bestowed upon him, by his neighbors, because of a just, good and blameless life.

Hugh had a good English education, which was finished at the Royal College at Belfast. His father's means being insufficient to send him to that institution, while yet a stripling, he earned enough himself, by teaching in his native place, to accomplish that object, and, late in life, when he appeared as a public writer to expose and denounce the political wrongs the people of his city and State were suffering, his terse and effective compositions, betrayed the culture of his early years.

When but little over age his eyes turned to America, as the eyes of so many had before and so many have since, as the Mecca of the poor, the industrious and the enterprising. He landed in one of the northern cities, whence, failing to find employment, he wended his way to the South and arrived in New Orleans, on Christmas day, 1838. A stranger, without a friend or acquaintance, in his new home, his purse light, unable to find a situation for which his education fitted him, he was constrained to seek any employment that he could get, rather than incur debt. He was wont, when prosperous and influential, to refer back to this period of his life, with a pride, which was commendable. Although of a slender frame and a by no means vigorous constitution, he worked as a laborer, laying gas pipes, in the streets of the city, and, month after month he toiled, with blistered hands, rather than eat the bread of dependence.

After a while he fell into a small ready-made clothing business, on the Levee, but did not succeed. Then he became an employe of Mr. Stevenson, who kept a soda and meal establishment, at the corner of Exchange Alley and Custom House streets, noted for the purity and excellence of the beverages. To that business Mr. McCloskey succeeded, and, thenceforth, was invariably a prosperous man, never relinquishing the trafic in which fortune first favored him.

Modest and unobtrusive, it was not until the year the civil war closed that public attention was drawn to the merits of this valuable citizen. His manly bearing, during the war, in maintaining his opinions, as a supporter of the Confederate cause, and his generous benevolences to the unfortunate, during that distressing period, impressed his fellow citizens with a high respect for his character and attracted the affectionate regard of good people in every rank of society. Upon the re-organization of the State government that year, he was, by a large majority, elected a delegate to represent the Third Ward, in the House of Representatives of the General Assembly. That Legislature of 1865–66, was distinguished in the annals of Louisiana for the high order of its average ability, for the moral elevation by which its deliberations were guided, and by the dignity with which its proceedings were conducted. Take it, in every aspect, no law-making body superior to it, has ever been assembled in any part of the Union and its equal has been rarely seen. It is not a small compliment to say that in that assemblage, Hugh McCloskey exercised no inconsiderable influence. He was an active member of several important committees, and he showed that with the private excellences which made him so estimable, he had talents and aptitudes for political affairs, which rendered him a most useful public servant.

Now the calls upon him to give his attention to matters, more or less public in their nature, became frequent. He assisted in organizing a company, which is permanently established, to secure, by importation, a constant and sufficient supply of ice for the city, and was one of the first directors. At a critical time with the Canal and Claiborne streets Railroad Company, he was chosen a director, and was largely instrumental in saving the corporation from bankruptcy and ruin. He was among those who initiated the project of the Hibernia Bank, a very successful institution, of which he became a Director and Vice-President. The last useful scheme of this sort, in which he was a pioneer, was the Hibernia Insurance Company, of which he was the first President. His services, in every one of these associations, were gratuitous. He sought none of these distinctions in business life, nor did he accept them as a money monger, for, personally, he adhered to the law of the middle ages, which forbade the lending of money on interest. Nor could he be prevailed upon, whatever the temptation of gain, to connect himself with any of those legislative schemes and monopolies, which have so multiplied since the General Assembly of 1865 and 1866, for public plunder, although repeatedly solicited and urged to

NATIONAL THEATRE,

Corner of Baronne and Perdido Streets, New Orleans.

do so. He would touch nothing that was adverse to the interests of the people.

So much in regard to him as a business man, a legislator, and a projector. We now come to his personal characteristics. He led no campaign, he made no notable speech, he wrote no book, he discovered no new principle in science or in art, nevertheless he is worthy of high eulogium, for he was one of the most exemplary and valuable citizens we have ever known, possessing moral traits which are very rarely found united in any one man.

He accumulated a handsome fortune, in a calling commonly thought belittling, which he had the sterling sense to stick to after he became affluent. Engaged in trade, during the greater part of his manhood, and successful in it, he was never known to utter an untruth or practice a deception. Profoundedly and practically religious few knew it, since the dawn of day was his favorite hour for attending mass, the hour when the lowly and the unostentatious, in the Catholic church, usually attend divine service. He was never known to turn away the distressed or the unfortunate with an empty hand or a cold look. In his own poverty and hardships he did not forget the duties of charity. As he prospered he became generous, and as he grew affluent his benevolences were munificent. The severe struggles of his youth did not harden his heart, nor did his advanced years bring with them avarice.

His life was sacrificed in the performance of a public duty, voluntarily undertaken, at the instance of his fellow citizens. As one of the great committee sent to Washington, to procure from the Federal authorities a redress of political grievances, he remained in the North several weeks, laboring in the cause with his accustomed zeal and enthusiasm, and in the extreme rigor of the weather, during December and January, he contracted a disorder, which resulted in his death, soon after his return. Whatever he was enlisted in, whether to advance the interests of a friend, to perfect some project of public utility, to aid a charity or to promote good government, his noble mind was absorbed in the matter until success attended his efforts, or until success was obviously impossible. And all this with the most perfect disinterestedness, entirely void of political ambition or design of pecuniary advantage.

No wonder that his funeral was a demonstration almost unequaled in its kind, in New Orleans. Hundreds of his good deeds that had been hidden, came to light when he was no more in this world. The beneficiaries and other inmates of most of the charitable institutions in the city, participated in the obituary ceremonies, and a great multitude surrounded his late dwelling, attesting, in every becoming way, the respect and veneration in which the memory of the good man and public-spirited citizen was held by all classes, by all nationalities, by all creeds.

ALGIERS is the great work-shop of New Orleans, for the building and repairing of vessels. It has its dry docks, and other facilities for the most extensive operations. In business times, it presents a scene of activity that is seldom observed in any other part of these regions, and reminds one of the bustling and enterprise of the North.

THE FORT ST. PHILIP CANAL.

THE Mississippi river has three principal outlet channels. They are the pass l'Outre, N.E., S.E., South, and West passes. Of these passes, the Southwest, is most used by vessels of the deepest draught, and this channel has been for two years past kept at a depth of 19½ feet by dredge boats, built and worked at the expense of the Federal Government. One vessel drawing 22 feet has entered the channel during the past season (1872). The navigation is, however, deemed precarious, and demands a more permanent outlet. Soundings at the north of the navigable channels of the Mississippi, run back for a century and a half, and show a bar of from one to two thousand feet across, with depth of from eleven to thirteen feet on the bars. It is the regimen of the river essential to regulations of its current. This depth on the bar continues though the bar itself advances annually into the gulf— the bar and outlet being over twelve miles lower down than it was a century and a half ago, while the water above the bar is from 60 to 50 feet deep. With this perpetual tendency to obstruction, the suspension of the dredge for even a short period allows the channel to fill, so that there has been at one time a number of ships loaded with cotton and other merchandize stranded on these bars, to the great detriment of the city and shipping interest. These obstacles long since led to scientific discussions, as to the best means of relieving navigation. Experiments and estimates were made for concentrating the current by wing draws, and caissons, lightering vessels, by canals and dredging. About the year 1832, Mr. Buisson, a civil engineer in the service of Louisiana, proposed to flank the passes by a ship canal leading from the river at a point about 27 miles above its mouth, into a deep water harbor in the gulf, a distance of seven miles. The studies and estimates of Mr. Buisson were adopted by the Legislature of Louisiana and Congress was asked to cause an examination of the practicability and cost of the work. A report was made by the topographical Bureau in 1837, expressing his opinion that the canal could be built at a cost of $10,000,000. This was an impossible sum at that period, and the prospect fell. About the year 1858-59, Mr. Montagu, a civil engineer, renewed the proposals, fortified by a re-survey and estimates, and proposed the formation of a joint stock company to construct the work and conduct the trade, for a compensation to be collected from tolls on the commercial tonnage. This plan, favored by the Insurances offices and the Chamber of Commerce, was prevented by the war, but was renewed in an application to Congress for a survey, and appropriations to construct the canal as a national ship canal, open in free passage to all vessels. The aggregate endowments mentioned were confirmed by a survey, made by the Federal government in 1871-72, with an estimate of cost at $6,000,000. A bill has been printed for this object at the present session of Congress. All the Western cities favor this work, and the National Board of Trade at its New York session, unanimously recommeded its construction.

The permanent deepening of this outlet i as assumed

new importance, since the immense increase in the production of corn in the States so distant from the sea board. From the western verge of this cereal area, it now costs from fifty-five to sixty cents to place a bushel in the markets of Europe. This leaves so small a balance to the credit of the cultivator, that corn is not worth in Iowa more than twenty cents a bushel. In some cases it has come to be used in the place of fuel. This cost of transportation is increased by the great quantity of corn sent forward just before and just after the ice blockade, it being greatly in excess of the motion stock. At this point the Mississippi affords a way always open and always adequate to this immense commerce. It thus becomes a regulator of freight on other waters. Now, as the rate of freight is always proportioned to the capacity of the ocean-vessel, it is plain that with a depth of thirty-five feet, proposed to be given by the outlet, canal vessels of such burden could be put in the bulk grain trade, as would carry from 90 to 100,000 bushels. The reduction of freight resulting from this enlargement of vehicles, would extend the cereal productions much further west, and add a value to the material domain much greater than the cost of the work, necessary to effect it.

As a general proposition ; the outlet to 850,000 square miles, occupied by little less that 20,000,000 of people, and producing $2,000,000 annually, should be opened without regard to cost. It may be remarked that it is the only obstruction to the principal navigable waters of the Mississippi, which remain to be provided for by the government. The Des Moines Rapids, the Falls of the Ohio and the Muscle Shoals of the Tennessee, being all completed or under construction.

The outlet canal completed, this noble river will be thrown open to commerce from its mouth, along its whole navigable courses, free from natural obstacles or tolls. In this result the whole Union is interested.

NAPOLEON JOSEPH PERCHÉ,

ARCH-BISHOP OF NEW ORLEANS.

ONE of the most disastrous draw-backs of biographical literature is, that the individuals, who most prominently figure in it, are precisely those who have done the least good or the most harm to humanity. The world's real benefactors have a peculiar secret in which they wrap themselves, just as if they were ashamed even of the treachery of effects in betraying them as their cause. To this modest but truly illustrious class of men, the subject of this sketch belongs, and, in our succinct notice of his beneficent career, we here assert, unhesitatingly, that he occupies in it no secondary place.

Napoleon Joseph Perché was born of pious and honorable parents at Angers, the capitol of the Department of Macrie-et-Soire, formerly called Anjou, on the 10th of January, in the year 1805. He was educated in the same city and in colleges of the vicinity; was ordained priest in 1829; came to the United States in 1837; was four years in the Missions of Kentucky; came to New Orleans in January, 1842 ; remained as Chaplain to the Nuns of the Ursuline Convent till 1870, when he was appointed Coadjutor to Arch-bishop Odin *cum jure succesionis;* was consecrated on the 1st of May of the same year ; at the death of Arch-bishop Odin, succeeded him, and received the *pallium* from his Holines, Pius IX, in December, 1870.

Arch-bishop Perché is largely identified with the history of religion and religious institutions, both in France and America, during the present century. The developments of his powerful intellect appeared at a very early period of his life. He read the French language with facility at four years of age. At fifteen, he studied philosophy with enthusiasm. At eighteen, he was promoted to a Professorship of it, and wore its mantle with grace and dignity. He is equally distinguished as a divine and a canonist. In the former august character, he writes French unction with intellectual vigor in the highest degree.

We do not know for which to admire this great man most, the paternity which he displays in the sphere of parochial and diocesan duty, or the championship he exhibits in the conduct of theological arguments. The characteristic traits of his genius are amenity and force.

He thinks for a whole community, and his affections are as diffusive as his thoughts. He understands the power exerted, in a free country, by the press as well as the pulpit, and has, for many years, been at the head of a catholic press in this city (which is his own property), and which has exerted immense influence. He is a charming conversationalist, always bringing wit, learning, good humor, knowledge of the world, and a varied experience to embellish his discourse.

Though a Frenchman by nativity, he is thoroughly identified with America and her institutions, and has attained to the mastery of a pure, forcible and elegant English style, which places him in the front rank of American writers. Nothing can be more finished than the Archiepiscopal letters which he, from time to time, communicates, when the condition of the Church requires it, to the numerous parishes in his diocese, and which, by all liberal and discriminating men outside of the Catholic church, as well as within its circles, are nearly equally admired, not only for their literary execution, but for the genial and apostolic tone which pervades them.

In looking through the annals of this time-honored Church for representative men, we find that there is one individual whom Arch-bishop Perché strongly resembles—we allude to Leo Tenth, who, to the manner and refinement of a polished gentleman, added the impressive carriage of a dignified ecclesiastic, equally cognizant of the affairs of the world and of the Church. We believe his Grace is on terms of excellent understanding with Pius Ninth, the Catholic Head of Christendom, whom he visited at Rome during his recent troubles, and that there is no dignitary of the Church, in the United States, in whom his Holiness places more entire confidence for upholding its integrity, maintaining its unsullied honor, and securing its triumphs over its enemies, than Arch-bishop Perché.

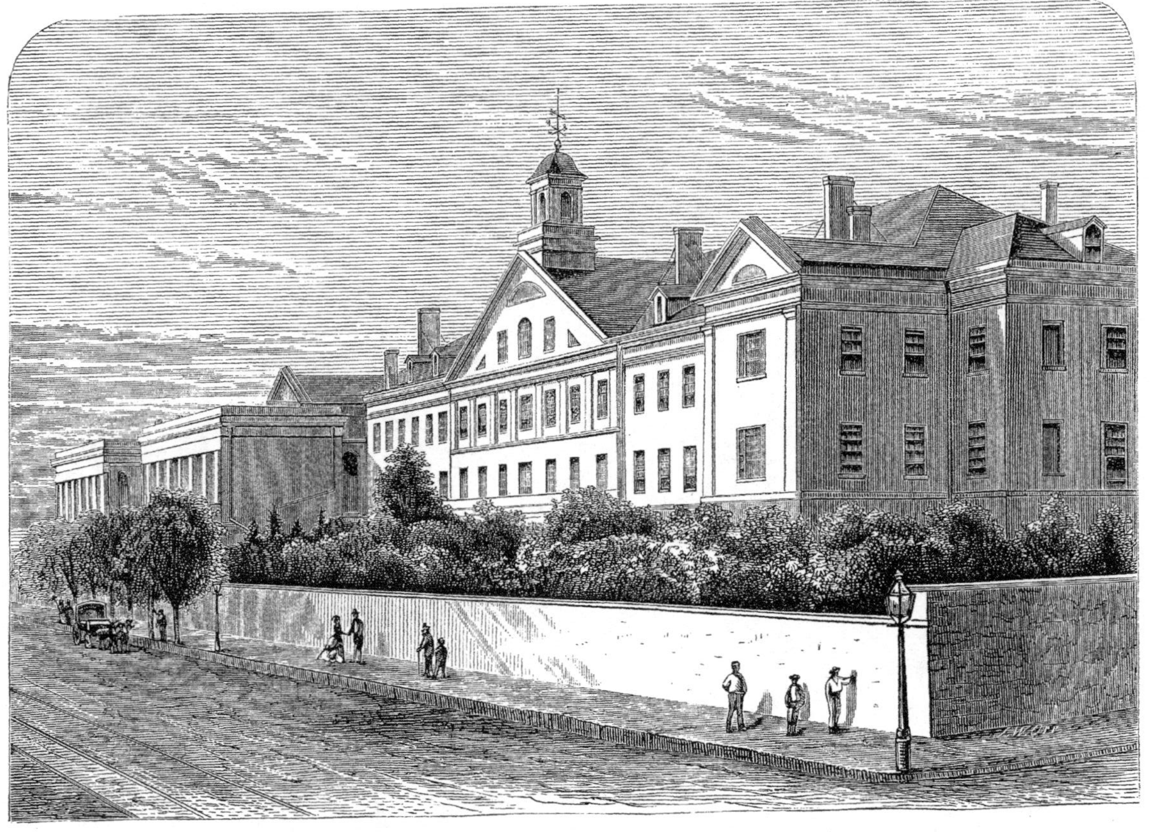

CHARITY HOSPITAL.

COLONEL ISAAC G. SEYMOUR.

In no other city in the United States, perhaps we might say in no other city in the world, have there been so many journalist soldiers as in New Orleans. Peter K. Wagner, so long editor of the Louisiana "Courier," and the recognized champion of the Democratic party of the State, was a lieutenant in the army with which Jackson defended New Orleans. John C. Larue of the "Delta," subsequently of the "Crescent," who was, in his day, among the ablest as an editor, as a jurist, and as a politician, served as a volunteer in the ranks of General Taylor's army, on the Rio Grande. General William Walker, the celebrated filibustero, who made his name famous, as a desperate fighter in Nicaragua, was a colleague of Larue on the "Crescent." Alexander Hays, the most capable practical newspaper man we have ever had in New Orleans, who was one of the founders of the "Delta," and one of those who established the "Crescent," sought dangerous adventures, during the Mexican war, as an amateur, under his friends, Captains Fairchild and Kerr, typos from New Orleans, who held commissions in the Louisiana cavalry. George Wilkins Kendall of the "Picayune," was one of the Texan band who undertook the main expedition, for the invasion of Mexico, the misfortunes of which are the themes of a melancholy history written by him, and, during the Mexican war with the United States, while corresponding with his paper, he was on the staff of General Worth, sharing the dangers and hardships of that enterprising and gallant officer. F. A. Lumsden, the associate of Kendall on the "Picayune," was, during the early period of that war, attached to the Texas Rangers, and was with them when they rendered themselves famous in the attack upon Monterey. In the civil war we had, in the Confederate army, J. O. Nixon, proprietor of the "Crescent," as Lieutenant-Colonel of the First Louisiana Cavalry; Israel Gibons, an attaché of the "Crescent," who served as a private, in the Nineteenth Louisiana, until physical disabilities incapacitated him for service in the line, and he was appointed quarter-master, with the rank of major; Lieutenant Wright of the "Bee," an officer of the Thirtieth Louisiana, killed in battle; Joseph Hanlon, of the "True Delta," who from captain rose to the command of the Sixth Louisiana, three of its colonels having been killed instantly, upon different battle-fields; Daniel Scully of the "Delta," and "True Delta," who, as correspondent of the "Picayune," saw service on the staff of General Joe Lane, the "Marion of the Mexican war," and, in the late war, was senior line officer of the Second Louisiana Batallion of Heavy Artillery; and Major William J. Seymour, son of the subject of this notice, and associate editor of the "Bulletin," who was Aid-de-Camp to General Duncan, during his defence of Fort Jackson, against Farragut's fleet, and, subsequently, until the close of the war, was on duty, as chief of staff, with the indomitable brigade of Louisianians, commanded by General Henry T. Hays.

Isaac G. Seymour, of whom we are writing, as one of those who dropped the pen, and buckled on the sabre or shouldered the musket, at the call of duty, was a man whose life and services deserve more than a passing notice. His family was a branch of that Connecticut stock of Seymours who have been so eminent for virtues and for talents, and, as publicists, have been so conspicuous for the courage and force with which they have maintained and constantly adhered to the great principles of constitutional liberty. He was born in Savannah, Georgia, in October, 1804. He graduated, creditably, at Yale College, and, soon after, established himself, as an advocate, at Macon, Ga. His practice gave early promise of an ample income, but he found the profession distasteful and abandoned it for journalism, when he became editor of the Macon "Messenger," which, while he was connected with it, was regarded as the organ of the whig party of the State. Civic honors came upon him too. For several successive terms, embracing a period of six years, he was chosen mayor, by his fellow citizens of Macon.

His advent, as a soldier, was made in the war with the Seminole Indians in Florida, in 1836, when he raised a company of Georgia Volunteers. He was favorably noticed by General Clinch and by General Scott, under both of whom, successively, he served. General Scott, particularly, seems to have been impressed with the martial aptitude and conduct of the captain, for the General repeatedly offered his influence to procure a commission for him in the regular army, which was declined because of the inertia and monotony of military life in time of peace. The Mexican war, however, which commenced in May, 1846, brought him to the "tented field" again. He organized a battallion of infantry in his native State, and was selected for its colonel. Shortly after the capture of Vera Cruz he reported for duty to his former commander-in-chief, General Scott. Cerro Gordo fought and won, La Hoya abandoned, Puebla fell, and a few months after our forces made their way into the City of Mexico. General Scott showed his appreciation of Colonel Seymour's ability, judgment and courage, by confiding to him the command of the town and castle of Perote, one of the most important posts on the line of communication from the capital to the American base at the Gulf. In command of that post he remained until the close of the war, in the summer of 1848, when he returned to Georgia, where his battallion was mustered out of service, and again he returned to private life.

In the autumn of that year he removed to New Orleans, to make it his permanent residence, and immediately purchased the "Bulletin" newspaper from Mr. William L. Hodge. Under Mr. Hodge the "Bulletin" had been a zealous propagandist of those extreme measures which were forced upon the whig party, by Northern and Eastern cupidity, and which compelled the abandonment of the National organization of that party by so many Southerners. Colonel Seymour brought the paper back to what it had been, under the control of William Carey Jones, son-in-law of Thomas H. Benton, and the immediate predecessor of Mr. Hodge. Thus Colonel Seymour made it the acceptable representative of the ideas and interests of the agricultural, as well as the mercantile communities of the State, and speedily it became a journal respected by, and popular with, all classes.

Associated all his life with a party tinged more or less,

according to place and occasion, with ideas antagonistic to the sovereignty of the States; circumspect in all things and especially in politics, and slow, therefore, to venture upon experiments, in public affairs, it can well be imagined that he thought long and thought deeply upon the election of a sectional man to the presidency, and upon all those issues which resulted in our civil war. His judgment was that the election of Mr. Lincoln left no honorable recourse to his native South but secession, and, if invaded, resistance. That judgment formed, thenceforth, with pen and with sword he maintained the cause of the Confederate States.

In 1861, when hostilities began, he was nearly fifty-seven years of age. He had reached a time of life when most men long for retirement and ease, but with him as with the illustrious Lee, duty was paramount. His reputation as a soldier induced the line officers of the Sixth Louisiana Regiment of Infantry to tender to him, unanimously, the command of the battallion, and it was instantly accepted. With his regiment, he was at the first battle of Manassas, and, during the retreat of General Joe Johnston upon Richmond, to him was assigned the honor of commanding the rear guard. He was with the heroic Jackson throughout that splendid campaign, in the Valley of Virginia, against Banks, Fremont, Shields and Milroy. He was engaged in the attacks upon McClelland's right, before Richmond, on the 26th and 27th June, 1862, and was instantly killed, on the last mentioned day, at the battle of Gaines Mill being the 2d days fight in the battles before Richmond—having been pierced by two minnie balls.

The reader will readily infer the esteem in which this admirable representative of Southern character was held. With professional talents as a journalist he had discreetness and a remarkably sound judgment. He was not more remarkable for these qualities than for the firmness and vigor with which he guarded the columns of his paper against wrong, or misrepresentation, and against every unseemliness that might give offence to the most fastiduous of well-bred people. As a soldier he was loved by his rank and file, as well as by his subordinate officers.

His latest command, composed of men of invincible bravery, demanded a high standard of courage in their leader. They regarded him as up to that standard, and loved and respected him accordingly. When not in active service, abounding animal spirits often made them mischievous and sometimes disorderly, but he never failed to enforce strict discipline when the good of the service demanded it. And that discipline was submitted to, without complaint. He demonstrated that volunteers, though prone to turbulence, as they often are, may be made equal to the best of soldiers when they see in their commander an officer without partialities, who never allows his men to be imposed upon, and who follows the advice of Luttrell of Arran to his son: "When perils are to be encountered never say go, always say come."

In no case was the conduct of General Butler more offensive to the people of New Orleans than when he suppressed the publication of the "Bulletin," confiscated the materials of the office, and turned them over to a pair of adventurers who had followed him. The paper was, at the time, conducted by Maj. Wm. J. Seymour, a pardoned prisoner awaiting exchange, and Mr. J. C. Dinnies, the commercial editor.

Both these gentlemen, Mr. Dinnies well advanced in years, were sent to Fort Jackson, where the latter was subjected to severe treatment for many months, and where the former remained a close prisoner until he was exchanged. It is imputed to General Butler, and not without reasonable grounds for belief, that his object was to secure to his followers to whom he gave the "Bulletin" office, the profits of a contract which the paper had as city printer.

Subjoined is an extract from an editorial notice of the death of Colonel Seymour, in the "Bulletin," written by Mr. Dinnies, which extract was quoted by General Butler, as justifying his proceedings. It simply did justice to the character and the fame of Isaac G. Seymour, and we reproduce it to aid us in illustrating the nobility of his nature:

"Others who have done their duty to their country as nobly, disinterestedly and bravely, were impelled by the ardour of youth and the stimulus of ambition, as well as by the dictates of patriotism. But with him, who had outlived the fires of youth, and was superior to mere aspirations for fame, the motive that carried him to the field was simply DUTY. It was DUTY that led him to accept the command of his regiment. It was DUTY that governed him in camp, in giving his men those lessons in the soldiers' science, which fitted them to fulfill the various requirements of the service with intelligence and efficiency. It was DUTY that kept him at his post, under all discouragements. It was DUTY that inspired him in his intrepid charge at Port Republic. It was DUTY that placed him in the front of danger at the battle of the Chickahominy; and, in fine, it was on the altar of DUTY that he offered up his life."

CARROLTON, a distance of six miles by the railroad, is an exceedingly pleasant resort. The line, for nearly a third of the way, passes through the suburbs of the city, and is dotted on either side with beautiful residences—the remainder passes through pleasant pastures, and delightful wood-lands. The road, like the country, is perfectly level shelled and kept in the finest condition. At the end of the route is situated the village; which is principally composed of tastefully built cottages, constructed in every variety of architecture that suited the individual fancy of the owner. Opposite the railroad depot, is one of the handsomest and most extensive public gardens, that is to be found in the vicinity of New Orleans. Here the genial and warm hearted Daniel Hickok presides with that ease and air of hospitality that have made him so popular and so widely known. He delights in showing the rare flours of his beautiful garden to the many strangers who visit him—and it is always his aim to please those who resort to the Carrolton Gardens for recreation and amusement.

At the commencement of the holydays, the city begins to put on a gay aspect. Visitors from all parts of the habitable globe, come here, either on business or pleasure. A general round of balls, masquerades, soirées and parties begin, and are continued without intermission during the season. Theatres and operas with their *stars* and *prima donnas*, circuses and menageries, bell-ringers and serenaders, are in full success.

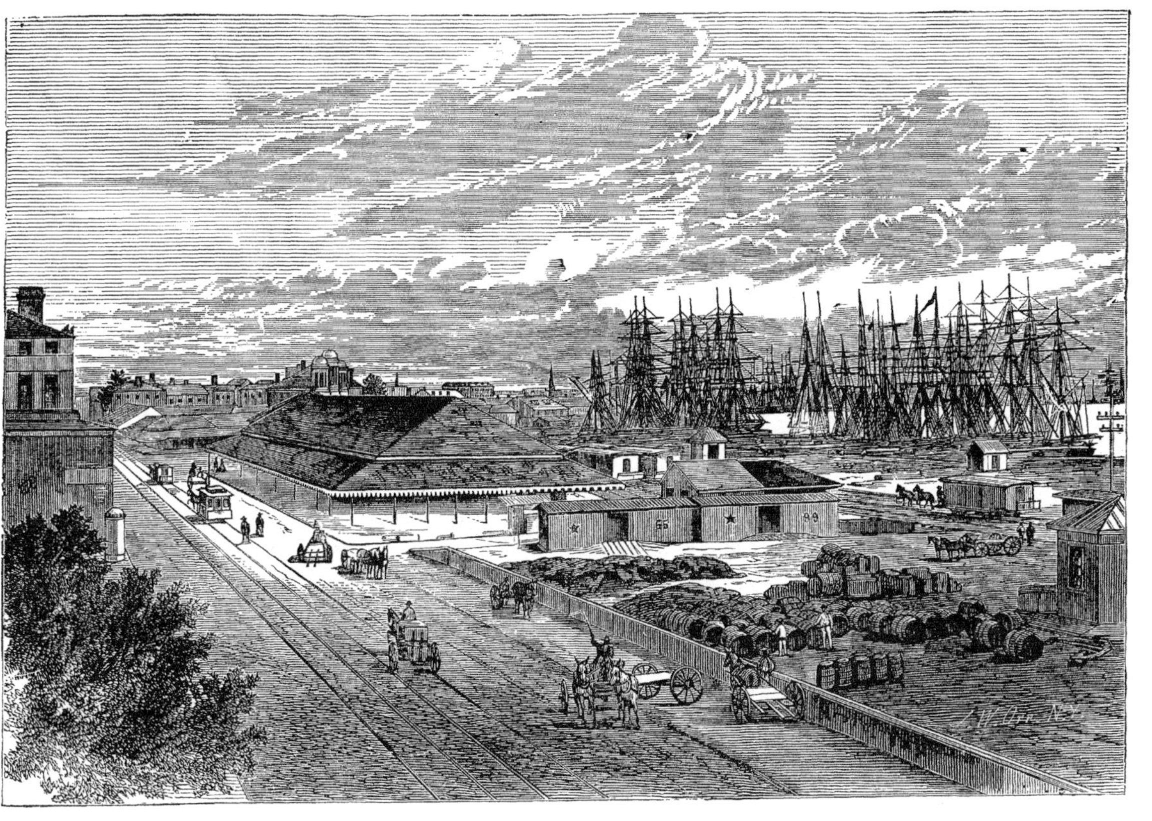

FRENCH MARKET AND SHIPPING.

JOHN DAVIDSON, ESQ.

JOHN DAVIDSON, the subject of this memoir, was the eldest son of James Davidson, of Dundee, Scotland, at which place John was born, on the 13th of December, 1816. His father emigrated to this country, in the year 1818, and settled at Monticello, in the State of New York. After an unsatisfactory trial of farming, he determined to embark in the slate business, in the city of New York; and for that purpose, made his home anew in that wonderful centre of industry, wealth and enterprise. It was there, amid the excitements and energy of the most rapidly developing emporium of the world, that the childhood and youth of our subject was passed. It was there, under those influences, that his character, which was afterward so distinguished by earnestness, energy, and practical judgment, was formed.

He received a good grammar-school education, and, at an early age, became connected with his father in business. It was not long before his intelligence, strict reliability and indefatigable industry made him complete master of that business, and placed upon his young shoulders the responsibility of its management.

At the age of twenty-two years, when most young men are commencing life, he left New York, and came to our sister city, Mobile, a complete business man. Mr. John Lyall, whose death has been so recently recorded, and who was so universally respected in this community, was then actively engaged here in the importation of slates. He was an intimate and old friend of the Davidson family, and had formed for young Davidson a strong friendship, which, as it was founded on respect for his real sterling merit, lasted through his entire life.

Mr. Davidson visited this city soon after he reached Mobile, and, in fulfilment of a promise made years before, called to see Mr. Lyall, and laid before him the plans and purposes of his opening career in the sunny South. The result was the immediate formation of a partnership between them, and thus commenced the history of a commercial firm whose standing and credit has never been surpassed in this busy mart of commerce. None of our old merchants will need an introduction to the firm of Lyall & Davidson. The story of their success and rapid growth in wealth, is inter-woven with the commercial history of the State. They were engaged, from 1839, when the partnership was formed, in the importation of slates from the quarries of Wales, and supplied, to a large extent, the whole southern market, and, indeed, the whole country bordering upon the Mississippi river, until 1850, when John Lyall retired from the firm with handsome capital, which he embarked in sugar planting on Bayou Lafourche. He was succeeded by James C. Davidson, a younger, and only, brother of John Davidson, and the style of the firm was then changed to J. & J. C. Davidson. From 1850 to the commencement of the war in 1861, the career of the new firm was one of unparalleled success in that line of business—yielding immense profits and rapidly enriching both partners. Their importations amounted to over two-thirds of the entire importations to the United States.

This business was conducted and developed by their good judgment and clear business sense. By well-directed movements and combinations, coupled with perfect mercantile reliability, they succeeded in bringing to New Orleans almost the entire control of this most valuable trade; thereby not only enriching themselves, and adding largely to the prosperity of the state, but at the same time setting an example, in the imitation of which by our people the material prosperity of Louisiana may yet be greatly enhanced.

The practical character of Mr. Davidson led him to make the safest investments of his capital, and, when the recent war commenced, it found him the owner of an immense amount of real property in and around New Orleans. He also had a large planting interest in the adjoining parish of St. Bernard. He suffered severely from the war. His property was taken possession of by the federal forces and large assessments laid upon him by the commanding officers of the Union army on account of his known sympathies with the confederate cause. He lost a large negro property, and was compelled to abandon his business during the occupancy of the city by the federal forces; but, such was the good sense displayed by the investment of his means, that, at the close of the war, he was still a man of large wealth.

So soon as he could make his arrangements to recommence business, his brother having retired, he formed a partnership with his nephew, Col. James D. Hill, a gallant and highly distinguished young officer of the confederate army, and the business of the firm was resumed under the style of J. Davidson & Hill. On the third day of January, 1872, his life, which had been a singularly useful and happy one, was brought to a sudden close by one of the most shocking calamities that ever startled this community. He was driving, in his buggy, upon the streets of New Orleans in the forenoon of the day, when he was most unexpectedly overtaken by a dummy-engine, drawing freight cars through the city, and, in attempting to escape from the perilous situation in which he was placed, jumped from the buggy and fell. He was struck by some portion of the train and so severely injured that death quickly ensued.

He was a member of the Presbyterian church. By a strange coincidence, one year from the day of his funeral services were conducted by Rev. Dr. Palmer, a like solemn duty was performed by the same divine over the remains of Mr. Lyall, who had died while visiting his old partner's homestead and family in the city of New Orleans.

His strongly marked qualities, both of head and heart, had made a deep impression upon the people of this city, and the news of his death was received everywhere, and by all classes, with unfeigned sorrow. The death of such a man at such a time, was indeed a public calamity. He not only possessed large means, but was full of enterprise, and, up to the last day of his life, was earnestly engaged in pushing forward every project which promised relief to our suffering people. There was nothing little or contracted about him. His views, upon all subjects of public interest, were broad and enlightened, and he never refused to embark his means freely in reasonable ventures for the restoration of our lost prosperity. He gave his time and counsel, without stint, upon all important public committees, and although for years before his death an invalid, yet he never failed to appear with punctuality at the council board of our various public institutions with which he was connected. But the supreme virtue of his character, to those who knew him best, was the loveliness of his private life. At home, he was the centre of happiness in a family circle of more than ordinary attractiveness. He was always cheerful, and, though by nature painfully sensitive, he bore all the vexations incident to such an active life as his was, with a quiet patience and gentleness which diffused around him a spirit of contentment. Such a man was John Davidson, and our country would be happier far if there were more such characters to delineate.

H. C. CASTELLANOS.

THIS eloquent criminal lawyer was born in New Orleans on the 12th of December, 1827.

He was educated at Georgetown College (D. C.,) and at St. Mary's, Baltimore, where he graduated with the degree of Bachelor of Arts, in 1847.

In 1848 he was admitted to the bar of New Orleans, and belonged to the first class of graduates in the University of Louisiana, his classmates being George Eustis, D. C. Labatt, Peniston and others.

At the age of twenty-four, he was elected delegate to the Constitutional Convention of 1852.

He was Editor of the "Louisiana Courier," of the "New Orleans Delta" and the founder of the "Attakapas Register."

As a criminal lawyer it is conceded that he has not a superior in the State.

JAMES McCONNELL.

THIS accomplished lawyer and worthy gentleman, is a native of Louisiana. He was educated at Washington College, Penn., and is a graduate of the Law Department of the University of Louisiana, having begun the practice of the law in this city in 1852.

During the late war he served as a Lieutenant in the First Regiment Louisiana Heavy Artillery.

He also served in the Legislatures of 1866 and '67.

Devoted entirely to the practice of his profession, in which he has attained success, he eschews politics and is quite popular.

Mr. McConnell is a vigorous speaker. The character of his argument is more of the solid and sensible than of the sensational and can be relied on usually. He has a noble heart located in the right place.

THE education of youth is of the utmost importance to a country—especially to one like this, that should be governed by the intelligence of its citizens. The portals to learning should be thrown wide open, equally to all—for upon knowledge is based the beautiful temple of liberty. Tear away this foundation and the fair edifice must fall.

GEN. ALBERT G. BLANCHARD.

GENERAL BLANCHARD. a distinguished Civil Engineer of this city, graduated at the West Point Military Academy, in the year 1829, in the 3d United States Infantry. In 1832, he married Miss Susan T. Thompson, from whom descended two children, a son, the Rev. H. Blanchard, of Lowell, and Mrs. S. B. Elder, one of our most popular Southern poets, known as "Hermine."

He married, a second time, Madamoiselle Herminie Benevist la Salle, from whom descended fifteen children, some of whom are living.

General Blanchard left the Army in 1840, and engaged in commerce until 1846, during which time he was an efficient Director of the Public Schools of New Orleans.

In 1846, he entered the Army as Captain of the 2nd Regiment of Louisiana Volunteers and went to Mexico. On the disbanding of General Smith's Brigade, he raised a company, called the Phœnix Company of Louisiana, served as the representative of Louisiana at the storming of Monterey and was complimented in General Orders, and subsequently at the siege of Vera Cruz, where the company was mustered out, their time having expired. He was then appointed Captain of Voltigeurs, which post he declined, but accepted that of Major of the 12th United States Infantry, in which capacity he served till the close of the war.

Returning to civil life, he became a teacher in the Public Schools, and was elected District Surveyor of Municipality No. 2, and Surveyor, on the death of G. T. Dunbar, Esq., who had previously occupied that position. He was subsequently, elected Deputy Surveyor of the City of New Orleans, and filled the place until the year 1854.

He is a Fellow, and was one of the original founders of the New Orleans Academy of Sciences.

From 1854, to 1861, he was Secretary and Manager of the Carrollton Railroad Company.

In 1861, on the occurrence of the late war was elected Colonel of the 1st Confederate Regiment from Louisiana, and went to Virginia. In September 1861, he was promoted to the office of Brigadier General, served through the war in Virginia, Louisiana, South Carolina and North Carolina, being in the last great battle of the war at Bentonsville, North Corolina.

Since then, he has been directly engaged in engineering on the Opelousas Railroad and the City Railroads, and in the City Surveyor's Department as Deputy Surveyor.

None of our citizens has led a life of more activity and usefulness than General Blanchard. Equally noted in military and civil life, he will never fail to be mentioned as one who has done the State good service, and his works and the shining record of them, are of a character to resist the corroding influence of Time. Of unobtrusive manners, his sole ambition seems to have been to perform all the duties devolving on him as the head of a family, a private citizen, and a member of the Commonwealth, constantly employed in the Public Service. His habits of temperance have preserved his health and strength, and, though past the prime of life, he is ready for any enterprise, and capable of any.

SHAKESPEARE CLUB.

THE claim of the Shakespeare Club for public favor is based on its usefulness to the community, and hence deserves the attention of all who have an interest in its welfare.

Members of the Louisiana Histrionics and Crescent Dramatic Associations are requested to meet on Sunday, March 17, 1867, at 10 o'clock, A.M., at No. 26 Commercial Place (up stairs), for the purpose of consolidating and forming a permanent organization. By request of   MANY FRIENDS.

The above notice, published by G. H. Braughn, Esq., who had at various times been President of the Association mentioned, brought together at the place indicated, Messrs. Braughn, T. O'Neil, Mark O'Rourke, F. G. Chamberlain and Peter Hart, and the Shakespeare Club was created.

Profiting by their ante-bellum experience, the club resolved that their theatrical entertainments should be private, and the expenses borne by its members. Meetings were frequently held thereafter, and to the rolls were, from time to time, added the names of some of the most prominent young men of this city.

On the 8th of May, 1867, the club, which then numbered about fifty members, adopted a constitution and by-laws, and was thoroughly organized by the election of the following officers:—Geo. H. Braughn, President; Dr. J. K. Walker, Vice-President; Walter H. Rogers, Secretary; J. G. Campbell, Treasurer; and T. O'Neil, Stage Manager; nearly every one of whom is still a member of the club, and Mr. Braughn has, from year to year, been re-elected as its President

On the 25th of May, 1867, the club gave its first performance at the National Theatre. The play was "The Wife; or, A Tale of Mantua."

On the 24th June following, the second entertainment was given, with "Love's Sacrifice" and to "Paris and Back for £5." On the 23d of the same month the third entertainment, "Money" and the "Loan of a Lover," occurred, and the fourth, "Hamlet," on the 19th August following. This last performance was given at the Opera House to unquestionably the largest and finest audience that ever filled that Theatre. On the 28th Augus, "The Wife" was repeated, for the relief of the yellow fever sufferers of New Iberia, which netted nearly two thousand dollars. On the 10th of September the last performance of the season was given at the old Varieties Theatre, producing "The Rivals." Since that time the club have produced "Lady of Lyons," "Marble Heart," "Dead Heart," "Richilieu" and "Ingomar."

During its existence the club has encountered many difficulties, which have been overcome by dint of intelligence and perseverance, its affairs have been carefully and judiciously administered, until it numbers two hundred members, comprising many of our most influential and respectable citizens, has a handsome sum in its treasury, and is in every way in a flourishing condition.

The social feature of the club, diminutive at first, has grown into splendid proportions; so much so that vaster quarters have been selected for the accommodation of its members. The Tilton Mansion, at the corner of Canal and Dryades streets, the new *locale* of the club, and represented by the above engraving, has been entirely repaired and refitted in a sumptuous style and provided with all the accessories of a modern club-house, which make it now the finest in New Orleans.

The club is literary, social and dramatic, the latter feature being participated in only voluntarily by the "active members," the others being termed "passive" members. It possesses a complete miscellaneous and dramatic library, keeps all the prominent magazines and periodicals, and presents many other pleasant club-life features.

HON. J. S. WHITAKER.

THIS prominent jurist and lawyer was born at New Bedford, Mass., March 8, 1817. While he was yet a child, his father, Rev. Jonathan Whitaker, removed with his family to South Carolina, where he united the duties of a clergyman with those of an instructor of youth. A graduate of old Harvard, a ripe scholar, and enthusiastically devoted to the training of the youthful mind, he presided over the education of his son and fitted him, at an early age, for entrance into college. Judge Whitaker, however became, without the advantages of a college course, the architect of his own fortunes, and few of our own citizens can claim to have been better educated.

He pursued the study of law at Charleston S. C., in the office of James L. Petigru Esq. one of the most eminent members of the legal profession in South Carolina, and having in 1838 successfully passed the ordeal of an examination before the Judges of the Supreme Court, received a license to practice in the Courts of law of that State as soon as he should attain the age of 21 years, which he had not then quite reached. In the mean time, and for a considerable period after he came of age, he devoted himself to the occupation of a teacher of youth, taking charge, in the first instance, of "the South Carolina School" at Charleston, a richly endowed institution and one of much note, but which was subsequently superceded by the establishment of the "Charleston High School," a classical institution, organized by the celebrated Mitchel King, a native of Scotland, on the plan of the Edinburgh High Schools. Mr. H. M. Burns, a fine scholar and teacher of long experience, was appointed to the first, and the subject of this notice to the second place in this school, being Latin teacher. He held this position, a highly respectable and important one in such a city as Charleston, for a couple of years.

Anxious now to enter on the profession of his choice, and the Charleston bar being crowded to repletion, with candidates for its honors and emoluments, he, in 1840, resigned his position and came to New Orleans, and became a student in the office of the late Alfred Hennen, one of the oldest and most esteemed of our Civil Law Lawyers.

Mr. John A. Shaw was then establishing the public school system in this city, and, among the first teachers of the new organization, we find the name of J. S. Whitaker enrolled. In the year 1845 he was invited to take the position of English Professor in Manderville College, in the Parish of St. Tammany, and subsequently became President of the Institution. Martin G. Penn, Judge of the 8th Judicial District Court, found him vegetating in this position, and advised him to return to the profession he had seemingly abandoned. On the 22nd of May, 1845, he was admitted, by the Supreme Court, to the practice of the law in this State, Judge Martin being then Chief-Justice.

With few clients and little to encourage him, he was by good fortune elected Attorney of the then Third Municipality of New Orleans, and, after a time, entered into partnership with the late John C. Larue, an able Judge, an acute advocate, well-versed in every branch of the law. This partnership continued for some years, and was a successful one. On the death of his partner, Mr. Whitaker remained for many months, laboring in his profession, single handed; but eventually took as a partner, a former student in his office, J. Q. A. Fellows, Esq., who remained with him till his appointment in 1862, to the position of Judge of the 2nd District Court of New Orleans. Mr. Whitaker was the first Judge appointed by the military Governor, General Shepley, after the occupation of the city. While filling this position, he received from the Governor, a commission as Associate Justice of the Supreme Court, but declined the honor, being unwilling to accept such position under Judge Peabody, then Judge of the U. S. Provisional Court, and holding at the same time, a commission as Chief Judge of the Supreme Court.

In 1864, Judge Whitaker resigned the office he held, and was subsequently appointed Chief Justice of the Supreme Court, by Governor Hahn, but was not confirmed by the Senate.

From the middle of April to July, 1864, he was employed by the then proprietors of the "Times" newspaper to write the leading editorials of that paper. The State Convention was then in session, and these articles had, it is said, a salutary influence upon their deliberations.

We find Judge Whittaker, about this time, again actively engaged in his profession, taking little part in politics, but known to be Republican in his principles, and a supporter of the administration.

The Degree of Master of Arts, recently conferred on him by Dartmouth College, (founded by his Grandfather) evinces the consideration which is entertained for his scholarship. We may add that no gentleman has taken a deeper interest in the cause of popular education than Judge Whitaker. He was, for several years, one of the most active as well as the most popular Directors of the Public Schools in this city.

During the late war, Judge W. was an outspoken Union man, though on all occasions affording such assistance as was in his power, to the citizens of his adopted state. He was, in 1864, solicited by many influential citizens, to become candidate for the office of Governor of the State, but declined.

It is said, by his friends, and intimates, that his talents are eminently judicial, and he is held in high repute as a counsellor and advocate. Many important cases are intrusted to his management. The habits of industry, which he acquired in youth, still adhere to him in mature life. He is very social and hospitable, and, when he entertains his friends, displays all the qualities of the urbane host, and abandon and buoyancy of the learned jurist enjoying a holiday.

His passion for gardening, flowers and trees, planted, trimmed and cultivated with his own hands, is evinced in the spacious and Eden-like grounds that encompass his fine residence on Carondalet street, the interior of which exhibits, in a rich and costly library, his taste for letters, and in all its domestic accompaniments and appointments his fondness for comfort and elegance.

PROFESSOR GREGORIO CURTO.

Professor Gregorio Curto is, we believe, the oldest teacher of musical composition and singing now living in New Orleans, where he arrived in 1830, and where he has resided uninterruptedly ever since. Mr. Curto is a native of Spain, but received his musical education in Paris, where he was admitted at a very early age into the celebrated Singing School of Choron, and had for his fellow pupils Dupuy, Monpou, Scudo, Marié, Rosina Stoltz, and a host of other musical and artistic celebrities. In one of his most charming *feuilletons*, published about fifteen years ago, Scudo relates a visit paid by Choron to the Minister of the Household (under whose superintendence all artistic and operatic matters were then placed), in company with three of his favorite pupils, his object being to give to that official a practical demonstratian of the efficiency and success of his method of teaching. The Duke De Larochefoucauld, the then Minister, was a man of taste and artistic accomplishments, and so well pleased was he with the performances of Choron's pupils that he forthwith granted a liberal appropriation for the support of the school. Young Curto was one of the scholars who figured upon the occasion, Dupuy and Scudo completing the trio. Before he had completed his fourteenth year, Mr. Curto received the appointment of organist of the Cathedral of Soissons, which he relinquished one year later to resume the study of musical composition with his old teacher, Choron, acting at the same time as "Maitre de Chapelle" at the church of the "Sorbonne," then a favorite place of worship for the Parisian *beau monde*. In 1830, Mr. Curto made a highly successful *debut* at the Italian Opera in Rossini's "Gazza Ladra," and shortly after was engaged as *primo basso cantante* by Mr. Davis, then manager of the Orleans Theatre. In this capacity Mr. Curto remained here for two seasons, performing with great success in "La Dame Blanche," "L'Italiana in Algieri," "Anna Bolina," the "Huguenots,' and also acting occasionally in Racine and Corneille's classical pieces, in connection with the distinguished *tragedienne*, Madame Closel, whom he subsequently married. In 1833, Mr. Curto left the stage to devote himself entirely to teaching and musical composition. Of his very great success as a teacher of vocal music no better proof is needed than the fact that two of his pupils, Mlle. Minnie Hauck and Mme. Fleury Urban have already achieved a European reputation, and that another one, Mme. Durand Hitchcock, bids fair to obtain very soon a no less enviable position as a lyrical artist. As a composer, Mr. Curto has written many operas and oratorios, several of which have been performed with great success in this country and in Europe. Among the latter may be cited "Le nouvel Ermite," three acts, performed in 1832; "Amour et Folie," three acts (1834); "Sardanapale," two acts and three tableaux (1838); "L'Héritiére," two acts; "La Mort de Jeanne D'Arc," two acts; "Le Lépreup," a dramatic scene, the words by Placide Canonge, and "La Mort d'Abel," oratorio, composed in 1866. We would exceed the limits of this sketch were we to enumerate Mr. Curto's church music, in which we find three Stabats, one intended exclusively for female voices, over fifty Masses, ten of which have been published, and more than two hundred *motets* solos, duetts, trios, quintettes, etc. His Stabat No. 1 was lately performed with great success at the church of St. Eustache in Paris, and his grand Mass of the Immaculate Conception, with full orchestra, was repeated three times in the same church. Professor Curto is the organist of St. Anne's Church, on St. Philip street, and still devotes a portion of his time to a select class of pupils who have prevailed upon him to give them the benefit of his invaluable services as a teacher of vocal music. As a master of this art, Mr. Curto occupies a very high rank in this country, and as far as this city is concerned, there is no one, with the single exception of Mr. Eugene Prévost, who can dispute the palm with him as a professor and composer.

NAPIER BARTLETT, ESQ.

Mr. Napier Bartlett for many years connected with the press of this city, and now the proprietor of the *Claiborne Advocate*, may be said to have inherited the editorial. His father, Myron Bartlett, established, fifty years ago, the Macon *Telegraph*, at the present day one of the most prosperous in Georgia, and his uncle, Cosam Emir Bartlett, is spoken of in "Sparks' Fifty Years' Recollections" as the leader of his party in that State.

Mr. Napier Bartlett graduated at Andover, Mass., in 1854, and had for his fellow students Edwin L. Jewell, Tobias Gibson, and many other Southern youth, who have since obtained honorable prëeminence. His first essay as an editor, was in connection with a paper then published by a literary society, and to the management of which he was elected by his classmates.

After being admitted to the bar in Georgia, and graduating in the Law Department of the University of Louisiana, Mr. Bartlett published the *Atlanta Confederacy*, two years before the name was applied to the seceded States, and was, for a short time, connected with the *Atlanta Intelligencer*.

Having fixed his abode in New Orleans a short time before the war, he contributed to the *Crescent* a number of stories and sketches, and upon the breaking out of hostilities a number of letters from camp, which were extensively copied. He went out as a volunteer in the Washington Artillery, a batallion made up of the best young men of the city, and remained with it until the close of the war. A reminiscence of army life in Virginia still remains in a story which was written on the straw of a soldier's tent, under the name of "Clarimonde."

Since the war Mr. Bartlett has been successively connected with the *Southern Star, Crescent, Bulletin,* and New Orleans *Times*. Besides the work before mentioned he is the author of stories of the "Crescent City," the entire edition of which was almost entirely sold the first week of its publication. A more extended work of a somewhat similar character will shortly appear from his pen.

PARISH PRISONS.

REV. THEODORE CLAPP.

Mr. Clapp was a native of the State of Massachusetts. He pursued his classical course at Yale College, and completed his theological studies at Andover Seminary—an institution preëminently evangelical. Such was the type of his own theology, when, at an early age, he came into the Valley of the Mississippi, and commenced his clerical career under the auspices of the Presbytery of that State. Thence, upon the death of the Rev. Dr. Larned, he came to this city, accepting a call from the First Presbyterian Church to become its pastor.

It appears that in the year 1830, or thereabouts, an entire revolution took place in the views he entertained on religious doctrines and discipline. These views assumed a particular shape, but no particular name. It was understood that he had become a liberal thinker on subjects of infinite scope and moment, and, had he not, at the same time, possessed a logical mind, enriched with varied learning, his renunciation of one creed and adoption of another, would have been a matter of comparatively little consequence to the public, or to the great and most respectable Presbyterian body politic, with which he was associated. It was because he was " a master in Israel"—a controlling mind in the church, that a radical change in his opinions produced a profound sensation, which culminated in a serious rupture of that church, and finally led to the exclusion of Mr. Clapp, and about one half of the congregation, composing his special friends and adherents, from its sacred precints and associations.

At the very moment when the excluded dissentients from orthodoxy were " without a local habitation and even a name," the late Judah Touro, Esq., an affluent and liberal minded Israelite, who had purchased, singularly enough at sheriff's sale, the church which then stood at the corner of St. Charles and Gravier streets, gave the use of it for an unlimited period, or, which was the same thing, for ninety-nine years, to Mr. Clapp and his congregation, for a permanent place of worship.

It was a large and commodious edifice ; and the popularity and eloquence of Mr. Clapp were such, that it was soon filled with hearers, even to overflowing. Mr. Clapp was in the habit of renting out the pews himself, and the proceeds, thence arising, constituted his income, which was not only adequate but large, even for a great and opulent city. He had the entire control of the society and its affairs, like a monarch in and over his own domain, and it was known, for a considerable time, only as Mr. Clapp's Society and Mr. Clapp's Church. Of the hundreds of individuals who reached New Orleans on Saturday evenings, coming from various States scattered along the banks of the great Father of Waters, the majority, on Sunday morning, would seek out and attend Mr. Clapp's church. Many would inquire, but nobody could inform them, with certainty, what were the doctrines inculcated in Clapp's church. The truth is, he dwelt more on precepts and facts than doctrines, and, when he handled the latter, (which he seldom did) wished to have the whole field of theological speculation open before him, in order to select " here a little

and there a little, line upon line and precept upon precept," as was suggested by his particular subject, the special occasion, or the character of his audience, composed, it might be, of men of all creeds, for the time being.

The divine authority of Revelation, of Jesus, man's relation to God, the universal Father, to the human race, individually and socially considered, to life with its fleeting hours, to eternity with its countless ages, to duty in its multiplied forms and extensive relations, these were his favorite themes, on which he dwelt with abounding power and touching fervor, now arresting attention by the force of his logic, anon opening the fountain of tears by his touching appeals, drawing his illustrations from the inspired volume, from the book of Nature, from human history, from the works of the poets and philosophers, and, more especially, from the course of events in his own day, of which he was an acute observer, and always an independent, outspoken critic.

In 1833, the legislature chartered Mr. Clapp's church, under the name of " the First Congregational Unitarian church in the city and parish of New Orleans." The corporation was to exist for twenty years, and had twenty corporators, viz: Samuel McCutchen ; Jacob Baldwin ; James McReynolds ; Richard Davidson ; Henry Babcock ; Peter Laidlaw ; John D. Bein ; Stephen Henderson ; Charles Lee ; P. S. Newton ; Wm. C. Bowers ; Henry Carleton ; James H. Leverich ; Wm. G. Hewes ; Isaac G. Preston ; Benj. Story ; Henry Lockett ; J. W. Lee ; Joshua Baldwin ; Abijah Fisk. The act was approved February 26, 1833.

In 1851, the church building which the society had occupied twenty years, through the liberality of Mr. Touro, without cost, was burned in the conflagration which, at the same time, reduced to ashes the stately and magnificent St. Charles hotel, which stood in close proximity to it. Mr. Touro again came forward and gave Mr. Clapp another church, which he had purchased, and which was originally built for the Baptists. It was also situated on St. Charles street, a little below the present edifice, and served for the temporary accommodation of the society till a larger and more commodious church could be built. Mr. Clapp officiated in it four or five years.

In 1853, the congregation resolved to build a church edifice, and to organize a society. A charter was drawn up for the purpose, but was never signed, adopted, or approved, by the District Attorney, or recorded as the law requires.

Samuel Bell, Henry D. Richardson, John D. Bien, H. S. Buckner, J. J. Day, A. M. Holbrook, Samuel Stewart, Isaac Bridge, John Leeds, Christian Roselius, Henry Renshaw, Lewis Soalles and Thomas A. Adams, were named as members in this inchoate charter. It purports to bear date March 17th, 1853. The title to the property bears date March 29th, 1853.

The church referred to, which is one of the most elegant edifices of the kind in the city, was finished in 1855. There was no dedication. Mr. Clapp was opposed to it. He would never consent to have the society called by the name of any particular denomination. As indicative of the nature of the organization, it was styled "Congregational or Independent." The edifice was called "the Church of the Messiah."

Mr. Clapp officiated only a few months in the new edifice, in consequence of failing health ; but his congregation, greatly attached to him, on his retiring and removing to Louisville, Kentucky, were in the habit of contributing liberally to his support up to the time of his death, which occurred in 1867. On that occasion, the Rev. Dr. Elliott, of St. Louis, Missouri, then on a visit here, delivered an appropriate and eloquent discourse, which was listened to with profound sensibility, by a thronged audience, composed of persons of all denominations, who hold the memory of the deceased in the highest esteem and ever veneration.

THE OPERA HOUSE.

Although its population was scarcely equal to fifty thousand inhabitants, during the greater part of that period, New Orleans enjoys the distinction of being the only city upon this continent which has supported, for more than half a century, a regular Opera Company.

There were two French theatres, one in St. Peter street, and another in St. Philip street, near Royal, which were in operation from 1808 to 1811. At the latter period, Mr. John Davis, a French *emigre* from St. Domingo, built the Orleans theatre, on the square, now partly occupied by the First District Court, near the Catholic Cathedral, and the adjoining court buildings, and engaged in Paris the first regular Opera Company that ever came into this country. The enterprise proved a highly successful one, and upon the death of Mr. John Davis the management of the theatre devolved upon his son, Mr. Piere Davis, (now residing in France), by whom it was most ably conducted during a period of over twenty-five years. It was under his management that those twin stars of the Parisian theatrical world, Mmes. Fanny Ellsler and Damoreau, were first seen and heard in this city, and that the great master-pieces of Rossini, Meyerbeer, Auber, Donizette, Herold, Mozart, Spontini and Mehul became familiar as household words to the highly-refined audiences which crowded the small but elegant and comfortable Opera house, which, after the one originally erected by Mr. John Davis, had been burnt down, was rebuilt the next year.

Mr. Varney, the author of " Le Chant des Girondiers." and afterwards leader of " Des Bouffes Parisiens," the late Eugene Prevost, (whose sketch may be found in another part of this book), Mr. John, and since the war Mons. E. Calabresi, have successively wielded the *baton* of leader of the orchestra.

In 1859, Mr. Chas. Boudousquié, having some years before succeeded Mr. Davis as manager of the Orleans theatre, the building was bought at the judicial sale of the estate of John McDonough by Mr. Parlange, who failed to agree with Mr. Boudousquié as to the lease of the theatre, whereupon a new company was formed, and the present splendid edifice on Bourbon street was built by Messrs. Gallier & Esterbrook, architects for the Opera House Association.

It was upon the boards of this theatre that the charming Adelina Patti made her *debut* in Meyerbeer's " Pardon de Ploermel," on which occasion the writer of this sketch remembers with pardonable pride and pleasure that he was among the few theatrical critics of the day who at once recognized and proclaimed her transcendent merits as a vocalist and actress. There, too, the dying notes of another great Italian artist, Madame Frezzolini, were heard just upon the eve of the great civil war, which, shortly after, led to the temporary suspension of all theatrical enterprises in New Orleans.

On the return of peace, a French strolling company, under Mr. Marcelin Alhaiza, proving highly successful, a number of subscribers furnished him at the close of the season with the means of engaging a complete dramatic and operatic company. The result was most unfornate, Mr. Marcelin Alhaiza having died on the eve of his company's departure from France, and the latter being shipwrecked and lost on the steamer in which they had taken passage from New York to this port.

Mr. Paul Alhaiza, the brother of the deceased manager, collected a few artists who had remained here, and engaged some of the members of another strolling company whose performances at the old Orleans theatre had been brought to a close in 1867, by the burning of that edifice. In 1868, he attempted, in partnership with Mr. Calabresi, to revive the opera, but the attempt proving unsuccessful, a new Opera House Association was formed, composed of leading capitalists and merchants of this city, by whom the opera house was purchased, and liberal provision was made for the engagement of a first-class opera company. Mr. E. Calabresi, was by them appointed manager and leader, at a very high salary, but although he succeeded in engaging two or three singers, of talent and reputation, such as Michot, Castelmary and Dumestre, most of the other artists brought over by him proved lamentably deficient, and after two seasons the members of the Opera House Association found themselves in debt after having expended the whole of their capital, and were therefore compelled to go into liquidation.

This happened at the close of the season of 1871-2, when Mr. Placide Canonge—a distinguished creole journalist and playwright, who had already given evidence of his tact and good taste in the selection of a dramatic company for the old Orleans theatre, obtained quite late in the summer a lease of the Opera House for the winter of 1872-3. The dramatic company brought over by M. Canonge has proved eminently successful, Mmes. Miller, Beauvais, Protal and Goslin, and M. M. Molina, Ariste, Deschamps, Schaub, and Scipiore, the leading comic and dramatic actors, having proved very acceptable to the public.

A strong effort is now being made by some of our leading citizens to form another Opera House Association, with the view of enabling Mr. Canonge to engage an Opera Company mostly of the past reputation of our lyrical stage—a task for which no one is better qualified than he is, and in which we most heartily wish him to succeed, as he can not fail to do if he is supported as he deserves to be by the " solid men " of his native city.

F. A. GONZALES.   A. GONZALES.

GONZALES BROS.

Importers of

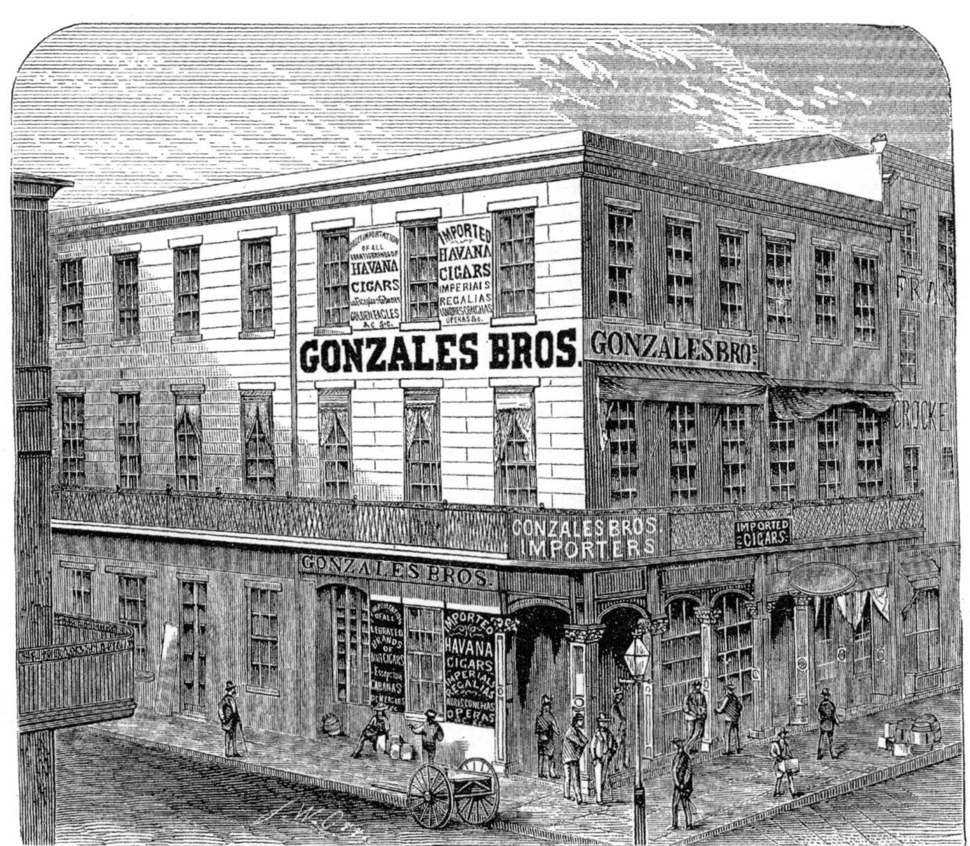

HAVANA CIGARS,

Corner of Camp and Common Streets,

OPPOSITE THE CITY HOTEL.

No. 2 Carondelet St., near Canal, and cor. Union and Carondelet Sts.

NEW ORLEANS, La.

All Cigars fully guaranteed imported and genuine brands.

PARTAGAS, UPMANN LA CARONA, LA ESCEPCION, ETC., ETC.

ALEXANDER HAY, ESQ.

ALEXANDER HAY, Esq., President of the St. Andrews Society of New Orleans, was born on the 26th of February, 1832, in Stranraen, a small sea-port town in Wigtonshire, Scotland, near the seat of the Earl of Stair, of "the Massacre of Glencoe" notoriety. Mr. Hay was educated at the old University of Glasgow, and, at the age of twenty-two, after an apprenticeship of three years, took the management of the large Tannery of Messrs. Thomas Pitling & Co., of Port Glasgow, which position he filled for eight years, until compelled by ill health to relinquish it.

From the time of his leaving the tan-yard till his departure to the United States, he traveled over the larger portion of Europe in pursuit of health, but seeking that blessing in vain. His physician then advised him to take passage on a sailing vessel and try a warmer climate. Complying with this recommendation, he set sail for the port of New Orleans, and by the time of his arrival here in June, 1865, after a long voyage, found his health completely restored. It was not in his nature to remain inactive. His old occupation among hides and leather had great attractions for him, and he thought there was a good opening here in that line of business. He was first employed as a clerk merely, but, in the course of a year from the time of his arrival, was able to set up business on his own account, when he established (taking into partnership a native of New Orleans) the firm of Hay & Mehle (50 Commerce and 120 St. Peters streets), one of the largest houses, if not the largest, in the trade of Hides and Wool in the city of New Orleans, and which has been exceedingly successful.

Mr. Hay furnishes an instance, not uncommon among his countrymen, in which the character of the industrious, persevering tradesman, is fully blended with that of the scholar and the gentleman. It is to the union of such characteristic traits (and which are worthy of all imitation where they are attainable) that he is largely indebted for his prosperity and success.

Mr. Hay was married in Bannockburn to a lady of that memorable village, Miss Miller, by whom he has two children alive, a son and a daughter. He had the misfortune to lose two fine boys in 1867.

In November, 1869, he was first elected President of the St. Andrews Society, and has had the unusual distinction conferred upon him of being annually reëlected the President of that most honorable and beneficent association ever since.

He is Agent for the Anchor Line of Trans-Atlantic Steamships, running twice a week between New York and Glasgow. This Company has a fleet of thirty-six steamers afloat, and seven more on the stocks. The career of the founder of this Line is somewhat remarkable, and affords evidence that colossal fortunes are often made in the Old World as well as the New. Forty years ago, three little Scotch boys started life together, owning first a sailing smack only ; gradually rising in the gradation of tonnage and rig, until they had served in schooners, brigs, barques, ships, and were conversant with every detail in connection with these different types of vessels. These little Scotch boys rapidly rose to be the world-wide known firm of Handyside & Henderson of Glasgow, the owners of the Anchor Line, a fleet that cost $180,000,000.

REV. GEORGE H. DEERE.

This highly esteemed pastor of the Unitarian Church in this city was born at Oswego, N. Y., September 4th, 1827. He was the son of an artist who entertained very liberal notions on the subject of Religion, took great pains in the personal training of his son. Owing to a defect in his eye-sight which became apparent in his infancy, his education was necessarily domestic.

The mother of young Deere was a Methodist, and as mothers are apt to exercise a controlling influence on the minds of their children, and do much towards shaping their character and opinions, it is not surprising that, shut out measurably from the world by his misfortune, and consequently addicted much to meditation and reflection, the youth should have adopted the maternal creed. In 1843, however, "a change came over the spirit of his dream," and at Brooklyn, N. Y., to which city he had removed, and where liberal views of theology had obtained a lodgment, he became an Universalist, the paternal recollections and influences now prevailing over the maternal.

Inclination and circumstances pointed him to the church as the department best fitted for him. He, accordingly, devoted himself to the study of theology, first under the tuition of Rev. Dr. Sawyer, now Packard Professor of Theology at Tuft's College, Boston, and, afterwards, under that of Rev. Dr. Thayer, of Brooklyn, N. Y., now editor of the *Universalist Quarterly*, and, in due time, became a licentiate, and ultimately an ordained minister of the gospel.

After a short ministry at Danbury, Conn., and Warren, Mass., he was settled as pastor at Brattleboro, Vt., where he remained seven years. Removing to Melrose, Mass., in September, 1860, and finding the climate of the New England sea coast prejudicial to the health of his wife, he accepted a call, at the close of a year, to a pastorate at Shellburne Falls, Mass., which continued six years. In October, 1867, he accepted an invitation to the charge of a parish at La Crosse, Wis., whence, after a ministry of four years, in October, 1871, he removed to New Orleans. The parishes which he has hitherto served have been in fellowship with the Universalist branch of the Liberal Christian Church ; and he has, thus far, been very acceptable as well as useful in his ministrations. The society over which he now presides, and which was very large under the ministry of the late Rev. Dr. Clapp, (but which declined after the war,) has taken a new start, and seems likely, under its new auspices to recover much of its former strength and influence.

Mr. Deere, like Dr. Clapp, is an extemporaneous preacher, and never writes a discourse before its delivery. His mind is clear, orderly, and didactic, and his manner serious and impressive without rhetorical display. His conversational powers are considerable, and whenever he appears in social circles with his intellectual and accomplished wife, he throws a certain charm over them.

REV. HENRY SAMUEL JACOBS.

Minister of the Hebrew Congregation, "Dispersed of Judah," was born at Kingston, Jamaica, in the British West Indies, on the 22d day of March, 1827. Exhibiting a decided inclination for the ministry from his youth, he early qualified himself for the sacred calling, beginning his theological studies under the Rev. Moses N. Nathan, who was subsequently the first minister of the Hebrew Congregation in this city, to which Mr. Jacobs is now attached. After officiating for three years as lay reader, he was, in his twenty-first year, placed in charge of the small congregation, "Habitation of Peace," at Spanish Town and Jamaica, till he was called to fill the important office of minister in the Kingston Congregation, "Gates of Righteousness."

His health having become impaired by too studious and sedentary a life, and feeling an irrepressible yearning to make the United States his home, he left his native island on the 3d of January, 1854, and reached New York the following week. His reputation as a zealous, devout, and indefatigable minister of his faith had preceded him, and this, together with the demand for English preachers (which has since assumed the largest proportions,) led to his receiving more than one call, terminating in his acceptance of that of the Portuguese Hebrew Congregation of Richmond, Va., the duties of which he assumed about a fortnight later. Here he labored successfully for nearly four years, when the pulpit of the Congregation, "Shearith Israel," of Charleston, S. C., then one of the largest and most influential in the Union, having become vacant, was tendered to him in the most flattering terms; but loath to leave his Richmond flock, he eventually consented to change his field of labor, only on the urgent advice of his numerous friends, who believed that his efforts in the holy cause would be more valuable in the wider ministrations to which he was so earnestly invited.

In this position he continued successful in his clerical charge, gaining many friends and winning golden opinions from all sorts of men—but "grim-visaged war" had overtaken the land—the battle of Secessionville had been fought—the "swamp-angel" had commenced shelling the chief city of South Carolina, and its streets were deserted of their many familiar faces. The Synagogue was "under fire," and the congregation had dispersed.

In this emergency, the Board of Trustees suggested to Mr. Jacobs to move to Columbia, where a large part of his flock had taken refuge, and he accordingly proceeded thither and organized public worship. This state of affairs continued till February 17th, 1865, when the Union Army, under General Sherman, reduced that beautiful inland city, the capital of the State, to a heap of ruins.

Sharing in the general calamity Mr. Jacobs lost all his earthly possessions, and escaped from his burning homestead with but the clothing on his back, finding temporary shelter with his family under the roof of a friend in the suburbs of the city, till opportunity offered of moving to Augusta, Ga., the nearest point of refuge and safety. For about a year he continued there still ministering in his holy avocation.

Peace, meanwhile, had been restored; but it was destined that he should not resume his clerical charge at Charleston; for the Synagogue there had been so injured by the shelling of the city that it could not be used in its then condition; whilst the few members of the congregation who remained were too impoverished either to repair it or provide the necessaries to continue public worship. Hence he had to resign the office he held there notwithstanding the attachment he felt to his Charleston flock.

Receiving several calls at this time he elected to accept the one coming from this city, which he now fills as minister of the Hebrew Congregation, "Dispersed of Judah."

Mr. Jacobs belongs to the conservative party of his denomination, which, whilst recognizing the necessity for some legitimate concessions to the scientific progress and inquiring spirit of our times, and the social condition of the country in which we live, yet respects the pious usages of antiquity, and holds firmly and uncompromisingly to the fundamental principles of Judaism, thus taking the intermediate position between Radical Reform and ultra-Orthodoxy.

Having been educated as a teacher, he has given much thought and labor to the cause of education. In his eighteenth year he was placed in charge of a Public School in his native country, and subsequently elected principal of the consolidated Hebrew schools. He was also engaged in the same duties in Richmond, Va., Columbia, S. C., and Augusta, Ga. In this city, at the establishment of "The Hebrew Education Society," he was its first President and afterwards became Superintendent,—a post which he has only recently relinquished. His interest in education has been most pronounced, and is his marked characteristic, and, it is expected, will continue to be exercised for the general welfare of the community.

None of our ministers, of any denomination, are more distinguished for learning, eloquence, and urbanity of manners, than the Rev. Mr Jacobs; and none exerts a more decided and high-toned influence in the various circles of society in which he moves.

MARKETS.

The markets are a prominent feature in a description of New Orleans. They are numerous, and dispersed, to suit the convenience of the citizens. The prices of many articles they offer are very fluctuating. Not dearer, however, on an average, than in New York. Stall-fatted meats are not so usual here as at the North, preference being given to the grass-fed. The mutton has no equal in America. Poultry and fish are fine; and vegetables, except potatoes, are abundant, and speak well for the soil that produced them. Fruit, from the West Indies and our own W   is not only plenty but of the best kind. The regulations are excellent, and are strictly enforced by officers appointed for that purpose. The greatest market day is Sunday, during the morning. The traveler, who leaves the city without visiting one of the popular markets on Sunday morning, has suffered a rare treat to escape him.

Accommodation Bank of Louisiana,

MASONIC HALL.

E. B. BENTON, PRESIDENT.   R. H. WOOD, CASHIER.

THIS BANK ALLOWS LIBERAL INTEREST ON DEPOSITS,

And advances MONEY in sums to suit, on every species of Personal Property, Warehouse Receipts, Stocks, Bonds, Warrants, Gold, Silver, Diamonds, Furniture, Pianos, Merchandise, and Valuables of every description,   Has large Warehouse and Store-rooms attached to the Bank.

DAVID BIDWELL.

In the theatrical world no name is more familiar or better known than that of Mr. D. Bidwell. Recognized throughout the country as one of the most enterprising and successful managers of public entertainments of the present day, he has achieved this reputation in a comparatively short space of time. Embarking in life at an early age he was thrown upon his own resources and forced to carve out his own future. That his career in life so far has been eminently successful, is fullly established by his present influential and wealthy position. Mr. Bidwell was born in the town of Stuyvesant, Columbia Co., N. Y., in the year 1821. He was educated at the Kinderhook Seminary, and, after leaving school, joined his father, Alex. Bidwell, who was at that time commander of a steamer on the Hudson River. After a term of service as clerk upon his father's boats, he became the proprietor of the Empire House, just in the rear of the Astor House, a place famous in the days of the Presidential Campaign of 1844, the year in which the noted Empire Club was organized and located at this place. In 1846, Mr. Bidwell came to New Orleans and engaged in business with his brother, Mr. H. Bidwell, as ship chandlers, under the style of H. Bidwell & Co. In 1852 the partnership was dissolved, when Mr. David Bidwell became the proprietor of the Phœnix House. In 1853 Mr. Bidwell took charge of the property now known as the "Academy of Music," and acted as agent for the proprietor in renting it to combination theatrical companies until 1856, when, in partnership with Spaulding & Rogers, he became the proprietor and manager of this theatre, and has continued to control and direct it until the present time, when he is the sole proprietor.

Mr. Bidwell's theatrical associations have not been confined exclusively to New Orleans. In 1867 he organized and took charge of the American Champion Circus Company and gave a series of performances in Europe, which created a great *furore* in the amusement circles of Paris. In connection with Dr. Spaulding, Mr. Bidwell also built the Olympic Theatre, in St. Louis, in 1867–8, and in 1869, with the same partners, he became interested in the New Memphis Theatre and the Mobile Theatre. Besides the present management of the "Academy of Music," Mr. Bidwell is the sole owner of the author's playwright of the Black Crook for a large portion of the country, and with one of the largest traveling combination companies ever organized, is making the tour of the United States, giving representations of this gorgeous spectacle. One secret of Mr. Bidwell's success is his thorough knowledge of the people of New Orleans and the peculiarities of their tastes, acquired by a long residence in their midst. Knowing their fancy he has always exerted himself to the utmost to please and gratify them. Money, time and labor have all been freely used to give eclat to every entertainment prepared by Mr. Bidwell for the citizens of New Orleans. That his efforts in this particular have been abundantly successful, is evidenced by the fact that he stands in the front rank of his profession, and is deemed the most successful theatrical manager in the country. Whilst catering to the amusement-loving portion of the people, Mr. Bidwell is not unmindful of the general interests and welfare of the entire city. His contributions for public works and improvements, for railroads and other enterprises, are liberal and numerous. Having accumulated a fortune here, thoroughly identified with every interest of the city, it is quite natural and proper that he should feel a deep concern for the future prosperity of the Crescent City and contribute, all in his power, to aid in the good work of developing its wonderful resources. In this respect he plays the part of a valuable and useful citizen, and as such commands the respect of the community of which he has been an exemplary member.

JAMES BARRY PRICE,

Was born in Pittsylvania County, Va., January 19th, 1832. His ancestors were prominent in the Revolution, and from them were directly descended the late distinguished soldiers and citizens, Generals Sterling and Thos. L. Price of Missouri. Among his not distant collateral relations were the late Admiral Barry. Mr. Price emigrated with his parents to Middle Tennessee at an early age. Few men during the last thirty years have been more prominent in the politics and business interests of that State than his father, Col. M. A. Price; while on his mother's side he is connected with the Sanders, Caruthers, Cahal, Donelson and Gentry families, than which none have been more conspicuous in the public affairs of Tennessee during the last two generations. Mr. Price has enjoyed all the advantages of wealth, education and travel, visiting all Europe, Egypt, Nubia, Arabia, Palestine, and the remote East as the *compagnon de voyage* of the late Lucius C. Duncan of New Orleans, and the distinguished and Hon. Edwin H. Ewing of Tennessee. His travels in America are probably more extended than those of any man in the States. He married and settled in St. Mary Parish in 1853, since which time he has been extensively engaged in agriculture, commerce and transportation. In transportation of the mails by steamboat and stage coach he had been more extensively engaged than any man in the South. He was one of the few bold enterprising spirits who established the Great Overland Mail Line of Stages connecting St. Louis and Memphis with San Diego and San Francisco, which practically demonstrated the feasibility of the existing and projected lines of travel and mail carriage across the Continent. Mr. Price has not confined himself to any specialty, but has taken a leading part in many enterprises with a large measure of success. During the war he and his partners, F. P. Lanyer and G. H. Giddiux, controlled nearly all the stage transportation in the Trans-Mississippi Department, through which means incalculable service was rendered to the people and soldiers, thousands of whom were transported to and from their homes gratuitously. Mr. Price more than once was offered high military rank, by reason of greater usefulness in the Civil Service of the Confederacy he was kept employed therein, and throughout the war he enjoyed the confidence of the Confederate rulers to the fullest extent. Mr. Price is accredited, by many familiar with his record, as having contributed as much material aid to the Confederacy as any other man in the South, though he was originally opposed to Secession. At the close of the war he at once went to work to aid in restoring the prostrate interests of Louisiana, especially in his own section, as the local papers abundantly testify. In 1866, in connection with those well known merchants, T. D. Hine of St. Mary, and G. Tupper of Charleston, S. C., he established the commercial firm in New Orleans of Price, Hine & Tupper. In 1867 he, Gen. Hersey of Maine, Robert Hare, and T. M. Simmons, and others of New Orleans, organized the Louisiana Petroleum and Mining Company of Calcasieu Parish, of which Mr. Price was elected President. In 1868 he induced his kinsman, Gen. T. L. Price, and Chas. P. Chauteau of Missouri, to lease and work the Avery Salt Mine, the firm of Price, Hine & Tupper being agents of the same. In 1867 he was appointed by Gov. Wells Special Commissioner to the Paris Exposition, and he doubtless deserves a considerable share of credit for the distinction which Louisiana there enjoyed. These things are all mentioned here to indicate that the subject of this sketch is one of that active, bold, enterprising, and intelligent class of men who are required to revivify Louisiana, and whose acts would all be vitalizing and beneficial, while those of mere politicians only tend—as we know by sad experience—to impoverish, to enervate, and to destroy. In June, 1872, the above facts and traits of character seem to have impressed the public mind to such an extent that those representative of public opinion, most of the delegates of the Democratic and Reform Conventions from the Third Congressional District of this State, paid him the remarkable compliment of inviting him to stand as an independent candidate to represent the District, saying, in their letter of invitation, substantially that his character for wisdom and intregity was all the declaration of principle required. His frank and manly letter of acceptance elicited the most complimentary notice of the Press, one of which held the following language—"No man is better acquainted with the wants and necessities of Louisiana, or more capable of relieving the same and promoting her welfare. He is much loved by his old servants, and is highly esteemed by his numerous employés. He is a good citizen, a thorough gentleman, a kind neighbor, and a true friend. A golden future awaits him," etc., etc.

From parental iufluence, liberal education, a large-hearted and broad-minded nature, with much travel and mixing with men, both in the old and new worlds, he is expanded in his feelings, liberal in his views, and thoroughly Cosmopolitan in his tastes. He is free alike from bigotry and sectionalism, and religion, education and morals find in him a hearty promoter.

In physique he is one of the best specimens of the Anglo-Saxon race, while a total abstinence throughout life, from beer, wine, spirits, and tobacco, and from any form of dissipation or gambling, has secured to him the multiplied blessings which flow from a good constitution and perfect health.

L. E. REYNOLDS, ESQ.

None of our architects is better known, few or none are more highly esteemed, than Mr. Reynolds. A passion for drawing, a fondness for handling tools, and a readiness in the use of them, marked his childhood, and seemed to indicate the special and important purpose to which his subsequent life was devoted. The training and experience through which he passed from the humbler labors of a carpenter, till, in maturer life, he adopted the nobler and more exacting profession of an architect, contributed to the gradual, but certain, development of powers essential to excellence in the Art of Design.

L. E. Reynolds was born at Norwich, Chenango County, in the State of New York, on the 29th of February, 1816. At an early age he went to Cincinnati, then rapidly rising into importance among the cities of the West, regarding it, as he did, a favorable locality for the commencement of his labors. The carpenter's trade first engaged his attention; but with the practical part of it, into which he was soon inducted, he united the study of architecture as a science—a study which he prosecuted with unceasing diligence, until figure, form, harmony and proportion became familiar ideas with him.

With a view to finish his education in the line of life he had adopted, he placed himself under the direction of distinguished architects in Louisville, and subsequently in New York, with whom he remained several years, diligently pursuing a prescribed course of study, and uniting the theory with the practice of the Art of Design as he had opportunity. He spent from ten to fifteen years in this way, building and designing buildings, before he considered himself competent to enter on the duties of a professional architect.

Having now become proficient as a draughtsman, and being inspired with a great love of his profession, as well for purposes of emolument as fame, he determined to teach its principles to others as a public lecturer. In this capacity, as well as that of an architect actively engaged in his profession, he visited New York, Philadelphia, Baltimore, St. Louis, Washington and New Orleans, and hundreds of young men in these cities, after the labors of the day were over, gathering around him, received their first instructions in building, architecture and civil engineering. He taught them a new system of prospective, reconstructed and improved many problems in carpentry and in cylindrical and conic sections. He invented five original methods of Hand-Railing, including all that have been of any practical use since the days of Peter Nicholson, and published a treatise on the subject accompanied with plates. The work is highly commended by skilled architects on both sides of the Atlantic, for the originality of its views and the beauty of its geometrical figures.

Mr. Reynolds paid his first visit to New Orleans in 1833, and came permanently to reside here ten years afterwards, viz: in 1843. Since that time he has pursued his profession with exemplary diligence and signal success. The monuments of his skill as an architect are scattered all around us. Many of the fine buildings that adorn the Third District were designed by Mr. Reynolds; and he

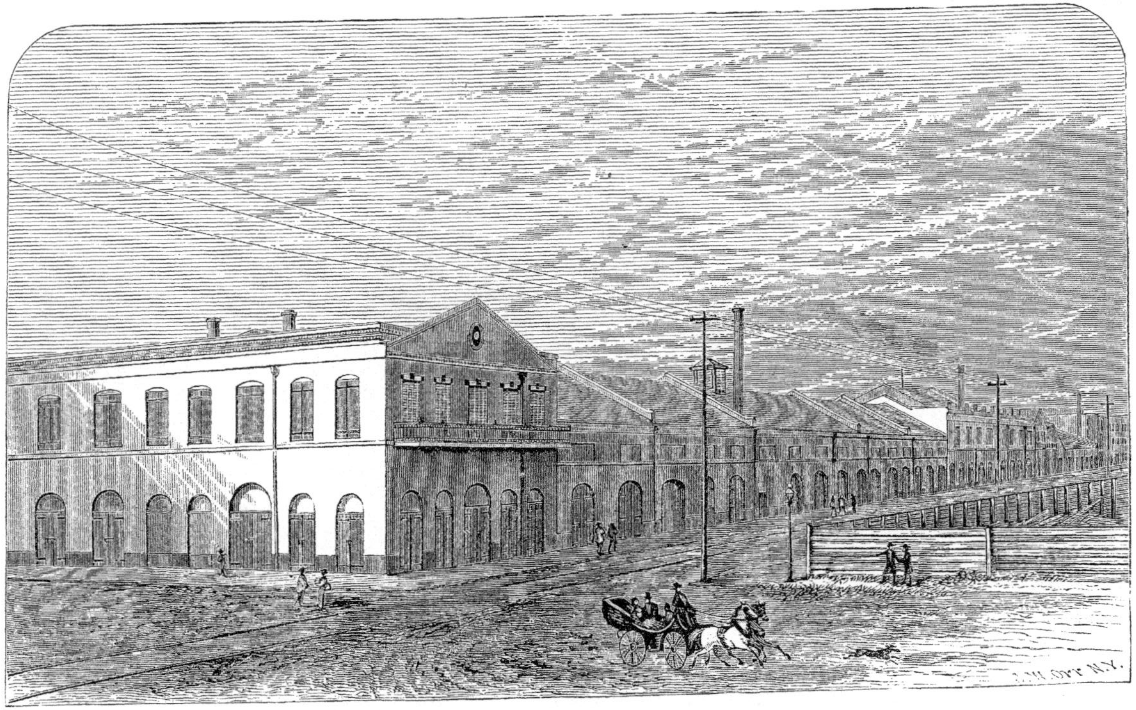

ORLEANS COTTON PRESS.

has, certainly among his brother architects, largely contributed to the beauty and permanent improvements of the city. The houses he has designed are models of elegance and high finish in their way. Among them we may mention Mr. Lafayette Folger's, corner of St. Charles and First streets; Dr. Campbell's, corner of St. Charles and Julia streets; Mr. Hale's corner of De Lord and Camp streets; the Canal Bank on Camp street; the Story Buildings, corner of Camp and Common streets: Mr. W. M. Perkins', corner of Jackson and Coliseum streets; St. James' Hotel on Magazine street; Crescent Mutual Insurance Building, Camp street; Mr. H. S. Buckner's house, corner of Coliseum and Jackson streets; the Factor's Row on Carondelet street; Row of Stores opposite St. James' Hotel; Mr. S. H. Kennedy's house, corner of First and Camp streets; Mr. Andrew Smith's house, corner of St. Charles street and Tivoli Circle; Jackson & Manson's extensive stores on New Levee streets, and many more firm and substantial buildings in the city than we have space or time to enumerate, and which testify to his genius and tasteful skill in execution.

By strict attention to order and system in his business arrangements, Mr. Reynolds has found considerable time for study, reading, writing and even publishing. He has one of the best, if not the very best, professional library in the city, and is thoroughly conversant with the architectural lore it contains. In his "Mysteries of Masonry," recently published by the Messrs. Lippincott of Philadelphia, he has treated a curious and transcendetal subject in a clear and philosophical manner. A large edition of the work has commanded a ready sale, and elicited favorable criticisms both in the United States and in England. He is now engaged on a work of still higher pretensions, entitled "The Science and Philosophy of Creation," which, when it appears from the press, will be likely to produce a sensation in literary and philosophical circles.

MRS. MYRA CLARK GAINES.

This remarkable lady, whose name is the common property of every part of the American Union, literally the heroine of a romance in real life; more familiar with the doctrines which regulates the succession of real estates than many of the learned civilians who frequent our courts of justice; an eloquent and able champion of her own rights in any and every forum where she has ever been permitted to appear in person; better acquainted with the great men who for the third part of a century have figured at the Bar, on the Bench, in the Senate Chamber, and other high and enveid places in America, than most of her masculine cotemporaries; bold, intrepid, undaunted, indomitable and successful in the pursuit of an object which deservedly occupied her whole mind and heart, was born at New Orleans in the year 1806, of the present century, of which she herself is one of those shining marks which green-eyed envy is said to love.

Her father, David Clark, Esq., an Irishman by birth and a large capitalist, by his enterprise contributed greatly to the advancement of the Crescent City, then in its infancy,

and was successfully employed in 1803 by Mr. Jefferson to negotiate the purchase of the great territory of Louisiana, and its cession to the United States by Napoleon, the Emperor of France. Her mother, Zulfrine, née Carrière, of French extraction, is said to have been endowed with the charms of a magical beauty, which rendered her, in her day, very celebrated.

We have not time to recapitulate the interesting events which checker the history of Mrs. Gaines. Suffice it to say, that she has been twice married, first to Mr. Wm. W. Whitney by whom she had several children, of whom two only survive, a son and daughter, both of whom are married and have children. The second marriage took place with Major General Gaines, of the United States Army, a gentleman and soldier, and whose well-known devotion to her amounted almost to idolatry.

Mrs. Gaines must have passed her climacteric, which has not, however, deprived her, as yet, of the coveted glory of youth which have rolled imperceptibly over her head, have scattered their roses while they have concealed their thorns. Her hair still retains its golden hue; her face is fair and unwrinkled by the cares of half a century, while her symmetrical form is as erect, her eye as lively and benignant, her laugh as ringing, and her step quick, light and buoyant as ever!

An ubiquitous person wherever she is, be it New Orleans, New York, Philadelphia, Washington, or Boston, her *petite figure* may be seen almost any day of the week, and at all hours of the day, moving rapidly along their great thoroughfares,—the very beau-ideal of nerve, enterprise, gracefulness, gaiety and good humor. Who would suppose, from her nonchalant air and smiling aspect, that the expectations of a millionaire fluttered around her heart strings?

But so it was! The highest judicial tribunal in the United States, after a controversy prosecuted, with zeal and enthusiasm, during a space of thirty years and upwards, has confirmed her *status* as entitling her to the largest estate that has ever fallen to the lot of any American female. Between her and the possession and fruition of her queenly wealth there still lie many difficulties, and those of no small magnitude.

She is aware that the glittering rewards that beckon her in the distance, and to which she is entitled, can only be reached at the expense of thousands of individuals, who have long been in the quiet and undisturbed possession of her property, and who can only be ousted from it by regular process of law.

What a world of litigation lies before her! Most women, endowed with sensibility, would shrink appalled from the prospect. But Mrs. Gaines is no ordinary woman, and with a heart overflowing with benevolence, retains a keen sense of the wrongs she has suffered from the willfulness, the mistakes or ignorance of others, and is upheld by a lively sense of the right and justice of her cause, and of the duty that devolves on her to prosecute it to the best of her ability. It is known that she is liberal and ready to make many sacrifices, provided she can be substantially righted. She has, accordingly, for the sake of humanity, and for the sake of peace, proposed to compromise with her debtors, whether individuals or corporate bodies, for refraction of her vast estates. Admitting that she has an unquestionable right to all that the courts have decided to be her property, however large the amount may be, if with a view to relieve those who are in possession of her rights, she is willing to surrender a considerable portion of her legal claims. Who can withhold from her the praise of nobleness and generosity?

It adds largely to the merit of Mrs. Gaines, that the prospect of untold wealth, which lies before her, has never roused within her those feelings of arrogance and pride which are often the accompaniments of large expectations. In her intercourse with society, her manners are simple, frank and genial, devoid of the slightest approach to assumption. She despises none because they are poor, but is ever disposed to aid them as she has opportunity; she respects none because they are rich, regarding wealth a blessing or a curse as it is employed to good or evil ends. No religious devotee seems more intensely conscious of the leadings of Providence, and no Christian entertains a profounder reverence for the Creator, whom, in her conversations with friends, she always styles, with evident affection and trust, her "Heavenly Father."

We cannot refrain from concluding our brief sketch of this distinguished woman, by quoting the significant opinion expressed by the Supreme Court of the United States on the subject of the Gaines' controversy:

"When, hereafter, some distinguished American lawyer shall retire from his practice, to write the history of his country's jurisprudence, this case will be registered by him as the most remarkable in the records of the courts."

JOSEPH ADOLPHUS ROZIER, ESQ.

ANY account of distinguished members of the New Orleans bar, and of prominent citizens, would be signally deficient, which omitted a proper notice of this gentleman.

Mr. Rozier, as we are informed, is of French extraction, and was born at St. Genevieve, Missouri, December 31st, 1817. After completing his classical course at St. Mary's College, Mo., he commenced the study of law at Kaskaskia, Ills., under the direction of Judge Nathaniel Pope, then District Judge of the United States; and, subsequently, under that of John Scott, Esq., a distinguished member of the St. Genevieve bar. It was doubtless fortunate for the future reputation of Mr. Rozier, that the gentlemen who presided over his legal education, were men of a high order of intellect, and well versed in their profession. It is always beneficial to young men of ingenuous temper and honorable ambition, to have influential examples constantly before their eyes when engaged in the prosecution of their studies; and such was the case with the subject of this notice. But his success, in after life, was more attributable to his own energy and his ardent devotion to the noble profession he had adopted, than even to the force of brilliant examples.

When he had completed his preparation for the bar, Mr. Rozier presented himself to the bench of judges for examination, and having successfully passed through that ordeal received his diploma.

It is an era in the career of the young advocate in our wide-spread country, when the question of an advantageous location for practice is first raised, and its solution is often attended with difficulties. Missouri was then, comparatively speaking, a young State, and its cities, now populous, were then small. He commenced the practice at home where his information and habits for business were duly appreciated; but, animated by the spirit of adventure, or seeing a wider scope for the exercise of his abilities in New Orleans, he removed to this place, and having, as a necessary step, first mastered the doctrines and problems of the civil law, (which is itself a science,) and been examined as to his proficiency, commenced practice in this community in the year 1840. Here he has since resided, occupying a position among the prominent members of his profession, greatly respected for the virtues which have adorned his career in the various relations of life—domestic, social, civil and religious. His practice has been lucrative, and his income adequate to all the requirements of taste and elegance. His habits are literary, his disposition social, and his acquaintance with men and events, in past times and present, large. He always prepares himself thoroughly in his cases, comes to trial fully armed with authorities, never loses sight of the interests of his clients, never trifles with grave topics, and uniformly speaks with fluency, dignity, grace and effect.

A trait, which eminently distinguishes Mr. Rozier, is decision of character—an invincible adherence to his principles. This was manifested, in a remarkable degree, during our late troubles. Though a member of the State Convention that resolved to resort to secession as a remedy for Federal grievances, he voted against the measure and refused to sign the ordinance of secession, being one of the only seven of the whole body comprising the Convention who pursued this course. In this instance, as in all cases, he was doubtless influenced by his convictions, being governed by a sense of what he regarded right. His Roman firmness and conscientiousness displayed on this occasion, have been much admired and even praised by those who, to this day, differ from him in political opinion.

The ability of Mr. Rozier, and his earnest devotion to the interests of the Federal Union, attracted the attention of President Lincoln who, regarding him the proper person for the place, appointed him District Attorney of the United States for Louisiana. Mr. Rozier possessing a remarkable share of that modesty which is always characteristic of minds of a certain elevation, could not be tempted either by the distinction or emoluments attending the office to accept it. He accordingly declined the appointment.

Unobtrusive in his manners, affable in his intercourse, *sans peur et sans reproche*, Mr. Rozier would be regarded a model man in any community.

Mr. Rozier is, at present and has been for several years, President of the Law Association, composed of the most distinguished members of the profession in this city.

LOUISIANA COTTON MANUFACTORY.

THE Louisiana Cotton Manufacturing Company was formed in 1869. The mill is near the Barracks, about three miles from Canal street, fronting (216 feet) on the Levee, the premises comprising about six acres on which the company propose to build houses for one hundred and fifty operatives. The capital of the company is $200,000 and over $100,000 is paid up. The mill runs about sixty looms and 3360 spindles. The fine machinery is from the works of Curtis, Parr, & Morley, Manchester, England. The operatives are all white, being chiefly creoles from Third District, who have proved to be excellent in industry and fidelity, and of more than average aptitude in learning difficult processes. At fair remuneration the supply exceeds the demand, and the poorer white people in the lower portion of the city are partial to the new industry that is here opened to them.

Although the products of this mill are comparatively small, the experiment has proved that cotton can be successfully spun and woven near to the place of production, thus avoiding compression, freights, duties, interest, commission, and risks by sea and land. The fabrics of this mill are in demand in this city, and have already gained favorable notice in Western trade centres. The Company readily sell all they make at paying rates, and for cash. The affairs of the Company are controlled and regulated by W. T. Hepp, L. Folger, F. Gueydan, M. A. de Lizardi, and J. C. Denis, who constitute the Board of Directors. The officers of the Company are: J. C. Denis, President; George Perrilliat, Secretary and H. V. Meigs, Superintendent.

For want of sufficient capital the operations of the Factory have been somewhat limited—but a reorganization of the Company with ample funds is contemplated.

DR. WILLIAM NEWTON MERCER.

Who now resides on Canal street, in this city, at the advanced age of eighty-one, is one of the most venerated and beloved of our citizens. His name has long been regarded as the epitome of benevolence, kind-heartedness, of genial hospitality, and refined learning and manners.

With these qualities he combines excellent judgment and good knowledge of men—a well-trained intellect, large information, and admirable powers of administration.

To this rare combination, Dr. Mercer owes his great success, and the accumulation of the large fortune which he now enjoys, and from which he derives the means of his highest enjoyment in life, that of relieving the wants and alleviating the distresses of the unfortunate, and promoting meritorous enterprises of Religion, Benevolence and Education.

Dr. Mercer was born in Cecil County, Maryland. He received a good education, and attended the course of lectures at the University at Pennsylvania, when Dr. Rush was principal professor at that institution. Graduating with distinction, he received the commission of Assistant-Surgeon in the regular army, about the beginning of the war with England, in 1812.

In this position Dr. Mercer served with great credit. The only action of the war in which he took active part was at the disastrous fight, or rather race, at Bladensburg, when the raw militia which had been hastily gathered for the defence of the National Capitol was so quickly put to flight by the Peninsular veterans, under General Ross. The only fighting done on that occasion was by Captain Barney, of Baltimore. with a small force of sailors and marines, and a few pieces of artillery. This little detachment held the British army at bay for some time, and only yielded their position when overrun by an overwhelming force, and their gallant commander was shot down at his post. Dr. Mercer was attached to that command, and bravely and faithfully performed his duty.

After the close of the war, Dr. Mercer remained in the army, and came, with a portion of it to this city, as a Post-Surgeon. This was in 1816. After remaining here for a short time, he was transferred to Natchez, Mississippi, where he resided for some years. At this time Natchez was a very important town—and its society was of a very distinguished character. The rapidly-increasing wealth of the cotton planters, and the attractive prospects of this commanding position in the south-west, had drawn thither a number of men from the old States of marked characteristics.

Then was laid the foundation of what was well known throughout the country as the Adams County Aristocracy. It was in this society Dr. Mercer obtained admission, through his gentlemanly bearing, refined and dignified deportment, and his many admirable and genial habits. He soon became a great favorite with all persons, especially with the ladies, who were always won by his graceful gallantry and playful wit. Among the gentlemen, the Doctor was regarded as first, on this account with some slight jealousy. This, and his freedom from the vices and dissipations, then quite prevalent in that section, led them to regard him as more of a beau and ladies' man, than was compatible with the manly qualities of the age. But this idea proved a delusion, the doctor's courage and power of will, were quite as conspicuous, when occasion demanded their exercise, as were his courtly ease and amiability of manners and deportment.

These virile virtues were not displayed in physical combats, or in deeds of violence, and indistinctiveness so common in the south-west, but in the higher forms of an immovable firmness in every duty, a tenacity in the maintenance of his convictions, and rights, and fearless intrepidity in the defences and relief of the oppressed and the unfortunate.

A striking example of this was related to the writer, by the late Robert Walker, who was for many years a distinguished citizen of Natchez. It happened that a large and brilliant company had assembled at one of the fashionable summer resorts in East Mississippi. A number of Natchez families were included in this company. One day there was an alarm, a cry of distress, a call for a doctor. Dr. Mercer, who happened to be in attendance, repaired to the spot, and there found a crowd, surrounding a negro boy, a slave of one of the families sojourning at the resort ; the boy was in an agony of fright and pain, and the spectators were all in wild panic what to do. The poor boy had been badly bitten by that most poisonous of snakes, the copperhead moccasin. Gently waving aside the helpless crowd, Dr. Mercer quickly examined the wound, drew from his pockets his surgical instruments, scarified it, and then applying his lips to it, sucked out the poison. The boy recovered, never experiencing any effect from the poison.

For a gentleman of such fastidious refinement and elegance as to incur the suspicion of effeminacy from his ruder and more boisterous contemporaries, this action of Dr. Mercer was justly regarded by the fair sex as one of the highest manifestations of real courage, such as is prompted by the triumph of true benevolence and philantrophy over the love of self—of an utter insensibility to danger in discharge of duty to supplying humanity.

These, and like incidents in Dr. Mercer's career, at Natchez, quickly dissipated the erroneous impressions in regard to his true character. It was discovered that whilst the most benevolent and most amiable of men, he was also, one of the finest, most positive and consistent.

An amusing illustration was given of this, when, during one of those spasmodic efforts, which used to characterize the legislation of the Southern States, a severe militia law was passed in Mississippi.

This law required frequent parades, provided for a thorough organization of the citizens into battalions and companies, who should elect their own officers, and that said officers should call out their companies, whenever they deemed it necessary, and should subject them to a thorough drill.

Under this law one of the companies, composed of the wealthy and aristocratic citizens of Natchez, thought it a happy practical joke to elect, as their captain, the courtly and elegant ex-surgeon of the army ; Dr. Mercer had resigned his commission in the army sometime before. Great was their surprise when they were assured by the doctor of his high appreciation of the honor conferred on him. And they were still more surprised when the doctor, buckling on his sword, and donning his epaulets, entered upon the duties of his command, and with such vigor and earnestness, that they quickly discovered that the joke had been turned on the engineers. There never was so unhappy a militia as that of Dr. Mercer's became, under his command. The frequency and severity of the drilling to which he subjected them, the pertinacity with which he marched them in the hot sun, and through the streets of Natchez, the vigor with which the fines were imposed and collected, and the general severity of his discipline produced so profound a disgust with themselves and the law, which their commander had so faithfully carried out, that petitions were got up and dispatched to Jackson for the immediate repeal of the law.

Dr. Mercer pursued his practice for some years in Natchez with great success. Marrying into one of the oldest families of the State, he found himself charged with the responsibility of administering a large cotton plantation. It was in the execution of this trust that the admirable administrative abilities of Dr. Mercer were displayed. His good sense, clear and practical views of financial management, and promptitude and firmness in all his transactions, rendered him one of the most successful planters in the South.

By a firm adherence to certain simple rules of management, and apparently without an effort, the estate of his wife was rapidly increased in value and productiveness. And, when her lamented decease occurred, a large fortune had been accumulated, mainly through the judicious management of Dr. Mercer.

The death of his wife clouded the remainder of Dr. Mercer's life—and some years afterwards the loss of his only daughter, just entering womanhood, and adorned with all amiable and attractive qualities of her sex, completed the cycle of his domestic calamities, and condemned him to long years of sorrowing and melancholy.

Even now, in his extreme age, the afflictions give a painfully perceptible tinge of melancholy and of conscious bereavement to the expression of his noble countenance, showing that his thoughts and memory have never been relieved of the heavy burden of grief, which fell upon him so many years ago.

Shortly after the death of his wife, Dr. Mercer removed to this city, and has resided here continually for nearly thirty years. Erecting an elegant residence on Canal street, and investing largely in this city, he has led the life of a retired gentleman, dispensing a most elegant hospitality, and enjoying himself in acts of charity of the most liberal and generous character.

The characteristic of Dr. Mercer's contributions to the relief and aid of humanity, has been the modesty with which they have been dispensed. A shrinking from all notoriety or ostentation, a desire " to do good by stealth," has been his chief ambition in life. His charity has been directed by the suggestion and emanations of his own mind and heart, rather than from concession to the demands or solicitations of others. It would not be appropriate here during the life of this modest old gentleman to refer to the various incidents of his life ilustrative of this quality of his benevolence. But there is one of these which has already gained a place in history to which we may be excused, for referring. It relates to that affecting incident in the life of Henry Clay, when that great man, having served his country for more than a quarter of a century, returned to his home to find that his financial afiairs, having been so long neglected, had fallen into a condition verging on bankruptcy. A note for a large sum held by the bank in Lexington was rapidly approaching maturity. It was impossible to meet this and his other liabilities.

If it were not renewed, but pressed for payment, it would involve the sale of his homestead. This was a very distressing circumstance for the great statesman. It may be imagined with what chagrin and distress the proud man proceeded to the bank on the day when the debt became due, to solicit its extension, to do that which, to Henry Clay, was one of the hardest of all sacrifices and struggles, to solicit a favor from men whom he looked down upon as his inferiors in all the claims and attributes of greatness and illustrious public service.

Imagine the surprise, the relief and the joy of the old gentleman, when, on applying at the bank for the renewal of his note, he was informed that it had been paid, and the cancelled instalment was handed to him.

It is said that the proud old man burst into tears at this announcement, and exclaiming, " Well, I must have some true friends after all," retired to his home, and his own reflections. No inquiry, however, could elicit the information as to the generous friend who had rendered him this great and timely aid, and thus smoothed and brightened the declining years of the great Kentuckian. We imagine, however, that his sagacity and knowledge of the character and of the affection so long manifested for him by his old friend with whom he had passed so many agreeable days in New Orleans, did not permit Mr. Clay to doubt who was that friend in need.

It was the timely intervention of Dr. Mercer, and his friend, Mr. Duncan, of Natchez, who had saved the great Kentuckian from the mortification and anxiety that threatened to darken his latter days, in his retirement from the active scenes of public life in which he had played so distinguished a part.

As we have said, we do not intend to repeat the many other instances of generous liberality and beneficence of this venerable gentleman. It would require a volume to narrate them all.

It was, however, especially during our civil war, that the sterling qualities, and courageous devotion to friends, to principle and duty, of Dr. Mercer were most conspicuously displayed. The doctor had earnestly opposed the secession movement. He was a warm, sincere and out-spoken Unionist. Unable to resist the impulse of the people to secession and civil war—but alway predicting its ultimate failure—he determined when war came upon us to share its calamities and burdens with his fellow citizens.

POYDRAS ASYLUM.

As president of the most solid banks of the city, he favored the aid and support of the authorities, who were engaged in the defence of the State from invasion. To that object, he contributed largely from his private means. On the approach of the Federal army and fleet to the city, he recommended to the directory of the banks of which he was president, to pay its large specie deposit of over two millions of dollars to the depositors. This proposition was objected to by the State authorities, as hostile to the credit of the Confederacy.

It was determined by them that the specie of the banks should be removed into the Confederacy to place it beyond the reach of the invader. This measure or mandate was most reluctantly yielded to by the president and directors of the bank of Louisiana, and the whole two millions of gold which had long lain in the vaults, were now transferred into the interior, where, after many abortive attempts to procure its release, and to guard it from seizure and expropriation, the whole amount finally disappeared in that charm, which had swollowed up so many more millions of the wealth of the South.

When Butler occupied the city, and commenced his career of bullying and persecution of the people, he threatened vengeance against the bank president for snatching from him this valuable spoil. They were all ordered before him, to answer for their conduct.

When they appeared—they were all citizens of the highest repute and wealth—Butler favored them with some of his choicest democratic oratory, and with unbounded denunciation, as a set of bank robbers, who had betrayed their faith to their depositors and note-holders, and had thus perpetrated a double treason to their country and to the people who had entrusted them with their hard earnings. After a long harrangue, full of abuse and bitterness, he asked them what excuse they could give for their conduct. Several of the presidents offered various pleas ; they had been coerced in the matter ; they had always opposed this transfer, and they had already set on foot measures to have their specie returned. It was very perceptible that the worthy gentlemen were not a little alarmed by the threatening tone and manner of Butler. Dr. Mercer alone, remained unmoved, and maintained a dignified silence under the fierce oratorical blast of the unblushing demagogue. At last Butler turned to him and asked : "What have you, Dr. Mercer, a Union man, to say in justification of your conduct in this matter ?"

"Nothing," replied the bland and brave old gentleman ; "but to bear my share of the responsibility and penalty for the act."

Not a word was said of his own earnest opposition to the measure ; no promise or pledge of reparation, no expression of regret or repentance, though of all present he might justly and honestly have availed himself of such pleas. It was not the time now, it would have been incompatible with true manhood, thus to separate himself from his associates in peril and misfortune. And so the doctor, not only maintained his self-respect, but managed to secure the confidence and admiration of Butler, who made vigorous efforts to win the confidence and regard of the brave but always courteous and dignified old gentleman.

It was due to this feeling of Butler toward Dr. Mercer, that the latter was enabled frequently to intervene in favor of his fellow citizens, who were subjected to the violent treatment of that officer, during the whole period of Butler's command in this city. Dr. Mercer was almost incessantly engaged in these acts of interposition and remonstrance against the hard orders and acts of the Federal General.

Finally, however, Butler became dissatisfied with the doctor. Of all our rich men, he alone refused to take the oath, which Butler required of all citizens, on the penalty of confiscation of all their property If this oath were not taken by a certain day, the non-jurors were commanded to hand over the schedules of their property.

When that day arrived, Dr. Mercer walked to the office of the Prevost Marshall, and duly delivered to him a complete list of all his large estate, retaining, as he stated, two thousand dollars in gold, for his necessities, which, however, he agreed to report to General Butler.

This adroit demagogue could not resist the opportunity for a display of his zeal for the Union, and his love of equal rights, and accordingly, he had published his letter refusing the doctor permission to retain this small sum referred to, stating that he, of all others, from his high position and great influence, over his fellow citizens, should set the example of a prompt renewal of his allegiance to this government.

It does not appear, however, that Butler intended anything more than to make a display before the people, for he never disturbed the doctor in the possession and enjoyment of this small remnant of his princely estate.

An incident, growing out of this event, may be here related as illustrative of the quiet humor and sharp repartee of Dr. Mercer. Shortly after the publication of the correspondence between Dr. Mercer and General Butler, the Dr. was taking his customary promenade on Canal street, when a hearty and robust young man, a native of the city, whose friends had been not a little mortified, that he should be absent from the scenes in which nearly all the able-bodied young men of the city were then playing their parts, saluting the doctor, inquired, jocosely, whether he had any of those two thousand gold dollars left.

"Oh ! yes," quickly responded the doctor, "I have a small sum left, which I keep for a special purpose."

"May I inquire what that purpose is ?"

"It is," whispered the doctor, looking around as if he intended to guard against Federal detectives, "to buy *you* a fine Confederate uniform."

Immovable in his purpose, the doctor remained in the city throughout the whole war, without taking the oath, or, as it was styled, renewing his allegiance.

But our sketch has extended beyond the limits we had prescribed, we must bring it to a close.

After the war, with a single interruption of a short visit to the North, Dr. Mercer has remained in New Orleans, a calm and philosophic, but not uninterested observer of passing events and characters ; a great reader, not only of the current literature of the day, but of the works of the great English and French authors, and the dispenser of the most cordial and sumptuous hospitality.

By every class of the people he is looked up to with the most profound veneration, love and respect, as the model of the Southern gentleman, patriot, philanthropist and Christian, as, indeed, the single survivor of a generation, whose standard of virtue, of dignity, of refinement and honor, was far higher than that which has succeeded it.

NEW ORLEANS CHAMBER OF COMMERCE.

This institution was founded and incorporated February 26th, 1830. The charter was renewed for an additional term of twenty years, on the 25th of April, 1853. Its earlier labors were very useful, and the decisions of its committees of arbitration were published, and were of analagous authority in the business transactions of the merchants. Suspended by what the resolutions of reorganization calls "fortuitous circumstances," the members on the 17th of February, 1864, and renewed their organization, by the election of Charles Briggs, Esq., as President, and of A. C. Waugh, Esq., Secretary and Treasurer. From that time it has continued in active usefulness. Its membership has steadily increased, although not so great as the population and interests of the city would justify. In the midst of the political contest which has raged for the past six or seven years, the Chamber of Commerce has devoted itself by pressing good measures of legislation, and preventing others tending, in its opinion, to injuries, or retard the commercial interests of the city.

Among the most prominent of the measures advocated by the Chamber, may be mentioned the limitation of State debt by constitutional amendment. Advocacy of a railroad system, with an investigation into their progress, or cause of their delayed completion. Application for Federal aid in improving the Mississippi from its mouths to its outlet canal, levee reparation, and postal appropriations for establishing postal connections with foreign countries. Also for such amendment of our commercial treaties as will give greater intercourse with the States on the continent and Island, south of the United States. An amendment and explanation of the law of lien on property, and endorsement of a system of Industrial education in the South and for the South. Such are some of the measures which have been commended, and enforced upon public adoption by the many active and able merchants of New Orleans. To enumerate them would occupy too much space, and to designate any of them as especially effective would be invidious. It is proper to be said that for the patriotism, integrity and wisdom of its action, as well as in the confidence of their fellow citizens, the Chamber of New Orleans has a most respectable record. The present membership number more than two hundred, and its officers are Joseph H. Oglesby, President ; J. M. Sandidge, Vice President ; C. E. Slayback, Second Vice President ; W. M. Burwell, Secretary and Treasurer. The Chamber holds its sessions on the 1st Monday of each month, in the hall over the Louisiana National Bank.

TWELFTH NIGHT REVELERS.

FIRST FESTIVAL, 1871.

IN the latter part of the year 1870, it was resolved by certain genial enterprising spirits in this city, to re-establish the ancient and honorable Festival of the 12th Night, so memorable in history.

It was found that these annual celebrations not only contributed to the public enjoyment, but, by giving the city a reputation for gorgeous public festivities, had the effect of drawing here that vast pleasure-seeking element, which is yearly becoming larger, and whose presence always acts as an impulse to every description of local business.

Accordingly, on the evening of the 6th of January, 1871, the initial pageant of the 12th Night Revelers made its appearance upon the streets.

Public curiosity had been greatly excited, and all the thoroughfares which were known to be included in the line of march, presented the spectacle of one dense mass of spectators.

The entire central district of the city, indeed, was one brilliant scene of life and gaiety. The whole population was in the streets, and, with the bright and balmy night, the gay throngs and the flashing lights, the *tout ensemble* was one which belongs only to New Orleans among American cities. When it was found that the pageant was to represent the familiar characters whom Mother Goose has made immortal, the delight of the spectators can be better imagined than described, and, as the costly, fantastic procession filed slowly by, each new tableau was greeted with shouts of enthusiastic recognition from the innumerable throng.

The pageant was headed by a grotesque and gorgeous figure with the title of the Lord of Misrule, who was followed in regular order by the characters who have been handed down to us in the old nursery rhymes of that mysterious poet Mother Goose.

We can not, perhaps, give a clearer idea of the nature of the procession and the elements which entered into its composition than by quoting the following clever verses which were written by a prominent member of the New Orleans press, one of the most versatile, piquant and brilliant of our writers, and on which the formation of the affair was based.

We will only premise that the representations were all gotten up in the most expensive and artistic style, and were aided by every accessory of color and illumination which it is possible to employ in such cases.

The poem itself is complete and perfect in construction, and although on the most familiar of subjects, is full of harmony, and will be read with pleasure by every one whose memories carry them back to the loving care of a mother and the innocent joys of childhood.

MOTHER GOOSE'S TEA PARTY.

I

Hink ! minx ! hink ! my eyelids wink ;
Marry I'll have a feast ;
Since all were out at my last rout
Is many a year at last.

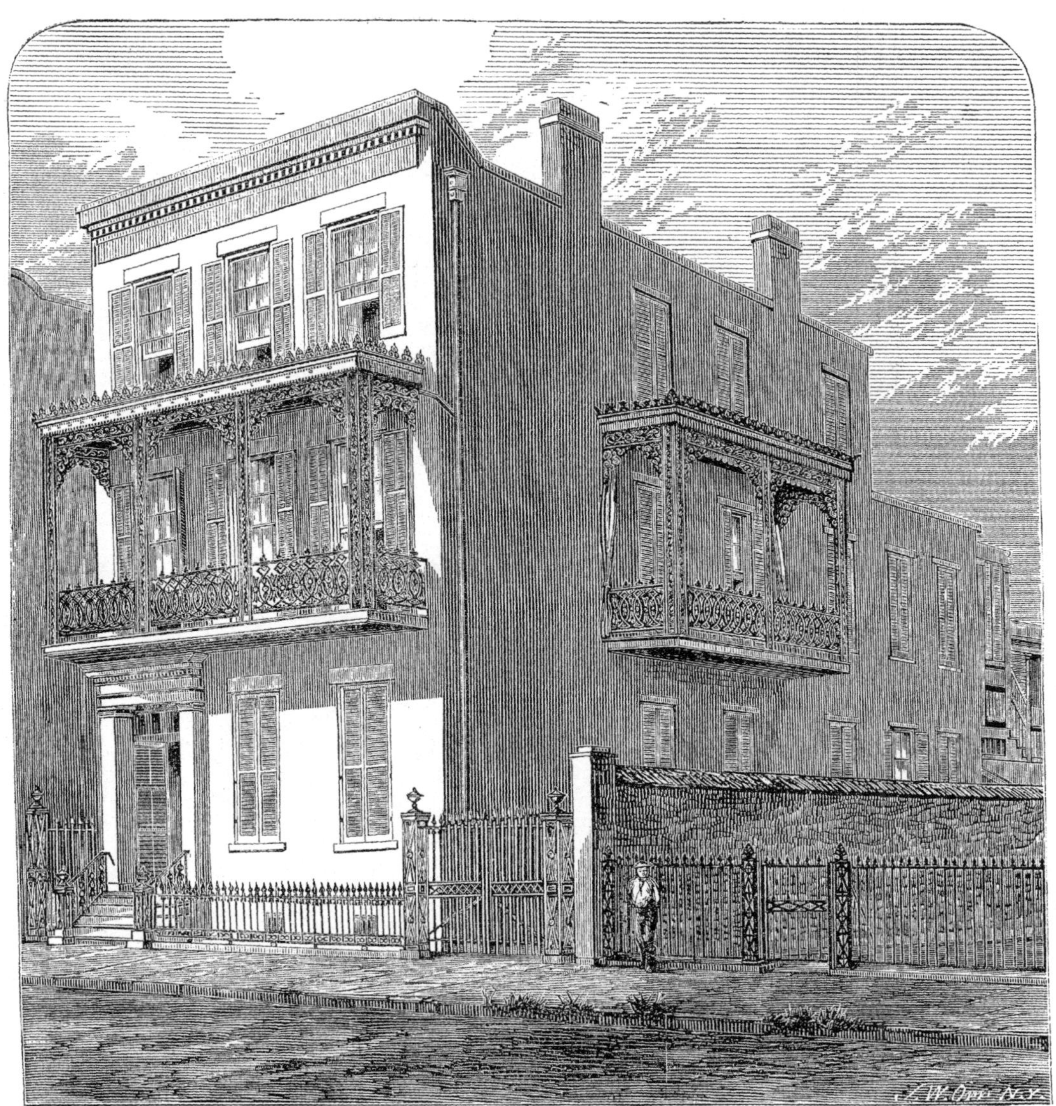

RESIDENCE OF JOS. H. OGLESBY, ESQ.,

206 ST. CHARLES STREET,

NEW ORLEANS.

The prating fools of modern schools
Would have me sound asleep :
'Tis time to call my children all
And give the world a peep.

So take the broom, sweep up the room
And then the table spread ;
We'll have one night as gay and bright
As any that have fled.

II

Wake Little Bo-peep, now fast asleep,
And rouse up Heart's good Queen ;
Bid Robin Hood from out the wood,
With his men in Lincoln green.

Bold Valentine, and Jack so fine,
Who cracked the Giant's pates,
To come with Spratt, who eat no fat,
And his wife who licked the plates.

Tell Jack and Gill, upon the hill,
And Humpty on the wall,
With Old King Cole, that good old soul,
They must obey the call.

III

We'll have a feast, where Beauty's Beast
Shall sup with Silver Hair,
Red Riding Hood and Orson good,
And Cinderella fair.

The children, too, who in the shoe,
Were all so poorly fed,
With Jenny Wren, and the little men,
Whose bullets were made of lead.

The summons sound till it shakes the ground,
So Fee-Faw-Fum may hear,
And Ogres come with Piper Tom,
To share our merry cheer.

IV

Quick, Saddle My Cock, hunt up the flock,
With a hop, step, jump away ;
Gather them all, both great and small,
Before the dawn of day.

There's Parson Rook, with solemn look,
Must bring young Johnny Grace,
Jack Horner too, with Buckle-my-Shoe,
Shall also have a place.

Nor maid forlorn, nor Crumple Horn,
Must either be passed by ;
Both girls and boys shall make a noise,
And sup on Blackbird Pie.

V

The fiddling Cat shall feed the Rat,
That quarrelled with the Frog ;
The Market Pig shall dance a Jig,
With Mother Hubbard's dog.

And Puss in Boots, in best of suits,
Shall pay Miss Muffet court ;
While Beanstone Jack rolls on his back,
With laughing at the sport.

Old Wondrous-Wise, with blinded eyes,
Shall mash Kriss-Kringle's corn ;
And Little Boy Blue, a hullabaloo,
Shall waken with his horn.

VI

Come out, come out, with song and shout,
Obey the grandame's call ;
To her bright eyes and golden skies,
We owe allegiance all.

The gems she wears distill no tears,
Her flowrets bloom for aye ;
Her castle walls and fairy halls,
Shall never pass away.

Like us who, back o'er life's dull track,
Our glance at Lapland throw ;
To hours of youth, to love and truth,
We never more may know.

——:o:——

SECOND ANNUAL FESTIVAL, 1872.

THE second Festival of these unknown Revelers was a splendid effort. With a more perfected organization, and with increased expenditure, they came to the front, determined to out-do their former effort and realize the brilliant expectations which their many admirers had founded upon the inaugural ceremony of their order.

They could scarcely have chosen a better theme than

THE TIDE OF ENGLISH HUMOR.

In all the realm of literature there is no richer field than this ; and our Revelers certainly culled its very fairest flowers as they wandered. Headed by Don Quixote (a pardonable theft from other lands) the pageant showed Humor, Its Gods, Its Fathers, Its Fountain, and Its Tide, in a splendid and harmonious sequence.

Shakespeare, Rare Ben Johnson, Gray, Swift, Sterne, Goldsmith, Burns, Scott, Irving, Dickens and Bret Harte !

These were figures which followed in the Tide of Humor ; each one set in a group of his own choicest creations, and clustered with them on their respective pedestals rivaling in chiseled spendor the majestic sculptures of Praxiteles himself.

In all the appointments of artistic elegance this display was considered as being yet unequalled. It was a daring flight into the realm of art, this attempt at marbleizing Humor, but the Revelers assuredly achieved a brilliant success.

The closing ceremonies, were, as on their first occasion, similar to those observed by the Mistick Krewe. There were two magnificent tableaux, representing

FIRST.

HUMOR'S PANTHEON.

" Above the smoke and stir of this dim spot
which men call earth."

SECOND.

THE APOTHEOSIS OF HUMOR.

" The mob of gentlemen who wrote with ease."

After the falling of the curtain on the closing tableau the usual ball commenced in which the fashionable company joined, finding no less delight therein by reason of their ignorance of their Hosts.

THIRD ANNUAL FESTIVAL, 1873.

This year the Revelers carried their representations into a still more elevated field of literatnre speaking with reference to utility and intrinsic dignity. In doing so they paid a merited tribute to the greatest genius ever produced by Louisiana—

JOHN JAMES AUDUBON.

> " That cheerful one who knoweth all,
> " The songs of all the winged choristers,
>   And in one sequence of melodious sound,
>   Pours out their music."

It was a specially happy conceit of theirs that, while they reproduced the birds of Audubon with the most astonishing fidelity, and while each individual figure was perfectly true in plumage, proportions and coloring, to the original which it was intended to represent, yet these were grouped in tableaux which were in most instances deliciously humorous in their meaning.

It was a curious and an artistic accomplishment, and, in that sense the 12th Night Revelers exceeded any similar effort of theirs.

This magnificent pageant was composed of seventeen immense cars or floats, fifteen of which bore groups of from five to ten figures. They were brilliantly illuminated with lanterns, transparencies and calcium lights, which, together with the gaudy coloring of the birds themselves, and the continuous blaze from the houses along their route, combined to make, not only one of the largest, but one of the most magnificent and imposing displays ever known in the history of our Carnivals.

There was also a novel idea shown in the management of the tableau. Instead of having a multiplicity of representations, the figures of the entire pageant were grouped in one colossal picture.

In the centre, on a raised pedestal was the immense statuary, composed of

AUDUBON AND HIS TWO COMPANIONS.

and round about him were the numerous birds which had followed him in the procession.

There were water, and marsh, and rocks, and sand, and trees and undergrowth, in which the birds were disposed appropriately ; thus making one grand tableau in which more than a hundred different contrasting figures were collected. The coup d'œil was inexpressibly striking, and when the curtain fell it was some time before the immense throng of spectators ceased their plaudits.

Thus, in a resumé of the past pageants which have made our city so famous over the whole continent, we cannot assert that anything in the past has exceeded this latest effort of the Revelers, all things considered.

It was in every sense a magnificent spectacle and it has proved that the Mistick Krewe have at last foemen worthy of their *steel*.

This chapter in the history of Revel'ry brings us up to the present day, when, if we may believe the mysterious hints which have been rife for weeks past, both Rex of the Carnival, and the Mistick Brotherhood of Comus intend to surpass all former displays.

THE BULK GRAIN TRADE.

THIS is comparatively a new commerce in the United States. It originated in Buffalo, upon the idea of applying the band and buckets employed by Oliver Evans in carrying grain and flour in a common flouring mill, and was adopted on a much larger scale as a means of handling cargoes.

Formerly, corn was received at New Orleans in the ear, shelled and sacked for sale Wheat was exported in considerable quantities before the war, and, on some occasions, grain in quantity was shipped to Europe by sail, and sometimes received in such condition that it had to be dug out of the hole with the spade. The plantation demand for corn at New Orleans, which, even now, reaches 4 to 5,000,000 bushels per annum, was sufficient to consume the surplus by the then West, which, until within the past twenty years, converted its surplus corn into cattle, hogs, horses and whisky. The vast growth of the West from foreign emigration, and the opening of canal and lake outlets to the East, has given a consequence to the grain trade which was not originally contemplated.

In the year 1868, L. J. Higby, Esq., having been for some years engaged in the Lake grain trade at Milwaukie, came to the conclusion that the Mississippi was the natural route for western grain to the ocean. Perhaps one of his strongest reasons for the opinion was that the ice blockade usually closed up from 20 to 30,000,000 bushels of grain, and subjected the grower and dealer to shrinkage, interest and insurance, or to the exaction of the Eastern Railroads.

He accordingly prospected this channel, and was the first person that put money into it as a practical proposition. In this enterprise it was necessary to provide for two transfers.

St. Louis had built a Grain Elevator, but like the canoe of Robinson Crusoe, it was as far from the water, that might have rotted down before it could be put to any use. This Elevator was, in the year 1869, and at the instance of Mr. Higby, brought into close connection by rail with the cars and shipping.

It was, however, in 1868 that pioneer of the bulk grain trade removed to New Orleans, purchased the ground, and erected the present Elevator, an illustration of which appears on another page of this work. He thus describes the installation and prosecution of the work in a letter to the Missouri " Democrat."

" After twelve days consultation in my own mind, I concluded to help New Orleans to a Grain Elevator—and make her the first grain mart in America. Consequently I brought my youngest son here, bought a block of land, built a wharf 275 feet long and 200 feet into the water, bought a steamboat, hauled her alongside, and made a boarding-house for ourselves and men, took off our coats on the first of June, and built an Elevator which is now, (25th December, 1868) able to hold and handle 120,000 bushels of grain in 24 hours. The building is 250 feet long, 100 feet wide, and 139 feet high, and will hold, when completed, 750,000 bushels of grain. The tower and Marine Elevator at the edge of the wharf is 102 feet high. The Marine Elevator is connected with the main elevator by a conveyor 33 feet high, and run-

W. B. SCHMIDT.   F. M. ZEIGLER.

SCHMIDT & ZEIGLER,

WHOLESALE GROCERS

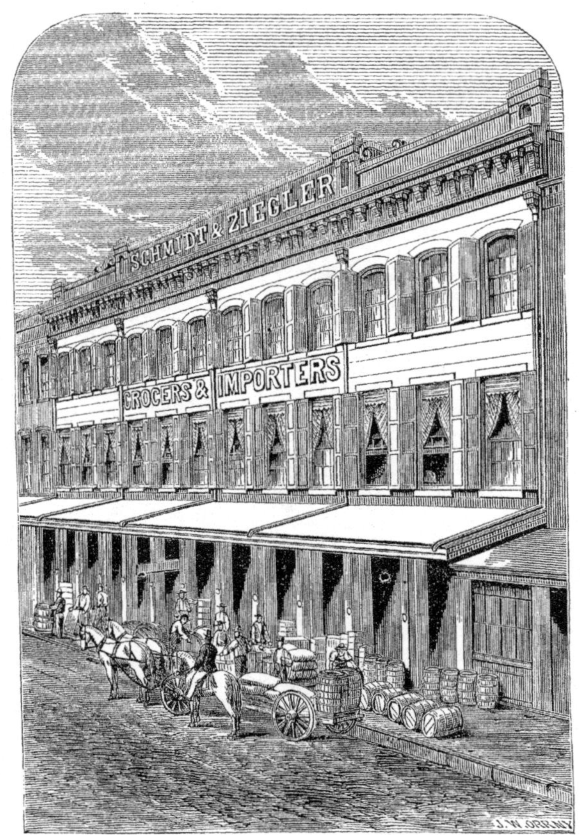

AND IMPORTERS OF

WINES AND LIQUORS.

Nos. 49, 51, 53 & 55 Peters Street,

Between Gravier and Poydras Streets,

NEW ORLEANS.

ning over the wharf and street. It is the only conveyor of the kind in America. The wharf Elevator can take grain out of a vessel at the highest or lowest water—there being a variation of 13 feet in the extreme stages. The wharf storage building is 200 by 275 feet, capable of storing 65,000 barrels of flour which can be loaded by machinery at the rate of 1,000 barrels per hour. The whole machinery is run by an engine of 500 horse power."

The enterprise of moving bulk grain by way of New Orleans was ridiculed by those who had not examined the subject, and especially by the Chicago Press. The "Times" said it would be as natural for Chicago to undertake the commerce of cotton, rice and sugar, as for New Orleans to control the grain of those high latitudes.

The St. Louis "Democrat," one of the earliest and staunchest advocates of the river grain trade, came to the rescue of New Orleans, and vindicated "De Bow's Review," from the imputation of having advocated an absurd proposition in maintaining the feasibility of the enterprise.

There was another imaginary impediment. All the Eastern interests maintained that grain could not be moved through the latitude of Louisiana without injury. Essays were written on the effects of humidity, and the temperature of the gulf stream was deemed fatal to a grain cargo.

This imputation was refuted by undoubted experiment. Grain was received by barges, transferred in elevator, sent by steam to England in the summer months, and was sold at a higher rate than other grain of its class, then in market. Some years later it having been assumed by some writer that grain must be dried at New Orleans before it could be exported safely, the indefatigable Mr. Higby published an account of sales of grain, sold abroad at a satisfactory profit; and produced proof that grain had been kept in his elevator 107 days in the summer time—and was sent sound into the English market. Since that it is admitted that the Mississippi and gulf is a sound route for sound grain; and western crops are fearlessly forwarded by this route.

There is in the opinion of the writer but one obstacle in the way of perfect success. The cotton crop comes to market at the same time with the western grain; the first commodity being worth ten times as much as the last, can afford to pay higher rates—the shipment of grain then arriving at New Orleans may find Orleans freights too high for profit—uncertainty embarrasses the foreign purchaser. By the time the cotton crop is off hand, the lakes and canals are open, and grain resumes its direct route to the East. If a line of grain propellers were established in close connection with the river craft to prorate with them and sign through bills between Liverpool and St. Louis, the shipment would be direct and continuous; the purchaser could tell what his grain would cost laid down at Liverpool, and we should have a steady business at least from October to May.

THE BARGE LINES.

In treating of the grain trade it would be improper to omit the influence resulting from the establishment of the river tow-boats and barges. This enterprise was started in 1866, and was the first to inaugurate the bulk grain trade.

When we consider that the grain crop of the United States is estimated at 2,500,000 bushels, and that it is grown chiefly on land west of the Mississippi, that a great part of this vast and increasing trade is frozen up for six months in the year, that the Mississippi is a sound and adequate route for the exportation of this crop at all seasons—the complete and independent organization of this trade is inevitable. We can not leave the subject without announcing that Chicago herself has modified her incredulity as far as to accept the agency of New Orleans in exporting her grain surplus, and as a relief against the exactions of Eastern Rail. The Illinois Central Railroad now delivers grain to barges at Cairo, and prorates for delivery at New Orleans. Efforts have been made to induce this company to emulate the example of the Baltimore and Philadelphia Railroad—and build barges, and even ocean steamers, to conduct the corn commerce with Europe.

NEW ORLEANS AND SPANISH AMERICA.

THE slightest reflection will show that it is the especial office and duty of the port of New Orleans to conduct the exchange trade between the valley of the Mississippi and the Rocky Mountain states, and the cis and citra-tropical countries lying south of the United States. The physical reasons are obvious on the map. The commercial causes are just as decisive. Trade and travel now move in right lines both over land and ocean. New Orleans is a deep water port on the direct line between the populations of which it is the outlet and of those who desire intercourse with them, in the sale of tropical and other products, and the purchase of food and manufactures. Trade lines drawn between those reciprocal and compensating consumers concentrate for collection and distribution at New Orleans. It is at once a depot and entrepot of all these exchangeable commodities. It is the natural point at which many of these Spanish American States will receive their European goods, immigrants and mails. The differential tariff alone prevents this, but this removed, the stock and selection of goods by the jobbers of New Orleans, supplied by the merchants and manufacturers of the Union, will present such an assortment as will command the custom of smaller cities in the South, and of the whole retail trade on the coast and in the interior. These obstacles will be removed by the rapid growth of the United States, and the mutual *promotion* of interest on the part of itself and of its neighbors. The trade lines between St. Louis, Chicago and Cincinnati, and Rio Janeiro and Valparaiso, taken as extreme southern points, pass through and are concentrated at New Orleans. The whole of the western coast of South America connects at Panama with a line of steamers from New Orleans. Central America, Mexico and Cuba will likewise conduct their trade with the cities named through New Orleans.

There is an especial reason why the postal and passenger routes between these great interests should be conducted from New Orleans as a postal centre. The mail service between the United States and Brazil, Central America and Mexico, is conducted by steamer by New York. These routes are respectively about 3500, 2700 and

2000 miles. They are all subjected to insurances along the whole coast of the Atlantic States. When it is remembered that from each of the principal cities of the Union to New Orleans the government has a double daily postal service already paid for, it will be seen that a steam postal service to the ports named could be organized with great economy of time, distance and rate of insurance. The cities of the interior could conduct their intercourse with the foreign countries named directly with New Orleans, thus saving the cost of an extra journey to and from New York as a point of departure. The travel and trade between the countries named and the United States would be conducted inland, over our own railroads and rivers, instead of coastwise and outside, over an ocean route affording no such incidental advantages. It is useless to encumber these pages with an estimate of the value of trade or the number of passengers to be calculated on by a perfect organization of these enterprises. Such statistics change constantly, but the natural advantages are permanent, and sooner or later they will be realized, either by public appropriation or private enterprise. The trade of New Orleans in sugar and coffee is very heavy and is increasing annually. We require, however, our freights to Brazil upon which to base a regular system of coffee imports. Coffee is brought from Rio principally by vessels which take cotton, corn, or tobacco to New York or Liverpool. The coffee import should be based upon a direct exchange of commodities between New Orleans and Brazil.

MESSRS. A. B. GRISWOLD & CO.

This firm, of whose establishment we give a fine interior view, is the oldest and largest house in their line of business in the South. And, in fact, there are probably not more than one or two firms in New Orleans that can carry the record of a continuous business under different styles so far back as these gentlemen.

In the year 1815, in the then central portion of the city, at the corner of St. Louis and Chartres Streets, the business was established by Mr. Hyde, who was shortly after joined by Mr. Goodrich, composing the firm of Hyde and Goodrich. This name, by many years of honest industry, enterprise, and fair dealing, was made familiar as a household word throughout the whole South. When the weight of years compelled the founders of this house to cease from their labors, their sons assumed control and continued its affairs with the same system of honesty and liberal dealing, and with a still greater share of pecuniary success, commensurate with the growth in wealth and prosperity of the city. They weathered successfully all the financial storms of the last half century, preserving intact, through every disaster, the mercantile credit and honor of the house. As the tide of trade in New Orleans set more and more towards the American portion of the city, the firm removed their place of business to No. 15 Chartres Street, which was henceforth connected with their name, and extensively known through the Southwest for more than twenty years. It was while in Chartres Street, in the year 1847, that the head of the present house, Mr. A. B. Griswold, became connected with

the firm; first as a clerk, then as a partner, and has, during this long period of over a quarter of a century, been identified with it under its different suyles of Hyde and Goodrich; Thomas, Griswold and Co., and A. B. Griswold and Co. In 1853, for the third time in their history, the firm made a change of location, and removed to their present admirable position at the corner of Canal and Royal Streets, into one of a number of stores just built by Judah Touro, and the completed row of which now forms one of the handsomest ornaments of Canal Street.

Here, for twenty years more, they have successfully prosecuted their business and preserved the ancient reputation of the house, as well as maintained its commercial credit on a solid and substantial basis, Having their own office and resident agent in New York, and with foreign connections in England, France and Germany, they have facilities for the conduct of their business not excelled in the United States, and can always furnish to their customers at short notice, by direct orders, what their own large stock fails to supply. They are also agents for two of the most substantial manufacturing firms in the country, viz: "The Howard Watch and Clock Co.," and the "Gorham Manufacturing Company," the largest manufacturers of Sterling Silver Ware in the *world*. The advantages offered to their retail customers by these agencies are a very large and well assorted stock to select from, and at the schedule prices of the companies.

The Howard Watch and Clock Company manufacture the most reliable American watch in the market, as well as the finest counting-house clocks, regulators, watchman detector clocks and electric clocks. They make no inferior or low-priced goods, as is the case with so many other American makers, and any purchaser of a genuine Howard watch can depend upon its being an accurate timepiece

The Gorham Manufacturing Company is universally known in this country, (and their fame is now also European,) for the originality of their designs in silver and plated ware, the exquisite beauty and finish of all their work, and that combination of elegance and taste with economy in fabrication, (effected by machinery) which enables them to furnish a choice and beautiful article of silverware at a price no greater than for ordinary goods. Messrs. A. B. Griswold and Co., notwithstanding the age of their firm, are by no means old fogies, but are fully alive to the exigencies of the times, and realize the fact that those who would do a successful business now, must do it on the basis of "quick sales and small profits." They guarantee their goods in every respect, and offer in all cases a first-class article at the lowest market price. With a record behind them of some *fifty-eight* years of honorable dealing, we think our readers, both citizens and strangers, cannot transact their business in New Orleans more safely and satisfactorily with any firm in that line, than with Messrs. A. B. Griswold and Co.

The Mechanics' and Traders' Bank, is situated on Camp street, occupying only an ordinary house, compared to some others, and requires no particular description. Capital $2,000,000.

CLAY STATUE AND CRESCENT HALL.

THE corner stone of the above statue was laid by the Clay Statue Association of New Orleans on the 12th of April, 1856.

The inauguration, which called out one of the grandest and largest public gathings that ever took place in New Orleans, was on the 12th of April, 1860. On that occasion, Col. J. B. Walton acted as Grand Marshal and Col. J. O. Nixon as First Assistant Marshal.

J. Q. A. Fellows appeard at the head of the Masons as Grand Master.

Gerard Stith, now of the "Pecayune" office, was Mayor of the city at that time.

Joel T. Hart, of Kentuky, the artist who gave form and proportions to the Clay Statue, was present at the inauguration.

Wm. H. Hunt, Esq., was orator of the day.

He said, that in 1852, a number of public spirited citizens determined to erect a bronze statue of Henry Clay. They entrusted the work of making the statue to Joel T. Hart, of Kentucky.

"We are here to-day to dedicate this statue, the statue of Henry Clay."

"Behold, his life-like image stands before you. No royal robes adorn his person ; no crown, no sceptre, no badges of ancestral glory. No sword is by his side to tell of battles fought and won ; no baton to indicate the pomp and power of authority.

"A plain man in the simple garments of a citizen ; his image challeges not our admiration through the adventitious aids of rank, or the tinsel ornaments of military glory. But he stands before us as we knew him, as we loved and honored him, the embodiment of the genius, of the wisdom, of the eloquence, of the courage, of the public virtue, of self-sacrifice, of the patriotism which filled the measure of his country's glory, and made his name and his fame immortal."

"A circle of fifty feet in diameter, surmounted with an iron railing, and a flight of hexagon shape granite steps, each one smaller than the one on which it rests, forms the foundation on which the pedestal and statue rest. The pedestal, like the firm foundation, is of granite, fitting emblem of the lasting fame of the subject of the lasting figure which stands upon its top.

"The statue itself is a perfect likeness of the illustrious statesman. Its height is about fifteen feet. This, with the height of the foundation circle, steps and pedestal, makes it stand some forty feet high, an ornament to our grand and beautiful thoroughfare, Canal street."

CRESCENT HALL.

THIS building was originally erected by Cornelius Paulding, Esq., about the year 1826. In 1858 it was purchased by Mrs. Cora A. Slocomb, and remodeled into a hotel, known as the "Merchants." In 1865, Col. A. W. Merriam transformed it into a Billiard Hall.

HENRY HOWARD, ESQ.

This well-known and accomplished architect was born in the city of Cork, Ireland, February 8th 1818, where he remained till he reached the age of eighteen years. He pursued his education at the Mechanics' Institute of that city, and received from his father, Thomas Howard, a noted builder, of Cork, the first rudiments of Architectural drawing and a knowledge of Mechanics. Owing to his father's death which took place when he was sixteen years of age, he emigrated, in the Spring of 1836, from his native city to New York, with a view to continuing the study of architecture with an American architect. In this particular he was at first disappointed. Arriving in New York on the 8th of May 1836, after the great fire, he had to go into a Looking-glass and Picture-Frame Maker's establishment, where he remained eighteen months.

Being desirous of seeing an older brother living, at that time in New Orleans, he left New York for the South, and arrived here on the 20th of September 1837, in the height of the prevalence of the Yellow Fever, a disease, which, notwithstanding its frequent occurrence in New Orleans, he has hitherto fortunately escaped. On arriving in this city, he undertook all kinds of carpenter's and joiner's work, including the most difficult branch of it, viz, stair building, commanding at first, only journeyman's wages. He shrank from no task on account of its difficulty, worked with diligence and rapidity, and always studied the welfare of his employers. After being engaged in this way about five years, he was promoted to a foremanship under the late E. W. Sewell, a well-known builder.

In 1849, he pursued the study of Architecture for a short time, with the late Col. James H. Dakin, an able architect of this city; also, during the same year, with Henry Molhausen, a Prussian, a good surveyor and civil engineer.

In 1845, Mr. Howard commenced the erection of a large brick country residence on Bayou Lafourche, for the late Thomas Pugh, Esq. After its completion, he opened in 1848, an Architect's office in Exchange Place, and, in order to execute and finish with despatch the large amount of business entrusted to his care, he was in the habit, during the first few years of his professional practice, of working and studying from eighteen to twenty hours a day. His employment and success were uninterrupted till the occurrence of the late war, during the continuance of which he was employed as principal draughtsman in the Confederate States Naval Iron Works at Columbus, Georgia.

After the war was over, he returned to New Orleans and resumed the practice of his profession, and, notwithstanding dull times, high taxation and other troubles, has had, up to the present time, a fair share of business, sufficient to give himself and his numerous family a handsome living.

In the year 1839, while working at stair-building, he married in this city Miss Richards, a native of New York, by whom he has had eleven children—eight girls and three boys. Of these, there are surviving six daughters and two sons; also grand-children, the oldest being eleven years of age.

The following is a list of the buildings erected in this city from designs and specifications furnished by Mr. Howard, and, in most instances, under his personal supervision.

PUBLIC BUILDINGS IN THE CITY:

First Presbyterian Church, Lafayette Square;
Second Presbyterian Church, Washington Square;
St. Peter's Roman Catholic Church, Third District;
Importers' Bonded Warehouse, Second District;
Hale's Warehouse, First District;
Buildings for Louisiana Fair Grounds;
Engine House and Engine Foundations for Commercial Water Works;
Zoelly's Brewery Buildings, corner of Magazine and Delord street;
Home Mutual Insurance Buildings, First District;
Crescent Mutual Insurance Building, First District;
Conery's Stores, corner of Common and Water streets:
Avendano's Store, corner of Delta and Common streets;
Remodelling Equitable (late Tulane) Building, Camp st.;
Extensive addition to Jewish Widows' and Orphans' Home, corner of Jackson and Chippewa sts., Fourth Dist.;
St. Elizabeth Asylum, Magazine street, Fourth District;
Protestant Boys' Orphan Asylum, on St. Charles avenue, Sixth District;
Catholic Orphan Boys' Asylum, Third District;
New Syphilitic Wards and Dissecting Rooms at the Charity Hospital, Common Street.

PRIVATE BUILDINGS IN THE CITY:

Pontalba Buildings, Jackson Square, Second District;
Hale's Five Dwellings, Camp Street, First District;
Conery's Dwellings, Prytania Street, First District;
Cyprien Dufours's Dwelling, Esplanade street;
Vredenburg's Dwelling, Esplanade street;
Burthe's Suburban Residence St. Charles avenue;
Palacio's Suburban Residence, St. Charles avenue;
Miltenberger's Dwelling, St. Charles avenue;
Grinnan & Short's Villa, Prytania street, Fourth Dist.;
Buildings Nos. 8, 9 and 13 Commercial place.

PUBLIC AND PRIVATE BUILDINGS IN THE COUNTRY.

Thomas Pugh's Residence, Bayou Lafourche, Parish of Assumptions;
W. W. Pugh's Residence, Bayou Goula, Parish of Iberville;
John H. Randolph's Residence, Bayou Goula, Parish of Iberville;
General R. Camp's Residence, Bayou Goula, Parish of Iberville;
Remodelling Louis La Bourgeois' Residence, Parish of St. James;
Court House and Prison, Carrollton, Parish of Jefferson;
Court House and Prison, Thibodeaux, Parish of Lafourche;
Court House, Donaldsonville, Parish of Terrebone;
Presbyterian Church. Houma, Parish of Terrebone;
Episcopal Church, Houma, Parish of Terrebone;
Episcopal Church, Bayou Goula, Parish of Iberville.

REV. JOSEPH P. B. WILMER, D.D., BISHOP OF THE EPISCOPAL CHURCH OF LOUISIANA.

This learned and eloquent prelate is of a Maryland family, well-known in the annals of that State. He removed in early childhood to Virginia. He was educated at Kenyon College, Ohio, from which he received his first degree. His ministerial life passed in Virginia, where he married into the Skipwith family, and where he lived in charge of a parish, until he accepted a call to St. Mark's Church in Philadelphia. He received his Degree of Doctor of Divinity from Union College, Schenectady, N. Y. He resigned his parish in Philadelphia, at the commencement of hostilities between the North and South, believing that the course pursued by the former towards the latter was not only unconstitutional but unchristian, and feeling that he could not conscientiously invoke the blessing of Heaven on the success of a cause essentially unjust. On thus severing his connection with the North, and with a people to whom he was greatly attached, and who regarded him with love and veneration, and deeply regreting the step which, from a sacred regard to principle and a deep sense of duty, he felt himself compelled to adopt, he returned to his estate in Virginia and remained in retirement with his family till the close of the war. He was, soon after, elected to the Episcopate of Louisiana, and removed to this city.

Bishop Wilmer is about five feet eight inches in height, compactly built, with strongly knit and well-proportioned limbs, blue eyes, broad forehead, fair complexion, open countenance, plants himself firmly on his feet, gesticulates but little, and has a clear, rich and ringing voice suited to an orator, and reaching, without difficulty, the remotest parts of a large church. His head is silvered over with the snows of nearly three score years, but his aspect in the pulpit, when animated by his subject, is that of a man of forty or forty-five at the utmost. His manner is rather calm and dignified than impassioned; but he immediately arrests attention by the strong and generous thoughts that spring from his heart, and by the order and convincing force of his arguments. No scholar is a greater master of pure, vigorous, flexible and elegant English. No divine of the Church of England, or of any other church, is more liberal and tolerant in his opinions, nor more free from cant. He makes no compromise, however, with vice, folly or egotism, which he regards proper subjects of rebuke or censure.

He is a fine conversationalist, and the attentive listener knows not which to admire most, the breadth of his intellect, the extent of his information, or the goodness of his heart. The interests of Christianity and of the church are uppermost in his mind, and those who are honored by his friendship never fail to be impressed by the loftiness of his motives, and the extent of his charity. His object, in his interviews with others, seems to be to render the obligations of truth more imperative, and the Christian virtues more attractive than they were before. He has a decided antipathy to political preachers, political sermons, and political prayers, regarding them fruitful sources of the skepticism that prevails in this country at this time.

When the illustrious General Lee, at the close of the late war, doubted as to the expediency of accepting the invitation he had received to take charge of Lexington (afterwards Washington) College, he visited Dr. Wilmer to consult with him on the subject of his duty in this matter. At first Dr. Wilmer endeavored to dissuade the General from accepting so humble a post, adding that the Presidency of the Virginia University would be more suitable for him. The people of Virginia, and of the whole South, would be proud, he said, to see him placed at the head of their time-honored University.

General Lee, thanking the Doctor for his flattering proposal and promised aid in consummating it, promptly but decidedly declined, saying that Providence seemed to have clearly opened the way to his acceptance of the Lexington College, where he thought there would be a sphere of usefulness which would task his powers to the utmost.

His friend was deeply affected by his arguments, yielded to the modesty of this truly great man, acquiesced in his judgment, and embraced him with a degree of warmth which honest sympathy alone could inspire. "Now,'' said the latter, "I listen to you with pleasure."

The two friends, it is said, then discussed, *in extenso*, the great questions of education, and General Lee proceeded to organize and establish the Washington College, and to place it on a footing which has made it one of the most celebrbrated and valuable educational institutions in the country. A fairer illustration of the spirit of true Christianity cannot be furnished than was exhibited by those two eminent men on this occasion.

Dr. Wilmer, for the space of two years, was a Chaplain in the American Navy, during which engagement he visited various centres of civilization, among others thrice visited England. Few Americans have enjoyed finer opportunities for observation, and an extensive knowledge of mankind. He has four children—a daughter and three sons. One of his sons is a practitioner at law in the City of Baltimore.

MAJ. JOHN H. NEW.

Maj. New within a few years has succeded in placing himself in the front rank of his profession.

He is a native of Louisville, Ky.

He commenced the study of the law in the University of Mississippi. He afterwards graduated with high honors in Harvard College, Mass.

He first went to practice at Baton Rouge, where he soon made himself known for his intellect and legal lore.

In 1861 when the South resorted to arms, Maj. New served in Gen. Hays' brigade as Adjutant Genral and distinguished himself for his ability, ready knowledge and efficiency, in the discharge of his duties.

After the war Maj. New settled in New Orleans and devoted his attention to the practice of his profession. He has since visited the principal cities of Europe.

As a lawyer he is noted for the quickness of his perception. In an examination he fathoms the inmost thoughts of witnesses. Although generally dispassionate, he is an excellent speaker.

JOCKEY CLUB RACE COURSE.

APPENDIX.

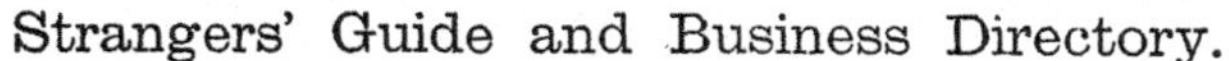

THE CITY GOVERNMENT

Incorporated 1804.

Organized 1804.

Reorganized 1852.

Reorganized 1870.

L. A. WILTZ, Mayor.

ADMINISTRATORS.

LOUIS SCHNEIDER,	Administrator of Finance.
JOHN CALHOUN,	" " Accounts.
H. F. STRUCKEN,	" " Assessments.
C. FITZENREITER,	" " Water Works.
JAMES LEWIS,	" " Public Improvements.
B. M. TURNBULL,	" " Commerce.
ROBERT REWSTER,	" " Police.

GEO. S. LACEY,	City Attorney.
HENRY WALSHE,	Assistant City Attorney.
J. B. CARTER,	Superintendent Public Schools.
S. WEEKS,	" Fire Alarm and Police Telegraph.
A. S. BADGER,	" Metropolitan Police.
J. E. DUTILLET,	" Insane Asylum.
J. A. NOBLE,	" Work House.
C. DAVISSON,	Librarian.
E. W. HALSEY,	Secretary of the Mayor.
DAN. SCULLY,	Secretary of the Board of Administrators.

W. H. BELL, - CITY SURVEYOR.
A. HERO, JR., - CITY NOTARY.

DISTRICT JUDGES.

EDMUND ABEL, - 1st District Court.
J. L. TISSOT, - 2nd   "   "
F. MONROE, - 3d   "   "
J. M. BONNER, - 4th   "   "
E. N. CULLOM, - 5th   "   "
A. SAUCIER, - 6th   "   "
T. W. COLLENS, - - - - - - - - - - - - - - - - - - - 7th   "   "
W. ELLMORE, - 8th   "   "

ATTORNEYS-AT-LAW.

ATTORNEYS AT LAW.

Atocha, A. A.
Augustin, D.
Augustin, J. D.
Baker, F. W.
Barnett, John J.
Barg, A.
Bartlette, T. A.
Beck, Thomas J.
Belcher, C.
Belden, J. K.
Belden, Simeon
Bemiss, C. T.
Bermudez, E.
Besancon, Clark W.
Besancon, C. W.
Bienvenu, Charles
Billings & Hughes
Blanc, S.
Bonner, John M.
Bradford, R. H. & J. L.
Braughn & Buck
Breaux, Fenner & Hall
Brewer, J.
Brice, A. G.
Brickell, J. N.
Brieugne, Anatole
Bright, George L.
Brown, George
Brown, S. R
Bryan, H. H. Jr.
Bryon, D. S.
Budd & Grover
Buddecke, C. B.
Cambray, E.
Cameron, Theodore
Campbell, Given
Campbell, J. A.
Canonge & Cazabat
Capdevielle, Paul
Case & Rouse
Castellanos, Henry C.
Chamberlain, F. G.
Charvet & Duplantier
Claiborne, Charles F.
Clarke, Bayne & Renshaw
Clerc, Charles
Clinton, J. W.
Clinton, Thomas P.
Cohen, Myer M.
Collins, T. S.
Colman, J. C.
Commandeur, Nicholas
Conrad & Son
Cooley, Thomas J.
Cooley, W. H.
Cooney, John M.
Cotton & Levy
Craig, Emmet D.
Crane, W. R.
Culbertson, John
Cullom, E. N.
Currell, J. R.
Cutler, R. King
Cuvellier, P. Chas.
Dalsheimer, Alex.
Dalton, Robert
Day, L. Madison

DeGray, R.
Dejean, J. A.
Denegre, C. Taylor
Denegre, W. O.
Dennee & Michel
Dinkelspiel, Max.
Dirrhammer & Kennard
Dooley, M. A.
Drouet, G.
Dubuisson, M. B.
Dugue, Henry
Dugue, Robert G.
Duvigneaud, Joseph
Earhart, F. B.
Edwards, W. W.
Egan, Bentinck
Elliott, B. C.
Elliott, John F.
Ellis, T. & J.
Elmore & King
Eustis, J. B.
Fellowes, E. T. & E. J.
Fellows & Mills
Ferguson, J. H.
Fernandez, G.
Field, A. P.
Filleul, E.
Finney, John J.
Forman, B. R.
Fouke, P. B.
Foute, M. A.
Fox Charles, H.
Freeman, John D.
Fuller, James
Fuselier, F.
Gastinel, Arthur
Gayarre, Charles
Gernon, M.
Gibson & Austin
Gifford, E.
Gill, T. M.
Gilmore, Thomas & Sons
Goldman, David
Gordan, W. Alex.
Graham, James
Grant, William
Grima, Alfred
Grivot, Maurice
Grow, John A.
Guillet, Edward C.
Hale, William G.
Hall, G. L.
Hall, H. H.
Harding, L.
Hart, T. B.
Hawkins & Tharp
Hays & New
Hornor & Benedict
Houston, W. T.
Howard, John B.
Howard, Thomas H.
Hudson, & Fearn
Hughes, D. M. C.
Hunt, Carlton
Hunt, Randal
Hunt, T. G.
Hunt, William H.
Huntington, Edward W.
Hunton & Grover

Hutcheson, R.
Hyams & Jonas
Ilsley, John H.
Jewell, E. L.
Johnson & Denis
Kelly, E. C.
Kelly, H. B.
Kelly, W. F.
Kendall, George W.
Kennedy & Chiapella
Ker, R. J.
Kerr & Slayden
Koontz, W. B.
Labatt & Aroni
Lacey & Butler
Lancaster, W. B.
Langdon, Thomas
Lauer, Etienne
Lea, Finney & Miller
Legendre & Poche
LeMonnier, John
Leovy & Monroe
Lewis, A. C.
Lewis, A. J.
Lingan, James
Livaudais, A. E.
Livaudais, M. E.
Livingston, J.
Lougue, Charles
Luzenberg, C. H.
Magioni, Joseph
Mansfield, E. S.
Marr, R. H.
May, C. Rodney
McCaleb, Howard E.
McCarty, A.
McCay, T. S.
McConnell, James
McGary, W. L.
McGloin & Kleinpeter
McPhelin, John
Meunier, E.
Meunier, Jerome
Michel, Julien
Micou, Augustin
Withoff, William, Jr.
Mix, E. C.
Morel, Christoval
Morel, Ernest
Morgan, H. G.
Morgan, P. H.
Murphy, William E.
Ogden, A. N.
Ogden, Charles G.
Ogden, Henry D.
Ogden, H. N.
Ogden, Robert N.
Ogden, W. F.
O'Sullivan, E.
Pierce, J. Caldwell
Philips, A. B.
Phillips, E.
Pitot, A.
Blanchard & Kramer
Poole, W. S.
Prentiss, S. S.
Preston, Robert S.
Price, H. H.
Quintero, Joseph A.

Race, Foster & E. T. Merrick
Randolph Singleton & Browne
Rawle, Edward
Reid, S. C.
Rice, Charles S.
Rice, Joseph A.
Richardson, Frank L.
Rightor, N. H.
Robert, Alexis
Roberts, Percy
Robertson, J. B.
Rogers, W. H.
Roman, J. J.
Roselius & Philips
Rozier, J. Ad.
Rozier, Valle J.
Sabourin, Ernest
Sadler, George W.
Sage, B. J.
Sambola & Ducros
Saucier & Michinard
Sawyer & Harding
Schmidt, C. E.
Schmidt, Gustavus
Schmidt, J. B. J.
Scott, W. T.
Seghers, Julian A.
Semmes, A. G.
Semmes & Mott
Shackleford, Richard
Shannon, Robert H.
Sheldon, L. A.
Simonds, L. E.
Smith, John P.
Smaer, S. R.
Soniat, Charles T.
Strawbridge, James
Taylor, Miles
Terrebonne, V. D.
Thomas, Q. A.
Thorpe, H. S.
Timony, James
Tissot, A. L.
Tissot, J. L.
Trist & Olivier
Trudeau, A.
Tully, John S.
Upton, Horace E.
Viavant, Augustin
Villere, A. J.
Voorhies, Albert
Walace, J. E.
Walker, Alexander
Walker, James C.
Walker, Samuel R. & C. L.
Wallace & Handlin
Waples, Rufus
Warren, E.
Washington, E. K.
Wenck & Hufft
Whitaker, J. S.
Whitaker, William R.
White, E. D.
Whitney, Charles E.
Whittemore, E. N.
Wilson, J. N. A.
Wooldridge & Thomas
Work, Phillip A.
Zacharie, F. C.

ACADEMIES.

ACADEMY OF SCIENCE. L. Unv., cor. Common and Barronne, ent. Barronne.

ACADEMY OF THE HOLY ANGELS. Cond. by the Sisters of the Holy Cross, Rampart, N. W. cor. Congress.

ACADEMY OF OUR LADY OF THE SA-CRED HEART. Cond. by the Marionite Sisters of the Holy Cross, 56 and 58 Hospital.

ACADEMY OF THE SACRED HEART. Emily Gardiner, Sup'r., 96 Dumain.

BOYS' CLASSICAL AND COMMERCIAL ACADEMY. R. M. Lusher, Prin. 247 St. Charles, op. Tivoli Circle.

BOYS' ELEMENTARY CLAS. AND COM-MERCIAL ACADEMY. A. Cordiers, Prin. 253 Johnson, cor. of Barracks.

ENGLISH, FRENCH AND GERMAN ACADEMY. Robinson, N. W. cor. St. Ann.

FRECH'S ACADEMY. Louis A. Frech, Prin. 82 Hospital.

ST. ALOYCIOUS' ACADEMY. Cond. by Bros. of the Sacred Heart, Chartres cor. Barracks.

ST JOHN'S COMMERCIAL ACADEMY, (private). John Dimitry, Prin. Dryades cor. Clio.

ST. FRANCIS ACADEMY, (girls). Sister Victoria Mensonier, 585 Villere, N. W. cor. Marigny, 3rd Dist.

ST. JOSEPH'S ACADEMY, (girls). Sister Stevens, superior, 337 St. Philip.

ST. VINCENT'S ACADEMY, Bro. Albian, Director, Napoleon av., bet. Magazine and Camp.

ST. VINCENT DE PAUL'S ACADEMY, (boys). Rev. Father Foltier, Director. Dauphin bet. Cluet and Montegut, 3rd Dist.

ST. VINCENT DE PAUL'S ACADEMY, (girls). Cond. by the Sisters of the Holy Cross. Dauphin bet. Cluet and Montegut.

ST. MAURICE ACADEMY. Trico, cor. Chartres

ASYLUMS.

ASYLUM FOR DESTITUTE ORPHAN BOYS—ss. St. Charles, bet. Valmont and Dufossat, Jefferson City.

ASYLUM FOR THE LITTLE SISTERS OF THE POOR—Sister Marie Claire, prin. Laharpe, bet. Johnson and Prieur.

BEAUREGARD ASYLUM—Pauline, bet. St. Claude and Rampart.

BOYS HOUSE OF REFUGE—Perilliat, se. cor. Magnolia.

CHILDREN'S HOME (Episcopal) — Miss Kate Lynn, prin., Jackson, bet. Chippewa and St. Thomas.

FEMALE ASYLUM OF THE IMMACU-LATE CONCEPTION—871 Rampart, cor. Elmira, 3d dist.

FEMALE ORPHAN ASYLUM OF OUR LADY OF MT. CARMEL—Sister St. Jean Baptiste, prin. 53 Piety, bet. Dauphine and Royal.

GERMAN PROTESTANT ASYLUM—P. Schumann, supt. State, bet. Camp and Chesnut, Burtheville.

GIRARD ASYLUM—Metairie rd., bet. St. Louis and Conti.

HOME FOR THE AGED AND INFIRM—Mary S. Griffin, directress, Tchoupitoulas, sw. cor. 2d.

HOME FOR THE AGED AND INFIRM—Mrs. Ann Gorman, matron, Washington av. cor. Locust.

HOUSE OF REFUGE FOR DESTITUTE GIRLS — Mrs. Eleanor Stokes, matron, Annunciation, sw. cor. Calliope.

HOUSE OF THE GOOD SHEPARD—Sister Mary Rose. superior, Bienville, bet. Broad and Dolhonde.

INDIGENT COLORED ORPHAN ASY-LUM—V. Dupart, pres. 393 Dauphine.

INSANE ASYLUM — John E. Dutillet, supt. Orleans, bet. Marais and Liberty.

JEWISH WIDOWS AND ORPHANS ASYLUM—Jackson, cor. Chippewa, Levi Shoenberg, supt.

LOUISIANA RETREAT INSANE ASY-LUM—Sister Savarrina, superior, Nashville av. sw. cor. Magazine, Hurstville.

NEW ORLEANS FEMALE ORPHAN ASYLUM—Sister Mary Margaret, prin. Clio, bet. Camp and Prytania.

NEWS BOYS' HOME—C. R. Ross, supt. 165 Franklin.

POYDRAS ORPHAN ASYLUM FOR FE-MALES—Magazine, bet. Leontine and Peters, Jefferson.

PROTESTANT ORPHAN HOME—Mrs. Pargoud, pres.; Mrs. Wilbur, vice-pres.; Mrs. Ginder, sec.; Mrs. Carroll, treas. 7th, cor. Constance.

PROVIDENCE ASYLUM FOR COLORED FEMALE CHILDREN—Mary B. Atkins, directress. Hospital, cor. Touti.

ST. ANNA'S ASYLUM—Mrs. James Clark, pres.; Mrs. R. Charles, sec. Prytania, cor. St. Mary.

ST. ELIZABETH ORPHAN ASYLUM—East side Magazine, bet. St. Andrew and Josephine.

ST. JOSEPH ORPHAN ASYLUM—Laurel, bet. Josephine and St. Andrew.

ST. MARY'S ORPHAN BOYS' ASYLUM—Chartres, bet. Mazant and French.

ST. VINCENT'S HALF-ORPHAN ASY-LUM—Sister Ernestine, superior. Cambronne, bet. 2d and Burthe, Carrollton.

ST. VINCENT'S HOME FOR BOYS—371 Bienville.

ST. VINCENT'S INFANT ASYLUM—Magazine, cor. Race.

BOARD OF BROKERS.

9 CARONDELET ST. UP STAIRS. Geo. C. Lawrason, pres.; Francis Rawle, vice-pres.

BANKING INSTITUTIONS.

BANK OF AMERICA—Canal st., cor. Exchange place. Incorporated 1857. Capital $507,800. Offering days, Tuesdays and Fridays. Discount days, Wednesdays and Saturdays.

BANK OF LAFAYETTE—Cor. Magazine and St. Mary sts., 4th dist.

BANK OF LOUISIANA—(In liquidation.)

BRANCH OF THE FREEDMAN'S SAV-ING AND TRUST COM'Y—114 Carondelet.

CANAL BANK—Camp, cor. Gravier. Incorporated 1831. Capital, $1,000,000. Discount days, Wednesdays and Saturdays.

CITIZENS BANK OF LOUISIANA—Custom House, cor. Royal.

CONSOLIDATED ASSOCIATION OF THE PLANTERS OF LOUISIANA — Henri Peychaud, pres.; H. L. Peire, cashier. 66 Toulouse.

CRESCENT CITY BANK—Carondelet, cor. Union. Capital $406.200. Offering day, Tuesday. Discount day, Wednesday.

GERMANIA NATIONAL BANK (late City National), 52 Camp. Capital, $300,000. Offering days, Mondays and Thursdays.

HIBERNIA BANK OF NEW ORLEANS —117 Camp. Capital, $500,000. Discount days, Tuesday and Friday.

THE LOUISIANA SAVINGS BANK AND SAFE DEPOSIT CO.—51 Camp.

MECHANICS' AND TRADERS' BANK OF NEW ORLEANS.—48 Canal. Capital, $750,000. Discounts every day.

MERCHANTS' BANK.—48 Camp.

MUTUAL NATIONAL BANK OF NEW ORLEANS—106 Canal. Capital, $500,000. Privilege, $1,000,000.

METROPOLITAN LOAN, SAVINGS AND PLEDGE BANK—14 Camp. Capital, $500,000.

NEW ORLEANS NATIONAL BANKING ASSOCIATION.—102 Canal. Capital, $600,000. Discount every day.

NEW ORLEANS NATIONAL BANK—54 Camp. Capital, $500,000.

NEW ORLEANS SAVINGS INSTITU-TION—187 Canal.

SOUTHERN BANK—11 St. Charles st. Incorporated 1852. Capital, $1,000,000. Discount days, Wednesdays and Saturdays.

STATE NATIONAL BANK OF NEW ORLEANS (late Louisiana State Bank)—31 and 33 Camp, and 131 Gravier. Offering days, Tuesdays; answers, 12 M., Wednesdays.

TEUTONIA NATIONAL BANK OF NEW ORLEANS.—28 Camp.

THE LOUISIANA NATIONAL BANK OF NEW ORLEANS—120 and 122 Common, bet. Camp and St. Charles. Capital, $1,000,000.

PEOPLE'S BANK OF NEW ORLEANS—Old Levee, corner St. Peter.

UNION BANK OF LOUISIANA—3 Carondelet. Incorporated 1854. Capital, $600,000. Discount days, Tuesdays and Fridays.

CEMETERIES.

American Cemetery, Basin, bet. St. Louis and Conti.

Cemetery of the Ev. Luth. St Johns Church, Canal, bet. Anthony and Bernadotte.

Charity Hospital Cemetery, head of Canal.

Cypress Grove Cemetery, No. 2, Metairie, ne. cor. Canal.

Fireman's Cemetery, ws. Canal, n. of Charity.

Girod Street Cemetery, Peter Barr, sexton, Liberty st. bet. Perrilliat and Cypress.

Greenwood Cemetery, Metaire, se. corner Canal.

Hebrew Cemetery, Canal, bet. Metairie and Anthony.

Hebrew Cemetery, Jackson, cor. White.

Lafayette Cemetery, No. 1, Washington, bet. Prytania and Coliseum.

CHAMBER OF COMMERCE.

Meets first Monday of each month at Merchant's Exchange Building, 120 Common st. Jos. H. Oglesby, pres.; Jas. T. Tucker, 1st vice-pres.; Edward Newman, 2d vice-pres.; Wm. M. Burwell, sec. and treas.

STANDING COMMITTEES.

Committee on Arbitration—Messrs. E. H. Sanford, Summers, W. Cooper, A. H. Peale. D. W. C. D. Chaffraix, J. H. Polhaus, Marshal J. Smith.

Committee on Appeals—Messrs. George A. Fosdick, Moses Greenwood, F. Dolhonde. W. B. Schmidt, Joseph West.

Executive Committee—Messrs. G. L. Laughland, J. L. Dunnica, C. E. Slayback, J. Prudhomme, Jules Vairin.

CCMMITTEE ON RIVER OBSTRUC-TIONS—Messrs. G. L. Laughland, Marshall J. Smith, Alfred Moulton, L. J. Higby, J. S. Copes.

N. O. BOARD OF UNDERWRITERS.

Meets at the offi e of the Crescent Mutual Insurance Company every Tuesday. Thos. A. Adams, pres.; Charles Briggs, vicepres.; H. P. Janvier, sec.; L. W. Cooper, inspector; Arthur C. Waugh, agent for the Boards of Underwriters of New York, Boston, Philadelphia, Baltimore, Lloyds Habaners, Havana: Lloyd's of London, and Underwriter's Association of Liverpool, England. Office, 33 Carondelet.

Dry Docks and Boat Builders.

GOOD INTENT—5th dist., ab. Canal (1st dist.) st. Ferry and head of Delaronde st.

MAHONY'S BOAT YARD—Bet. 2d dist., (French Ferry) from St. Ann st. to Bouny.

OCEAN DOCK—Two blocks below 2d dist. Ferry.

MARINE DOCK—Three blocks below 2d dist. Ferry, foot of Laverone.

VALLET DOCK—one block below 3rd dist. Ferry and foot.

DRIVES for Pleasure Carriages.

Canal st. to Metaire Ridge; Bienville st. to Metaire Ridge; Common st. to Metaire Ridge; Delord st. (New Shell Road) to Lake; St. Charles st. to Carrollton.

ELEVATOR (GRAIN) BUILDINGS AND WHARF—Tchoupitoulas, bet. Harmony and Pleasant. L. G. Higby & Son, props.

EXPOSITION HALL—E. fr. on St. Charles, bet Girod and Julia, W. fr. Caronde let.

FAIR GROUNDS AND BUILDINGS—N. s. Esplanade, nr. Bayou St. John.

Foreign Consuls and Consular Agents in New Orleans.

Austria, Bavaria and Baden, A. Eimer Bader, Consul, 17 Carondelet.

Belgium, Alexander Marks, vice consul, 38 Chartres.

Brazil, A. F. Elliot, vice consul, 184 Gravier.

Costa Rica, J. A. Quintero, consul, 5 Carondelet.

Danish, H. Frellsen, consul, 30 Magazine.

France, Charles Fauconnet, acting consul, 11 St. Louis.

Great Britain, Denis Donohoe, consul. Henry V. Ogden, acting, 13 Carondelet

Greece, N. M. Benachi, consul, 2 Carondelet.

Italy, Fabio Sanminiatelli, consul, 208 Royal.

Mexico, R. S. Dias, consul, 196 Chartres.

Netherlands, A. M. Coutourie, 30 Decatur.

Nicaragua, John E. Beylle, consul, room C. Gallier Court.

Norway and Sweden, William M. Perkins, 64 Carondelet.

North German Confederation, John Kruttschnitt, consul, 42 Perdido.

Portugal, A. J. DaSilva, consul, 57 Decatur, 2d dist.

Republic of Mexico, Ramon Dias, consul, 196 Chartres.

Russia, J. F. Schroder, vice consul, 192 Gravier.

Spain, Carlos Pie, consul 113 Dauphine.

Switzerland, X. Wessenbach, consul, 44 Carondelet.

Venezuela, Anderson D. Dieter, consul, 27 Carondelet.

Wurtemburg, H. F. Klumpp, consul, 42 Union.

FERRIES.

First dist.—New Orleans and Algiers ferry landing, Canal st.

Second dist.—New Orleans and Algiers ferry landing, St. Ann st.

Third dist.—New Orleans and Algiers ferry landing, Elysian Fields st.

Fourth dist.—New Orleans and Gretna ferry landing, Jackson st.

Morgan's La. and Texas Railroad ferry—from foot of St. Ann st., to railroad depot, Algiers.

Slaughterhouse Co's ferry—from and to slaughterhouses, Algiers.

Bobb's Ferry—starts from foot of Louisiana av. to Gretna.

GASLIGHT COMPANIES.

Jefferson City, F. G. Lockwood, sec. St. Charles, se. cor. Napoleon av.

New Orleans Gaslight Co. James Jackson, pres., W. S. Brown, Treas. Office, 159 Common. Works, Gravier, bet. Freret and Magnolia.

HOTELS.

Carondelet House—M. Ainslie, prop. Carondelet, ne. cor. Poydras.

Carrollton Hotel—Daniel S. Hicock, prop. St. Charles, opp. Dublin, Carrollton.

Cassidy's Hotel—Hugh Cassidy, prop., 38 Carondelet and 172 Gravier.

Central House—Mrs. M. J. Fisher, prop., 130 and 132 Camp.

City Hotel—R. S. Morse, prop., Camp, cor. Common.

Commercial Hotel—John C. Usener, prop., 48 Girod.

Conti Verandah—Mrs. Louisa Schwartz, prop., 23, 25 and 27 Conti.

Louisiana Hotel—213 and 215 Tchoupitoulas street.

Murphy's Hotel—Alex. Taylor, prop., 98 and 100 St. Charles.

Oviatt House—Silas Oviatt, prop., 11 Dauphin.

St. Charles—Rivers & Lonsdale, proprs., St. Charles, bet. Common and Gravier.

St. James—R. S. Morse, prop., es. Magazine, bet. Gravier and Natchez.

St. Louis—St. Louis, bet. Chartres and Royal.

Texas—J. J. Cheney, prop., Thayer, sw. cor. Verret, 5th dist.

Waverly Hotel—T. W. Kidder, prop., 101 Camp and 129 Poydras.

HOSPITALS AND INFIRMARIES.

Hospitals.

Charity Hospital—Common, bet. Locust and Howard. Officers: Dr. H. Hire, secretary and treasurer. Dr. A. W. Smith, house surgeon. Board of Administrators: Gov. H. C. Warmoth, pres. Jacob Hawkins, vice-pres. Hon. Michael Hahn, R. W. Watson, J. C. LeClare, Sidney Thezan, John Stump, Dominic Urbau.

City Hospital—Elysian Fields, near Miro.

Hayes' House of Health—431 Elysian Fields.

Hospital de la Saint Famille, for colored widows. Francois Lacroix, supt. 40 St. Bernard.

Hotel Dieu—ss. Common, bet. Johnson and Bertrand. Sister Theresa, supt.

Marine Hospital—W. H. Hire, physician, Broad, bet. Common and Gravier.

Smallpox Hospital—Common, bet. Hagan av. and Genois.

Infirmaries.

Cireus Street Infirmary—132 and 134 Rampart, 1st dist.

Infirmary of the Sisters of Charity, Hotel Dieu, Common, bet. Bertram and Johnson. Dr. P. C. Boyer, attending physician and surgeon. Dr. Warren Stone, consulting surgeon.

Orleans Infirmary—142 Canal st., conducted by Drs. S. Choppin, C. Beard, D. W. Brickell, and J. D. Burns.

Touro Infirmary—L. B. Kane, pres. ws. Peters, bet. Calliope and Gaiennie.

INCORPORATED COMPANIES.

Crescent City Ice Company. J. F. Kranz, pres.; J. J. E. Massicot, treas. 21 Camp.

Crescent City Stock Landing, (left Bank), Front Levee, below Jackson Barracks.

German Building Association, office, No. 10 St. Peter st. Business hours from 9.30 a. m. to 3 p. m. R. H. Schmidt, pres.

Good Intent Tow Boat and Balize Telegraph Company; W. G. Coyle, pres., Edward A. Yorke, supt.; Eugene Morris, sec.; 35 Carondelet.

Louisiana Ice Manufacturing Company—Tchoupitoulas, bet. Delachaise and Aline. William T. Hepp, pres.; D. Pochelu, sec. and treas.; office, 58 Camp.

Louisiana State Lottery Company—St. Charles, cor. Union.

New Orleans Elevator and Warehouse Company—office, Louisiana National Bank Building, 120 Common st. L. J. Higby, pres.; Len. Higby, sec.

New Orleans Gas Light Company—office, 159 Common st. James Jackson, pres.; Theobald Forstall, gen'l supt.; William S. Brown, treas.; John Van Slooten, engineer.

New Orleans Law Library Association—Courthouse, Chartres, opp. Jackson sq. J. Ad. Rozier, pres.; T. L. Bayne, sec.

New Orleans Sanitary and Fertilizing Co. Dr. F. Formento, jr. pres.; E. G. Golden, secretary. Freret, cor. Clio.

National Steam Transportation Company—office, 122 Gravier. Officers: Theo. W. Buddecke, pres.; J. M. Wagner, vicepres.; W. A. Bartlett, sec.; D. DeHaven, supt.

New Orleans Sugar Shed Co—Office, 41 Carondelet. Jules Blanc, pres.; Gustave Cuculu, sec.

New Orleans Wrecking and Salvage Co.—E. K. Converse, pres.; Greenleaf Andrews, supt.; Walter S. Crawford, sec. 84 Magazine.

Southern Paving Co.—E. J. Hart, pres.; C. McRae Selph, sec.; J. C. Riddle, supt. 77 Tchoupitoulas.

The Loan and Pledge Association Accommodation Bank. E. B. Benton, pres.; R H. Wood, Cashier. Office, St. Charles, cor. Perdido.

CHURCHES.

CONGREGATIONAL CHURCHES.

ALGIERS CHURCH, ALGIERS—(col'd)—Valette, near Eliza. Sabbath services, 11 a. m. and 7.30 p. m.; Sunday school, 3 p. m. Prayer and conference meeting, Thursday evening.

FIRST CHURCH—Prytania, nr. Calliope. Rev. M. W. Reed, pastor. Sabbath services, 11 a. m., and 7.30 p. m.; Sunday school, 9.30 a. m. Prayer and conference meeting, Wednesday evening. Industrial School and Mite Society, Saturday afternoon, in chapel.

GRETNA CHURCH, GRETNA (col'd)—Sabbath services, 11 a. m. and 7.30 p. m.; Sunday school, 9 a. m. Prayer and conference meeting, Thursday evening.

HOWARD CHURCH—(col'd)—Spain, nr. St. Claude. Sabbath services, 11 a. m. and 7.30 p. m.; Sunday school, 3 p. m. Prayer and conference meeting, Thursday evening.

MORRIS BROWN CHURCH—(col'd)—467 Villere, 3d dist. Sabbath services, 11 a. m. and 7.30 p. m.; Sunday school, 3 p. m. Prayer and conference meeting, Thursday evening.

ST. ANDREW STREET CHURCH (col'd)—St. Andrew, cor. Willow. Sabbath services, 11 a. m. and 7.30 p. m.; Sunday school, 3 p. m. Prayer and conference meeting, Thursday evening.

UNIVERSITY CHURCH—Esplanade, cor. Derbigny. Sabbath services, 11 a. m. and 7.30 p. m.; Sunday school, 3 p. m. Prayer and conference meeting, Thursday evening.

ZION CHURCH (col'd)—123 Johnson. Sabbath services, 11 a. m. and 7.30 p. m.; Sunday school, 3 p. m. Prayer and conference meeting, Thursday evening.

EPISCOPAL CHURCHES.

DIOCESE OF LOUISIANA—Office, 92 Camp. Right Rev. J. P. B. Wilmer, D.D., LLD., bishop; W. McW. Wright, treas.; Rev. Herman C. Duncan, sec.

ANNUNCIATION CHURCH—Cor. Race and Camp. Rev. John Percival, rector. Sunday services, 11 a. m. and 7.30 p. m.; Sunday school, 9 a. m.

CALVARY CHURCH—Prytania, nr. 6th. Rev. D. S. Lewis, rector. Sunday services, 11 a. m. and 7.30 p. m. Sunday school, 9 a. m.

CHRIST CHURCH—Canal, cor. Dauphine. Rev. W. S. Leacock, rector; W. T. Leacock, pastor. Sunday services 11 a. m. and 7.30 p. m.; Sunday school, 9 a. m.

EMANUEL CHURCH—Jefferson City. Rev. Chas. Morrison, rector. Sunday services, 11 a. m.; Sunday school, 9.30 a. m.

L'EGLISE PROTESTANT FRANCAIS.

MOUNT OLIVET CHURCH, ALGIERS—Rev. C. W. Hilton, rector. Sunday services, 11 . m. and 7 p. m.; Sunday school, 9 a. m.

ST. JOHN'S CHURCH—Third, cor. Annunciation.

ST. PAUL'S CHURCH—Camp, cor. Gaiennie. Rev. W. F. Adams, rector. Sunday services, 11 a. m. and 7.30 p. m.; Sunday school, 9 a. m. Daily service at 10 a. m.

ST. ANNA'S CHURCH—177 Esplanade—Rev. J. F. Girault, rector. Sunday services, 11 a. m. and 7.30 p. m.; Sunday school, 9 a. m.

ST. TRINITY ORTHODOX CHURCH—Rev. Father Gregorius Lagias, Dorgenois, bet. Hospital and Barracks. Service every Sunday at 9.30 a. m.

TRINITY CHAPEL—Dryades, cor. Euterpe. Rev. A. Marks, rector. Sunday services, 11 a. m.; Sunday school, 9 a. m.

TRINITY CHURCH—Jackson, cor. Coliseum. Rev. S. S. Harris, rector. Sunday services, 11 a. m. and 7.30 p. m.; Sunday school, 9 a. m.

AFRICAN CHURCH—Coliseum, bet. Bordeaux and Valence.

JEWISH SYNAGOGUES.

DISPERSED OF JUDA—Rev. H. S. Jacobs, minister. A. H. D'Meza, pres. 218 Carondelet. Services, Fridays, 5 p. m. and Saturdays, 9 a. m.

GATES OF MERCY—Rev. J. L. Leucht, minister. F. Hollander, pres. Rampart, bet. Conti and St. Louis. Services, Fridays, 5 p. m. Saturdays, 9 a. m.

GATES OF PRAYER—Rev. Mr. Moshe, Minister. L. Bodenheimer, pres. Jackson, bet. Chippewa and Annunciation. Services, Fridays, 5 p. m., Saturdays, 8 a. m.

THE RIGHT WAY—B. E. Jacob, minister. William Davis, pres. Carondelet, bet. Poydras and Lafayette. Services, Fridays, 5 p. m., Saturdays, 8.30 a. m.

TEMPLE SINAI—Rev. Godheim. Es. Carondelet ab. Delord-Worship

TEMIME DERECH—Rev. Jacobs. Es. Carondelet, bet. Lafayette. Worship, 6.30 p. m. Saturday, 9 a. m.

LUTHERAN CHURCHES.

BETHLEHEM CHURCH—368 Felicity rd. Henry Kleinhagen, pastor. Sabbath services, 10 a. m. and 3 p. m. Sunday school, 9 a. m.

EVANGELICAL CHURCH (German)—Milan, sw. cor. Camp. Frederick Judt, pastor. Sabbath services, 10 a. m. and 3 p. m. Sunday school, 9 a. m.

FIRST EVANGELICAL CHURCH—Port, cor. Burgundy. Christian Moedinger, pastor. Sabbath services, 10 a. m. and 7 p. m.

GERMAN CHURCH—Branch of Zion German Lutheran Church. Chippewa, cor. 4th. M. Tirmenstein, pastor.

FIRST GERMAN PROTESTANT CHURCH—Clio, bet. St. Charles and Carondelet. Rev. H. J. Perpeet, pastor.

GERMAN PROTESTANT CHURCH—Chippewa, cor. Philip. P. L. Heintz, pastor. Sunday services, 10 a. m. and 7 p.m. Sunday school, 9 a. m.

GERMAN PROTESTANT CHURCH, CARROLLTON—Zimpel, cor. Monroe. Rev. T. A. Polster, pastor.

MADISON STREET CHURCH—Madison, bet. Burthe and 3d. Carrollton.

ST. JOHN EVANGELIST CHURCH—Customhouse, cor. Prieur. C. F. Leibe, pastor. Sabbath services, 10 a. m. and 3 p. m.

ZION GERMAN—Euterpe, bet. Baronne and Dryades. M. Tirmenstein, pastor.

METHODIST EPISCOPAL CHURCHES.

AFRICAN CHURCH—Valence, cor. Chestnut. Rev. Joseph Gould, pastor.

AMES CHAPEL—St. Charles, cor. Calliope. Rev. J. C. Hartzell, pastor. Sabbath services, 11 a. m. and 7 p. m. Sunday school, 9 a. m. and 3 p. m.

BETHEL AFRICAN CHURCH—Roman, nr. Bienville.

BETHLEHEM CHURCH (colored)—357 Camp

FIRST STREET CHURCH (colored), Winan's Chapel—Dryades, ne. cor. 1st. Sabbath services, 11 a. m. and 7 p. m. Sunday school, 9 a. m. Prayer meeting, Thursday evening.

GERMAN CHURCH (colored)—Felicity rd., bet. Dryades and Rampart. Sabbath services, 11 a. m. and 7 p. m. Sunday school, 9 a. m. Prayer meeting, Thursday evening.

LAHARPE STREET CHURCH (colored)—Laharpe, bet. Roman and Prieur. Sabbath services, 11 a. m. and 7 p. m. Sunday school, 9 a. m. Prayer meeting, Thursday evening.

SOULE CHAPEL (colored)—Marais, near Bienville. Sabbath services, 11 a. m. and 7 p. m. Sunday school, 9 a. m. Prayer meeting, Thursday evening.

PORT STREET CHURCH (col'd)—Green's Chapel—93 Washington. Sabbath services, 11 a. m. and 7 p. m. Sunday school, 9 a. m. Prayer meeting, Thursday evening.

SIXTH STREET CHURCH (col'd—6th, near Constance. Rev. Eugene Royal, pastor. Sabbath services, 11 a. m. and 7 p.m. Sunday school, 9 a. m. Prayer meeting, Thursday evening.

ST. PAUL'S CHURCH (col'd) 132 Liberty, 1st dist.

ST. MARY'S STREET CHURCH (col'd)—Chippewa, cor. St. Mary. Sabbath services, 11 a. m. and 7 p. m. Sunday school, 9 a. m. Prayer meeting, Thursday evening.

UNION BETHEL CHURCH (col'd)—St. Mary, cor. St. Thomas.

WESLEY CHAPEL—(col'd)—St. Paul, bet. Poydras and Perdido. Rev. James Haywood, pastor. Sabbath services, 11 a. m. and 7 p. m. Sabbath school, 9 a. m. Prayer meeting, Thursday evening.

ZION CONGREGATION (colored)—123 Johnson. 1st district.

METHODIST EPISCOPAL (South.)

ALGIERS CHURCH—Algiers. Rev. J. Gorton Miller, pastor. Sabbath services, 11 a. m. and 7 p. m. Sunday school, 9 a. m. Conference and prayer meetings, Wednesday evening.

DRYADES STREET CHURCH—Dryades, cor. Felicity rd. Rev. John A. G. Rabe, pastor. Sabbath services, 11 a. m. and 7.30 p. m. Sunday school, 9 a. m. Prayer meeting, Tuesday evening. Preaching, Thursday evening.

FELICITY CHURCH—Felicity rd., near Chestnut. Rev. John Matthews, pastor. Sabbath services, 11 a. m. and 7.30 p. m. Sunday school, 9 a. m. Prayer and Conference Meeting, Thursday evening.

GERMAN CHURCH—Burgundy, bet. Washington av. and Music. Rev. J. B. A. Ahrens, pastor. Sabbath services, 11 a.m. and 7.30 p. m. Sunday school, 9 a. m. Prayer and conference meeting, Monday evening. Preaching, Thursday evening.

CADIZ STREET CHURCH—Cadiz st., cor. Coliseum. Rev. P. M. Goodwyn, pastor. Sabbath services, 11 a. m. and 7.30 p. m. Sunday school, 9 a. m.

LOUISIANA AVENUE CHURCH—Louisiana av., cor. Magazine. Rev. James A. Ivy, pastor. Sabbath services, 11 a. m. and 7 p. m. Sunday school, 9 a. m.

McGHEE CHURCH—Carondelet, bet. Lafayette and Girod. Rev. W. V. Tudor, pastor. Sabbath services, 11 a. m. and 7 p. m. Sunday school, 9 a. m. Prayer and conference meeting, Thursday evening.

MOREAU STREET CHURCH—Chartres (late Moreau) cor. Lafayette. Rev. Thos. B. White, pastor. Sabbath services, 11 a. m. and 7 p. m. Sunday school, 9 a. m. Prayer and conference meeting, Friday evening.

SORAPARU CHURCH—Soraparu, corner Chippewa. Rev. J. B. Ahrens, pastor. Sabbath services, 11 a. m. and 7.30 p. m. Sunday school, 9 a. m.

ST. JOHN'S CHAPEL (colored)—Market st., Algiers. Rev. J. B. Woods, pastor.

MISCELLANEOUS.

CHAPEL OF THE URSULINE CONVENT—Third District. Mass on Sunday at 6.30 and 8.30 o'clock.

ST. ANTOINE'S (funeral Chapel)—Rampart, cor. Conti.

HOLY CROSS (male orphan asylum)—Independence st., 3d dist. Rev. F. Toohey, C. S. C., pastor.

HOLY NAME OF MARY—Verret, bet. Alix and Eliza. Rev. F. Denis, pastor.

NOTRE DAME DEBONSECOURS(French) Jackson, bet. Laurel and Constance. Rev. Father DeHam, C. SS. R. and Rev. F. Fevere, C. SS., R., pastors. Week day mass, 5 o'clock; on Sunday, first mass, 7 o'clock, and high mass at 10 o'clock; sermon at 10 o'clock; evening sermon at 5.30 o'clock in summer and 5 in winter.

ST. ALPHONSUS'—Constance. bet. St. Andrew and Josephine. Rev. J. B. Duffy, pastor. Week day mass, 5.30, 6 and 8 o'clock; Sundays, 6, 8 and 10 o'clock; sermon, 10 o'clock; vespers, 3 o'clock; evening devotion and sermon, 7 o'clock.

ST. ANN'S CHURCH—St. Philip, bet. Roman and Prieur. Rev. Father Tumoine, pastor. Week day mass, 7 o'clock; Sunday, 7 and 9.30; sermon, 9.30; vespers, 3.30 o'clock.

ST. AUGUSTINE'S CHURCH—Hospital, cor. Franklin. Rev. Father Joubert, Rev. Father Sublieau, pastors. Week day mass, 7 o'clock; Sunday, 7, 8 and 10; sermon, 10 o'clock; vespers, 4 o'clock.

ST. HENRY, BOULIGNY (German)—Berlin, bet. Live Oak and Magazine. Rev. J. Bogaerts, C. M., pastor. Mass and sermon, 10 o'clock; vespers and benediction, 3 o'clock.

ST. JOHN THE BAPTIST CHURCH—Dryades, bet. Calliope and Clio. Rev. Father Moynihan, pastor. Week day mass, 7 o'clock; Sundays, 7, 8.30 and 10; sermon, 10; vespers, 4 o'clock.

ST. JOSEPH'S CHURCH—Gretna. Rev. M. Halbedl, pastor. Sunday mass, 7 and 10 o'clock; sermons in English and German on every alternate Sunday; vespers and benediction, 3.30.

ST. JOSEPH'S—Common, bet. Marais and Villere. Father T. J. Smith, pastor; Rev. C. Boglioli, C. M.; Rev. D. Leyden, C. M.; Rev. C. Beecher, C. M.; Mass, week days, 5.30 and 7 o'clock; Sunday mass, 6, 7.30, 8.30 and 10; sermon, 8.30 and 10 o'clock; vespers and benediction, 7 o'clock.

ST. LOUIS CATHEDRAL—Chartres, bet. St. Ann and St. Peter. Rev. G. Raymond, pastor; Rev. C. Feric, Rev. J. Millet, assts. Week day mass, 6 and 7 o'clock; Sunday, 6, 7, 8 and 10. Sermon in French, 10 o'clock; vespers and benediction, 4.30 o'clock.

ST. MARY'S CHURCH (Archbishop's residence—Chartres, bet. Ursulines and Hospital. Very Rev. G. Raymond, D. D. V. G., Rev. C. Denoyelle, Rev. A. Mascaroni, chaplains. Week days, 6 o'clock; Sunday, 6, 7 and 10; sermon, 10; vespers, 5 o'clock.

ST. MAURICE'S CHURCH—Hancock, cor. Royal. Rev. A. Duval, pastor.

ST. BARTHOLEMEW'S CHURCH—Algiers. Rev. F. Bellanger, S. M., Rev. F. Gautherin, S. M., Rev. M. Chapin.

ST. MICHAEL'S CHURCH—Annunciation square. Rev. M. Sheehan, pastor.

ST. PATRICK'S CHURCH—Camp, bet. Girod and Julia. Rev. J. Flanagan, Rev. P. Allen and Rev. Thomas Heslin, pastors. Week day mass, 6.30 and 7 o'clock; Sunday, 6, 7 and 10; sermon, 10 o'clock; vespers, 4 o'clock.

ST. PETER'S CHURCH—Burgundy, bet. Marigny and Mandeville. Rev. Father C. Moynihan, pastor. Week day mass at 6.30 o'clock; Sunday, 7, 8.30 and 10; sermon, 10 o'clock; vespers, 4.

ST. ROSE DE LIMA CHURCH—Bayou, bet. Dorgenois and Broad. Rev. F. Mittelbron, pastor. Week day mass, 7 o'clock; Sunday 7.30 and 10; sermon, 10 o'clock; vespers, 4 o'clock.

ST. TERESA'S CHURCH—Erato, cor. Camp. Rev. Thos. J. Kenney, pastor. Mass, Sunday, 6, 7.30 and 10 o'clock; sermon 10 o'clock; vespers and benediction, 4 p. m.

ST. TRINITY CHURCH (German)—St. Ferdinand, bet. Dauphin and Royal. Rev. Mr. Thevis, Rev. J. Koergerl, Rev. M. Halbedl. Week day mass. 7 o'clock; Sunday, 7 and 10; sermon, 10 o'clock; vespers, 3 o'clock.

ST. VINCENT DEPAUL—Dauphine, bet. Montegut and Clouet. Rev. E. Foltier, Rev. F. Heslin. Week day mass, 7 o'clock; Sunday, 7 and 10; sermon, 10 o'clock; one Sunday in French and one Sunday in English; vespers, 4.30 o'clock.

ST JAMES (African) M. E. Church. I. R. V. Thomas, pastor. Roman, bet. Customhouse and Bienville.

PRESBYTERIAN CHURCHES.

AFRICAN CHURCH—465 Villere, 3d district. Rev. William Brown, pastor.

CARROLLTON PRESBYTERIAN CHURCH—Carrolton. Sunday services, preaching, 4 p. m. Sunday school, 3 p. m.

FIRST GERMAN PRESBYTERIAN CHURCH—First, near Laurel. Rev. John Hollander, pastor. Sunday services, at 11 a. m. and 7.30 p. m. Sunday schoo at 9.301 a. m.

FIRST PRESBYTERIAN CHURCH—Lafayette Square. Rev. B. M. Palmer, pastor. Sunday services at 11 a. m. and 7.30 p. m. Sunday school at 9 a. m.; prayer meeting, Wednesday at 7 p. m. Pastor resides 63 Prytania.

FOURTH PRESBYTERIAN CHURCH—Liberty, nr. Gasquet. Rev. A. F. Dickson, pastor. Sunday services at 11 a. m. and 7.30 p. m. Sunday school, 9.30 a. m. Prayer meeting, Thursday evening. Pastor's residence,————.

JEFFERSON CITY PRESBYTERIAN CHURCH—ss. Camp, bet. Valence and Cadiz. Rev. Benjamin Wayne, pastor. Sunday services at 11 a. m. and 7.30 p. m.; Sunday school at 9.30 a. m. Pastor's residence, Coliseum, cor. Napoleon.

LAFAYETTE PRESBYTERIAN CHURCH—Magazine, nr. Jackson. T. R. Markham, pastor. Sunday services, 11 a. m. Sunday school, 9 a. m.; prayer meeting, Wednesday evening. Pastor resides 179 Constance.

PRYTANIA STREET PRESBYTERIAN CHURCH—Prytania, cor. Josephine. Rev. R. Q. Mallard, pastor. Sunday services, 11 a. m. and 7 p. m. Sunday school, 9.15 a. m.; prayer meeting, Friday at 7 p. m. Pastor's residence, 15 Coliseum.

SECOND GERMAN PRESBYTERIAN CHURCH—St. Bernard, cor. Claiborne. Rev. F. O. Koelle, pastor.

THALIA STREET PRESBYTERIAN CHURCH—Thalia, cor. Franklin. Rev. William Flynn, pastor. Sunday services, 11 a. m. and 7.30 p. m. Sunday school, 9 a. m. Prayer meeting, Wednesday evening, 7.30 p. m. Seats free. Pastor's residence, 298 Franklin.

THIRD PRESBYTERIAN CHURCH—Washington Square. Rev. H. M. Smith, pastor. Sunday services, 11 a. m. and 7 p. m. Sunday school, 9 a. m.; prayer meeting, Thursday, 7 p. m. Pastor resides 533 Chartres st.

SWEDENBORGIAN.

NEW JERUSALEM CHURCH—Glendy Burke, Reader. Melpomene, cor. Camp.

UNITARIAN CHURCHES.

CHURCH OF THE MESSIAH—St. Charles, cor. Julia. Rev.————, pastor. Sabbath services, 11 a. m. and 7.30 p. m. Sunday school, 9 a. m.

CITY HALL—See City Government.

CITY WATER WORKS—Tchoupitoulas, Richard Bldg. and office 32 Dryades.

COLLEGES.

BLACKMAN'S COMMERCIAL COLLEGE—78 Camp st., J. W. Blackman, Proprietor.

DENTAL COLLEGE—67 Carondelet.

DOLBER'S COMMERCIAL COLLEGE—Founded 1832. 164 & 166 Canal st.

LA COLLEGE—J. Choppin, supt. 274 Burgundy.

JESUIT COLLEGE—Rev. F. Gautrelet, S. J., pres.; Rev. F. Lespes, S. J., vice-pres.; Rev. F. Butler. S. J., treas. Baronne, bet. Canal and Common sts.

PEOPLE'S COMMERCIAL COLLEGE—A. T. Selover, prin, 114 Carondelet.

SOULE'S COMMERCIAL COLLEGE—Camp, sw. cor. Common.

ST. MARY'S COMMERCIAL COLLEGE—Bro. Thurlan, prin. Constance, ne. cor. Poyfarre.

ST. MARY'S COLLEGE—Constance, cor. Poyfarre st.

CONVENT OF MERCY—Josephine, cor. Constance.

MT. CARMEL CONVENT—Sister Julia Theresa, prin., 200 Hospital.

ST. JOSEPH CONVENT—Sister Stephene, superior. St. Philip, cor. Galvez.

ST. MARY'S DOMINICAN CONVENT—Sister Mary, mother prioress. Dryades, cor. Calliope Branch ss. St. Charles, bet. Broadway and Upper Line.

SUSANE—John E. Dutillet, supt. Orleans, bet. Liberty and Marais.

URSULINE CONVENT—Sister Seraphine, superior. Peters, bet. Treasure and Goodwill.

BOARD OF HEALTH.

OFFICE, 159 CANAL.

Dr. C. B. White, president; Dr. S. C. Russell, sec. and treas.; John S. Walton, Dr. A. W. Smythe, H. D. Baldwin, W. H. Hire, M.D., B. Maas, M.D., M. P. Avila, M.D., J. S. Clark, M.D.

Sanitary Inspectors—Dr. J. S. Clark, 1st dist. office, Delord, cor. St. Charles; Dr. F. B. Albers, 2d dist. office, 29 Canal; A. W. Perry, 3d dist. office, 409 Chartres; J. A. Mathieu, 4th dist. office, 756 Magazine; Dr. C. P. Ames, 5th dist. office, Patterson, nr. Lavergne; Dr. T. D. Worrall, 6th dist. office, Magazine, cor. Berlin.

Commissioners of the Consolidated Debt of New Orleans.

ROOM, CITY HALL.

Mayor B. F. Flanders, pres. ex.officio; Alfred Shaw and John S. Walton, coms.

CORONERS.

Patrick Creagh, 1st, 4th, 5th and 6th dists., office, St. Charles, cor. Lafayette.

J. F. Jackson, M.D., 2d and 3d dists., office, 45 St. Peter.

METROPOLITAN POLICE.

Board of Commissioners— ——, pres. ex-officio; J. A. Ranyall, treas.; W. Baker, W. M. Robinson, Thos. Isabelle and G. A. Baldey, coms; E. E. Adams, chief clerk, Central Department, cor. Carondelet and Girod; A. S. Badger, supt., office, cor. Carondelet and Girod sts.

First Precinct—Bounded by Canal st., Delord, New Canal and Broad. Station house, cor. St. Charles and Lafayette sts., J. G. Schriber, captain.

Second Precinct—Bounded by Delord st., Felicity road, Land Boundaries of Harbor Prect. and Broad st. Station house, cor. Terpsichore and Chippewa sts., Boyd Robinson, captain.

Third Precinct—Bounded by Canal st., Esplanade, Rampart and Land Boundaries of Harbor Prect. Station house, Jackson square, nr. the Cathedral, Wm. McCann, captain.

Fourth Precinct—Bounded by Canal, Rampart, Esplanade and Broad sts. Station house, cor. Marais and Orleans sts., Octave Rey, captain.

Fifth Precinct—Bounded by Esplanade st., river, lower limits and rear of city. Station house, Elysian Fields, nr. Greatman. Sub-precinct, Parish of St. Bernard, Eugene Rapp, captain.

Sixth Precinct—Bounded by Felicity road, river, and upper limits of city to Broad st. Station house, Rousseau, nr. Jackson st., R. B. Edgeworth, captain.

Seventh Precinct—Station house, City Hall, cor. Magazine and Berlin sts. Sub-precinct, city of Carrollton and left bank of Parish of Jefferson, D. C. Woodruff, captain.

Eighth Precinct—Fifth dist., with Gretna as Sub-precinct. Station house in Court House. H. Fuentes, sergeant.

HARBOR PRECINCT.

OFFICE, HEAD OF CANAL STREET.
Thomas Flanagan, captain.

SUBURBAN SUB-PRECINCT.

STATION, COMMON STREET, OPP. CAR STABLE.
Philip Taylor, sergeant.

JUSTICE OF THE PEACE COURTS.

FIRST JUSTICE COURT.

Office, 150 Julia st. ——, justice; Daniel Crowley, constable; B. F. Sadler, clerk.

SECOND JUSTICE COURT.

Office, 26 Commercial bl. and 82 St. Charles. ——, justice; ——, constable; F. M. Mohrmann, clerk.

THIRD JUSTICE COURT.

Office, 26 Exchange pl. ——, justice; ——, constable; ——, chief clerk; ——, clerk.

FOURTH DISTRICT COURT.

Office, 3 and 5 Frenchmen. ——, justice; ——, constable.

FIFTH JUSTICE COURT.

Office, Villere, bet. Seguin and Bartholomew, 5th dist. ——, justice; ——, constable.

SIXTH JUSTICE COURT.

Office, 570 Magazine. ——, justice; ——, constable.

SEVENTH JUSTICE COURT.

——, justice; S. V. Stalzberg, constable.

EIGHTH JUSTICE COURT.

——, justice; ——, constable.

BOUNDARIES OF WARDS.

First Ward—From Felicity st. to Thalia.
Second Ward—From Thalia st. to Julia.
Third Ward—From Julia st. to Canal.
Fourth Ward—From Canal st. to St. Louis.
Fifth Ward—From St. Louis st. to St. Philip.
Sixth Ward—From St. Philip st. to Esplanade.
Seventh Ward—From Esplanade st. to Elysian Fields.
Eighth Ward—From Elysian Fields st. to Lafayette av.
Ninth Ward—From Lafayette avenue to lower limits of the city.
Tenth Ward—From Felicity st. to First.
Eleventh Ward—From First to Toledano.
Twelfth Ward—From Toledano st. to Napoleon av.
Thirteenth Ward—From Napoleon av. to Upper Line.
Fourteenth Ward—From Upper Line st. to Lower Line.
Fifteenth Ward—All of the Fifth Dist.

FIRE ALARM AND POLICE TELEGRAPH.

ROOM 3, CITY HALL.

Superintendent, S. Weeks; Assistant-Superintendent, Charles A. Adams; Operator, Fred; Welschans; Operator, H. Strouder; Operator. T. J. Rogers, Lineman, George W. Packard. Assistant Lineman, Chas. Penot.

N. O. FIRE ALARM STATION BOXES.

FIRE DISTRICT No. 1—TOLEDANO TO WASHINGTON ST.—Alarm from this District is One Blow on the bells, repeated twenty times, with an interval of fifteen seconds between each blow.

BOXES.

No. 1. Corner Harmony and Levee sts.
No. 2. Corner Washington and Chippewa sts.
No. 3. Ninth Street Market.
No. 4. Corner Apollo and Eighth sts., R. R. Depot.
No. 5. Seventh, corner Laurel.
No. 6. Sixth, corner Prytania.
No. 7. Sixth, corner St. Denis.

FIRE DISTRICT No. 2—WASHINGTON ST. TO FELICITY ROAD.—Alarm is Two Blows, repeated fifteen times, with an interval of fifteen seconds between each alarm.

No. 1. Engine House No. 22.
No. 2. Corner Rousseau and St. Mary's.
No. 3. Lafayette Hook and Ladder No. 2.
No. 4. Corner Constance and First strs.
No. 5. Corner Magazine and St. Andrew.
No. 6. Engine House, No. 23 Washington st.
No. 7. Corner Dryades and First sts.
No. 8. Corner Dryades and St. Andrew.
No. 9. Keller Market.
No. 10. St. Patrick, corner Second st.
No. 11. Chestnut, corner Second st.

FIRE DISTRICT No. 3—FELICITY ROAD TO THALIA ST.—Alarm is Three Blows, repeat thirteen times, with an interval of fifteen seconds between each alarm.

No. 1. Corner Market and Levee sts.
No. 2. Corner Henderson and Levee sts.
No. 3. Engine House, No. 12 Tchoupitoulas st.
No. 4. Engine House, No. 1 Hunter st.
No. 5. Corner Market and Chippewa sts.
No. 6. Robin st. Police Station.
No. 7. Corner Melpomene and Camp sts.
No. 8. Horse Station, Dryades st.
No. 9. Engine House, No. 20 Thalia st.
No. 10. Terpsichore, corner Franklin st.
No. 11. Race, corner Annunciation st.

FIRE DISTRICT No. 4—THALIA TO JULIA ST.—Alarm is Four Blows, repeated ten times, with an interval of fifteen seconds between each alarm.

No. 1. Corner Gaiennie and New Levee st.
No. 2. Engine House, No. 6, St. Joseph st.
No. 3. Corner Constance and Erato st.
No. 4. Corner Camp and St. Joseph st.
No. 5. Engine House, No. 18 Calliope st.
No. 6. Corner New Basin and Triton Walk.
No. 7. Corner Calliope and Freret, Fassman's Press.
No. 8. Corner Magnolia and Erato, Lurges' Foundry.
No. 9. Liberty, corner Erato st.

FIRE DISTRICT No. 5—JULIA TO CANAL ST.—Alarm is Five Blows, repeated nine times, with an interval of fifteen seconds between each alarm.

No. 1. Corner Julia and Levee sts.
No. 3. Corner Canal and Levee sts.
No. 4. Corner Magazine and Girod sts.
No. 5. Engine House, No. 2, Tchoupitoulas st.
No. 6. Corner Canal and Camp sts.
No. 7. Engine House, No. 5, and City Hall.
No. 8. Engine House, No. 13 Perdido st.
No. 9. Corner Carondelet and Common.
No. 10. Rampart, corner Canal st.
No. 11. Poydras, near Rampart.
No. 12. Engine House, No. 14 Common st.
No. 13. Work House, Girod st.
No. 14. Common and Rocheblave, R. R. Depot.
No. 15. Claiborne, cor. Poydras st.

FIRE DISTRICT No. 6—CANAL TO ST. PETER ST.—Alarm is Six Blows, repeated seven times, with an interval of twenty seconds between each alarm.

No. 1. Corner Bienville and Old Levee sts.
No. 2. Corner St. Louis and Royal sts.
No. 3. Engine House, No. 7 Dauphine st.

No. 4, Corner Burgundy and Toulouse sts.
No. 5. Pelican Hook and Ladder, No. 4 Basin st.
No. 6. Corner Canal and Robertson sts. Wood's Press.
No. 7. Bienville, corner Johnson st.
No. 8. Derbigny, corner Conti.

FIRE DISTRICT NO. 7—ST. PETER TO ESPLANADE ST.—Alarm is Seven Blows, repeated seven times, with an interval of twenty seconds between each alarm.
No. 1. Corner Old Levee and St. Philip.
No. 2. Police Station, Jackson square.
No. 3. Corner Hospital and Dauphine sts.
No. 4. Engine House, No. 10 Dumaine st.
No. 5. Corner Treme and Esplanade sts.
No. 6. Treme Market and Parish Prison.
No. 7. Engine House, No. 21 Clairborne.
No. 8. Corner Bayou road and Clairborne.
No. 9. Engine House, No. 3 Bayou road.
No. 10. St. Ann, corner Miro st.
No. 11. Bayou Bridge.

FIRE DISTRICT NO. 8—ESPLANADE TO ST. FERDINAND ST.—Alarm is Eight Blows, repeated six times, with an interval of twenty seconds between each alarm.
No. 1. House of Hook and Ladder No. 3.
No. 2. Engine House, No. 9 Esplanade st.
No. 3. Engine House, No. 8 Decatur st.
No. 4. Police Station, Elysian Fields.
No. 5. Bourbon and Esplanade.
No. 6. St. Claude and St. Antoine.
No. 7. St. Claude and Elysian Fields.
No. 8. Clairborne and St. Bernard.
No. 9. Laharpe and White R. R. Depot.
No. 10. Bagatelle, corner Roman.
No. 11. Mandeville, corner Clairborne.
No. 12. Port, corner Urquhart.

FIRE DISTRICT NO. 9—ST. FERDINAND ST. TO THE BARRACKS.—Alarm is Nine Blows, repeated six times, with an interval of twenty seconds between each alarm.
No. 1. Cotton Press and Levee.
No. 2. Washington Market.
No. 4. Engine House, No. 24 Dauphine st., nr. Port.
No. 5. Corner Independence and Dauphine sts.

A GENERAL ALARM sounded after a DISTRICT ALARM will be indicated by TWENTY SUCCESSIVE BLOWS upon the bells.

AN ADDITIONAL District alarm will be indicated by striking upon the bells THREE ROUNDS of the number of the District.

The SIGNAL for ADDITIONAL and GENERAL alarm can only be given by the CHIEF ENGINEER or his ASSISTANTS.

FIRE DEPARTMENT.

Chief Engineer, Thomas O'Connor, 120 Carondelet st.
Assistant Engineer, First District, John Connors, of No. 14.
Assistant Engineer, Second District, P. Lacour.
Assistant Engineer, Third District, Patrick Swan, of Hook and Ladder No. 3.
Assistant Engineer, Fourth District, Adam Frery.
The Department consists of fifteen Steam Engines, fifteen Hose Carriages, five Hand Engines, four Hook and Ladder Trucks, all with horses and harness complete.
The companies are located as follows:
First District—7 Steam Engines, 3 Hand Engines, 1 Hook and Ladder Truck.
Second District—3 Steam Engines, 1 Hand Engine, 1 Hook and Ladder Truck.
Third District—3 Steam Engines, 1 Hand Engine, 1 Hook and Ladder Truck.
Fourth District—2 Steam Engines, 1 Hook and Ladder Truck.

FIRST DISTRICT.

Volunteer, No. 1 (steam), es. Hunter, between Peters and Tchoupitoulas sts.
Mississippi, No. 2 (steam), 45 Tchoupitoulas st.
Columbia, No. 5 (hand), Girod, bet. St. Charles and Carondelet sts.
Mechanics, No. 6 (hand), St. Joseph, cor. Commerce st.
Irad Ferry, No. 12 (steam), ss. Common, bet. Race and Orange sts.
Perseverance, No. 13 (hand), 12 Perdido st.
Philadelphia, No. 14 (steam), ss. Common, bet. Liberty and Howard sts.
Jackson, No. 18 (steam), Calliope, bet. St. Charles and Carondelet sts.
Washington, No. 20 (steam), Thalia, bet. Baronne and Dryades sts.
American Hook and Ladder Company, No. 2, Girod, bet. St. Charles and Carondelet sts.
Louisiana Hose (steam), Carondelet, cor. Perdido st.

SECOND DISTRICT.

Vigilant, No. 3 (steam), Bayou road, cor. Galvez st.
Eagle, No. 7 (steam), ns. Dauphine, bet. Customhouse and Bienville sts.
Louisiana, No. 10 (steam), Dumaine, bet. Rampart and St. Claude sts.
Orleans, No. 21 (hand), St. Peter, ne. cor. Claiborne st.
Pelican Hook and Ladder, No. 4, Conti, ne. cor. Basin st.

THIRD DISTRICT.

Milneburg, No. 1 (hand), Town of Milneburg.
Phœnix, No. 8 (steam), ss. Decatur, bet. Marigny and Mandeville sts.
Creole, No. 9 (steam), Esplanade, cor. Decatur st.
Crescent, No. 24 (steam), Dauphine, bet. Post and Ferdinand sts.
Hope Hook and Ladder, No. 3, Peters, se. cor. Marigny st.

FOURTH DISTRICT.

Jefferson, No. 22 (steam), 783 Tchoupitoulas st.
Chalmette, No. 22 (steam), Washington av., cor. Camp st.
Lafayette Hook and Ladder, No. 1, Jackson, bet. Rousseau and Fulton sts.

FIFTH DISTRICT.

Pelican Engine Co. No. 1, Peter, cor. Verret st.
Brooklyn Engine Co. No. 2, Bouny, bet. Delaronde and Peter sts.
Washington Hook and Ladder Co. No. 1, Alix, cor. Verret st.

Mayor's Office.

CITY HALL, ROOM 9.
L. A. Wiltz, Mayor; E. W. Halsey, secretary; E. L. Bower, clerk.

Administrator of Accounts.

John Calhoun, Aministrator.

Administrator of Finance.

Louis Schneider, Administrator; ———, chief clerk; ———, bookkeeper.

Administrator of Water Works and Public Buildings.

OFFICE, ROOM 23, CITY HALL.
C. Fitzenreiter, Administrator; ——— general clerk.

Administrator of Police.

ROOM 12, CITY HALL.
Robert Brewster, Administrator.

Administrator of Commerce.

ROOM 14, CITY HALL.
B. M. Turnbull, Administrator.

Administrator of Assessments.

H. F. Sturcken, Administrator.

Administrator of Improvements.

OFFICE, ROOM 16, FIRST STORY.
James Lewis, Administrator; ———, secretary.

City Attorney's Office.

CITY HALL, ROOM 21.
Geo. S. Lacey, Attorney; ———, assistant city attorney; ———, clerk.

Surveyor's Department.

CITY HALL, ROOM 19.
Wm. Bell, city surveyor; ———, assistant city surveyor; ———, chief clerk.

The City Hall.

On St. Charles street, fronting Lafayette square, is where the city business is transacted. The following shows the location of the various offices in the building:

BASEMENT.
Room 1, Administrator of Accounts.
" 2, Administrator of Finances.
" 3, Fire Alarm Telegraph.

FIRST STORY.
Room 9, Mayor's office.
" 10, City Library.
" 11, Mayor's Clerks.
" 12, Administrator of Police.
" 14, Administrator of Commerce.
" 15, Administrator of Assessments.
" 16, Administrator of Improvements.

SECOND STORY.
Room 17, Lyceum Hall.
" 18, Council Chamber.
" 19, City Surveyor.
" 20, School Board.
" 21, City Attorney.
" 23, Department of Water Works and Public Works.

THIRD STORY.
Room 28, City Archives.

INSURANCE COMPANIES.

Crescent Mutual Insurance Company.

Camp, cor. Commercial pl. Thos. A. Adams, pres.; Samuel B. Newman, vice-pres.; Henry V. Ogden, sec. Trustees—C. T. Buddecke, Samuel B. Newman, John Phelps, S. H. Kennedy, P. H. Foley, A. G. Ober, A. Thompson, J. J. Garrard, E. H. Summers, B. Newgass, P. N. Strong, Victor Meyer, Jos. Bowling.

Commercial Insurance Company.

45 Camp st. Joseph H. Oglesby, pres.; John T. Hardie, vice-pres.; Walter Huntington, sec. Directors—J. H. Oglesby, Edward A. Yorke, E. H. Fairchild, J. S. Copes, P. Poursine, J. N. Beadles, J. L. Dunnica, Thomas Smith, Joseph West, Julius Weis, B. Newgass, R. L. Adams. T. J. McMillan, William Flash, George R. Preston, E. H. Wilson, J. M. Witherspoon, J. J. Irby, Joseph O'Brien, W. T. Blakemore, John T. Hardie. E. Kirkpatrick, J. G. Parham, and Charles Pleasants.

Cosmopolitan Mutual Aid Life Insurance Association.

50 Camp. A. Marks, pres.; M. L. Block, sec.

Delta Insurance Company.

Common, cor. Carondelet. E. Ganucheau. pres.; A. Baldwin, vice-pres.; L. W. Baquie. sec. Directors—A. Baldwin, G. P. Blancand, A. Eimer Brader, O. Bercier, A. Tertrou, B. Hufft, R. F. Theurer. M. A. de Lazardi, C. J. Leeds, F. Laborde, A. H. D'Meza, Emile Dupre. Jno. Brunaso, D. Bouligny, A. Palacio, T. M. Simmons, E. Ganucheau, L. H. Gardner, J. Lapene. O. Hopkins. C. H Mouton, W. B. Couger, E. Bordelois, T. L. Airey, Jos. Aleix.

Factors' and Traders' Insurance Company.

No. 39 Carondelet st. Harmon Doane. pres.; Moses Greenwood, vice-pres.; Edward A. Palfrey, sec. Trustees—Moses Greenwood, W. A. Johnson, John I. Noble. John Chaffe, Marshall J. Smith, Richard Milliken, Samuel E. Moore, J. J. Warren, Simon Bloch, R. T. Buckner, Perry Mugent, Samuel Friedlander, H. Frellisen, W. S. Pike, H. W. Farley, A. A. Yates, John I. Adams, Isaac Scherck. R. M. Walmsley, Michael Musson, William Morrisson, John. Carroll, A. Brittin, and J. T. Pace.

Germania Insurance Company, of New Orleans.

124 Common st. D. Michel, pres.; Frederick Del Boudio. vice-pres.; E. Maier, sec. Directors—Frederick Del Boudio, D. Michel, A. Eimer Bader, Thomas Schorr. August Koenig, A. Marks, H. F. Klump, J. J. Weckerling. J. F. Krantz, George Merz, S. Friedlander, W. Goldenbow, F. M. Ziegler, P. W. Dielmann, Philip D. Meyer. N. A. Baumgarden. R. F. Theurer. T. Hassinger, A. Gassie., Louis Redor. G. H. Braughn, M. Stern, Louis Grunewald, H. Oerthling.

Great Western Mutual Insurance Company.

26 Carondelet st. West Steever, pres.; J. Mitchell, sec. pro tem. Trustees—W. A. Shropshire, Z. Foley, Jas. J. Stewart, R. Bleakley, Thomas M. Scott, F. Eugster, W. S. Wren, West Steever, I. R. Hastings, Jno. G. Fleming, J. F. Spearing, Wm. Golding, W. H. Buck, Sam'l. Stafford, A. Thomas, A. Wheless, Geo. T. Converse.

Home Mutual Insurance Company of New Orleans.

Office, No. 78 Camp st. Alfred Moulton. pres.; William N. Perkins, vice-pres.; A. W. Hunter, sec. Trustees—Archie Woods, Robert Hare, B. M. Horrell, William Chambers, A. Moulton, A. H. May, John T. Moore. John C. Rogers, W. M. Perkins, M. C. Randall, William F. Tutt, Adolph Meyer.

Hope Insurance Company of New Orleans.

Office, No. 21 Camp st. Incorporated in 1857. H. Peychaud, pres.; Jno. I. Adams, vice-pres.; Lewis Barnett, sec.; Johnson & Denis, attorneys. Directors—John I. Adams, M. L. Navra, F. A. Ducros, F. E. Bernard, J. C. Denis, William Alexander Gordon, T. N. Blake, P. Malochee, H. Peychaud.

Lafayette Fire Insurance Company.

Magazine, sw. cor. St. Andrew. Kaspar Auch, pres.; Louis Mathis, sec.

Louisiana Branch of the Mound City Life Insurance Company of St. Louis.

33 Carondelet. F. H. Hatch, pres.; E. T. Merrick, vice-pres.; B. B. Simmes, sec. Directors—Gov. C. H. Mouton, Robt. Hare. T. Fitzwilliam, L. Alfred Wiltz, E. T. Merrick, James Jackson, F. H. Hatch, Octave Voorhies, B. B. Simmes.

Hibernia Insurance Company of New Orleans.

Office, No. 37 Camp st. Hugh McCloskey, pres.; John Henderson, vice-pres.; Thos. F. Bragg, sec. Directors—Hugh McCloskey, Patrick Irwin, Robert Carey, Edward Conery, John T. Gibbons, Wm. Conway, Thos. Markey, Thos. King, R. M. O'Brien, Michael McQuade, David Jackson, Thos. Dunne, Edward Sweeney, William Hart, John Lockhart, Michael Duffy, John Henderson, Thos. Gilmore, Thos C. Walsh, John McCaffrey, Jno. Farrell, Thos. McKenna, Nicholas Burke. Jno. T. Moore, jr., Thos. Fitzwilliam, Edward Burke, James D. Martin, Jno. Henderson, jr., E. B. Briggs, Patrick Dwyer, Jno. G. Ryan.

Louisiana Equitable Life Ins. Co. of New Orleans.

Office, Carondelet, ne. cor. Gravier, New Orleans. Jas. H. Low, pres.; J. W. Stone, vice-pres.; Wm. Henderson, sec.; W. C. Robins, manager of agencies. Directors—E. A. Tyler, C. H. Slocomb, Geo. A. Fosdick, J. W. Stone, A. Thomson, D. B. Penn, Marshall J. Smith, Edward Rigney, W. B. Schmidt, Alexander Marks, E. B. Briggs and B. T. Walshe. Medical Examiners—B. H. Moss, Henry Smith. Sam. Choppin, and J. H. Lewis; Y. R. Lemonier, physician; G. A. Breaux, attorney.

Louisiana Mutual Insurance Company.

Office, 120 Common street. Charles Briggs. pres.; Antoine Carriere, vice-pres.; J. P. Roux, sec. Directors—Charles Briggs, Antoine Carriere, George A. Fosdick, R. Brugier, Chas. Lafitte, P. Anderson, A. Fredrichs, George W. Dunbar, E. F. Stockmeyer, Geo. W. Hinson, Arch'd Montgomery, Henry J. Vose. E. Marqueze. Chas. Weishaar, A. R. Montgomery, A. Lecourt, Frank Williams, Thomas Byrne, John Thornhill, Jno. S. Wallis, George Foster. Andrew Stewart, L. B. Pothier, R. Piaggio, Budolph Sieg, H. F. Given, W. C. Black, Geo. C. Garner, Thomas H. Hunt. Chn. Honold, O. Carriere, R. S. Howard.

Mechanics' and Traders' Insurance Company.

Office, 14 Carondelet street. Lloyd R. Coleman, pres.; James A. White, sec. Trustees—C. W. Allen, A. J. Aiken, J, A. Braselman, W. T. Blakemore, A. Eimer Bader, I. Bloom, E. B. Briggs, T. B. Bodley, John D. Cobb, George W. Church, J. E. Campbell, Benjamin Gerson, C. A. Green, I. L. Haas, Jno. N. Harrison, T. H. Hunt, J. A. Lane, Geo. Wm. Logan, Robert L. Moore, John Myers, Wm. Moran, R. C. Oglesby, G. W. Sentell, J. P. Smith, W. H. Sutton, W. B. Thompson, J. P. Todd, Frederick Wing, Louis A. Wiltz, T. S. Waterman.

Merchants' Mutual Insurance Company of New Orleans.

104 Canal street. Paul Fourchy, pres.; G. W. Nott, sec, Directors—P. Fourchy, D. D. McCoard, L. F. Generes, S. Z. Relf. D. A. Chaffraix, P. Maspero, M. Puig, P. S. Wiltz, Joseph Hoy, Charles Lafitte. J. J. Fernandez.

Mutual Aid and Benevolent Life Insurance Association of Louisiana.

Officers—John Davidson, pres.; I. N. Marks, vice-pres.; R. W. Young, sec.; L. A. Fournier, treas. Directors—John Davidson, I. N. Marks, E. F. Schmidt, Wm. Cooper, L. H. Joseph, R. E. Revers, Anthony Sambola, John C. Sinnot, R. N. Ogden, I. Schenk, J. Hassinger, W. B. Schmidt, J. D. Hill, W. H. Thomas, F. Dolhonde, C. A. Eager, W. C. Kennedy, Thos. McKenna, Joseph O'Brien. Medical Examiner—Alex. Hart. Office, 120 Carondelet st., Davidson's row.

The Economy Mutual Aid Association of New Orleans.

Louis Schneider, pres.; J. B. Guthrie, sec. 110 Gravier.

New Orleans Mutual Insurance Association.

Office, 102 Canal street. Charles Cavaroc, pres.; G. Lanaux, sec. Directors—C. Cavaroc, C. DeRuyter, A. Reichard, L. Haas, jr., E. F. Mioton, W. Agar, S. Cambon, U. Maranoni, A. Poiney, Ant. Lanata, F. E. Bernard, J. Egli.

New Orleans Mutual Insurance Company.

Office, cor. Camp and Canal streets. J. Tuyes, pres.; J. W. Hincks, sec. Directors—George Urquhart. A. Rochereau, G. W. Babcock, August Reichard, T. B. Blanchard, W. B. Schmidt, M. Payro, E. Miltenberger, J. Tuyes, A. Schreiber, Charles Lafitte and P. Forstall.

Salamander Insurance Company.

25 Royal. Charles Roman, pres.; Jules Le More, sec. Directors—Charles Roman, James Wood, Domingo Fatjo. T. Bailly Blanchard, Placide Forstall, Francois Gueydan, Felix Linet, C. E. Girardey, M. A. DeLizardi, Christian Roselius, Felix Grima, J. Villarrubia, Arthur Forstall, Charles Lafitte, Emile Dupre, Clement Millaudon, B. Saloy, C. Tiblier, Ant. Lanata, Louis Mathe.

Sun Mutual Insurance Company.

Camp, cor. Commercial pl. Thomas Sloo. pres. ; J. G. Gaines, vice-pres. ; Thomas Anderson, sec. Directors — John G. Gaines, Henry Renshaw, B. Biscoe, W. E. Seymour, Hugh Wilson, E. J. Hart, B. F. Taylor. J. C. Weis, I. H. Stauffer, I. N. Marks, Thomas Sloo.

Teutonia Insurance Company.

Office, 111 Gravier. A. Eimer Bader, pres. ; C. Engstfeld, vice-pres. ; George Stroemeyer, sec. Board of Trustees—A. Eimer Bader, L. Schneider, S. L. Nasits, R. Sieg, J. Hassinger, H. R. Cogreve, H. Eicke, L. Schwarz, William Davis, C. H. Millet, C. L. L. Mayer, H. Pohlmann, E. F. Del Bondio, T. Lillienthal, F. Rickert, J. M. Schwarz, C. Engotfeld, I. Scherk, N. A. Baumgarden, Frank Roder, W. B. Schmidt, M. Frank, H. Weisenbach, Joseph Keller.

The Economy Mutual Aid Association of New Orleans.

110 Gravier st., cor. Bank pl. Louis Schneider, pres.; J. B. Guthrie, sec. Trustees— J. G. Gaines, William H. Holcombe, Louis Schneider, W. G. Robinson, J. S. Walton, W. Van Norden, J. B. Guthrie, J. C. Morris, J. A. Blaffer, Julius Weis. Dr. Jules Font, medical examiner.

The Howard Mutual Aid Association.

46 Camp. A. Fortier, pres. ; B. L. Brown, sec.

The Live Stock Insurance Company of New Orleans.

Office, Carondelet. T. S. Williams, pres.; W. J. Johnson, sec.

The Peoples' Insurance Company.

Office, 5 St. Peters st. R. M. Davis, pres.; A. Granger, sec. Directors—R. M. Davis, A. Socola, Rich. England, J. K. Gourdain, N. A. Llambias, Jos. David, F. Jaufroid, J. J. Reiss, E. L. Fevre, F. Sancho, H. Manuel, A. Haber, R. Dumestre, S. Cambon, Ernest Prangst, P. H. Mousseaux, V. Battalora, F. Schumacher, B. Saloy, J. B. Solaai, J. Newhauser, Jos. Mizzi, M. Draskovich.

Union Insurance Company of New Orleans.

3 Carondelet st. A. Chiappella, pres. ; J. M. Crawford, sec.

Workingmen's Mutual Life Insurance Society.

A. B. Bacon, pres. ; John Roy, sec.

LEVEE REGISTER.

Posts in 1st District.

ASCENDING RIVER.

Nos.
1. Opposite Common.
2. Between Common and Gravier.
3. Opposite Gravier.
4. Poydras.
5. Between Poydras and Lafayette.
6. Opposite Lafayette.
7. Between Lafayette and Girod.
8. Opposite Girod.
9. Between Girod and Notre Dame.
10. Opposite Notre Dame.
11. Opposite Julia.
12. Between Julia and St. Joseph.
13. Opposite St. Joseph.
14. Opposite St. Mary's Market.
15. Opposite Delord.
16. Opposite Calliope.
17. Opposite Gaiennie.
18. Between Gaiennie and Erato.
19. Opposite Erato.
20. Between Erato and Thalia.
21. Opposite Thalia.
22. Between Thalia and Terpsichore.
23. Between Thalia and Terpsichore.
24. Between Thalia and Terpsichore.
25. Between Thalia and Terpsichore.
26. Opposite Terpsichore.
27. Between Terpsichore and Henderson.
28. Opposite Henderson.
29. Between Henderson and Robin.
30. Opposite Robin.
31. Near Robin.
32. Between Robin and Race.
33. Opposite Race.
34. Between Race and Orange.
35. Opposite Orange.
36. Between Orange and Richard
37. Opposite Richard.
38. Between Richard and Market.
39. Opposite Market.
40. Between Market and St. James.
41. Opposite St. James.
42. Between St. James and Celeste.
43. Opposite Celeste.
44. Between Celeste and Nuns.
45. Between Celeste and Nuns.
46. Between Nuns and St. Mary.
47. Between Nuns and St. Mary.
48. Between Nuns and St. Mary.

Posts in 2d District.

DESCENDING RIVER.

Nos.
1. Opposite Canal.
2. Between Canal and Customhouse.
3. Between Canal and Customhouse.
4. Opposite Customhouse.
5. Between Customhouse and Bienville.
6. Opposite Bienville.
7. Between Bienville and Conti.
8. Opposite Conti.
9. Between Conti and St. Louis.
10. Opposite St. Louis.
11. Between St. Louis and Toulouse.
12. Opposite Toulouse.
13. Between Toulouse and Jefferson.
14. Opposite Jefferson.
15. Opposite St. Peter.
16. Opposite Jackson Square.
17. Opposite Jackson Square.
18. Opposite St. Ann.
19. Between St. Ann and Madison.
20. Opposite Madison.
21. Opposite St. Philip.
22. Between St. Philip and Ursulines.
23. Opposite Ursulines.
24. Between Ursulines and Hospital.
25. Between Ursulines and Hospital.
26. Between Ursulines and Hospital.
27. Opposite Hospital.
28. Opposite Barracks.
29. Opposite the Mint.
30. Opposite the Mint.
31. Opposite Esplanade.

Posts in 3d District.

DESCENDING RIVER IN CONTINUATION FROM THE 2D DISTRICT.

Nos.
32. Opposite Elysian Fields.
33. Between Elysian Fields and Marigny.
34. Opposite Marigny.
35. Between Marigny and Mandeville.
36. Opposite Mandeville.
37. Opposite Spain.
38. Opposite Lafayette av.
39. Between Lafayette av. and Port.
40. Between Port and St. Ferdinand.
41. Opposite St. Ferdinand.
42. Between St. Ferdinand and Montegut.
43. Between St. Ferdinand and Montegut.
44. Opposite Montegut.
45. Between Montegut and Clouet.
46. Between Montegut and Clouet.
47. Opposite Clouet.
48. Between Clouet and Louisa.
49. Opposite Louisa.
50. Between Louisa and Piety.
51. Opposite Piety.
52. Between Piety and Desire.
53. Between Desire and Elmira.
54. Opposite Desire.
55. Opposite Congress.
56. Opposite Bartholomew.
57. Between Bartholomew and French.
58. Between Bartholomew and French.

Posts in 4th District.

ASCENDING RIVER IN CONTINUATION FROM THE 1ST DISTRICT.

Nos.
49. Opposite St. Mary.
50. Between St. Mary and St. Andrew.
51. Opposite St. Andrew.
52. Between St. Andrew and Adele.
53. Opposite Adele.
54. Between Adele and Josephine.
55. Between Josephine and Jackson.
56. Between Josephine and Jackson.
57. Between Jackson and Philip.
58. Opposite Philip.
59. Between Philip and Soraparu.
60. Opposite Soraparu.
61. Between Soraparu and First.
62. Between Soraparu and First.
63. Between Soraparu and First.
64. Opposite First.
65. Between First and Second.
66. Between Second and Third.
67. Opposite Third.
68. Opposite Fourth.
69. Between Fourth and Washington.
70. Opposite Washington.
71. Between Washington and Sixth.
72. Between Washington and Sixth.
73. Opposite Sixth.
74. Between Sixth and Seventh.
75. Between Seventh and Eighth.
76. Opposite Eighth.
77. Opposite Ninth.
78. Between Ninth and Harmony.
79. Opposite Harmony.
80. Between Harmony and Pleasant.
81. Opposite Pleasant.

MISCELLANEOUS.

LOUISIANA OIL WORKS, Office 187 Gravier.

LA. ICE WORKS, Tchoupitoulas bet. De-Lachaise and Aline, Office 58 Camp.

LA. MASONIC RELIEF ASSOCIATION, Office, Masonic Hall, cor. Perdido and St Charles.

LA. JOCKEY CLUB HOUSE, Esplanade nr. Bayou Bridge, Office 27 Carondelet.

LA. COTTON FACTORY, J. C. Denis, Pres. 57 Carondelet, Mill 3d District.

LA. LIBRARY, Mrs. H. S. Ball, Librarian. N E. cor. Common and Dryades.

MASONIC HALL, (old) S. M. Todd, G. M. St Charles.

MASONIC HALL, St John, Peter cor. Oliver 5th District.

METAIRIE RACE COURSE, Duncan F. Kenner, Pres. New Shell Road, west end Canal.

MECHANIC'S INSTITUTE, E. S. Dryades, bet. Canal and Common.

MORGAN'S N.O. & TEXAS R. R. DEPOT, Verrett Av. 5th District.

MORGAN'S U. S. MAIL LINE & R. R. OFFICE, cor. Magazine & Natchez.

MORGANS' FERRY, Foot of St Ann.

MORESQUE BUILDING, Poydras, Camp, South and St Francis.

NEW ORLEANS AND BAY ISLAND FRUIT CO., F. Pace, Jr. Pres. Peter Torre Sec. 6 St. Peter.

NEW ORLEANS CONSERVATORY OF MUSIC, Theopilus Masac, pres. 90 Baronne

NEW ORLEANS COTTON EXCHANGE, E. H. Summers, president, H. G. Hester, Superintendent and Secretary, 187 Gravier

NEW ORLEANS FEMALE INSTITUTE, Mme. Loquet Leroy, Principal, 280 Camp.

NEW ORLEANS, FLORIDA AND HAVANA STEAMSHIP CO., J. K. Roberts, Secretary, 120 Common.

Monuments.

CLAY, Canal, opp. Royal and St. Charles.

JACKSON, Decatur, St. Peter, Chartres and St. Ann.

DE SOTA AND JACKSON STATUES, Rotunda of Custom House.

Military Organizations.

LOUISIANA LEGION.—Organized June 28, 1870. Barracks and Headquarters, Davidson's ct., 120 Carondelet st. Officers, A. P. Mason, brig. gen. comd'g; W. P. Harper, maj. and asst. adjt. gen.; W. E. Fitzgerald, maj. and Q. M.; G. A. Williams, capt. and insp. gen.; Henry Puissan capt. and aid-de-camp. Dr. J. Dickson Bruns surgeon.

Markets.

Bazaar Market, bet. Decatur and St. Phillip, Peters and Dumaine.

Carrollton Market, Dublin bet. Hampson and 2d Carrollton.

Claiborne Market, Claiborne, bet. Gasquet and Common.

Dryades, Dryades, bet. Terpsichore and Thalia.

French Market, bet. Peters and Decatur, from St. Ann and Ursulines.

Jefferson City Market, Magazine, n.w. cor. Berlin

Keller, bet. Felicity and St. Andrew, Locust and Magnolia.

LeBreton, Bayou rd, s. w. cor. Dolhonde.

Magazine, Market bet. Magazine and Camp, St. Mary and St. Andrews.

Ninth Street Market, Magazine, bet. 9th and Harmony.

Pilie, Poydras, bet. Rampart and Basin.

Port Market, Elysian Fields, cor. Levee.

Poydras, bet. N. and S. Poydras, Baronne and Rampart

Soraparu, Tchoupitoulas, bet. Sorparu and Rousseau.

St. Bernard Avenue, St. Bernard Av. cor. Claiborne.

Treme, Orleans, bet. Marais and Robertson.

Washington, Chartres, ne. cor. Louisia.

Merchant's Exchange.

E. S. Royal bet. Canal and Custom House.

Mechanic's Institute.

E. S. Dryades bet. Canal and Common.

Newspapers and Publications.

GERMAN GAZETTE (daily), J. Hassinger. propr. 108 Camp.

L'AVENIR (French) (sem-weekly), L. E. Marchand, publisher, editor and propr. 111 Chartres.

LA RENAISSANCE LOUISIANNAISE (French), published weekly by Henry Dubos, 48 Conti, cor. Exchange pl.

LE PROPAGATEUR CATHOLIQUE, (French), a weekly religious paper. Am. Lutten, editor, Madison, cor. Chartres.

LOUISIANIAN, W. G. Brown, editor, 114 Carondelet.

MORNING STAR AND CATHOLIC MESSENGER, published weekly by the New Orleans Catholic Publication Co., at No. 124 Carondelet. Directors—The Most Rev. Archbishop N. J. Perche, pres; Rev. Cornelius Moynihan, Rev. T. J. Kenny Rev. Jeremiah Moynihan, Mr. Hugh McClosky; Mr. John McCaffrey, treas; Mr. T. Fitzwilliam, sec.

NEW ORLEANS BEE (French) published daily and sem-weekly by Dufour & Limet, 73 Chartres st.

N. O. COTTON AND PRODUCE CIRCULAR, Philip J. Punch, editor, 122 Gravier.

NEW ORLEANS PRICE CURRENT, Young, Bright & Co., editors and proprietors, 129 and 131 Gravier st.

NEW ORLEANS REPUBLICAN, (daily and weekly), published by N. O. Republican Printing Co., Wm. R. Fish, editor, 94 Camp st.

NEW ORLEANS TIMES (daily and weekly) C. A. Weed, publisher, 70 Camp st.

OUR HOME JOURNAL (weekly), J. H. Hummel, publisher, 106 Camp st,

PICAYUNE (daily and weekly), D. C. Perkins, editor, 66 Camp St.

RURAL SOUTH LAND (weekly), E. F. Russell, editor, 78 Carondelet.

SOUTHERN PLANTATION, (semi-monthly), T. Watters & Co., publishers, 27 Commercial pl.

SOUTHWESTERN PRESBYTERIAN, published by the Trustees of the Depository. Heny M. Smith, D. D. editor, Office, 36 Camp st.

THE MAGNOLIA. (weekly), A. M. C. Messena, editor, 118 Carondelet.

THE NATIONAL REPUBLICAN, 109 Gravier.

New Orleans Gold and Stock Exchange.

W. Frazer, agt., 57 Camp.

New Orleans Merchants' and Auctioneers' Exchange.

19 Exchange Pl. and 20 Royal.

New Orleans Free Medical Dispensary.

H. Shilly, dispenser. 164 Carondelet.

New Orleans Dental College.

Cor. Carondelet and Perdido Sts.

New Orleans Gymnasium.

Scott & Hammersly, Managers, 170 Canal.

New Orleans Homœpathic Dispensary.

No. 4 Rampart St., bet. Canal and Common Sts. Free consultation daily.

New Orleans Law Association Library.

J. H. Rozier, President, Thomas L. Boyne, Secretary, Court House, cor. St. Ann and Chartres.

New Orleans Military High School.

(private), 188 Race. T. B. Edwards and Samuel H. Lervis, Principals.

New Orleans School Medicine.

Common cor. Villere.

New Orleans Sugar Shed Company.

Julius A. Blanc, President. Levee bet. and from Custom House to St Louis.

New Orleans Transfer Company.

Frank Borge, Superintendent, 22 Camp.

North German Lloyds Steam Ship Line.

42 Union, 1st Dist.

North German Union Consulate.

42 Perdido.

Orleans Draining Machine.

Carondelet walk bet. Orleans and St. Peter.

Orleans Fencing Club.

(private), 150 Royal.

Orleans Institute.

Mrs. Fornet, Directress, 99 Toulouse.

Orleans Oil Manufacturing Company.

Office, 17 Exchange Place, C. E. Girardy, President, J. H. O'Conner, Secretary, M. H. Sheppard, Superintendent. Building on Patterson, from Chestnut to Elmira, two blocks above 3d District Ferry.

Odd Fellow's Hall.

118 Camp, opp. South St.

Ponchar Train Railroad Depot Building.

Front foot of Girod.

Parish Hall.

Villerie, bet. Seguin and Bartholomew.

Parish Prison.

Orleans bet. Liberty and Marais, Robert W. Johnson, Superintendent.

Phyisicians and Surgeons.

E. Adler, F. B. Albers, F. R. Alpuente, C. P. Ames, Edward Ames, O. Anfoux, Richard Angell, S. M. Angell, (homeopathic), W. G. Aussin, A. F. Axson, Walter Baily, E. D. Beach, C. Beard, J. G. Beldon, S. M. Bemiss, Joseph Bensadon, Eugene Berjot, William H. Berthelot, Charles Bickham, C. J. Bickham, Weldemar Billie, William W. Black, P. C. Boyer, J A. Bradbury, D. Warren Brickell, T. E. Broaddius, M. Brown, J. Dickerson Burns, A. H. Burritt, R. O. Butler, J. W. Caldwell, Thomas Campbell, J. A. Cantrelle, Augustus Cadeville, St. Case Carlos. D. Castellanos, S. E. Chille, A. Chastant, Samuel Choppen, Julius Clark, Mrs. T. Cook, L. Coursault, Leondas M. Cowan, I. L. Crowcour, N. J. Crow, J. M. Cullen, Henry D'Aquin, T. M. Davieson, J. D. Davis, R. Gretna Davis, Ernest DeBlanc, John DelArto, F. H. Dennis, Abel DeRoaldes, A. B. DeVilleeuve, G. Devron, W. B. Dodson, E. S. Drew, M. Drew, A. Ducatel, Auguste Dupagneer, D. Durac, Pierre F. Durel, J. G. Dyer, J. E. Eylandt Charles Faget, L. Ferrier, T. Ferris, James Finney, J. A. G. Fisher, A. F. Follin, J. N. Folwell, Jule Font James Ford, Felix Formento, W. R. F. Fryer, F. B. Gaudet, J. O, Guimbellot, J. W. Hallisy, A. Hanneman, Edward Harrison, Aiexander Hart, F. Hartman, Jene Hava, John B. Henderson, Stephen Herrick, W. H. Holcombe, D, C. Holliday, Joseph Holt, S. R. Hurd, Paul Jegon, J. B. Johnson, A. A. Jones, James Jones, Joseph Jones, W. B. Jones, George Kellogg, Thomas Kennedy, W. E. Kennedy, Otto Kratz, Isidore Labatut, Alexandre Landry, Y. R. LeMonnier, Ernest Lewis. E. S. Lewis, George Lewis, J. H. Lewis, J. S. Lewis, J. E. Lockwood, F. Loaber, Samuel Legan, T. R. Lurton, John J. Lyons, Benjamin Maas, J. B. Mailhe. William R. Mandeville, L. Marette, Sabin Martin, Alfred Mercier, J. J. Meylor, Uriel R. Milner. W. S. Mitchel, Jacob F. Majonner, George Monelte, Joseph T. Moreau, Mrs. Cora Moret, A. W. Morse, B. H. Moss, B. F. Mullen, E. A. Murphy, I. Nagel. W. N. Naudain, Thomas Nicholson, Theodore Oriad, J. D. Petez. Joseph Demi Pique, B. A. Pope, J. J. Reily. Francois Ribot, T. G. Richardson, G. Ridgely, W. H. Bartholomew Rily, J. B. Ritchie. L. Roesch, A Roth, Louis Charles Roudanez, L. C. Roudanez, S. C. Russell, Charles Sabourin, Antoine Samsot, H. D. Schmidt, Joseph Schmittle, J. W. Shoenecker, M, Schuppert. Joseph T. Scott, G. Scratchley Edward T. Shepard, L. B. Sholes. H. Smith, Liberto L. Solanas. Edmund Souchon, John C. Stickney, Nathaniel Stolzenburgh, N. Stolzenburgh, Warren Stone, James Syme, F. L. Taney, J. A. Thurber, Just Touatre, P. Tricou, DeBeaumnont L, Trigant, Charles C. Turpin, Theodore Ulrichs, W. H. Watkins, Barack A. Wefelsburgh, C. B. White, F. Wilhoft, W. C. Wilson, Sidney S. Wood, I. R. S. Zehender.

RAILROADS.

NEW ORLEANS AND LAKE POINT-CHARTRAIN R. R. George Pandely, pres. and supt,; Wm. J. Carter, sec. New Depot, foot of Lafayette. Stations, foot of Canal, French Market, Claiborne, Gentilly station.

NEW ORLEANS, JACKSON AND GREAT NORTHERN R. R. CO. H. S. McComb, pres.; E. Q. Sewell, gen. supt.; R. S. Charles, sec. and treas.; J. B. Morey, freight and passenger agt.; J. T. J. Anderson, storekeeper, Principal office, Odd Fellows' Hall, 118 Camp. Depot foot of Calliope. Through Ticket office, Camp, cor. Common.

MORGAN'S LOUISIANIA AND TEXAS R. R. George Pandely, supt.; C. E. Whitney & Co., agts. Office, Magazine, ne. cor. Natchez.

NEW ORLEANS BATON ROUGE AND VICKSBURGH R. R. S. C. Pomeroy, pres.; Geo. W. Cochran, vice-pres. and gen. supt.; Porter Farley, sec. and asst. treas. 44 Perdido.

NEW ORLEANS, MOBILE AND TEXAS R. R. James A. Raynor, pres.; G. W. R. Bayley. gen. supt.; William J. Phelps. gen. freight agt.; Geo. G. Sanborn, gen. ticket agt.; A. Kingsbury, Cashier's Offices, 2 Exchange ct., New York, and Camp, cor. Common, New Orleans.

City Railway Lines.

Canal and Claiborne St. Railway Co., office, 6 Camp st. E. J. Hart, pres.; J. H. DeGrange, see, ; Francis Bone, supt.

Cresent City Railway Co., office, 46 Canal. David McCoard, pres.; Charles Pitts, sec, ; P. Irwin, E. J. Hart, M. McGraw, P. Maspero, directors.

Magazine St., 6th Dist., Kaiser & Judt, proprietors, Magazine bet. Peters Av. and Octavia.

New Orleans City Railway Co., office, 124 Canal st. Frederick Wintz, pres.; Wm. P. Sinnott, sec. and treas.; C. R. Evans, supt.

New Orleans and Carrollton, Railway Co., office, 17 Baronne st. Gen. G. T. Beauregard. pres.; P. McBride, sec.; J. M. Reid, supt.

Orleans Railway Co., office, at station, Laharpe, cor. White st. B. Saloy, pres.; P. Tinse, sec.; John Langles, treas.

St. Charles St. Railway Co., office, 8th. cor. Caroudelet sts. Alden McClellan, pres.; Samuel S. McCuen, sec.

Notaries Public.

The following list contains the names of all Notaries, date of their appointment in the Parish and City of New Orleans. to the 15th of October. 1870, also, where all records may be found: W. D. Ash. Jan. 18th, 1 69, Charles G. Andry, July 29th. 1869. James D. Augustin, Aug. 9th. 1869. Alphonse Barnett, July 29th, 1869. Edward Barnett, 18 Royal, July 26. 1869. Thomas J. Beck, July 22d, 1869. John Bendernagel, 13 St. Charles app'd July 23d, 1869, has records of Michael Hahn, D. J. Richards, 1844 to 185 and Hugh Wadden, 1861 to 1867. A. E. Beinvenu, July 31st, 1869. Eusebe Bouny, July 26th, 1869. Theodule Buisson, Aug. 18th, 1969. Geo. W. Christy, July 22d, 1869. Joseph Cohn, July 26th, 1869. Theodore Guyol, July 4th, 1869. Joseph Cuvillier, 80 Exchange pl. July 20, 1869, has records of J. B. F. Peddesclaux, 1828, to 1830. P. Charles Cuvellier, July 24th, 1869. J. Morris Day, Feb. 2d, 1869. Octave DeArmas, July 26th, 1869. Henry C. Dibble, Dec. 18th, 1868. Andrew D. Doriocourt, Aug. 3d, 1869. Antonio Doriocourt Aug. 3d, 1869, Abel Dreyfous, Aug. 18th, 1869. Oscar Drouet, Aug. 5th, 1869. Amedee Ducatel, July 29th, 1869. Marcel T. Ducros, Sept. 10th, 1869. Ferdinand B. Earhart, Feb. 2d, 1869. Ernest Eude, Aug. 26th, 1869. John G. Eustis, July 27th, 1869. James Fahey, July 29th, 1869. Charles Victor Foulon, August 13th, 1869. Michael Gernon, July 3d, 1869. E. G. Gottschalk, Aug. 24th, 1869 James Graham, 17 Commercial pl. Dec. 11th, 1868. Edgar Grima, Aug. 11th, 1869. A. Hero, jr., 17 Commercial pl., Dec. 8th, 1868. John H. Isley, jr., April 8th, 1869. F. W. Jones, St. Charles st., cor. Melpomene, Dec. 11th, 1868. William McC. Jones, July 26th, 1869. Alcec J. Ker, Aug. 19th, 1869. Robert J. Ker, July 22d, 1869. W. B. Kleinpeter, July 26th, 1869. Paul E. Laresche, Aug. 19th, 1869. Gustave LeGardeur, July 26th, 1869. A. J. Lewis, Aug. 11th, 1869. Charles W. Lowell, April 15th, 1869, Charles Martinez, Dec. 12th, 1868. Adolph Mazureau. July 20th, 1869. Christoval Morel. July 26th, 1869. Octave Morel, Aug. 3d, 1869. John N. Ogden, Aug. 2d, 1869. Sanders D. Oliver, April 10th, 1969. F. C. Remick. Jan. 16th, 1869. F. D. Seghers, Aug. 23d, 1869. N. B. Trist. Sept. 2d, 1869. Arthur Waugh. July 27th, 1869. E. G, Well, July 24th, 1860. F. A. Woolfley. Nov. 24th, 1868.

The following has been appointed since Jan. 1st, 1870. : William J. Castell. Chas. Stringer, Robert Hutchinsou, Wynne Rogers, Alfred Ingraham, C. A. Scott, O. L. Kernion, John F. Coffee, Thomas Layton, Felix Grima, Armand Pilot, jr., Etienne Lauer, Edward Allen

A. Hero, jr., 17 Commercial pl. custodian of notarial records, has the following records: A. Abat, 1847 to 1862. J. Agaisse, 1843 to 1862. A. C. Ainsworth, 1845 to 1850. A. Almonester, 1770 to 1782. J. Amand, 1827 to 1829. J. J. Add, 1846 to 1847. A. A. Baudouin, 1850 to 1855. P. Bertus, 1833 to 1835, and 1841 to 1843 A. Blache, 1868. C. Brown, 1853 to 1859 William Boswell, 1825 to 1838. J. W. Breedlove, 1857 to 1868. A. Brocard, 1860 to 1862, Henry Brown, 1804 to 1805. F. Brouten, 1790 to 1799. A. Cuvellier, 1850, H. B. Cenas, 1834 to 1859. J. W. Cable, 1850 to 1856. J. Castanie, 1866 to 1867. William Christy, 1827 to 1849, and 1853 to 1857. M. DeArmas, 1809 to 1823. Christoval DeArmas, 1815 to 1828. Felix DeArmes, 1823 to 1839. Carlos DeArmes, 1833 to 1835. James Dunlap. 1857 to 1859. Clude Dejan, 1813 to 1815. Guy Duplantier. 1854 to 1857. E. Duplessis, 1843 to 1846. J.

W. Duplessis, 1855 J. N. Duncan, 1826 to 1829. A. A. Ducros, 1860. Horatio Davis, 1837 to 1840. S. B. Davis, 1843 to 1853. A. Devall, 1850. F. DeArmes, jr., 1861 to 1862. John L. Davis, 1866 to 1867. C. O. Dugue, 1866 to 1867. C. T. Estlin, 1855 to 1856. Jos. Fernandez, 1768 to 1770. E. Fitch, 1805 to 1810. Louis Feraud, 1827 to 1838. C. E. Fortier, 1859 to 1862. J. B. Garie, 1771 to 1779. H. K. Gordon, 1825 to 1830. P. F. S. Godfrey. 1808 to 1809. J. P. Gelly, 1847 to 1850. F. L. Hubbard, 1863. L. Hermann, 1839 to 1850. John E. Holland, 1845 to 1853. John H. Holland, 1859 to 1863. F. N. Haralson, 1847 to 1851. W. U. Howe, 1867. Andrew Hero, 1864 to 1867. E. Heriart 1850 to 1851. J. E. Jarreau, 1857 to 1862. C. Janin, 1828 to 1833. R. Jacobs, 1829 to 1833. T. A. James, 1862. John Jones, 1859 H. Keating, 1852 to 1855. C. L. Kerman, 1854 to 1857. J. M. & J. G. Kennedy, 1851 to 1856. P. P. Labarre, 1840 to 1850. C. C. Ladrayere, 1849 to 1856. P. Lacoste, 1838 to 1862. M. Lafitte, 1810 to 1826. W G. Latham, 1845 to 1864. H. Lavergne, 1819 to 1827. G. Legardeur, 1833 to 1837. Jos. Lisbony, 1846 to 1860. G. Lugenbuhl, 1850 to 1862. Jno. Lynd, 1804 to 1821. W. R. Leckie, 1851. U. Y. Lewis, 1835 to 1848. S. H. Lewis. 1838 to 1847. E. L. Lewis, 1854 to 1856. H. Lucas, 1846 to 1850. L. Laugrin, 1863 to 1866. H. J. Labatt, 1866 to 1867. J. B. Marks, 1836 to 1851. N. Brouton, 1799 to 1819, J. B. Beard, 1847 to 1850. T. J. Beck, 1849 to 1862, and 1865 to 1867. T. A. Bartlett, 1854. C. Boudousquie 1838 to 1850, and 1865 to 1866. A. Boudousquie, 1850 to 1866. R. Brenan, 1852 to 1867. P. S. Biron, 1853 to 1857. C. T. Caire, 1826 to 1850. P. H. Caire, 1850 to 1858. John Claiborne, 1850 to 1854. H. L. Castellanos, 1861. A. Chaipella, 1839 to 1855. A. Commandeur, 1858 to 1862. L. F. Maureau, 1843 to 1846. J. M. Maureau, 1846 to 1850. D. L. McCay, 1836 to 1847. W. Monaghan, 1850 to 1855. Albin Michel. 1838. A. Mazureau, 1829 to 1861. Jules Mossy, 1833 to 1847. E. Mazange, 1780 to 1783. B. W. Miller, 1833 to 1834. J. A. Mendiverre, 1863 to 1865. C. L. Marshall, 1855 to 1856. P. Pendergrast, 1850 to 1852. R. Perdonne, 1782 to 1790. Peter Pedesclaux, 1787 to 1816. Philip Pedesclaux, 1817 to 1826. Hugh Pedesclaux, 1830 to 1837, and 1853 to 1862. Felix Percy, 1839 to 1862, Denis Preiur, 1850 to 1853. Carlisle Pollock. 1815 to 1845. O. H. Perry, 1850 to 1853. W. L. Poole. 1850 to 1862. Barnard Phillips, 1844 to 1854. W. L. Poindexter, 1854. J. G. Poindexter, 1854 to 1857. Walter H. Peters, 1853 to 1866. S. Quinones, 1805 to 1815. J. A. Quinters, 1866 to 1868. George Rareshide, 1851 to 1858. H. Rareshide, 1803 to 1856. P. W. Robert, 1852 to 1854. George J. Ross, 1810 to 1813. F. Rodreguez, 1783 to 1788. Theo. Seghers, 1828 to 1842. Jacob Soria, 1850 to 1855, Neville Soule, 1857 to 1860. G. R. Stringer, 1823—1843, to 1849. P. E. Thread, 1853 to 1857. T. F. Thienemann, 1845 to 1847. T. Tureau, 1837 to 1845. L. Turgeau. 1838 to 1848. B. Van Pradelies, 1806 to 1808. J. H. Van Dalson, 1850 to 1852. W. H. Wilder, 1847. W. W. W. Wood, 1850 to 1862. J. R. Winchester, 1867. C. Ximines, 1790 to 1805. Savinien Blanc, not found. Jno. V. Bogart, not found. Dennis Corcoran, 1849. John Craig, 1850. Paris Childress, destroyed by fire. Alfred Ducros, not found. Edward Floyd, destroyed by fire. —— Guriot, destroyed by fire. Jno. F. Lowell, not found. C. Maurian, not found. F. Munhall, not found. R. D. Mudge, not found. J. M. G. Parker, not found. L. Pinelle, not found. Chas. W. Seaton, not found. W. T. Spear, not found. W. H. Shepperd, not found. E. A. Tailarie, not found. Jno. Truro. not found. M. G. Beck, John G. Holland, E. Commagere. S. Wagner, D. Corcoran, John Cragg, E. A. Conand, C. Martinez, E. Burthe, L. Duigneaud, A. Robert, L. R. Kenny, J. A. Drogstede, D. Clark, jr., J. B. G. Arnoult, S. Powell, F. J. Larzer, W. H. Pascoe, T. McCormack, J. T. Michel, P. E. Davis, C. C. Porter, J. Hotard, J. Fabor, B. Campbell.

Crescent City Yacht Club.

189 Common.

Recorder of Births, Deaths and Marriages.

L. Pessou, 24 St. Anthony's al.; A. A. Lafferranderie, chief clerk; Henry Colin, assistant clerk.

Recorder's Court.

FIRST DISTRICT.

Office, St. Charles, cor. Lafayette, G. P. Houghton, Recorder; R. McDonnell, chief clerk; John James, affidavit clerk; A. E. Adams, and Henry Fish, assistant clerks.

SECOND DISTRICT.

Office in Criminal Court, 2d floor, A. H. McArthur, recorder; A. Lusto, chief clerk; J. E. Mathieu, affidavit clerk; John E. Stacs, bond clerk; Alfred Capla, subpœna clerk.

THIRD DISTRICT.

Office, Elysian Fields, bet. Royal and Dauphine, D. V. Leclerc, recorder; John O. Lozo, chief clerk; E. D. Farr and O. J. Rigaud, assistant clerks.

FOURTH DISTRICT.

Office, Rousseau st. near Jackson, A. E. Billings, recorder; J. D. O'Connell, recorder's clerk.

FIFTH DISTRICT.

Office, Villere, bet. Seguin and Bartholomew, John Parsons, recorder; Charles Hill, clerk.

SIXTH DISTRICT.

Office, Magazine, bet. Berlin and Napoleon av. Benjamin Campbell, recorder; Harold Percy, chief clerk.

ASSISTANT RECORDERS.

1st dist., T. H. Drapel; 2d dist., Henry Heidenham; 3d dist., Louis Pessou; 4th dist., William Wright; 5th dist., Wm. H. Toy; 6th dist., Henry M. Van Solingen.

City Workhouse.

PERILLIAT ST., OPP. LOCUST.

Patrick Buckley, warden; J. B. Walsh, deputy warden; J. L. Dupart, clerk; William Stewart, under warden; E; Millieur, under warden; A. A. Maurice, under warden.

Sheriffalty of Parish and City of New Orleans.

Sheriff's office in Court House.

CRIMINAL DEPARTMENT.

J. A. Massicot, criminal sheriff; J. V. Bofill, act'g chief deputy, first district.

PARISH PRISON.

Robert W. Johnson, deputy sheriff, keeper.

CIVIL DEPARTMENT.

C. S. Sauvinet, sheriff; F. M. Sicard, chief deputy; J. Degan, bookkeeper; Joseph Presas, cashier; Robert Swain, J. P. Walden, writ clerks; W. J. Grady, G. Laurent, docket clerks; Michael DeArmas, E. Ricker and Albert DeArmas, sales department; A. F. Lynd, city writ department; A. Reggio, collector of fees.

Industrial School of our Lady of the Holy Cross.

Father Chas. Villandre, prin. Front Levee, bet. Reynes and Tennessee.

Members of the Board of Directors, City Schools of New Orleans.

Hon. H. C. Dibble, President. J. B. Carter, superintendent. Office, room 20, City Hall. N. T. Kendall, secretary. Directors—Michael Hahn, Thomas Lynne, P. B. S. Pinchback. J. R. Clay, B. F. Joubert. C. W. Boothby, J. B. Cooper, J. T. Jackson, James Longstreet, L. C. Matlack, W. H. Toy; W. Rollinson, sec. 39 Burgundy,

Names and Locations of City Schools.

N. O. Central High School (for Boys), 37 39 and 41 Burgundy st.

Girls' High School, 1st, 4th and 6th dist. Chestnut, bet. Jackson and Philip sts.

Girls' High School, 2d, 3d and 5th dist. Royal cor. Hospital.

Jackson, boys—corner Magazine and Terpsichore sts.

Jackson, girls—Magazine, bet. Terpsichore and Robin sts.

Jefferson, boys—Dryades, bet. Erato and Thalia sts.

Webster, girls—corner Dryades and Erato sts.

Clio. boys and girls—Clio, bet. St. Charles and Prytania sts.

Paulding, boys and girls—Corner Constance and Gaiennie sts.

Marshall, boys—Church, bet. Girod and Julia sts.

Franklin, girls—St. Charles, bet. Girod and Julia sts.

Fish, boys, and branch—Corner Franklin and Perdido sts.

Madison, girls, and branch—Corner Prieur and Palmyra sts.

Fish and Madison, branch, boys and girls—Basin, bet. Poydras and Perdido sts.

Howard, boys and girls—Corner Howard and Cypress sts.

Gravier, boys and girls—Gravier, bet. Liberty and Howard sts.

Perdido, Boys and girls—Perdido, bet. Boliver and Bertrand sts.

Johnson, boys and girls—Johnson bet. Perdido and Gravier sts.

Mason, boys and girls—Genois, bet. Gravier and Common sts.

Beinville, boys—Corner Beinville and Robertson st.

Derbigny, boys and girls—Derbigny, bet. Custom house and Beinville.

Rampart, girls—Rampart, bet. St. Louis and Toulouse sts.

Claiborne, boys—Corner Claiborne and St. Peter sts.

St. Ann, girls—St. Ann, bet. Marais and Villere sts.

St. Philip, boys—St. Philip, bet. Royal and Bourbon sts.

Barracks, girls—Barracks bet. Dauphine and Burgundy sts.

Ursulines, girls—Ursulines, bet. Rampart and St. Claude sts.

Bayou Road, girls—Bayou Road, bet. Derbigny and Roman sts.

Chartres, boys and girls—Corner Chartres and Esplanade sts.

Beauregard, girls—Union, cor. Good Children.

Fillmore, boys—Bagatelle, bet. St. Claude and Marais sts.

Villere, boys and girls—Villere, bet. St. Anthony and Bagatelle sts.

LeBreton, boys and girls—Corner Tonti and Onzaga sts.

Laharpe, boys and girls—Laharpe, bet. Roman and Prieur sts.

Bayou Bridge, boys and girls—Bayou St. John.

Gentilly, boys and girls—Gentilly Station, Elysian Fields st.

Pontchartrain, boys and girls—Columbia st. Milneburg.

Marigny, boys and girls—Corner Marigny and Urquhart sts.

DeSoto, girls—Mandeville, bet. Rampart and St. Claude sts

Chalmette, boys—Corner Port and Royal sts.

Washington, girls—Corner Chartres and Piety sts.

Elmira, boys and girls—Elmira, bet. Royal and Dauphine sts.

McCarty, boys—Pauline, bet. Chartres and Royal sts

Hancock, boys and girls—Peters, bet. Monroe and Hancock sts.

Dauphine, boys and girls—Corner Dauphine and Hancock sts.

Fulton, boys and girls—Corner Fulton and Josephine sts.

Laurel, boys—Corner Laurel and Philip sts.

McDonough, girls—Laurel, bet. Philip and First sts.

Laurel and McDonough Branch, boys and girls—St. Mary, bet. Rousseau and Religious sts.

Magnolia, boys—Carondelet, bet. Jackson and Philip sts.

Magnolia, girls—Carondelet, bet. Jackson and Philip sts.

Keller, boys and girls—Magnolia, bet. Felicity and St. Andrew sts.

St. Andrew, boys and girls—Corner St. Andrew and Willow sts.

Live Oak, girls—Corner Constance and 9th sts.

Live Oak, boys—Corner Constance and 9th sts.

Dryades, boys and girls—Corner Dryades and 6th sts.

Greenville, boys and girls—Market bet. Chestnut and Walnut sts.

Leontine, boys and girls—Live Oak, bet. Valmont and Leontine sts.

Cadiz, boys and girls—Corner Cadiz and Coliseum sts.

Jersey, boys and girls—Jersey bet. Valence and Bordeaux sts.

Napoleon Avenue, girls—Napoleon avenue, bet. Magazine and Camp sts.

Valence, boys—Valence, bet. Camp and Chestnut sts.

Coliseum, girls—Coliseum, bet. Valence and Bordeaux sts.

Austerlitz, boys and girls—Austerlitz bet. Magazine and Live Oak sts.

Marengo, boys and girls—Marengo bet. Magazine and Live Oak sts.

Magazine, boys and girls—Magazine bet. Toledano and Louisiana avenue.

Delaronde, boys and girls—Delaronde, bet. Bouny and Villere sts.

Villette, boys and girls—Villette, bet. Alix and Eliza sts.

Tunisburg, boys and girls.

Cut-off Road, boys and girls.

St. Mary's School, Combronne, nr. 2d st. Carrollton.

St. Michael School, Rev. M. Sheehan, director, 80 Chippewa st.

St. Patrick's School, by the Christian Brothers, es. Constance, bet. Julia and St. Joseph st.

St. Paul's School, Miss. J. Falconer, prin., Gaiennie cor. Camp st.

St. Peter's School, es. Marigny, bet. Royal and Dauphine sts.

St. Simeon's Select School, 131 Annunciation st.

St. Teresa, 131 Erato.

St. Vincent's Academy, Rev. Father Mundine, prof., Rev. Father Albian, director, Napoleon av., bet. Magazine and Camp sts., Jefferson.

School of the Holy Trinity Church, Henry Spord, prin., Ferdinand, cor. Royal st.

Third Presbyterian Church School, Royal, bet. Elysian Fields and Frenchmen st.

Schools Parochial.

Annunciation Episcopal, 456 Camp.

Christ Church Parochial School (boys and girls), Beinville ne. cor. Rampart.

Prytania Parochial School, Uhic Bettison, prin., Prytania, sw. cor. Josephine.

St. Boniface School, Galvez, cor. Lapeyrouse.

St. Joseph, Sister Angelica, superior, Jena, cor. Prytania.

St. Joseph's Parochial School, (boys), Bro. Cadoc, prin. Howard, bet. Common and Gasquet.

St. Mary's Parochial School, directed by the Marionite Sisters of the Sacred Heart, 56 and 58 Hospital.

St. Mary's Parochial School directed by the clergy of St. Mary, Chartres, cor. Ursulines.

St. Patrick's Parochial School, (girls), conducted by the Sisters of Mercy, Sister Catharine, superior, 139 Magazine.

St. Rose de Lima, Rev. F. Mattelbron, prin., Bayou rd., bet. Dolhonde and Broad.

Trinity Chapel, Mrs. J. Abott, prin., 476 Rampart, 1st dist.

Calvary Parish School, 8th, nw. cor. Prytania.

Catholic Institution, for instruction of destitute orphans and children. Victor Dupart, pres.; A. Henry Duhart, sec. P. Adolphe Duhart, prin., 393 Dauphine st.

Evangelical Lutheran, Congregration School, C. Zeige, prin., Port, cor. Burgundy st.

Evangelical Lutheran School, O. Steinmeyer, prin., Chippewa, cor. 4th st.

First German Prostestant School, ss. Clio, bet. St. Charles and Carondelet sts.

First Mission School, 3d, ne. cor. Dryades st.

German Evangelical Protestant School, F. Hufft, teacher, St. Philip, cor. Chippewa street.

Hebrew Educational School, Calliope, bet. Prytania and St. Charles sts.

Holy Trinity, directed by Rev. T. Leonard, Royal, bet. St. Ferdinand and Press.

Mount Carmel, Seguin, se. cor. Alix, 5th dist.

Southern Methodist High School, D. I. Rust, prin., 473 Dryades st.

St. Francis School, 2d, nr. Franklin av.

St. Alphonsus School, J. H. Heslin, prin., St. Andrews, bet. Constance and Magazine sts.

St. Henry, Berlin, bet. Magazine and Constance sts.

St. John's Parochial School, Dryades cor. Clio st.

St. Joseph Parish School, Gretna.

St. Joseph's School, for boys, ns. Howard, bet. Gasquet and Common sts.

St. Joseph's School, for girls, Common, cor. Villere sts.

St. Louis School, directed by clergy of St. Louis Cathedral, 18 St. Anthony al.

St. Mary's boys' school, Daminson Litz director, Josephine, cor. Constance st.

St. Mary's girls' school, in charge of Sisters De Notre Dame, Constance, bet. Josephine and Jackson sts.

Seminaries.

St. James' Hall Seminary, Derbigny bet. Customhouse and Beinville.

INDIVISIBLE FRIENDS COMMANDERY. No. 1—Perseverance Hall. Officers, Sir John G. Fleming, E. C. M. A. Colongne, Recorder.

JAQUES DE MOLAY COMMANDERY, No. 2—Grand Lodge Hall, Sir James B. Scott, E. C. Gustave Sontag, Recorder.

ORLEANS COMMANDERY, No. 3—Grand Lodge Hall. Sir George Baldy, E. C. Sir S. B. Wright, Recorder.

ACTIVE MEMBERS OF THE SUPREME COUNCIL OF THE 33d D. FOR THE S.∙. J.∙. OF THE U.∙. S.∙. FOR LOUISIANA—James C. Batchelor, M. D. 33d, New Orleans. Samuel Manning Todd, 33d, New Orleans. J. Q. A. Fellows, 33d, New Orleans. Achilles R. Morel, 33d, New Orleans.

M.∙. P.∙. GRAND CONSISTORY OF SUB.∙. PP.∙. OF THE R.∙. S.∙. 32d, DEGREE. ANCIENT ACCEPTED SCOTTISH RITE. IN AND FOR THE STATE OF LOUISIANA—Officers, Ill. Dan. E. Scruggs, 32d, Gr. Com'r in-Chief. Ill. James B. Scott, 32d, 1st Lieut. Com'r. Ill. John A. Stevenson, 32d, 2d Lieut. Com'r. Ill. Thad. D. Van Horn, 32d, Gr. Constable. Ill. Zet. M. Pike, 32d, Gr. Admiral. Ill. John G. Fleming 32d, Gr. Minister, of State. Ill. J. P. Horner, 32d, Gr. Chancellor. Ill. B. Sternklar, 32d, Gr. Almoner. Ill G. Sontag, 32d, Gr. Registrar. Ill E. Blessey, 32d, G. Keeper of Seals. Ill. H. P. Buckley, 32d, Gr. Treas. Ill. H. Breen, 32d, Gr. Primate. Ill. J. B. Walton, 32d, Gr. Master of Ceremonies. Ill. R. L. Bruce, 32d, Gr. Expert. Ill. John N. Wood, 32d, Beausenifer. Ill. Mo·es Mayer, 32d, Bearer Vexillum Belli. Ill. S. M. Brown, 32d, Master of Guards. Ill. Thomas Cripps, 32d, Gr. Chamberlin. Ill. George B. Ittmans, 32d. Gr. Steward. Ill. W. C. Chamberlain. 32d, Aid de-Camp. Ill. Timothy Carroll, 32d, Gr. Tyler.

TRINOSOPHES COUNCIL OF KADOSH, No. 1—M. A. Colongne, 30th. T. P. G. M. Charles Colongne, 30th Rec.

POLAR STAR COUNCIL OF KADOSH, No. 3—Polar Star Hall. Officers, James Trudeau, 33d, T. P. G. M. Ph. Bidault, 30th, Chancellor.

ST. ANDREW COUNCIL OF KADOSH, No. 4—J. F. L. Lamarre, 33d, T. P. G. M. J. Leicher, 30th, Chancellor.

PERFECT UNION COUNCIL OF KADOSH, No. 5—Rampart bet. Dumaine and St. Philip sts. Rene Lafon de Ladebat, 30th, T. P. G. M. H. Damieus, 30th, Chancellor.

EAGLE COUNCIL OF KADOSH, No, 6—Grand Lodge Hall. Joseph P. Hornor, 32d, V.∙. E.∙. C.∙. Robert Strong, 32d, Chancellor.

LOS AMIGOS DEL ORDEN COUNCIL OF KADOSH, No. 7—Perseverance Hall. Officers, Angel Martin, 33d, T. P. G. M. Enrique B. D'Hamel, 30th, Chancellor.

FOYER MACONNIQUE COUNCIL OF KADOSH, No. 8—Perseverance Hall. U. Marinoni, 30th, T. P. G. M. P. Brugier, jr. 30th, Chancellor.

SILENCIO COUNCIL OF KADOSH, No. 9—Polar Star Hall. Officers, G. Segui Gahona, 32d, T. P. G. M. Martin Perez, 30th, Chancellor.

UNION COUNCIL OF KADOSH, No. 10—Cor. Commercial al. and Camp st. Officers, Samuel H. Brown, 32d, T. P. G. M. Charles Assenheimer, 30th, Chancellor.

TRINOSOPHES CHAPTER, ROSE CROIX, No. 1—Perseverance Hall. M. A. Colongne, 30th, M. W. J. M. Cessac, 18th, sec.

POLAR STAR CHAPTER ROSE CROIX, No. 3—Polar Star Hall. Officers, Jas. Trudeau, 30th, M. W. Ph. Bidouit. 30th, sec.

LOS AMIGOS DEL ORDEN CHAPTER, ROSE CROIX, No. 4—Perseverance Hall. Officers, Jaime Triay, 30th, M. W. E. B. D'Hamel, 30th, sec.

ST. ANDREWS CHAPTER, ROSE CROIX, No. 5—Conti, bet. Villere and Robertson sts. Officers, A. Lercher, 30th, M. W. J. Pausas, 30th, sec.

FOYER MACONNIQUE CHAPTER ROSE CROIX, No. 6—Perseverance Hall. Officers, P. Brugier, jr. 30th, M. W. A. S. Picard, 18th, sec.

SILENCIO CHAPTER, ROSE CROIX, No. 9—Polar Star Hall. Officers, P. Ugarte, 32d M. W. Felix Gilbert, 18th, sec.

PERFECT UNION CHAPTER, ROSE CROIX, No. 10—Rampart, bet. Dumaine and St. Philip sts. Rene Lafonde Ladebat, 30th, M. W. H. Damiens, 18th, sec.

PELICAN CHAPTER, ROSE CROIX, No. 11—Grand Lodge Hall. Officers, Jas. B. Scott, 32d, M. W. Gustavus Sontag, 32d, sec.

KOSMOS CHAPTFR, ROSE CROIX, No. 12—Cor. Commercial al. and Camp street.

UNION CHAPTER, ROSE CROIX, No. 13—Cor. Commercial al. and Camp st. Officers, H. Breen, 32d, M. W. Chas. Assenheimer, 30th, sec.

ALBERT PIKE COUNCIL, P. P., OF JERUSALEM, No. 1—Grand Lodge Hall. Officers, R. L. Bruce, 32d, sov. master.

ALBERT PIKE LODGE OF PERFECTION, No. 1—Grand Lodge Hall. Officers, Samuel H. Brown, 32d, T. P. M. Charles Assenheimer, 30th, sec.

I. O. O. F.

R. W. GRAND LODGE, I. O. O. F., of the State of Louisiana, meets semi-annually on the fourth Tuesday in January and July, in New Orleans, in the Grand Lodge Room, Odd Fellows' Hall. Officers for 1871—Frank Pfister, M. W. Grand Master Eugene P. Brugere, R. W. Deputy Grand Master. Jules A. Florat, R. W. G. W. Josiah Folger, R. W. G. S. F. W. Delesdernier, R. W. G. T. W. C. Wilson, Geo. Nungesser, R. W. Grand Representatives to the R. W. G. L. U. S. John G. Dunlap, W. G. C. Fergus Fuselier, W. G. M.——, W. G. C. G. F. Mathes, G. G. H. Office of the Grand Sec., Odd Fellows' Hall, Camp street.

Subordinate Lodges.

LOUISIANA LODGE, No. 1, meets every Friday evening in Lodge Room No. 2, Odd Fellows' Hall.

WASHINGTON LODGE, No. 2, meets every Thursday evening in Washington Hall, 3d dist.

UNION LODGE, No. 6, meets every Monday evening in Lodge Room No. 2, Odd Fellows' Hall.

CRESCENT LODGE, No. 8, meets every Thursday evening in Lodge Room No. 4, Odd Fellows' Hall.

JEFFERSON LODGE, No. 9, meets every Thursday evening in Jefferson Hall, cor. Magazine and Philip sts., 4th dist.

TEUTONIA LODGE, No. 10, meets every Tuesday evening in Teutonia Hall, cor. Customhouse st. and Exchange al.

ORLEANS LODGE, No. 11, meets every Tuesday evening in Lodge Room No. 4, Odd Fellows' Hall.

COMMERCIAL LODGE, No. 12, meets every Wednesday evening in Lodge Room No. 2, Odd Fellows' Hall.

HOWARD LODGE, No. 13, meets every Tuesday evening in Lodge Room No. 2, Odd Fellows' Hall.

HOPE LODGE, No. 14, meets every Wednesday evening in Lodge Room No. 4, Odd Fellows' Hall.

DELTA LODGE, No. 15, meets every Monday evening, in Lodge Room No. 4, Odd Fellows' Hall.

COVENANT LODGE, No. 17, meets every Tuesday evening in Odd Fellows' Hall, 3d dist.

POLAR STAR LODGE, No. 19, meets every Wednesday evening in Polar Star Hall, St. Louis st.

MAGNOLIA LODGE, No. 22, meets every Tuesday evening in Lodge Room No. 2, Odd Fellows' Hall.

INDEPENDENCE LODGE, NO. 23, meets every Thursday evening in Lodge Room No. 5, Odd Fellows' Hall.

COLUMBUS LODGE, No. 24, meets every Friday evening in their new hall, Algiers.

GERMANIA LODGE, No. 19, meets every Friday evening Tchoupitoulas, bet. Jackson and Philip sts., 4th. dist.

PACIFIC LODGE, No. 33, meets every Wednesday evening in Jefferson Hall, 6th, dist.

HERMAN LODGE, No. 39, meets every Wednesday evening, in Odd Fellows' Hall, 3d dist.

SOUTHWESTERN LODGE, No. 40, meets every Wednesday Evening in Lodge Room No. 5, Odd Fellows' Hall.

HELVETIA LODGE, No. 44, meets every Thursday evening, in Helvetia Hall, cor. Cadiz and Tchoupitoulas sts., Jefferson City.

ORIENT LODGE, No. 46, meets every Thursday evening, in Odd Fellows' Hall, 3d dist.

EAGLE DEGREE LODGE, No. 1, meets first and third Saturday in each month, in Lodge Room No. 2, Odd Fellows' Hall. Officers for 1871, S. B. Sifers. D. M. Charles A. Barnes D. D. M. John H. Windelkin, sec. and treas.

R. W. GRAND ENCAMPMENT I. O. O. F. State of Louisiana, holds its regular sessions on the Third Tuesday in January and July of each year, in the

St. Joseph's Seminary, Jean LeFebre, prin. 212 Orleans.

Peabody's Normal Seminary, R. M. Lushe, supt., 247 St. Charles.

St. Mary's Theological Seminary, Ursuline, cor. Chartres. Rev. Gilbert Raymond, V. G. supt.

St. Vincent's Seminary, Napoleon av. bet. Camp and Chestnut. Father Mandim, supt.

SOCIETIES, SECRET AND BENEVOLENT.

Masonic.

MOST WORSHIPFUL GRAND LODGE OF THE STATE OF LOUISIANA.

Officers for 1871.

Samuel Manning Todd, M. W. Gr'd Mas.
Amos Kent, R. W. Deputy Gr'd Mas.
Wm. Robson, R. W. Sen. War'n.
John B. Saraparu, R. W. Jun. War'n.
Hy R. Swasey, R. W. Gr'd Treas.
Jas. C. Batchelor, M. D. R. W. Gr'd Sec.
Rev. J. C. Carpenter, W. Gr'd Chap'n.
W. L. DeGraffenreidt, W. Sen. Gr'd Dea'n.
M. E. Girard, W. Jun. Gr'd Deacon.
James B. Walton, W. Gr'd Mars'l.
James B. Dunn, W. Gr'd Sword Be'r.
Samuel Humes Brown, W. Gr'd Pursivant.
William Carson, W. Gr'd Steward.
Timothy Carroll, W. Gr'd Steward.
Rene Lafton deLadebat, W. Gr'd Steward.
Fred. Dentzel, W. Gr'd Tyler.

Constituent Lodges.

Officers for 1871.

PERFECT UNION, No. 1.—Rampart st. bet. Dumaine and St. Philip, 2d Wednesday and 4th Friday. Officers, Rene Lafon deLadebat W. M. Paul F. Laborde, sec.

POLAR STAR, No. 1.—Polar Star Hall, cor. Rampart and Kerlerec sts. 1st and 3d Fridays. Officers, W. Maylic, W. M. F. Levasseur, sec.

CONCORDE LODGE, No. 3.—Perseverance Hall, cor. Dumaine and St. Claude sts. 1st Wednesday of each month. Officers, Louis Prados, W. M. E. A. Devron, sec.

PERSEVERANCE LODGE, No. 4.—Perseverance Hall, cor. Dumaine and St. Claude. 2d and 4th Sunday. Officers M. A. Calongue, W. M. Jean Magendie, sec.

LOS AMIGOS DEL ORDEN LODGE, No. 5.—Perseverance Hall, cor. Dumaine and St. Claude sts. Officers, Angel Martin, W. M. Manual Blanco, sec.

ST. ANDREW LODGE, No. 5—Conti, bet. Villere and Robertson sts. Officers, A. Leicher, W. M. Romaine Lafontaine, sec.

SILENCIO LODGE, No. 9—Polar Star Hall, cor. Rampart and History sts. Officers, F. DeA. Ribot, W. M. Felix Gilbert, sec.

FOYER MACONNIQUE LODGE, No. 44—Perseverance Hall, cor. Dumaine and St. Claude sts., 2d and 4th Tuesdays. Officers, B. Campiglio, W. M. P. Brugier, jr., sec.

GERMANIA LODGE, No. 46—St. Louis, bet. Derbigny and Roman sts., 2d and 4th Wednesdays. Officers, Chas. Koerrenzig, W. M. Ed. Ehrhard, sec.

FRIENDS OF HARMONY LODGE, No. 58—Grand Lodge Hall, South Wing, every Tuesday. Officers, Alex. Frelford, W. M. Hilel Marks, sec.

MT. MORIAH LODGE, No. 59—163 Camp, bet. Girod and Julia sts., every Tuesday. Officers, W. H. Moon, W. M. Jas. Furneaux, sec.

GEORGE WASHINGTON LODGE, No. 65—Grand Lodge Hall, South Wing, every Wednesday. Officers, Z. M. Pike, W. M. F. A. Dentzel, sec.

DUDLEY LODGE, No. 66—Grand Lodge Hall, South Wing, every Saturday. Officers, Ed Marks, W. M. J. B. Fox, sec.

MARION LODGE, No. 68—Grand Lodge Hall, South Wing, every Thursday. Officers, James W. Davis, W. M. Thos. Cripps, sec.

HIRAM LODGE, No. 70—Grand Lodge Hall, North Wing, every Friday. Officers, William H. Sims, W. M. Wm. D. Taylor, sec.

ALPHA HOME LODGE, No. 72—Grand Lodge Hall, North Wing, every Tuesday. Officers, Fendal Horn, W. M. Jos. G. P. Sumner, sec.

QUITMAN LODGE, No. 73—Odd Fellows' Hall, Camp st., every Friday. Officers, George Johnson, W. M. J. D. Tilden, sec.

ORLEANS LODGE, No. 78—Grand Lodge Hall, South Wing, every Friday. Officers, C. F. Hufft, W. M. A. Queant, P. M., sec.

HERMITAGE LODGE, No. 98—Tchoupitoulas, bet. Jackson and Philips sts., every Thursday. Officers, A. W. Skardon, W. M. P. L. Boulocq, sec.

LOUISIANA LODGE, No. 102—Odd Fellows, Hall, Camp st., every Thursday. Officers, C. H. Luzenburg, W. M. A. Waugh, sec.

OCEAN LODGE, No. 144—Polar Star Hall, cor. Rampart and Kerlerec sts., every Wednesday. Officers John Robinson, W. M. John A. Letten, sec.

ST. JOHN'S LODGE, No. 153—Algiers Parish of Orleans, La., every Tuesday. Officers, John McCloskey, W. M. W. H. Martin, sec.

EXCELSIOR LODGE, No. 166—Grand Lodge Hall, North Wing, every Wednesday. Officers, R. L. Bruce, W. M. W. Star, sec.

LINN WOOD LODGE, No. 167—163 Camp st., every Thursday. Officers, Charles A. Scott, W. M. Hy Able, sec.

ORUS LODGE, No. 170—Conti, bet. Villere and Robertson sts. Officers, L. Haubtman, W. M. L. Jollisaint, sec.

KOSMOS LODGE, No. 171—Cor. Commercial al. and Camp st. 2d and 4th Mondays. Officers, L. P. Heintz, W. M. B. Ambruster, sec.

UNION LODGE, No. 172—Cor. Commercial al. and Camp st., every Thursday. Officers, Charles Assenheimer, W. M. H. Meister, sec.

ORIENT LODGE, No. 173—Grand Lodge Hall, cor. St. Charles and Perdido sts., every Monday. Officers, Alfred Shaw, W. M. Vincent Mielly, sec.

DANTE LODGE, No. 174—Cor. Rampart and Kerlerec. Every Monday. Officers, G. B. Rossi, W. M. S. Delfini, sec.

PERFECT HARMONY LODGE, No. 176—Grand Lodge Hall, North Wing, every Monday. Officers, J. O. DeCastro, W. M. L. L. Miller, sec.

CORINTHIAN LODGE, No. 190—163 Camp st., 1st Friday of each month. Officers, William Carson, W. M. Thomas D. Clark, sec.

JEFFERSON LODGE, No. 191—City of Jefferson, opp. City Hall, every Friday. Officers, George G. Garner, W. M. H. P. Phillips, sec.

MOST EXCELLENT GRAND ROYAL ARCH CHAPTER OF THE STATE OF LOUISIANA—Officers, for 1871: M. E. Girard, M. E. Gr'd H. P. Joseph P. Horner, R. E. D. Gr'd H. P. W. R. Whittaker, R. E. Gr'd K. William Robson, R. E. Gr'd S. Hy. R. Swasey, E. Gr'd Treas. Jas. C. Batchelor, M. D. R. E. Gr'd Sec. Rev. R. S. Trippet, E. Gr'd Chaplain. J. H. DeGrange, E. Gr'd C. H. H. Hamburger, E. Gr'd P. S. Wm. W. Leake, E. Gr'd. R. A. C. J. G. McWilliams, E. Gr'd G. M. 3 Veil. John L. Barret, E. Gr'd G. M. 2 Veil. James Todd. E. Gr'd G. M. 1. Veil. R. S. Burke, E. Gr'd. Guard. John C. Gordy, R. E. Gr'd. Lecturer.

ORLEANS R. A. C., No. 1—Grand Lodge Hall, every Monday. Officers, Joseph H. Degrange, E. H. P. F. A. Dentzel, sec.

CONCORD R. A. C., No. 2—163 Camp st., every Monday. Richard Lambert, E. H. P. Jas. Furneaux, sec.

PERSEVERANCE, R. A. C., No. 3—Perseverance Hall, cor. St. Claude and Dumaine sts., 1st Monday in each month. Officers, Rene Lafon deLadebat, E. H. P. J. M. Cessac, sec.

DELTA, R. A. C. No. 15—Grand Lodge Hall, every Thursday. Officers, A. Queant, E. H. P. Hitel Marks, sec.

POLAR STAR, R. A. C., No. 21—Isaac W. Homan, E. H. P. John S. Barnes. sec.

GRAND COUNCIL ROYAL AND SELECT MASTERS—Hugh Green, M. P. Gr. Mast. J. P. Horner, P. Dep. Gr. Mast. William Robson, T. I. Gr. Mast. Amos Kent, G. P. C. Work. James Ray, Gr. C. G. R. Lambert, Gr. Treas. Gus Sontag, Gr. Rec'r. Rev. Thomas B. Lawson, Gr. Chap. F. W. Delesdernier, Gr. Com'r. J. L. Barret, Gr. Stew'd. Richard Burk, Gr. Sen'l.

HOLLAND COUNCIL NO. 1—163 Camp st. F. Holyland, T. I. G. M. James Ferneaux, Becorder.

LOUISIANA COUNCIL, No. 2—G—— Hall. Samuel M. Todd, T. I. G. M. F. A. Dentzel, Recorder.

GRAND COMMANDERY OF KNIGHTS OF TEMPLAR AND APPENDANT ORDERS OF THE STATE OF LOUISIANA—Officers, Sir John E. Stevenson, R. E. Gr'd Com'r. Sir Richard Lambert, V. E. Dep'y Gr. Com'r. Sir William R. Whitaker, E. Gr. Generalisimo, Sir Hugh Breen, E. Gr. C. G. Sir H. C. Duncan, E. Gr. Prelate. Sir John H. Clark, E. Gr. Sr. Warden. Sir W. L. Stanford, E. Gr. Jr Warden. Sir Emanuel Blessey, E. Treasurer, Sir Gustave Sontag. E. Gr. Recorder. Sir Daniel E. Scruggs, E. Gr. Standard Bearer. Sir John A. Peel. E. Sword Bearer. St. Charles A. Scott, E. Gr. Warder. Sir Raymond S. Burk, E. Gr. Captain of the Guards.

Grand Lodge Room, Odd Fellows' Hall, Officers for 1871—J. R. Walker, M. W. G. P. Jules A. Florat, M. E. G. H. P. George Ritter, R. W. G. S. W. Josiah Folger. R. W. G. S. B. da Silva, R. W. G. T. Charles C. Neis, R. W. G. J. W. A. J. Vandegrief, R. W. G. R. to the R. W. G. L. of the U. S. Frank H. Drake, W. G. M. Henry Tiemann, W. G. S. M. Frankford, W. D. G. S.

Subordinate Encampments.

WILDEY ENCAMPMENT, No. 1, meets the first and third Saturday of each month, in Lodge room No. 5, Odd Fellows' Hall.

HOBAH ENCAMPMENT, No. 3, meets the second and fourth Saturday in each month, in Lodge Room No. 5, Odd Fellows' Hall.

WASHINGTON ENCAMPMENT, No. 6, meets second and fourth Monday in each month, in 3d dist.

LAFAYETTE ENCAMPMENT, No. 7, meets first and third Wednesday, in Jefferson Hall, cor. Magazine and Philip sts., 4th dist.

CENTRAL ENCAMPMENT, No. 11, meets first and third Monday, in room 5, Odd Fellows' Hall.

Interior Encampments.

DIRECTORS OF THE ODD FELLOWS' REST meet in the office of the Grand Secretary, second Monday in January April, July and October each year, and a meeting on the third Monday in January for the organization of the new Board. Officers for 1871—Benjamin Moses, pres.; Josiah Folger, sec.; Stephen Voullemet, treas.; John Quinn, sexton.

GENERAL RELIEF COMMITTEE meets the first Friday of each month, in the office of the Grand Secretary. Election for president first meeting in January and July. Officers for 1871—A. W. McDonald, pres.; Josiah Folger, sec.

WIDOWS' AND ORPHANS' GENERAL RELIEF ASSOCIATION.—Delegates meet in the office of the Grand Secretary last Saturday of each month. Officers for 1871—George Nungesser, pres.; Josiah Folger, sec.; A. Wallace Hunter, treas.

MUTUAL AID ASSOCIATION meets the fourth Monday of each month, in the office of the Grand Secretary; election of trustees on the third Tuesday in January of each year. Officers for 1871 —Benjamin Moses, pres.; Josiah Folger, sec.; F. W. Delesdernier, treas.

ODD FELLOWS' LIBRARY, room over the office of the Grand Secretary.

ODD FELLOWS' HALL ASSOCIATION—Board of Directors meets first Monday in each month in the office of the Grand Secretary. Election for Directors first Monday in May each year. Board for 1871—Edwin M. Rusha, pres.; L. F. Tower, treas.; Frank Pfister, M. W. G. M.; A. Wallace Hunter, Eugene P. Brugere, S. E. Moore, Luther Homes, George Nungesser, George W. Roper. W. C. Wilson, John G. Dunlap, E. H. Fairchild and Howard Millspaugh; Josiah Folger, sec.

Order of S. W. M., or Heptasophs.

GRAND CONCLAVE OF LOUISIANA—THIRD DEGREE.

This body was incorporated by the Legislature, on March 15th, 1854. Meets at Ætna Hall, No. 3 Carondelet st. near Canal, annually first Monday in January, and quarterly, in January, April, July and October. It is composed of three delegates from each and every Conclave under its jurisdiction.

OFFICERS FOR 1871.

Grand Chief, A. J. Lewis, of Crescent Conclave, No. 13.

Grand Chancellor, V. Grosjean, of Aurora Conclave, No. 14.

Grand Provost, G. W. Sniff, of Ætna Conclave, No. 15.

Grand Prelate, M. A. Calongne, of Ionia Conclave, No. 11.

Grand Scribe, J. H. Hardy, of Gem Conclave, No. 22.

Grand Financial Scribe, J. T. Butler, of Washington Conclave, No. 20.

Grand Treasurer, H. P. Walter, of Oliver Conclave, No. 16.

Grand Inspector General, O. S. Babcock, of Gem Conclave, No. 22.

Grand Herald, P. M. Hields, of Algiers Conclave, No. 23.

Grand Guide, G. Weil, of Deborah Conclave, No. 25.

Grand G. of Threshold, D. Spangler, of Schiller Conclave, No. 6.

Grand Sentinel, I. H. Horton, of Ætna Conclave, No. 15.

GRAND EXECUTIVE COMMITTEE Meets monthly at 33 Exchange Alley.

A. J. Lewis, Grand Archon, Chairman. V. Grosjean, Grand Chancellor. G. W. Sniff, Grand Provost. J. T. Butler, Grand Financial Scribe. H. P. Walter, Grand Treasurer. Central Office of Communication. Box 1360, Post office, New Orleans.

THE HEPTASOPH, Organ of the Order. Issued on the 15th of every month, by the Literary and Printing Association of S. W. M., under the supervision of a Board of administrators, at New Orleans, La. Office, cor. Exchange alley and Customhouse st.

GRAND CONCLAVE FOR THE STATE OF LOUISIANA—SIXTH DEGREE—This body was incorporated by the Legislature, meets quarterly, first Monday in January, April, July and October, at Ætna Hall, 3 Carondelet st. Officers—Wm. Woelper, Grand Chief; G. H. Braughn, Grand Chancellor; T. I. Beck, Grand Provost; Edward Kohnke, Grand Scribe; Jas. T. Butler, Grand Financial Scribe; E. Heldingsfelder, Grand Treasurer; B. Onerato, Grand Inspector General; J. H. Baker, Grand Herald; M. A. Calongne, F. Rhode, Grand Guide; J. A. Strasser, Grand G. of Threshold.

SUBORDINATE CONCLAVES IN THE STATE.

GUTTEMBURG, No. 5 (German)—H. C. Brehop. M. E. C.; 1. Speck, chan; L. Schmidt, provost; H. A. Herrlitz, inspector general; E. Benson. H.; I. M. Braun. scribe; A. Werner, treasurer. Meets every Friday, cor. Camp and Commercial al.

SCHILLER, No. 6 (German)—Jno. Haas, M. E. C.; A. Lieve, chan.; U. Herman, provost; F. Fuhr, inspector general; H. Brehof. herald; H. Aurich, scribe; D. Spengler. treasurer. Every Monday, Tchoupitoulas, nr. Jackson, 4th dist.

SOLON, No. 8 (Spanish)—Jos. Barba, M. E. C.; F. Luque, chan.; M. Arxe, provost; F. D. Alme, inspector general; I. A. Valdez, herald; F. D. Villasana, scribe; L. P. Santos, treasurer. Meets on Wednesday, at 48 St. Louis st.

WATERMAN, No. 9—Fred. B. Earhart, M. E. Archon; J. A. Strasser, chan.; H. W. Canney, provost; E. A. Ducros, scribe; Y. Sambola, treasurer; Chas. H. Schenck, inspector general; W. Stumpff, herald; Lewis Lehman, warder. Meets at Teutonia Hall, cor. Exchange al. and Customhouse st., on the first and third Fridays of each month.

IONA, No. 11 (French)—M. A. Calongne, M. E. C.; E. Levy, chan.; E. A. Louis, provost; M. I. Pons, inspector general; H. Lecrocq, H.; G. Barbier, scribe; A. Pons. treas. Meets at 46 St. Louis st., 1st and 3d Friday of each month.

MAGNOLIA, No. 12—Chas. Brill, Archon; A. V. Ward, chan. H. L. Thelberger, provost; M. C. Murrray, scribe; D. E. Sullivan, treas.; S. M. Terrell, financial scribe; J. E. Jaquet, inspector general; P. Thebould, herald; Jos. Lion, warder; J. Holskamper, prelate. Meets 1st and 3d Fridays in the month, at cor. Commercial al. and Camp st.

CRESCENT, No. 13—A. J. Lewis, M. E. C.; G. Cuculla, chan.; M. I. Leroy. provost; P. I. Ludwig, insp. gen.; J. Cornelia, H.; E. Dunn, scribe; G. Leroy jr. treas. Meets 2d and 4th Tuesday of each month, in Washington Hall, Marigny bldgs. 3d dist.

AURORA, No. 14—Eugene May, M. E. C.; W. DeLacy, chan.; I. L. Villa, provost; W. E. Clark, insp. gen.; Jas. Jackson, H.; W. W. Schermerhorn, scribe; E. R. May, F. scribe; W. Matherson, treas. Meets every Saturday night, at Tuetonia Hall, cor. Customhouse and Exchange al.

ÆTNA, No. 15—Geo. W. Sniff, M. E. C.; Geo. Crena. chan.; Charles Richards, provost; J. A. Betat, insp. gen.; T. H. B. Taylor, herald; T. Taquino, scribe; Macellus Banister, treas. Meets every Tuesday night, at No. 3 Carondelet st.

OLIVER CONCLAVE, No. 16 (German) —H. P. Walter, M. E. C., P. Reis, scribe. Meets in Temperance Hall, No. 67 Josephene street. 4th dist., every Wednesday.

ALLEN No. 18—F. H. Wilson, M. E. C.; J. T. Carey, chan.; J. L. Lewis, provost; J. Grasser, insp. gen.; J. P. Nobles, H.; J. G. Wire, scribe; Will Frazer, treas. Meets every Thursday, at No. 3 Carondelet st.

BOEHLER No. 19—Meets cor. Customhouse and Exchange al. every Thursday night.

WASHINGTON, No. 20—Francis M. Brooks, M. E. Archon; Emanuel Johnson, chan; E. Kohnke, provost; G. A. Stemper. scribe; John Butler, treas.; H. Millspaugh, prelate; John W. Taylor, insp. gen.; James F. Butler, herald;

John Doyle, warder ; P. J. Ludwig, sent. Meets every Friday evening, at Washington Hall, No. 9 Marigny Building, 3d dist.

SOUTHERN, No. 21—C. O. Gerlein, M. E. C. ; O. Dalliet, chan. ; J. B. Duff. provost ; P. Godchaux, insp. gen.; N. Burga, H.; A. Worner, jr., scribe ; H. Sarran, treas. Meets every Friday night at No. 48 St. Louis st.

GEM, No. 22—J. P. Zatarin, M. E. C. ; L. I. McNeill, chan. ; O. S. Babcock, provost; D. Cronan, jr., insp. gen. ; L. Hermaize, scribe ; M. Gombert, treas. Meets every Monday night, at No. 18 Royal st.

ALGIERS, No. 23—W. I. Channing, M. E. C. ; P. N. Hield, chan. ; T. V. Wicklaus, provost ; J. A. Reinas, insp. gen.,; W. Bethel, H.; J. J. Pugol, scribe ; E. H. Brockman, treas. Meets every Wednesday in Algiers.

DEBORAH, No. 25—E. Heidingsfelder, M. E. C. ; H. Myers, chan ; F. Gimbel, provost ; Gus. Weil, insp. gen. ; L. Benjamin, H.; G. Huhner, scribe ; D. Katzenstein, treas. Meets every Wednesday night. cor. Customhouse st. and Exchange al.

KNICKERBOCKER, No. 26—F. W. Weishemier, M. E. C. Meets in Washington Hall, 3d dist.

SHAKESPEARE, No. 27—G. H. Braughn, M. E. C. ; J. G. Campbell, chan.; E. F. Lhoste, provost ; T. D. Vanhorn, insp. gen. ; J. M. Baldwin, H. ; N. C. Forstall, scribe ; J. H. Collins, treas.

Encampments.

GRAND ENCAMPMENT OF LOUISIANA—Meets semi-annually, on the first Tuesday of May and November, at Gem Hall, No. 19 Royal st.

OFFICERS:

Grand Commander—M. A. Calongne, of Ionia, No. 5.

Grand Chancellor—J. Barba, of Solon, No. 2.

Grand Provost—H. P. Walter, of Oliver, No. 10.

Grand Prelate—A. J. Lewis, of Crescent, No. 7.

Grand Scribe—V. Grosjean, of St. George, No. 8.

Grand Treasurer—A. Sambola, of Waterman, No. 3.

Grand Inspector General—E. Fuhr, of Schiller. No. 4.

Grand Herald—E. Headingsfelder, of Deborah, No. 11.

Grand Guide, F. M. Brooks, of Crescent, No. 7.

Grand Warder—J. Metzger, of Solon, No. 2.

SUBORDINATE ENCAMPMENTS.

Solon, No. 2—Meets at 48 St. Louis st., on first Wednesday of each month. J. Baba, commander, Fernando Gutierez, scribe.

Waterman. No. 3—Meets at Teutonia Hall, cor. Exchange al. and Customhouse st., on first Friday of each month, F. A. Earhart, commander, E. A. Ducros, scribe.

Schiller, No. 4. Meets at Hall on Tchoupitoulas, bet. Philip and Jackson, 4th dist. on first and second Mondays. Joseph Schindler, commander; H. Aurich, scribe.

Iona, No. 5—Meets at 48 St. Louis st. on first Friday of each month. M. A. Calongne, commander; Gabriel Barbier, scribe.

Crescent, No. 7—Meets at Washington Hall, Marigny building, 3d dist. on second Tuesday of each month. C. E. Keller, commander ; J. Lefevre, scribe.

St. George, No. 8—Meets at Teutonia Hall, cor. Customhouse and Exchange al., on first and third Saturdays. Eugene May, commander ; E. R. May, scribe.

Oliver, No. 10—Meets at Temperance Hall, 67 Josephene st., near Rousseau, 4th dist. on first Wednesdays. Peter Rausch, commander ; H. P. Walter, scribe.

Ætna, No. 11—Meets at Ætna Hall, No. 3 Carondelet st., on first Tuesday of each month. J. B. Williams, commander ; F. L. Place, scribe.

Orleans, No. 6—Meets at cor. Commercial pl. and Camp st., on first and third Fridays. M. C. Murray, commander ; Charles Brill, scribe.

Deborah, No. 13—Meets at Teutonia Hall, cor. Exchange al. and Customhouse st., on first and third Wednesdays. E. Heidingsfelder, commander ; E. Nesbit, scribe.

Temperance Societies.

GRAND DIVISION SONS OF TEMPERANCE, meets quarterly in January, April, July and October. S. M. Angell, G. W. P.; Thomas H. Jones, grand scribe, 305 Gravier and P. O. Algiers.

PELCIAN DIVISION, No. 1—Meets every Friday evening, over the Bible House, 163 Camp st.

CRIYSTAL FOUNT, No. 4—Meets every Wednesday evening. at 163 Camp st., over the Bible House.

HARMONY DIVISION, No. 6—Meets every Tuesday evening, Magazine, cor. Philip.

HOPE DIVISION, No. 10—Meets every Thursday evening, over Bible House, 163 Camp st.

LOUISIANA STATE TEMPERANCE UNION, (auxilliary to the National Temperance Union of New York.)—W. W. McGarity, pres. 48 Union st., H. S. Bell, rec. sec., 173 Camp st. ; Thos. A. Jones, cor. sec., 305 Gravier st., and P. O. Algiers.

Temple of Honor.

GRAND TEMPLR OF LOUISIANA—Meet semi-annually. Thomas Keets, G. W. T. ; Thomas Hall, G. W. R.

HOWARD TEMPLE, No. 2—Meets every Wednesday evening, in Franklin Temperance Hall, cor. Rampart and Spain sts., 3d dist.

WADSWORTH TEMPLE, No. 8—Meets every Monday evening, over Bible House, 163 Camp st.

WASHINGTON TEMPLE, No. 9.—

Meets every Friday evening at the old Odd Fellows' Hall, Patterson, bet. Lavergne and Verret sts., Algiers.

Knights of Temperance.

CRESCENT ENCAMPMENT, No. 1—Meets every Wednesday evening in Odd Fellows' Hall, Camp st. room No. 1.

ONWARD ENCAMPMENT, No. 2—Meets every Friday evening in Odd Fellows' Hall, Magazine, cor. Philip st.

U. A. O. D.

THE GRAND GROVE OF LOUISIANA UNITED ANCIENT ORDER OF DRUIDS.—Meets in annual session on Dec. 8th, and in same annual session on the third Monday in May. Officers—John M. Wiemann, N. G. A. ; George B. Ebling, D. G. A. ; Valentine Fuchs, G. Sec.; John Reich, G. Treas. ; H. Birrcher, G. Mar.; B. Gelder, G. Guard ; F. Haag, G. O. Guard.

Subordinate Groves Under Jurisdiction of the Grand Grove of Louisiana.

MAGNOLIA GROVE, No. 1 (German)—Meets first and third Thursdays, cor. Customhouse and Exchange al. Officers—P. Schneller, N. A. ; F. Barckes, sec.

OAK GROVE, No, 2 (German)—Meets every first and third Tuesday, at Union Hall, cor. Camp and Commercial al. Officers—F. A. Knoll, N. A. · F. Buckmann, sec.

GOETHE GROVE, No. 4 (German)—Meets every second and fourth) Tuesday, cor. Camp and Commercial al. Officers—H. Gleffers, N. A. ; F. Rohling, sec.

MISPEL GROVE, No. 6 (German)—Meets at Hermitage Hall, on Tchoupitoulas, nr. Jackson every second and fourth Wednesday. Officers—Anton Braun, N. A. ; George Unger, sec.

ESPERANZA GROVE, No. 8 (Spanish and French)—Meets every first and third Wednesday, 49 St. Louis. Officers—M. Brisolaro, N. A. M.; M. Sacerdote sec.

MISTLETOE Grove, No. 9 (English)—Meets every second and fourth Friday, cor. Customhouse and Exchange al. Officers—M. O. Lawrence, N. A. ; Samuel Burns, sec.

ORIENT GROVE, No. 10 (English)—Meets every Thursday, at Hermitage Hall, Tchoupitoulas, nr. Jackson. Officers—W. Whiteside, N. A. ; C. Engel, sec.

GERMANIA GROVE, No. 11—Organized April 4, 1869. Meets every first and third Wednesday, at 742 Tchoupitoulas. Officers H. Brand, N. A. ; B. Mickler, sec.

NORMAL SUPREME ARCH CHAPTER, No. 3.—Meets first and Second Mondays, at Hermitage Hall. Officers—George H. Pabst, E. S. A.; F. Rohling, S. sec.

Red Men.

OSYKA TRIBE, No. 1.—Improved Order of Red Men. Founded Nov. 11, 1855. Meets every Wednesday evening, at cor. Commercial pl. and Camp. H. Clarence, sachem ; F. Ritter, senior sagamore ; R. Mogal, junior sagamore ; Charles Habeney, chief of records ; P. Becker, keeper of wampum.

Good Fellows.

GRAND LODGE OF LOUISIANA, ANCIENT ORDER OF GOOD FELLOWS, holds annual meetings in November, and special meetings at call of Grand Master. Officers B. Planellas, Gr. M. A. L. Tissot, Dep. Gr. M. Julien Michel, Gr. C. G. Barbien, Gr. Sec.

LIBERAL LODGE, No. 5, meets at Polar Star Hall, St. Louis st., 2d and 4th Tuesdays of each month. Jose. Planellas, W. Gr. Juan Suarez, V. Gr. Felipe Gaen, chaplain. Vincente Planellas, treas. H. Thanni, sec.

Knights of Pythias.

GRAND LODGE OF LOUISIANA— Meets semi-annually, 3d Monday in January and July. E. R. Hogan, G. V. P. J. M. G. Parker, G. C. W. F. Dunham, V. G. C. H. Clarence, G. R. and C. Scribe. Theo. Guyol, Grand Banker. M. H. Nicoll, Grand Guide. R. Von Stoltzenberg, G. I. S. L. Lorenz, G. O. S.

IVANHOE LODGE, No. 1, meets first and third Mondays of each month, at Ætna Hall. No. 3. Carondelet st. H. C. Caulkins, W. C. R. Von Stolzenberg, sec.

LOUISIANA LODGE, No. 1, meets 2d and 4th Monday, at 48 St. Louis st. J. H. Manuel, V. P. E. J. Sullivan, sec.

TEMPLAR LODGE, No. 3, meets on Saturday evenings, at Commercial al., cor. Camp. W. M. C. Jones, W. C. T. R. Duval, sec.

BAYARD LODGE, No. 4, meets every Wednesday. R. A. Chattborne, W. C. E. R. Bochler, sec.

ÆTNA LODGE, No. 5, meets at Ætna Hall, No. 3 Carondelet st., every Friday evening. J. C. Branick, W. C. Thomas Taquino, recording and financial sec.

CRESCENT LODGE, No. 7, meets every Monday in Algiers. Charles Hill, W. C. T. M. Field, sec.

TEUTONIA, No. 8, meets at Ætna Hall, No. 3 Carondelet st., every Saturday night. Dr. J. Hentz, W. C. Charles Lochbruner, sec.

LIBERTY, No. 10, meets every Friday at Masonic Hall, 6th dist. John Garstkamp, W. C. Charles Jackson, scribe.

ANDREW JACKSON, No. 11, meets every Friday at Odd Fellows' Hall, 3d dist. Gustavus Devron, W. C. H. Kleinfeller, scribe.

B. B. G. Y. M.

LOUISIANA WIGWAM, NO. 1— Meets at Odd Fellows' Hall, Marigny bldgs. 1st and 3d Monday of each month. Chas. E. Retz, chairman. H. Eck, rec. sec. G. Brunin, per. sec.

Benevolent.

FIREMEN'S CHARITABLE ASSOCIATION, No. 120 Carondelet—Officers—I. N. Marks, pres. No. 13 C. C. Flanagin, sec. No. 13.

Financial Committee—C. Hemard, Vigilant No. 3, chairman ; E. A. Burke, Mississippi No. 2 ; Charles T. Howard, La. Hose.

Board of Commissioners—1. N. Marks, chairman, No. 13 ; M. Lardner, No. 13 ; Frank Rawle, H & L. No. 4 ; George H. Braughn, No. 2; W. H. Manning, No. 12.

General Relief Committee—John Fitzpatrick, No. 13, chairman.

Widows' and Orphans' Committee—Philip Hoffman, No. 5, chairman.

Cemetery Committee—John McCaffrey, No. 6, chairman; John Quinn, sexton.

Fifth dist. (Algiers) Thomas H. Jones, pres. No. 1; L. Peterson, sec. No. 2.

BENEVOLENT ASSOCIATION OF THE SONS OF LOUISIANA—Meets 1st Sunday of each month, at Stonewall Jackson Hall, F. J. Levis, 247 Burgundy, pres.. L. J. Courtin, sec.

CLERKS' BENEVOLENT ASSOCIATION OF LA.—Meets every Thursday at 8 p. m. 17 Royal. O. S. Babcock, pres.; D. H. Buckley, sec.

FRENCH BENEVOLENT, ASSOCIATION—T. Girod, pres., St. Ann, bet. Roman and Derbigny.

GERMAN ASSOCIATION, 1st dist.— Meets Dryades, cor. Lafayette, on the 2d Sunday of each month. H. Paul, pres.; J. Baumann, rec. sec.

GERMAN ASSOCIATION, 2d dist.— Meets 51 Beinville, Coliseum Hall, Valentine Fuchs, pres.; Franz Ritter, rec. sec.

GERMAN EMIGRANT AID SOCIETY—Office, 10 St. Peter. William de la Roue, pres. ; L. Schwartz, rec. sec. ; Charles Becker, manager.

GERMAN MECHANIC'S ASSOCIATION—4th dist. F. Lauer, pres.; J. Frischhertz, sec.

GERMAN BROTHERHOOD (United Brethren)—Meets at Franklin Temperance Hall. Adolph Smith, pres.; Bernhard, Muckler, sec.

GERMAN WORKINGMEN'S ASSOCIATION—Meets 303 Bayou rd., every Sunday. R. E. Kurfurst, pres.; A Weisborn, sec.

GREEK AND SLAVONIC ASSOCIATION—P. N. Benachi, sec. No. 2 Carondelet, 3d floor.

HIBERNIAN BENEVOLENT ASSOCIATION, Board of Delegates—John McPhelin, pres. ; H. H. Ward, sec. ; Philip McCabe, treas.

No. 1—Meets first Monday of each month at 120 Carondelet st. John McCaffrey, 83 Boliver st., 1st dist., pres. ; Thomas Rice, rec. sec. 139 Magazine st.

No. 2—Meets first Thursday of each month at schoolhouse on Marigny st., bet. Royal and Dauphine sts. R. H. Bartley, pres. ; P. Marti, sec.

No. 3—Meets on first Tuesday of each month at St. Joseph's Hall, Common, cor. Derbigny st. Philip McCabe, 100 Camp, pres.; P. J. Hackett, rec. sec.

No. 4—Meets on first Wednesday of each month at St. John's schoolhouse, Dryades st. nr. Clio. M. Whelahan, pres. ; John C. Murray, sec., *Picayune* Office.

No. 5—Meets on first Tuesday of each month on Erato st. nr. Camp R. E.

Diamond, pres. 89 Felicity ; M. Houlahan, sec. 65 Constance.

No. 6—Meets on second Thursday of each month at Temperance Hall, Josephine st. nr. Rousseau. H. H. Ward, sec.

HOWARD BENEVOLENT ASSOCIATION—Office, 58 Camp st. E. F. Schmidt, pres. ; John P. Caldwell, sec.

ITALIAN SOCIETY—"Tiro-al-Bersaglio." Meets 18 Royal st. Chartered March 10, 1869. Civil Officers : G. Minere, pres. *protem* ; C. Remili, vice-pres.; J. S. Tredo, sec. Military Officers : J. Delda Valle, captain ; A. Sidoti, 1st lieut.

JACKSON BENEVOLENT ASSOCIATION—Meets at Franklin Temperance Hall, Rampart cor. Spain st., on the first Tussday of each month, at 7 p. m. C. Melchor, pres. Peter, bet. Montegut and Ferdinand sts., John Fitzwilliam, per. sec., St. Claude, bet. Manuel and Spain.

LAFOURCHE AND BAYOU SARA PILOTS' BENEVOLENT ASSOCIATION—Emile F. Gross, pres. ; Ernest Riviere, sec. ; E. Charlet, treas. Hall, Toulouse, cor. Bourbon st.

LOUISIANA BENEVOLENT ASSOCIATION—Meets at Wollrich's Hall, 357 Decatur, 3d dist., on the third Sunday of each month. John Strobel, pres., Union, cor. Solidelle st. ; L. Ackerman, rec. sec., Elysian Fields, bet. Prosper and Claiborne sts. ; Peter Siebert, treas., 60 Urquhart st.

LOUISIANA DRAYMEN'S ASSOCIATION (German)—Meets at Association Hall, on the first Sunday of each month. George Eschbacher, pres.; Clemens Huner, rec. sec. 59 Exchange pl.

LUTHERAN BENEVOLENT SOCIETY (colored)—James Haywood, prin. director, 318 Gravier st.

NEW LUSITANOS BENEVOLENT ASSOCIATION OF NEW ORLEANS—Hall on Old Levee, bet. Ursulines and St. Philip sts. Founded and incorporated Sept, 12th, 1858. 600 members. The affairs of this association are under the control and supervision of a board of administrators, which meets on the first Thursday of each month. General meetings are held on the third Monday of January, April, July and October.

The Tomb of this society, containing 100 vaults, is situated in Girod Street Cemetery—Officers, V. Camugl, pres. Fee Ripoll, 1st vice-pres. ; A. A. Marchand, sec. A. Sambola, treas. ; R. V. Relimpio, asst. treas. ; Dr. J. J. Castellanos, physician ; J. P. Grossir, collector, Charles Leon, grand marshal.

NEW ORLEANS RIFLE CLUB, meets at Magnolia Garden, Bayou bridge, every Sunday morning. E. J. Wenck, pres., 3 St. Clarles st. L. Moses, sec.

NEW ORLEANS TURNER ASSOCIATION, meets every Tuesday and Thursday, at Turner Hall, Lafayette, cor. Dryades. L. Mieg, 1st speaker ; W. M. Debus, speaker.

ORLEANS DRAMATIC RELIEF ASSOCIATION.—3½ Carondelet st. C. F. Buck, pres.; E. M. Stella, sec.

RED RIVER PILOTS' BENEVOLENT ASSOCIATION—Offices and rooms, 25 St. Charles, nr. Canal st. J. H. Lewis, pres.; John A. Mouchon, sec. and treas. Meetings first Tuesday of each month.

STEAMBOAT CAPTAINS' UNION BENEVOLENT ASSOCIATION—Offices and rooms, 9 Delta, nr. Canal st. John E. Hyde, pres.; C. T. Reader, sec.

SWISS RIFLE CLUB—M. Winteler, pres., 142 Podras st.,; R. Hirzel, sec., Gravier st. Meeting the first Saturday in each month, 51 Beinville.

SWISS BENEVOLENT ASSOCIATION—M. Wintella, pres.; C. F. Pelot, vice-pres.; George Fatzer, treas.; A. Haggman, sec.

TRINITY BENEVOLENT ASSOCIATION—J. W. Norris, pres.; 27 Canal st.; H. W. Ogden, vice-pres. 69 Camp st.; Charles Breuff, sec.; Eug. G. Meslier, treas.

WASHINGTON ARTILLERY ASSOCIATION—Meets third Tuesday in each month, at Hawkins' Club Rooms, 182 Common st., J. B. Walton, pres., 162 Common st.; Louis A. Adam, sec.; W. J. Behan, treas.

WASHINGTON BENEVOLENT ASSOCIATION—Meets at Franklin Temperance Hall, Spain, cor. Rampart st., on the first Monday of each month, at 7½ p. m. Joseph Armbruxer, pres.; John Schneidmuller, 1st vice-pres.; George Frank, 2d vice-pres.; H. Kleinfeller, cor. sec.; H. Hauschild, financial sec.; Balthasar Kerner, treas.

YOUNG MENS' BENEVOLENT ASSOCIATION—Meets first Monday of each month, Customhouse st., ne. cor. Exchange pl. Geo. H. Braughn, pres.; C. Strobel, rec. sec. 89 Camp st.

YOUNG MENS'S CATHOLIC FRIENDS SOCIETY—D. A. Mullane, pres.; D. T. Cummings, sec.

YOUNG MENS' CHRISTIAN ASSOCIATION—A. H. Brown, pres; J. Talbot Sauyer, cor. sec.; Robt. Gribble, rec. sec. W. H. Foster, treas.; W. H. Barremore, librarian, 82 Camp.

YOUNG MENS' CRESCENT AND STAR BENEVOLENT ASSOCIATION—Meets on the first Sunday of every month, at 12 o'clock. m.. at Ætna Hall, 3 Carondelet st. Officers—Wm. E. Fitzgerald, pres. Henry Messonier, 1st vice-pres.; John G. Guerin, 2d vice-pres.; Louis Hardell, sec.; P. N. Benachi, treas. Louis Kuntz, marshal.

SOCIETE ALSACIENNE ET LORRAINE DE BIENFAISANCE ET D'ASSISTANCE MUTUELLE DE LA NOUVELLE ORLEANS—J. Lorber, pres.; John Ramstein, sec. 252 Chartres; C. Duvic, treas. Meets Perfect Union Hall, Rampart st., bet. Dumaine and St. Philip sts., on the first Monday of each month.

SOCIETE FRANCAISE de BIENFAISANCE et d' ASSISTANCE MUTUELLE—Hall and Asylum, ws. St. Ann, bet. Roman and Derbigny. Administration, J. Girod, pres., res. 72 Dumaine. Committee on Help—J. Leblanc, res. 255 Old Levee; A. Barbier, sec. res. 342 Robertsou; P. J. Chabert, col., res. 345 Chartres; J. Tonatre, physician res. 342 Dumaine. Tomb in St. Louis Cemetery, No. 1.

ST. VERONIQUE BENEVOLENT SOCIETY (colord female)—216 Kerierec.

SOCIETY ITALIANA di MUTUA BENEFICENZA in NUOVA ORLEANS (Italian)—Hall, St. Louis st., nr. Levee. G. Massa, act. pres., res. 146 Old Levee. E. Troise, sec., res. Chartres, cor. Jefferson; J. B. Solari, treás.

TIDAL WAVE CLUB—T. H. Farrell, pres.; W. M. Hicks, sec., 17 Royal.

UNITED BROTHERS BENEVOLENT ASSOCIATION—Temperance Hall, Rampart, cor. Spain. Louis Leonhardt, pres., Dauphine, cor. Calliope; Aug. Freschper, sec. Chartres, cor. Congress.

Social, Literary and Dramatic.

BOSTON CLUB—4 Carondelet. Gen. R. Taylor, pres.; W. Bell, sec.

CHALMETTE CLUB—Rooms, Carondelet, cor. Canal. John M. Witherspoon, pres.; L. C. Lawton, sec.

CLERKS' BENEVOLENT ASSOCIATION OF LOUISIANA—Meets every Thursday, 8 p. m., at the room, 3 Carondelet. O. S. Babcock. pres.; E. A. Louis, sec.

GERMANIA CLUB—Rooms, Customhouse, cor. Royal st. Charles Potthoff, pres.; Charles Engstfend, vice pres.; E. Berje, sec.; Frank Oberheuser, treas.

MINERVA SOCIAL CLUB—67 Josephine.

NEW ORLEANS CONSERVATORY OF MUSIC—T. Masac, pres.; 90 Baronne.

PICKWICK CLUB—Rooms, 6 Exchange pl. T. C. Herndon, of Star Cotton Press, pres.; E. A. Barker, 11 Magazine, sec.

SHAKESPEARE CLUB—Meets at their rooms, 107 St. Charles. George H. Braughn, pres.; Numa Forstall, sec.

VARIETIES CLUB—Composed of stockholders of the Varieties Theatre—Rooms, Varieties Theatre. T. M. Simmons, pres.; John Crickard, sec. and treas.

OPERA ASSOCIATION—House, Bourbon, cor. Toulouse st. John G. Gaines, pres.; Emilie Wiltz, sec. and treas.

GOVERNING COMMITTEE—John G. Gaines, Augustus Reichard, Henry Frellsen.

ST. ALOYSIUS LITERARY ASSOCIATION—Meets every Thursday evening, at the schoolhouse, on Marais st., nr. Common. J. J. Finney, pres. and treas.; John T. Markey, rec. sec.

CRESCENT CITY YACHT CLUB—Rooms, 189 Common st. J. O. Nixon, commodore; H. Rareshide, 1st vice commodore; S. W. Scott, treas.; W. T. Perry, sec.

MECHANICS' INSTITUTE, Est. 1806—Dryades, bet. Canal and Common. John McIntyre, pres.; 120 Carondelet; Luther Homes, rec. sec., 15 Dryades.

MECHANICS' AND AGRICULTURAL FAIR ASSOCIATION OF LOUISIANA—Officers and members are elected to serve from May, 1871, to May, 1872: I. N. Marks, pres.; N. E. Bailey, 1st vice-pres.; James Jackson, 2d vice-pres.; C. H. Slocomb, 3d vice-pres.; John Davidson, W. B. Schmidt, E. M. Rusha, G. A. Breaux, Charles J. Leeds, K. W. Merriam, E. A. Tyler, Wm McCulloch, Willamson Smith, Lafayette Folger, A. M. Fortier, G. W. Dunbar, W. A. Shropshire, J. L. Gubernator, Geo. G. Garner, Jos. L. Harris, and R. G. Musgrove. Offices, Mechanics' Hall, Dryades st. The annual fair is held at the Fair grounds in April. The grounds are always open to visitors.

MECHANICS' AND DEALERS' EXCHANGE ASSOCIATION—51 St. Charles. R. Roberts, pres.; 391 Gra-

vier; F. Wing, treas.; W. M. Grant, sec., Delord, cor. Rampart.

MEDICAL ASSOCIATION OF NEW ORLEANS—University Building, Prof. Warren Stone, M. D., pres., 314 Canal; C. H. Tebault, M. D., sec., 496 Baronne.

NEW ORLEANS COTTON SHIPPERS' ASSOCIATION—A . T. Elliot, pres.; Edw. A. O'Brien, sec. and treas.

NEW ORLEANS TYPOGRAPHICAL UNION, No. 17—Meets first Sunday of each month, at Louisiana Hose Co s. Hall. John C. Murray, pres., *Picayune* office; P. A. Vanderdoes, rec. sec., *Times* office.

SHOO FLY CLUB—Rooms, Ætna Hall 3 Carondelet, 3d floor. Alfred Meilleur, pres., W. E. Fitzgerald sec., 2 Carondelet; P. N. Benachi, treas., 14 Union. Strictly social and private club.

TEXAN CLUB—Rooms, cor. Camp and Common.

YOUNG BACHELORS' SOCIAL CLUB—116 Carondelet.

TURN GEMEINDE OF N. O.—Hall, Dryades, cor. Lafayette. L. Mieg, pres.; W. Debus, rec. sec.; B. Keuss. cor. sec.; S. Schmidt, treas.; H. Spiring, turn war.; John Reheege. asst. turn war.; C. Stohl, librarian. Meets twice each month, on Wednesdays.

TURNER SCHUTZEN (German Rifles)—Meets Turn Halle, cor. Lafayette and Dryades, every Monday. H. Loga, capt.; J. Koch, first lieut.; Frank Huss, first sergt.. 229 Rampart.

LOUISIANA GEWERBE VEREIN—Meets every 2d Thursday at their hall, St. Philip. cor. St. Claude. Herbert Wax, pres.; Henry German, treas., M. Schulz, sec.; Urban Theurer. fin'l sec.; Dr. A. de Blanc, physician, 15 Dauphine street; Balthasar Mer z. first halle ward.; Edward Claus, second halle ward.

WASHINGTON TERPSICHOREAN PHILHARMONIC ASSOCIATION—John H. O'Dowd, pres.; J. F. Markey, vice-pres.; G. J. Pritchard, sec.; P. F. Curley, treas.

Places of Amusement.

SHAKESPEARE CLUB, 107 Story Building, (Iron front), se. cor. Camp and Common.

ACADEMY OF MUSIC, David Bidwell, proprietor and manager, es. St. Charles, bet. Commercial pl. and Poydras.

NATIONAL THEATRE, (German) Perdido, from Baronne to Carrol st. Oscar Gutman, manager.

NATIONAL HALL, Davis & Jackson, proprietors, S. Poydras, bet. Franklin and Liberty.

OPERA HOUSE, ASSOCIATION BUILDING, Bourbon, sw. cor. of Toulouse.

ST. CHARLES THEATRE, Benedict De-Bar, proprietor and manager, es. St. Charles, bet. Podras st. and Academy of Music.

VARIETIES THEATRE, Lawrence Barrett, director, Lorain Rogers, business manager, Front on Canal, bet. Dauphine and Burgundy.

MUSEUM OF ANATOMY AND PHYSIOLOGY, University Buiding, for the inpection of students and the faculty.

Public Squares.

ANNUNCIATION SQUARE, Annunciation, Chippewa, Race and Orange, 1st dist.

CLAY SQUARE, Chippewa Annuciation, 3d and 4th sts. 1st dist.

COLLISIUM SQUARE, junction of Camp. E. and Collisium W. bet. Melpome, ne. and Euterpe, 1st dist.

CONGO SQUARE, or Place d'Arms, Rampart. E. St. Peters S. St. Claude, W. and St. Ann, N. 2d dist.

DOUGLAS SQUARE, bounded by Third Washington, Howard and Freret, 4th dist.

FREDERIC 'S SQUARE, bounded by Fifteenth, Hamilton, Edingburg and Laurel Grove, Carrolton.

INDEPENDENCE SQUARE, bounded by Urquhart, Robertson, Spain and Music, 3d dist.

JACKSON SQUARE, bounded by Decatur, St. Peter, Chartres and St. Ann, 2d dist.

LAFAYETTE SQUARE, bounded by Camp S. St. Charles and North sts. 1st dist.

ST. ANTHONY SQUARE, bounded by St. Louis Passengers N. and S. by Royal W. and by St. Louis Cathedral, E. 2d dist.

TIVOLI CIRCLE, St. Charles and Delord, 1st dist.

WASHINGTON SQUARE, bounded by Elysian Fields, N. Royal, E. Frenchman S. and Dauphine W. 3d dist.

TULANE BUILDING, iron, w. s. Camp, bet. Gravier and Common.

TOURO ALMS HOUSE, (Ruins) Levee, ab. Barracks.

UNION LEE CLUB, 32 Royal.

U. S. POST OFFICE, Customhouse Building. Ladies delivery, 2d door from Canal on Decatur. General delivery and boxes from 3d door to centre. Newspaper Department, Centre of west front.

U. S. (Jackson) BARRACKS, Gen. Alfred Sully, Lieut-comd'g. Front Levee cor. Dellery.

UNIVERSITY OF LOUISIANA.

Common, bet. Dryades and Baronne. Hon. Randall Hunt, LLD., President.

ADMINISTRATORS, EX-OFFICIO.—His Excellency. H. C. Warmoth, Governor of Louisiana ; Hon. John T. Ludeling, Chief Justice of Louisiana ; Hon. John Isley, Hon. P. H. Morgan, J. Q. A. Fellows, George S. Lacey, Newton Richards, B. H. Moss, M. D., Thomas Sloo, Hon. Ed. Rawle.

MEDICAL FACULTY—A. H. Cenas, M. D., emeritus professor of obstetrics and diseases of woman and children ; James Jones, M. D., professor of obstretrics and diseases of women and children ; Warren Stone, M. D., professor of surgery ; T. G. Richardson, M. D., professor of anatomy, and dean of the faculty ; Samuel M. Bemiss, M. D., professor of the theory and practice of medicine ; Stanford E. Chaille, M. D. professor of physiology and pathological anatomy ; Frank Hawthorn, M. D., professor of materia medica and thcrepeutics ; Joseph Jones, M. D. (late of the University of Nashville), professor of Chemistry ; C. J. Bickman, M. D., demonstrator of anatomy ; E. Souchon. M. D. John M. Cullen, assistant demonstrators.

LAW DEPARTMENT.—Hon. Randall Hunt, LLD., professor of commercial and criminal law ; the law of evidence and insurance. Christian Roselius, LLD., professor of civil law and practice ; the jurisprudence of Louisiana and the land laws of the United States. Hon. Carleton Hunt, professor of admiralty and maritime law. and of International law. Christian Roselius, LLD, dean of the faculty. Thomas A. Clark, professor of common law.

STRAIGHT UNIVERSITY, Esplanade, cor. Derbigny st. Established 1869. Rev J. W. Healey, AM., pres., assisted by a full corps of professors and teachers, in the collegiate, normal, medical and theological departments.

WASHINGTON HALL, (odd fellows') 8 Marigny Building.

WASHINGTON,—Painting of—on Horseback. Mayors' office, City Hall.

------◄•►------

Warehouses.

Alabama Warehouse, Marshal J. Smith, & Co., proprs., Delord, bet. Clara and Willow.

Batture Warehouse, Girod, bet. Front and Delta.

Blessey Warehouse, Julia, sw. cor. Locust. Boston Warehouse, H. M. Isaackson & Co., proprs., ns. Julia, bet. Magazine and Tchoupitoulas.

Bull's Head Tobacco Warehouse, Tchoupitoulas, bet. Nuns and Celeste.

Chandler's Warehouse, Water, bet. Philip and Saraparu.

Commercial Warehouse, 57 and 59 Lafayette.

Delta Warehouse, W. C. Harrison, propr., 81 to 85 Front.

Eagle Warehouse, P. M. Tourne, propr., 64 Notre Dame.

Fulton Warehouse, Fulton, bet. Delord and South Market.

Great Western Warehouse, Constance, cor. Julia.

Gretna Warehouse. Gretna.

Harrison, Warehouse, Fulton, bet. Girod and Lafayette.

Homes Inspection Warehouse, John Homes & Co., proprs., 157 to 167 Tchoupitoulas.

Home Warehouse, 57 to 67 Fulton.

Hunter Street Tobacco Warehouse, Tchoupitoulas, cor. Hunter.

India Warehouse, 143 and 145 Tchoupitoulas.

Iron Warehouse, bet. Fulton and Peters, Julia and St. Joseph.

Kentucky Tobacco Warehouse, Peters, bet. Gaiennie and Erato.

Lafayette Warehouse, A. A. Maginnis, propr., 107 Magazine.

Liverpool Warehouse, 61 Peters, nw. cor. Montegut. R. Y. Chamburg, propr.

Merchants' Warehouse, and Bonded Yard Gretna ; office, 49 Carondelet.

Mississippi Warehouse, Front, bet. Julia and St. Joseph.

Montgomery Warehouse, Peters, bet. Fulton and St. Joseph.

Paragon Warehouse, J. R. Kane, propr. 121 Fulton.

Pelican Bonded Warehouse, P. M. Tourne, propr., 50 to 56 Girod.

Rio Warehouse, P. M. Tourne, propr., Tchoupitoulas, sw. cor. Notre Dame.

Rondeau Warehouse, Magazine, cor. Julia.

Sheriff's Warehouse, 74 St. Ann.

St. Louis Warehouse, Knower & Walden, propr., Fulton, bet. Girod and Lafayette.

Star Warehouse, Wm. A. S. Rondeau, propr., Commerce, cor. Notre Dame.

State Warehouse, Magazine, bet. Girod and Julia.

Tobacco Internal Revenue Warehouse, B. F. Flanders, propr., Julia, cor. Constance.

Tunnard Warehouse, Delord, sw. cor. Clara.

Uncle Sam Warehouse, (closed), 158 to 164 Peters, 1st dist.

Union Warehouse, John Holmes & Co., proprs., 128 Tchoupitoulas st.

Virginia Warehouse (closed), St. Peters, cor. Race.

Wabash Warehouse, (closed), 75 and 77 Fulton st.

Whitehead Warehouse. bet. Julia and Notre Dame, New Levee and Fulton.

------◄•►------

Wharfingers and Ex-Officio Collectors of Levee Dues.

1st dist. C. A. Waldo. 2d dist. A. H. McArthur. 3d dist. A. B. Chace. 4th dist. J. G. Chadwich.

------◄•►------

WHARVES, LANDINGS, FERRIES.

DIVISION OF WHARVES.

The wharves of the city of New Orleans are divided into twelve sections, as follows:

First Municipal District, three sections—Nos. 1, 2 and 3.

Second Municipal District, three sections—Nos. 4, 5 and 6.

Third Municipal Districts. three sections—Nos. 7, 8 and 9.

Fourth Municipal District, three sections—Nos. 10, 11 and 12.

------◄•►------

Landings.

FIRST SECTION—1st district.

Steamboat Landing—From Canal st. Ferry landing to the upper line of Notre Dame.

SECOND SECTION—1st district.

Steamship, Barge, Flatboat and Coalboat Landing—From Notre Dame st. to Thalia.

THIRD SECTION—1st district.

Sea-going Vessels and Coalboats of N. O. Gas Light Co.—From Thalia st. to upper limits of 1st dist. (Felicity rd.)

ADVERTISEMENTS.

PHILIP WERLEIN'S

Piano, Organ and Music

WARE-ROOMS,

80, 82 AND 90 BARONNE STREET, NEW ORLEANS.

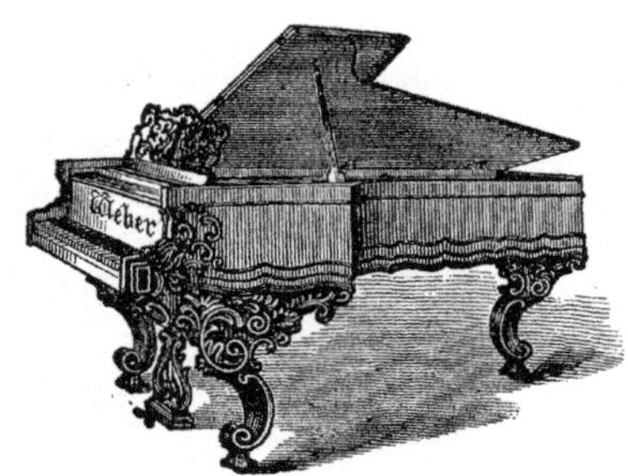

We occupy almost one half of an entire block frontage. Our stock consists of the Largest Collection of First=class Pianos, Square and Upright, Comprising **Weber's, Dunham's, Hale's, Zeigler's, Malhushek & Colibri's, Grovestein's, Pleyel's, Etc., Etc.,** *which will sell for cash at low prices, and on monthly payments, if preferred, with full guarantee.*

ORGANS:

Our stock consists in Needham's World=renowned Organs, which are the best manufactured, and sold at prices not higher than those of many inferior Organs.

Whoever purchases a Piano or Organ without first calling on or writing to us, for our prices and terms, acts without reasonable prudence and care.

We have Second-hand Pianos guaranteed at $125 to $225. New Pianos, a dozen different grades in price, from $290 to $600.

PHILIP WERLEIN.

S. N. MOODY,

Manufacturer of

THE CHAMPION SHIRTS,

And Importer of

MEN'S FURNISHING GOODS.

Highest Premiums at the State Fairs of Lousiana, Texas, Alabama, Mississippi, the Great Paris Exposition of 1867, and endorsed by thousands of customers who have worn no other Shirts for the past Twenty Years.

SEASONABLE

UNDER GARMENTS,

HOSIERY,

Neck Dressings,

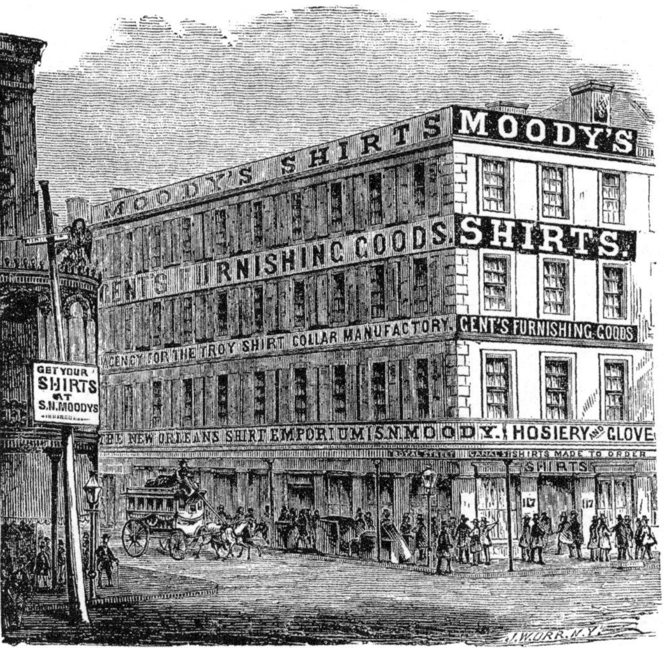

ALSO

GLOVES,

Suspenders,

Shirt Collars

And Every Requisite for a Gentleman's Toilet.   Boys' Shirts and Under Wear.

Shirts Made to Order in THREE DAYS.   A Fit Guaranteed.

Send for Circular, Tape Measure and directions for self=measurement, Gratis.

GOODS SHIPPED C. O. D. TRADE SUPPLIED.

Corner of Canal and Royal Streets,

NEW ORLEANS.

Printed in Dunstable, United Kingdom

85055947R00152